W9-DAC-959

MULTILINGUALISM IN
LATER MEDIEVAL BRITAIN

The languages of later medieval Britain can no longer be regarded as separate or separable, but must be treated and studied together to discover the linguistic reality of medieval Britain and make an assessment of the relationship between the languages and the role, status, function or subsequent history of any of them. This is the theme which emerges from the articles collected here, by leading international experts in their fields, dealing with law, language, Welsh history, sociolinguistics and historical lexicography. The documents and texts studied include a Vatican register of miracles in fourteenth-century Hereford, medical treatises, municipal records from York, teaching manuals, gild registers, and an account of work done on the bridges of the river Thames.

Professor D. A. TROTTER is Professor of French and Head of the Department of European Languages at the University of Wales, Aberystwyth.

MULTILINGUALISM IN LATER MEDIEVAL BRITAIN

Edited by D. A. TROTTER

D. S. BREWER

First published 2000
D. S. Brewer, Cambridge

ISBN 0 85991 563 8

D. S. Brewer is an imprint of Boydell & Brewer Ltd
PO Box 9, Woodbridge, Suffolk IP12 3DF, UK
and of Boydell & Brewer Inc.
PO Box 41026, Rochester, NY 14604–4126, USA
website: http://www.boydell.co.uk

A catalogue record for this book is available
from the British Library

Library of Congress Cataloging-in-Publication Data
Multilingualism in later medieval Britain / edited by D.A. Trotter.
    p. cm.
    Includes bibliographical references and index.
    ISBN 0–85991–563–8 (alk. paper)
    1. English language – Middle English, 1100–1500 – Foreign
elements.   2. English language – Great Britain – Foreign
elements.   3. Multilingualism – Great Britain – History –
To 1500.   4. Language and languages – Influence on English.
5. Manuscripts, Medieval – Great Britain.   6. Great Britain –
Languages.   I. Trotter, D. A.
PE664.A3 M85 2000
420'.42'0902 21–dc21   99–042630

This publication is printed on acid-free paper

Printed in Great Britain by
St Edmundsbury Press Ltd, Bury St Edmunds, Suffolk

Contents

Contributors

PAUL BRAND — Oxford
BEGOÑA CRESPO GARCÍA — A Coruña
TONY HUNT — Oxford
LUIS IGLESIAS-RÁBADE — Santiago de Compostela
LISA JEFFERSON — Oxford
ANDRES M. KRISTOL — Neuchâtel
FRANKWALT MÖHREN — DEAF, Heidelberg
MICHAEL RICHTER — Konstanz
WILLIAM ROTHWELL — AND, Manchester
HERBERT SCHENDL — Vienna
LLINOS BEVERLEY SMITH — Aberystwyth
D. A. TROTTER — Aberystwyth
EDMUND WEINER — OED, Oxford
LAURA WRIGHT — Cambridge

Item, a mon plus que pere . . .

In memoriam
Jonathan Harris Cass
21.9.17–23.12.99

Preface

With the publication of these proceedings from a Colloquium which took place two years ago, I have at last the opportunity to register my thanks to those who have helped it all happen. The agreeable informality and unintrusive efficiency with which the Colloquium itself ran owed much to Jim Wallace, of the Conference Office in Aberystwyth, and his staff. The administration of the Colloquium was very largely the work of Carol Marshall, who then took over the first stage of the editorial work, which subsequently passed to Alison Vaughan for the demanding task of standardisation and finalisation of the typescript. My thanks go, too, to the Sir David Hughes Parry Fund of the University of Wales, Aberystwyth, for generously providing a grant to support publication. Finally, I record here my gratitude to colleagues from many academic disciplines for their support and interest. Aberystwyth seems to me a model of how scholarly co-operation can and does work in a spirit of genuine collaboration and enquiry. And it would be hard for any historical linguist to live and work in an energetically bilingual environment like this without thinking about how matters must have been in the past, and wishing to know more.[1] I hope now that the publication of these papers will help others to know more, and to want to know more, about the patterns of multilingualism across Britain as a whole, and what they can tell us about past societies and past, and present, languages.

D.A.T.
Aberystwyth
December 1999

---

[1] For an attempt to address this in one respect, see 'L'anglo-français au Pays de Galles: une enquête préliminaire', *Revue de linguistique romane* 58 (1994), pp. 461–88.

Abbreviations

AND or AND1	William Rothwell et al., eds, *Anglo-Norman Dictionary* (London, 1977–92).
AND2	William Rothwell, Stewart Gregory and D. A. Trotter, eds, *Anglo-Norman Dictionary*, 2nd edn (in preparation).[1]
ANTS	Anglo-Norman Text Society
DEAF	Kurt Baldinger, ed., *Dictionnaire étymologique de l'ancien français* (Tübingen/Québec/Paris, 1971–).
DHLF	Alain Rey, ed., *Dictionnaire historique de la langue française* (Paris, 1992).
DMLBS	R. E. Latham and D. R. Howlett, eds, *Dictionary of Medieval Latin from British and Irish Sources* (Oxford, 1975–).
Du Cange	Charles du Fresne, Sieur Du Cange, ed., *Glossarium mediae et infimae latinitatis* (reprinted Graz, 1954).
FEW	Walther von Wartburg, ed., *Französisches Etymologisches Wörterbuch* (Bonn/Leipzig/Basel, 1922–).
G	Frédéric Godefroy, *Dictionnaire de l'ancienne langue française* (Paris, 1880–1902).
G Comp	*Complément* to the above (volumes 8–10 inclusive).
MED	Hans Kurath et al., eds, *Middle English Dictionary* (Ann Arbor, MI, 1956–).
OED	J. A. Simpson and E. S. C. Steiner, eds, *Oxford English Dictionary*, 2nd edn (Oxford, 1989).
RMLWL	R. E. Latham, ed., *Revised Medieval Latin Word-List* (Oxford, 1965).
TL	A. Tobler and E. Lommatzsch, *Altfranzösisches Wörterbuch* (Berlin, 1925–).

In addition, a number of chapters use their own abbreviation system, for which the reader is referred to the notes to individual chapters.

---

[1] The academic work for A–E is substantially complete, but publication has been blocked by a contract and copyright dispute.

Multilingualism in Later Medieval Britain: Introduction

'Monoglots are not good critics': so says no less an *auctoritas* than Frank Kermode, in his 1998 Presidential Address to the Modern Humanities Research Association, on *The Discipline of Literature*.[1] He makes the point that with the demise (at least in Britain) of an insistence on Anglo-Saxon and Middle English linguistic study as a compulsory element of a degree in English, 'it became possible to undertake the university study of "English" without troubling about languages that were both difficult and, in the opinion of many, irrelevant to their interests'.[2] The present volume shows only too clearly that medievalists cannot be permitted simply not to bother with 'difficult languages', still less to remain monoglot. Not one of the papers here would be thinkable, let alone achievable, for a monoglot. Other languages, 'difficult' or not – and most of them are 'difficult' –, are not irrelevant to the interests of those who write here: they are central to them. Many literary scholars clearly believe that they can function with English alone, can write at length on literature in sublime ignorance of rudimentary linguistic knowledge, and (in the case of all too many literary theorists) can indulge in extensive exegesis of translated versions of their canonical texts. Of course, another peculiarly British phenomenon, the disastrous divide between 'literature' and 'language', an idiocy thankfully not adopted elsewhere, has obscured the elementary fact that these are two aspects of one subject, not two independent disciplines.[3] But those whose interest lies in language find that one language alone is not sufficient if they wish to examine a period and a society where one language was emphatically *not* enough. The monolingual approach makes it impossible to apprehend this world, and it simply perpetuates the compartmentalised and misleading information transmitted by outdated, but consistently revered and no less regularly reprinted, manuals of the history of English or French. The study of the linguistic situation of medieval Britain cannot be carried out by specialists working in isolation, but requires a convergence of attention, and a determined refusal to hide behind the artificial barriers of either allegedly separate languages, or (perhaps above all) conveniently separated academic disciplines, each hermetically sealed against the dangers of contamination from adjacent fields of enquiry, and each buttressed by its own traditions or (less charitably) insulated by its own uncritical and self-preserving preconceptions. The *garoil* (see Möhren, this volume), both the real institutional and structural barrier, and above all

---

1 'The Discipline of Literature', printed in *Modern Language Review* 93 (1998), p. xxxvii.
2 Ibid., p. xxxvi.
3 In a forthcoming essay on 'The Anglo-French lexis of the *Ancrene Wisse*: a re-evaluation', to appear in a collection edited by Yoko Wada, I have discussed this very real problem at greater length.

the flimsy psychological palisade erected to keep out invading ideas, must be torn down and be put firmly in the museum of intellectual history where it belongs. The lawyer needs the Anglo-French expert, who needs the Latinist, who needs the Middle English scholar, who depends on the historian. The lexicographer needs them all, and many more besides. It was thus encouraging to find scholars from so many disciplines (and indeed, so many countries) willing to come to Aberystwyth to discuss such matters and in so open a manner; and it is my hope that the Collo-quium, far from concluding a discussion, will rather continue one, and will demon-strate the need for a concerted move forward to a truly interdisciplinary approach to the languages of medieval Britain.[4]

This volume contains thirteen of the twenty papers given at an international conference held at the University of Wales, Aberystwyth in September 1997.[5] The intention of the colloquium was to explore the languages of post-Conquest medieval Britain from a deliberately multilingual perspective. There have been colloquia on such themes before, but it seems that this was the first gathering which attempted this for that period in British history. By bringing together specialists in the various languages of medieval Britain, together with lexicographers currently preparing dictionaries of their respective languages, and scholars with an interest in phenomena such as language contact and language mixing, I hoped that it would be possible to get some way towards understanding the reality of multilingual medieval British society. Only too often, the study of the languages of medieval Britain is carried out within the distinct disciplines of the languages concerned, often with the implicit or unconscious assumption that modern monolingualism is a valid model for the investigation of the past; often, too, discipline-specific preconceptions and methodologies hamper an ability to compare and contrast. Yet this is an artificial divide, and an unhelpful one: no one can work on individual medieval languages without being acutely aware of the level of interference and contact with adjacent and competing languages, vernacular and Latin. Many writers, major, minor and anonymous, in all registers, were clearly at ease in two or more languages. Outside literary texts, documents in two or more languages, and language-mixing within the same text, were widespread, and this phenomenon, an oddity to modern eyes, patently created no obstacle to effective communication. Much of what is recorded from the law-courts in one language may well have been spoken in another. Multi-

---

4   To make an obvious point: extreme as the British case may be (all the more so as one moves into the Celtic-speaking areas), it is unlikely that the basic situation was radically different from that obtaining at least amongst the educated classes in the rest of Europe. Everywhere, there is at least Latin and vernacular; often, and increasingly with the standardisation of the vernacular, there is also a measure of diglossia within the vernacular. Much work (in the first instance archival) remains to be done in this general area.

5   The paper by Patrick SIMS-WILLIAMS, 'Breton *conteurs* and the *matière de Bretagne*', has now been published in *Romania* 116 (1998), pp. 72–111. The argument of David HOWLETT's 'Towards a history of literary languages in the British Isles' may be found in his 'Insular Latin Writers' Rhythms', *Peritia* 11 (1997), pp. 53–116; *Cambro-Latin Compositions: Their Competence and Craftsmanship* (Dublin, 1998); *Sealed from Within: Self-Authenticating Insular Charters* (Dublin, 1999, forth-coming); *English Origins of Old French Literature* (Dublin, 1997), and in *Pillars of Wisdom: Irishmen, Englishmen, Liberal Arts* (Dublin, 2000, forthcoming).

lingual glossaries are common, and their authors often seem uncertain as to which language is which. Their modern successors, compiling dictionaries of the languages of medieval Britain, have to contend with the same problem of deciding at what point words are part of 'their' language, and when what some would call 'loan-words' become a naturalised part of the target language. The whole question of lexical borrowing in the medieval context raises major problems, both theoretical and practical, which remain largely unresolved. What all this means is that the monolingual approach is neither appropriate nor adequate for the investigation of language use in a society where multilingualism was endemic and where, for the educated at least, monolingualism was the exception and not the norm.

The chapters below fall into three major groups: those which discuss and describe the historical evidence and reasons for language contact; those which deal with the phenomenon of language-mixing or code-switching in the medieval period; and those which tackle the practical consequences of language contact from a lexicographical perspective. Such a division seems neat in theory but (like the subject-matter of the conference itself) proves not so straightforward in practice.

A number of essays within the collection provide syntheses and overviews of what might be called the social background within which language contact exists. Llinos Beverly SMITH provides an authoritative account of the relationship between English and Welsh in medieval Wales, thus setting the scene for other studies within this volume which focus on the textual evidence of such proximity.[6] Begoña CRESPO reviews the historical background of multilingualism with specific reference to Middle English. Here, too, the paper offers a panoramic backdrop against which some of the more detailed contributions of other authors in this volume may be viewed. Two further essays fall halfway between historical sociolinguistics, and detailed textual analysis, in many respects drawing on the latter in order to furnish the former: Andres KRISTOL looks at the manuscript evidence which shows how one Anglo-Norman author responded to the challenge of multilingualism, and what the manuscript tradition can tell us about not only the relationship between the languages in play, but (perhaps more importantly) concerning speakers' and writers' attitudes towards the different vernaculars. Michael RICHTER, building on a series of previous studies, revisits the documents in the Vatican dossier concerning the canonisation of Thomas Cantilupe in the early fourteenth century, and elicits from them detailed but generalisable findings regarding patterns of language use in the Hereford area. Finally, Paul BRAND provides a masterly synthesis of data from a range of sources regarding the use of different languages within the legal system.

It will be readily apparent that the classification of these studies into the first group ('historical') is misleading, since most if not all would be equally at home in my second group, where the focus is language mixing and contact within texts or

---

6 The paper by Ceridwen LLOYD MORGAN, on loan words in medieval Welsh, not included in the published proceedings, revealed one of the major difficulties from a Welsh perspective: namely, that it is often difficult, indeed impossible, to determine with any measure of certainty whether a given word in medieval Welsh comes from French, or English, or even from both.

documents. At least three of the articles in the volume fall reasonably squarely into this category. Herbert SCHENDL and Luis IGLESIAS-RÁBADE both explore, in different ways, the influence of French on Middle English. Schendl looks closely at the phenomenon of code-switching at a predominantly lexical level, deploying a corpus of data from which it emerges that the phenomenon is both widespread and specific in the way in which it operates. Iglesias-Rábade surveys the well-documented pattern of phrasal verb structures (involving *take(n)/nime(n)*) which were clearly appropriated from medieval French (more precisely, in fact, Anglo-Norman) into Middle English as part of the contact process. The issue of code-switching in medical texts is addressed by Tony HUNT, with an analysis which demonstrates how in this text-type, the pattern is rule-governed, productive, and extensively found. Hunt's comments on language contact and its implications should be read by all those who imagine that they can manage by studying one language on its own. Laura WRIGHT, finally, reviews what she describes as the 'everyday tri-lingual activity' of the business world of later medieval England: where, again, code-switching, language-mixing, and mixed language texts are not merely wide-spread, but are the defining characteristics of this type of discourse. Not the least of the questions which her work (here and elsewhere) raises is that of the remarkable linguistic versatility displayed by an admittedly educated, but hardly socially elite group.

For those who attempt to record in dictionaries the type of data which the authors of these papers discuss, there are major problems of methodology, and indeed of ideology, to confront and to overcome. Four articles explicitly tackle some of the lexicographical consequences of the type of language-mixing discussed by many other contributors to this collection. For Frankwalt MÖHREN the word *garoil* is an object-lesson which enables him to spell out a number of conclusions for the lexi-cographer, prominent amongst which is the suggestion that, in order adequately to account for the development of the word's form and meaning, in medieval French, the historical lexicographer must range widely not only in his sources but also in the languages which he considers. Monolingual lexicography in a multilingual environ-ment does not work. Similar conclusions emerge from Edmund WEINER's account of the revision of the OED, from which it is clear that reliance on multilingual text-types is radically altering (some would say belatedly) the accepted chronology of many words in the history of English.[7] It is evident that OED3 will be a genuinely new edition, and will transform our knowledge of English. Lisa JEFFERSON provides a survey of Anglo-French words in the records of the Goldsmiths' Company; not only does the article provide a host of words not hitherto attested, it also points to significant levels of language-mixing, borrowing, and code-switching throughout

---

[7]   Another unpublished paper given at the Aberystwyth colloquium, that by Gareth BEVAN (editor of the *Geiriadur Prifysgol Cymru*) indicated a similar, radical revision of datings, this time in Welsh and as a result of a major series of editions being produced within the Centre for Advanced Welsh and Celtic Studies of the University of Wales. Paul SCHAFFNER's 'Towards an interlingual lexicon', from the standpoint of the MED, reached similar conclusions to Weiner's.

this important corpus of late-medieval documents. Finally, in this group of contributions by practitioners, William ROTHWELL's contribution, on lexical and morphosyntactical mixing, picks up on themes discussed also by Schendl, Wright, and Hunt, as well as (more implicitly) by those of nearly every contributor to this volume. Rothwell is concerned to explore what might be called the limits between languages: his main conclusion, and it is one which is fully in keeping with that of the conference as a whole, is that those limits are far from watertight. The modern (post-medieval) urge is to label words as belonging explicitly to one language, implicitly available for borrowing from that language to others, but fundamentally remaining distinct entities within distinct sets of lexical items. Modern studies of bilingualism, in societies as diverse as Haiti, French Canada or Wales, have conclusively demonstrated that this pattern is by no means general: it does not hold at all for the bilingual individual, still less for such an individual within a society characterised by bilingualism or multilingualism. Patently, it does not work in medieval Britain. An interesting question, though something of a footnote to a volume on medieval multilingualism, is whether this rigid demarcation between languages holds good even for monolinguals in a Europe increasingly dominated by, and infiltrated by loanwords from, English. Herbert Schendl, at the close of his article, remarks that the study of documents of the past can be every bit as exciting for the linguist and sociolinguist as the study of present-day language varieties. The normal approach of course is to apply the findings of modern bilingualism to the study of the past. It could equally be argued, and as much is implicit in many of the articles in this volume, that the study of linguistic and sociolinguistic patterns of the past has much to tell us about the present.

The Welsh and English Languages in Late-Medieval Wales

LLINOS BEVERLEY SMITH

TOWARDS THE middle of the fifteenth century a Welsh poet, probably Tudur Penllyn, a modest landowner from Penllyn in Merionethshire and one who practised the profession of drover, composed a *cywydd* recording a conversation which he had, apparently, conducted with a young English girl. *Dydd daed, Saesnes gyffes, gain, Yr wyf i'th garu, riain* ('Good day to you, fine handy Englishwoman, I really fancy you, girl') is the poet's opening salvo in the encounter. *What saist, mon? . . . Ffor truthe, harde Welsman i tro* retorts the young lady. As the *cywydd* proceeds, as the poet becomes ever bolder in his suggestive remarks and as the maiden becomes ever more indignant at his unwelcome advances, it becomes evident that neither understands a word of the other's language. *I am not Wels, thow Welsmon, Ffor byde the, lete me alone*, exclaims the woman. *Na fydd ddig, Seisnig Saesnes, Yn war gad ddyfod yn nes* ('Don't be angry, English Englishwoman, be gentle and let me come closer') implores the poet, and it is this situation of mutual incomprehension which he wickedly and deliciously exploits for maximum comic effect.[1] Yet the very fact that a mid-fifteenth-century Welsh poet had sufficient command of the English language to compose several couplets in fluent *cynghanedd* is in itself suggestive of familiarity with English on the part of the author himself and, perhaps, on the part of his audience. It is with the inter-relationship of Welsh and English in the period from the final conquest of Wales in 1282–3 to the Union legislation of 1536, and its celebrated 'language clause', that this paper will be concerned and with the historical and cultural contexts in which the two languages accommodated to each other in late-medieval Wales.[2]

By the mid-fifteenth century the English language had long been a natural mother tongue among inhabitants of urban and rural communities both in the borderland and within Wales. Although direct evidence of language-use is exiguous, the comments of medieval and later observers are illuminating. In his account of an

---

[1] For the text of the *cywydd* see T. Roberts, *Gwaith Tudur Penllyn ac Ieuan ap Tudur Penllyn* (Cardiff, 1958), pp. 53–4 and D. Johnston, *Medieval Welsh Erotic Poetry* (Cardiff, 1991), pp. 75–7. Reference is made here to the text and translation contained in the latter edition.

[2] For a fuller discussion and documentation of some of the issues in this paper see Llinos Beverley Smith, 'The Welsh Language Before 1536', *The Welsh Language Before the Industrial Revolution*, ed. G. H. Jenkins (Cardiff, 1997), pp. 15–45.

incident at Cardiff Gerald of Wales related how a knight from the region (*de finibus illis oriundus*) translated the king's French speech into English; at the end of the fourteenth century John Trevisa, in his translation of Higden's *Polychronicon*, could assert how 'the Flemmynges that woneth in the weste side of Wales haueth i-lleft her straunge speche and speaketh Saxonliche i-now'; while the Elizabethan antiquary, George Owen of Henllys, admittedly a late witness, was firmly of the opinion that 'the greatest parte of these people that came into Pembrokshere with these [Norman] Earles were Saxons and Englishmen', and that 'manye of them yf not maior pars were Saxons, for otherwise the Englishe tongue had not ben theire comon and mother speache as it was'.[3] Moreover, there is also some evidence that such early settlers were reinforced in the twelfth and thirteenth centuries by successive waves of new colonists who braved the perils of the Severn Sea and set down their roots in South Pembrokeshire and the Vale of Glamorgan. Much the best documented movement of settlers into Wales, however, was that which took place in the immediate aftermath of the conquest of 1282–3 when English settlers were attracted into the nascent castle-boroughs of Wales and, in some instances, to the rural townships of the north-eastern lordships and imparted a distinctively English flavour to the parts where they settled.[4] The use of English words and phrases is sometimes revealed in surviving court rolls. Those of Rhuthun, the caput of the lordship of Dyffryn Clwyd for which an outstanding series of court rolls survives, show that in the fourteenth century words such as *barmcloit, aelstake, yarnwindle, buffin, rewet, maesfat, borcloth* and *paltok* are included in inventories of goods and chattels and, if it reflects colloquial usage as well as scribal practice, this suggests that the English language was widely used in such milieux. Seignorial account rolls, likewise, regularly employ stock English terms such as *lathnail, bordnail, groundwerk, waturwalk* or *fflodyetes* in recording expenditure on mill-works and buildings.[5] By the fifteenth century the English ambience of the town of Caernarfon is attested not only by the presence of English place names and field names within the town and its liberties but also by the fact that one of Sir John Wynn's ancestors, as he claimed, had been

3   B. Scott and F. X. Martin, eds, *Expugnatio Hibernica: the Conquest of Ireland, by Giraldus Cambrensis* (Dublin, 1978), p. 110; C. Babington, ed., *Polychronicon Ranulphi Higden Monachi Cestrensis* (9 vols, London, 1865–86), II, p. 159; H. Owen, ed., *George Owen: The Description of Penbrokshire* (4 vols, London, 1892–1936), I, pp. 36–7.

4   See, in general, R. R. Davies, 'Colonial Wales', *Past and Present* 65 (1974), pp. 3–23; D. Huw Owen, 'The Englishry of Denbigh: An English Colony in Medieval Wales', *Transactions of the Honourable Society of Cymmrodorion* [*THSC*] (1975), pp. 57–76; R. I. Jack, 'Welsh and English in the Medieval Lordship of Ruthin', *Transactions of the Denbighshire Historical Society* 18 (1969), pp. 23–49; A. D. M. Barrell and M. H. Brown, 'A Settler Community in Post-Conquest Rural Wales: The English of Dyffryn Clwyd, 1294–1399', *Welsh History Review* 17 (1994–5), pp. 332–56.

5   References to the Dyffryn Clwyd Court Rolls calendared in a database compiled at Aberystwyth are to the database record number. The work was funded by ESRC (Awards Number R000232548 and R000234070) whose support is gratefully acknowledged. All other references to the court rolls of Dyffryn Clwyd are to the relevant roll and membrane number. For English words and phrases see e.g. GC1/1809, 2321; GC3/2115; GC4/787; GC7/543 and OED s.v. From among many examples of expenditure on mill-works in seignorial accounts, see National Library of Wales (hereafter NLW) Chirk Castle D9, D40.

sent there to school where, in addition to acquiring a knowledge of Latin, he 'learnt the English tongue'.[6] Because of the importance and the interest attached to these movements and their possible consequences for the development of English as it was spoken and written in late-medieval Wales it is worth pausing briefly to examine the settlers in greater detail.

A number of characteristics deserve our attention. In the first place, the wide migration-fields which even a small late-thirteenth century Welsh castle-borough could command need to be noted, a pattern which in England can only be matched by the very largest of towns, and, more especially, the great city of London. Second, we can be certain that the colonists, for such they may be called, came directly from the town or village which lent them their label of origin and indeed, on occasion, there is direct evidence of their provenance. When, for example, in 1358 a Rhuthun burgess set out his claim to the urban estate of his kinsman Thomas Don, through a line of descent which stretched back to a certain Thomas Carpenter of Rothwell in Yorkshire, he was described as a 'stranger from Rothwell in the county of York whose kindred is unknown in these parts' (*dictus Hugh extraneus de Rothwell de comitatu Eborac' de cuius parentela incognita est in partibus istis*).[7] Third, the wide social diversity of the colonists is attested by the fact that their numbers included not only functionaries of seignorial administrations (although these certainly formed a self-conscious and distinctive group) but also craftsmen and tradesmen who set down their roots in the towns where they settled. Finally, within the small compass of a Welsh castle-borough there lived men and women who were often drawn from regions of strong and contrasting dialectal diversity as a few illustrative examples will show. At Rhuthun, a town for which much detailed evidence in the form of a series of court-rolls spanning almost the whole of the fourteenth and fifteenth centuries survives (as was noted above), it can be shown that immigrant families from Northamptonshire and Bedfordshire, evidenced by such surnames as Weedon, Flitwick and Helpston, intermingled with Leicestershire Grobys and Hinckleys, with families from Yorkshire and Lancashire as well as from the border counties of Cheshire, Shropshire and Herefordshire with which the Grappenhalls, Bunburies, Egges, Ludlows and Landingates were associated.[8] Such a mixing bowl of dialects (*mutatis mutandis)* can be replicated in towns such as Denbigh or Conwy, Caernarfon or Carmarthen and certainly deserves to be taken into account in any analysis of the character of the English language spoken and written in Wales.[9]

6   J. G. Jones, *Sir John Wynn, History of the Gwydir Family and Memoirs* (Llandysul, 1990), p. 49.

7   PRO, SC2/218/7, m. 5v.

8   See the detailed study by O. J. Padel, 'Locational Surnames in Fourteenth-Century Denbighshire', *Names, Places and People: An Onomastic Miscellany for John McNeal Dodgson*, ed. A. R. Rumble and A. D. Mills (Stanford, 1997), pp. 279–300, esp. pp. 294–300.

9   For e.g. Carmarthen see T. James, 'Medieval Carmarthen and its Burgesses: A Study of Town Growth and Burgess Families in the Later Thirteenth Century', *The Carmarthenshire Antiquary* 25 (1989), pp. 9–26, esp. pp. 18–25; R. A. Griffiths, 'Carmarthen', in idem, ed., *Boroughs of Medieval Wales* (Cardiff, 1978), pp. 131–65. The poet Dafydd ap Gwilym (fl. c.1320–70), referred to the *lediaith lud* ('persistent alien speech') of the wife of an Aberystwyth burgess (T. Parry, ed., *Gwaith Dafydd ap Gwilym* (Cardiff, 1952), p. 266).

By the early fifteenth century, if not earlier, clear evidence of the infiltration of English into domains hitherto dominated by Latin and French can be adduced, in a process which parallels the development of the English language in England. Despite the continuing importance of Latin as a language of record, the replacement of French by English as a language of documentary literacy is clear. Once again, a few illustrative examples of the spheres in which English was used must suffice. Property deeds written in English survive, such as the gage relating to land in Beaumaris to be found in the Baron Hill collection at the University of Wales Bangor or the indenture, in English, relating to land in the town of Rhuthun. Increasingly, arbitration awards and marriage contracts were drawn up in English and correspond almost precisely to the format of such documents in fifteenth and early-sixteenth century England. Conditional bonds, deployed by the same period, are commonly endorsed in English. Wills, when they were not written in Latin, were almost invariably recorded in English and, of the three hundred and fifty or so wills of Welsh provenance so far identified, nearly a half were written either partly or entirely in English.[10] By then, too, petitions which in the fourteenth century were expressed in French are far more commonly written in English and, if the testimony of George Owen of Henllys is to be credited, the habit, familiar enough among literate Welshmen and women of a much later age, of penning their personal correspondence in English was already firmly established. Noting the low prestige accorded the English tongue in the wake of the Norman conquest of England and the preference among English speakers then for writing in French, he referred to the selfsame tendency at work within Wales where Welshmen 'allthoughe they vsuallye speacke the welshe tongue, yett will they writte eche to other in Englishe, and not in the speache they vsuallye talke'.[11] The letter written by or on behalf of the outlaw Gruffudd ap Dafydd ap Gruffudd and dated at the park of Bryncyffo in the lordship of Dyffryn Clwyd during the second decade of the fifteenth century, and the brief exemplars preserved in the commonplace or formulary book of Edward ap Rhys, a volume of early-sixteenth-century date, are illustrative examples.[12] Equally suggestive of the important presence of English in Wales is the inclusion of texts written in English in manuscripts of Welsh provenance. As Dr William Marx comments, in some of the surviving manuscripts Welsh is the first language and English the minority language in what appear to have been single campaigns of compilation,

---

[10] See University of Wales, Bangor, Baron Hill Collection 476; NLW Trovarth and Coedcoch Deeds and Documents 793; NLW Brogyntyn 3450 (a marriage agreement between John Owen ap John ap Maredudd and Lowri, daughter of Madog ab Ieuan ap Gruffudd). For arbitration awards written in English see Llinos Beverley Smith, 'Disputes and Settlements in Late-Medieval Wales: The Role of Arbitration', *English Historical Review* 106 (1991), pp. 835–60; references have been confined to illustrative examples. For wills in English see Helen Chandler, 'The Will in Medieval Wales to 1540' (unpublished University of Wales M.Phil. thesis, 1991), Appendix.

[11] See e.g. PRO SC2/222/1, m. 52; SC2/223/2, m. 6a; SC2/223/3, m. 5. Herefordshire Record Office O/29, p. 109b (a petition from the parishioners of the parish of Hyssington in the diocese of Hereford); Owen, *Description*, I, p. 36.

[12] D. Gray, ed., *The Oxford Book of Late Medieval Verse and Prose* (Oxford, 1985), pp. 34–5; NLW Peniarth 354.

while in others English language items have been added to Welsh-language manu-scripts. Whatever the precise linguistic balance, however, it is noteworthy that manu-scripts of mid- to late-fifteenth-century date such as Peniarth 26, Peniarth 50 and Peniarth 53 include English-language medical texts, prophecies, recipes and poetry.[13] The celebrated 'Hymn to the Virgin', attributed to Ieuan ap Hywel Swrdwal and rightly described as a *tour de force*, whatever the precise circumstances of its composition, is possibly the first attempt by a Welsh writer to write in English in strict metre *cynghanedd* and is, likewise, a work of the mid- or late-fifteenth century.[14]

What can be said of the character of the English language spoken and written in late-medieval Wales? Until the entire corpus of English language texts which can be reliably sourced within Wales is subjected to detailed and critical analysis, it is diffi-cult to be certain whether a Cambro-English comparable to the Irish-English identi-fied in late-medieval Ireland ever existed.[15] Of those texts which have been scrutinised, it is suggested, for instance, that the Hymn to the Virgin shows traces of a West Midlands dialect although analyses of other texts done so far provide little material of dialectal interest. The most recent overview of 'Welsh' English has suggested, for instance, that before the twentieth century the English language docu-mented in the usage of native Welsh writers is that of standard English seldom distinguishable from that of England; while Shakespeare's treatment of his native Welsh characters and their speech combines dialectally locatable features, such as strongly aspirated plosives and non-standard verb-forms which can be described as 'Welsh', with other features which reflect a more general vernacular usage, the whole deployed to suggest a comic scenario rather than a specifically regional loca-tion.[16] However, in any investigation of the language of English medieval texts of Welsh provenance, some thought might be given to the historical evidence not only of language contact between speakers of English and Welsh but of dialect contact among speakers of English. Trudgill in his analysis of dialects in contact, for instance, has suggested that colonial English varieties are what they are 'because of the way in which people behave linguistically in face-to-face interaction', and that when dialects are mixed 'large numbers of variants will abound and, through the process of accommodation, interdialect phenomena will begin to occur'.[17] What, for

---

13 I am most grateful to Dr William Marx, University of Wales, Lampeter, for letting me see his comments on the manuscripts in his Introduction to the Handlist of Manuscripts in NLW containing Middle English prose.

14 E. J. Dobson, 'The Hymn to the Virgin', *THSC* (1954), pp. 70–124; G. Williams, *The Welsh Church from Conquest to Reformation* (Cardiff, 1962), p. 424.

15 See, in general, A. McIntosh, M. L. Samuels and M. Benskin, eds, *A Linguistic Atlas of Late Medi-aeval English* (Aberdeen, 1986), I, pp. 59 and 269–70. On the English of Ireland see J. L. Kallen, 'English in Ireland', in R. Burchfield, ed., *The Cambridge History of the English Language*, V (Cambridge, 1994), pp. 148–96 and A. Bliss, 'Language and Literature', in J. Lydon, ed., *The English in Medieval Ireland* (Dublin, 1984), pp. 27–45.

16 See A. R. Thomas, 'English in Wales', *Cambridge History of the English Language*, V, esp. pp. 107–10.

17 P. Trudgill, *Dialects in Contact* (Oxford, 1986), pp. 1–83, 126.

example, was the consequence for the spoken English language in Wales of the intermingling, through day to day contact and through marriage, of families from contrasting English regions? When, to take one instance, the daughter of Nicholas de Lidley, a family of Shropshire origin in its third generation in late-fourteenth-century Rhuthun, married the newcomer William Groby from Leicestershire, in what ways, if at all, was their offsprings' language affected? Or in what ways were the speech patterns of the grandchildren of Andrew de Landingate, who hailed from the Herefordshire borders, influenced by the marriages of his three daughters with husbands of different dialectal traditions?[18] To be sure, the implicit comparison between the late-thirteenth and fourteenth-century English colonies in Wales and the experiences of later colonial movements should not be pressed too far. The English language in Wales did not, after all, develop in relative isolation from the speech of the home land. The settler community did not weather a lengthy sea voyage nor, indeed, was their language an intimate, secret lingo of a shared prison experience. They did not confront a strange vegetation or landscape nor, on the whole, a people of unfamiliar customs and habits. Even so, this early colonial venture and settlement, it may be suggested, left some permanent imprint on the English language in Wales and should certainly be taken into account when the sorely needed analysis of English texts of Welsh provenance is accomplished.[19]

Turning from English to the spatial distribution and domains of the Welsh language in Wales, a number of features deserve particular emphasis. In the first place, there can be little doubt that in geographical terms the Welsh language was far more widely disseminated in the medieval centuries than was true of later periods. Indeed, there is good reason to believe that the language had been able to survive and to re-establish its strength in areas which, in earlier times, had been won for the Saxons and for the Norman invaders. In the area between Clun and Montgomery, to take one example, it was claimed in 1307 that the residents of three townships had command of only the Welsh language with the result that Thomas Cantilupe, bishop of Hereford, was constrained to make use of an interpreter when he preached in the region, just as in the late fourteenth century the parishioners of the parish of Garway in Archenfield maintained that their parish priest was unable adequately to minister to their needs 'for he knew no Welsh and many of them had no knowledge of English'.[20] We might note that these border lands, including some areas comprised within the counties of Shropshire and Hereford, were not only regions where settled Welsh-speaking inhabitants were to be found but also experienced an influx of Welshmen and women, many of them harvest workers drawn to the ripening

---

[18] For the Lidleys, Grobys and Landingates see, from among numerous references, Reliefs/257; D/623; D/6575.

[19] See the discussion by L. Bauer and G. W. Turner in *Cambridge History of the English Language*, V, pp. 277–327.

[20] M. Richter, *Sprache und Gesellschaft im Mittelalter: Untersuchungen zur mündlichen Kommunikation in England von der Mitte des elften bis zum Beginn des vierzehnten Jahrhunderts* (Stuttgart, 1979), p. 196; A. T. Bannister, 'Visitation Returns of the Diocese of Hereford in 1397', *English Historical Review* 44 (1929), p. 289.

harvests of lowland England, whose presence, albeit temporary, must have created a demand for a spiritual ministry in Welsh and accustomed the permanent settlers to the speech and culture of their Welsh neighbours. A chance reference in the rich records of the bishop of Hereford's consistory court shows how the Welsh poet, Ieuan Dyfi, had sojourned, and elicited the attentions of the functionaries of ecclesiastical justice, at Norton near Presteigne, while equally indicative of the Welsh texture of many of the border settlements is the fact that several of the poets of the fourteenth and fifteenth centuries were regular visitors to gentry homes in the area.[21] Owain ap Llywelyn ab y Moel, to take one example, was one for whom Offa's Dyke, once the acknowledged boundary between the Welsh and the English, held little significance for, although he referred to the dyke in his *cywyddau*, his patrons were to be found on either side of the traditional line. Caurse castle, for all its self-consciously Norman nomenclature, was, by the fifteenth century 'a court which fostered the language' under the kindly tutelage of its master, while the poet Lewys Glyn Cothi saluted his patron, Sion ap Hywel ap Tomas of Ewias Lacy, as *clo'r Dre-hyr* (the lock of Longtown).[22] Indeed, rightly or wrongly, the impression conveyed by the evidence is of a distinct rejuvenation of the Welsh language within several communities in the course of the fifteenth century, although whether such an apparent renaissance resulted in an absolute increase or rather a redistribution of existing Welsh speakers into areas and social milieux where the language was unknown at an earlier date is an important but unanswerable question. By the early sixteenth century, the poet Thomas ab Ieuan, although noting the English speech of the dwellers of the village of Wick in the Vale of Glamorgan, was also accustomed to seeking sustenance and alms in the manors of Laleston, Llangewydd and Ogmore where English or Anglo-Norman settlers had once held sway.[23] Even if the circumstances which may have encouraged the increasing colloquial use of the Welsh language in some parts of Wales require more detailed investigation, the fact of its resurgence seems clear enough.

What may be said of the standards of the written and spoken language and the domains of its use? In so far as the spoken language is concerned, the existence of strong local dialects is attested by several writers, including Gerald of Wales. In one of the most fascinating and revealing passages of his *Descriptio Kambriae*, Gerald comments as follows: 'it is thought that the Welsh language is richer, more carefully pronounced and preferable in all respects in north Wales, for the area has far fewer foreigners. Others maintain that the speech of Ceredigion in south Wales is better articulated and more to be admired, since it is in the middle and the heartland of Wales.'[24] Likewise, some of the thirteenth- and fourteenth-century poets, by referring to *y Wyndodeg* (the Welsh of Gwynedd in north Wales) or *y Wenhwyseg* (the

---

21 The episode concerning Ieuan Dyfi is discussed in Llinos Beverley Smith, 'Olrhain Anni Goch', *Ysgrifau Beirniadol* 19 (1993), pp. 107–27.

22 E. Rolant, ed., *Gwaith Owain ap Llywelyn ab y Moel* (Cardiff, 1984), pp. 2, 5, 14; D. Johnston, ed., *Gwaith Lewys Glyn Cothi* (Cardiff, 1995), pp. 274–5.

23 D. H. Evans, 'Thomas ab Ieuan a'i "Ysgowld o Wraig"', *Ysgrifau Beirniadol* 19 (1993), pp. 86–106.

24 J. F. Dimmock, ed., *Giraldi Cambrensis Opera*, 8 vols (London, 1861–91), V, p. 177.

Gwentian speech of the south-east) attest to the regional distinctiveness of the spoken language.[25] But variegated as the dialects of spoken Welsh may have been, its written standard had achieved a remarkable degree of uniformity at an early period. It may well be that a 'northern written standard' was already exerting its influence on the written standards of other regions, but the task of identifying the geographical associations of medieval Welsh texts has proved difficult even though new methodological and analytical approaches are beginning to uncover interesting dialectological perspectives. In general, however, and most certainly in comparison with the fortunes of English in the thirteenth and fourteenth centuries, it is the standardisation not the dialectal variation of written Welsh which is deserving of emphasis.[26]

Turning to the domains of its use, we might note that in addition to the abundant corpus of vernacular poetry and prose, increasingly committed to writing, a rich harvest of functional prose texts, both works of translation and original compositions, may be identified. Despite claims made of the difficulty of rendering texts into the vernacular (a common enough *topos* of the medieval translator) they reveal a supple language fully capable of sophisticated scientific and philosophical expression. The domain of the Welsh language, it has been well said, 'was not purely that of Celtic romance and magic, of archaic legalism, heroic praise poetry and love lyrics, but of a complex mixture of philosophy, religion, science, music and grammar which underlay and enriched the native literary genres.'[27] Historical writing in Welsh of which *Brut y Tywysogyon* (The Chronicle of the Princes), a translation into Welsh of a now lost Latin original, is the outstanding example, shows not only how a profound national consciousness was sustained in the post-conquest period but also how Welsh had become, in the monastic *scriptorium*, a medium as worthy as Latin for preserving the nation's history.[28] In the sphere of legal literature, the use of Welsh had long been established and the surviving texts, which date from the middle of the thirteenth century onwards, constitute one of the most impressive examples of the use of the vernacular among the medieval nations of Europe. The texts reveal rich resources in technical terms and a capacity for precise legal expression. Pleading in Welsh was taken for granted (as is shown by the tractate on pleading incorporated in thirteenth-century redactions) while, by the sixteenth century, the rich technical vocabulary of the law texts had extended far

---

[25] N. G. Costigan (Bosco) et al., *Gwaith Dafydd Benfras ac Eraill o Feirdd Hanner Cyntaf y Drydedd Ganrif ar Ddeg* (Cardiff, 1995), p. 445; T. B. Pugh, ed., *Glamorgan County History*, III (Cardiff, 1971), p. 483.

[26] See P. W. Thomas, 'Middle Welsh Dialects: Problems and Perspectives', *Bulletin of the Board of Celtic Studies [BBCS]* 40 (1993), pp. 17–50; R. A. Lodge, 'Language Attitudes and Linguistic Norms in France and England in the Thirteenth Century', in P. R. Coss and S. D. Lloyd, eds, *Thirteenth Century England, IV: Proceedings of the Newcastle Upon Tyne Conference 1991* (Woodbridge, 1992), pp. 73–83; J. Milroy, 'Middle English Dialectology', in Blake, ed., *Cambridge History of the English Language*, II, pp. 156–206.

[27] M. E. Owen, 'Functional Prose: Religion, Science, Grammar, Law', in A. O. H. Jarman and G. R. Hughes, eds, *A Guide to Welsh Literature*, I (Cardiff, 1992), pp. 248–76.

[28] T. Jones, 'Historical Writing in Medieval Welsh', *Scottish Studies* 12 (1968), pp. 15–27.

beyond the courts of law. It has been shown that in the luxuriant lexis of Salesbury's New Testament translation there are a substantial number of terms derived from the medieval Welsh lawbooks of which one, Peniarth MS 30, was liberally annotated in Salesbury's hand.[29] In the north-east march it is clear that landowners might commit their private financial accounts and personal memoranda to writing in Welsh, as is suggested by a late-fifteenth-century manuscript volume which includes a number of property deeds written in Welsh. Likewise, a volume comprising texts in Welsh, Latin and French and attributed to John Edwards of Chirk shows how legal vocabulary of English or French derivation had been absorbed into the Welsh language. Words such as *ysgutor* (executor), *yndeintur* (indenture) and *gweithred ffi-tail* (a deed of fee-tail) appear alongside native legal vernacular terms such as *cynhysgaeth* and *tremyg* and even the 'writ of novel disseisin' is felicitously rendered into Welsh as *cwyn newydd-ddifeddiant*. From north-west Wales a document in Welsh recorded the partition of the lands of Hywel ap Gruffudd Fychan of Abererch in Llyn, while arbitration awards drawn up in both the lordship of Denbigh and in the county of Carmarthen reflect the continuing use of Welsh in bringing disputes to conclusion in extra-curial proceedings.[30] In all of these instances, chance survivals from a body of evidence which was once, perhaps, substantial, the Welsh language comes into view not as an archaic and cumbersome medium but as one with a capacity to express contemporary technical concepts and as a language of practical, functional use.

If the volume owned by John Edwards of Chirk suggests the broad linguistic repertoire of its owner, it is equally clear that competence in more than one language was by no means universal in late-medieval Wales. On the contrary, the language divide is abundantly evidenced in a number of sources. In the thirteenth century, the poet Dafydd Benfras (c.1220–58), while he displayed an acute and early awareness of the various languages in use in his time, nonetheless confessed that his own linguistic abilities were modest:

> Ni wybum erioed medru Saesneg,
> Ni wn ymadrawdd o ffrawdd Ffrangeg;
> Pan geisiais-i esill o Ennilleg
> Cam oedd, neud ydoedd yn Wyndodeg![31]

> (Ability in English I never had, Neither knew I phrases of passionate French, When I attempted a syllable of Scandinavian, It was all wrong, it came out as the language of Gwynedd.)

Likewise, agents of secular and ecclesiastical authority had found it necessary to make use of interpreters or latimers. Their use is referred to at several points in the

---

29 T. M. Charles-Edwards, '*Cynghawsedd*: Counting and Pleading in Medieval Welsh Law', *BBCS* 33 (1986), pp. 188–98: D. Ifans, *William Salesbury and the Welsh Laws* (Aberystwyth, 1980).

30 Cardiff MS 51; BL Add. MS 46846; NLW Edwinsford 3366; University of Wales, Bangor Library, Mostyn 786; NLW Trovarth and Coedcoch 573.

31 *Gwaith Dafydd Benfras*, p. 445; see also the general comments of M. Richter, 'Monolingualism and Mutlilingualism in the Fourteenth Century', in idem, *Studies in Medieval Language and Culture* (Dublin, 1995), pp. 77–85.

writings of Gerald of Wales; in the march of Wales men might hold land in return for their services as latimers while their use by the seignorial regimes of the fourteenth century can be securely documented. Equally revealing is the evidence presented at Swansea in the course of the canonisation proceedings of Thomas Cantilupe, bishop of Hereford. William ap Rhys, a convicted felon whose miraculous survival through the bishop's intercession had prompted the enquiry, not only gave his evidence in Welsh through interpreters and was specifically described as one who knew no Latin, no French and no English, but had confessed his sins to a Welsh-speaking priest 'because he knew not how to speak English'.[32] It is significant that William ap Rhys, although he hailed from Llanrhidian in the Gower peninsula, a village situated on the very border of two linguistic and cultural zones, nonetheless, was, by his own clear admission, a monoglot Welshman. Several centuries later, the profound linguistic dichotomy of Pembrokeshire was vividly described by George Owen in a celebrated and compelling passage:

> You shall finde in on parish a pathe waye parteinge the welshe and Englishe, and on the on side speake all Englishe, the other all welshe . . . And nowe this diversitie of speeches breedeth some inconveniences, soe that often tymes it is founde at the Assises, that in a iurye of xii men there wilbe the one half that cannot vnderstand the others wordes; and yett must they agree upon the truth of the matter, before they departe; and I have seene two tryers sworne for tryall of the rest of the pannell, the on meere Englishe, the other not vnderstandinge anye worde of the Englishe, have lasted out three daies vpon the matter: the on not able to speake to the other.[33]

Moreover, he also contended that the 'meaner sorte' of both cultures did not normally join together in marriage nor engage in commercial transactions with one another. Whether or not this was the case, it may well be that in some areas of Wales there existed linguistically homogenous communities where, even when mixed marriages and commercial exchanges can be securely documented, discrete language groups tended to assimilate the speakers of other tongues.[34]

Even so, the language divide was by no means unbridgeable. Although George Owen made much of the fissures in culture, habits and language in his own native county, he also commented on the important bilingual element in Pembrokeshire society, for the inhabitants of about six parishes, so he averred, spoke both English and Welsh.[35] These six parishes, 'as it were the marches betweene both those Nations', according to Owen, reflected in microcosm the greater march between England and Wales where the use of several languages can scarcely be doubted.[36] Although it is far easier to document the linguistic repertoire of individuals than

---

[32] Richter, *Sprache und Gesellschaft*, pp. 197–201.
[33] Owen, *Description*, I, p. 40.
[34] Ibid., p. 39; see also the discussion by Janos M. Bak, ' "Linguistic Pluralism" in Medieval Hungary', in M. A. Meyer, ed., *The Culture of Christendom* (London, 1993), p. 278.
[35] Owen, *Description*, I, p. 48.
[36] See, in general, Smith, 'The Welsh Language', pp. 33–5 and the references cited.

communities, the evidence is, even so, suggestive. Among people of high social rank there is much direct or indirect evidence for the acquisition of language skills. The epithet Sais (Englishman or English speaker), although by the fourteenth century it is, perhaps, less reliable as an indicator of competence in English, may, for earlier periods, betoken the ability to speak English. For interpreters and translators such skills were a matter of professional necessity and pride, but it may well be that a knowledge of French and possibly of English had already been growing apace more generally in the period before the conquest of 1282–3. Leading servants of Prince Llywelyn ap Gruffudd had spent long periods in England as prisoners or servants of King Henry III while members of important lineages were sent to England as hostages, often as children, so that opportunities to learn the tongue of their captors may have been many. Indeed, we might note that although references are made to the use of interpreters in the course of diplomatic negotiations in documents of the twelfth century, references to their use in the far more voluminous records of the thirteenth century are exiguous, a point which suggests an increasing linguistic competence on the part of prominent Welshmen.[37] In the march between England and Wales there were, by the late middle ages, high-ranking families whose members, according to poetic evidence, were competent in English and Welsh. The fifteenth-century poet, Bedo Brwynllys, specifically commended his patron, Thomas ap Rosier of Hergest, scion of an exceptionally distinguished and cultured lineage, for cultivating two languages in his home, just as Lewys Glyn Cothi, in a *cywydd* addressed to the same lineage, reflects the bilingual character of his patron's household. *Doeth ieithydd teg* (a fair and wise linguist) was how the poet Tudur Aled addressed John Edwards of Chirk, and we may be sure that English was included in the linguistic repertoire so fulsomely praised by the poet.[38] A handsome and well-executed grammar book of the kind used to inculcate the elementary principles of Latin grammar, almost certainly written in John Edwards's hand, suggests the copious use of English as a medium of instruction, for the Latin vocabularies which it contains are interlineated with their English equivalents and a treatise on heteroclite nouns is accompanied by illustrative material in English. Within this social milieu, sophisticated, lettered and cultured, it may be suggested that a full competence in English was already taken for granted.[39]

As for peasants and artisans, although little direct information concerning their language and speech-patterns has yet been uncovered, a measure of linguistic contact can be assumed. For one thing, geographical mobility and seasonal, itinerant labour, a well-documented phenomenon characteristic of many Welsh communities,

---

[37] Ibid.

[38] F. G. Payne, *Crwydro Sir Faesyfed* (Llandybie, 1966), p. 33; *Gwaith Lewys Glyn Cothi*, p. 285; T. Gwynn Jones, ed., *Gwaith Tudur Aled* (Cardiff, 1926), II, p. 254. For the English works of a distinguished descendant of a Welsh marcher family, see V. J. Scattergood, *The Works of Sir John Clanvowe* (Cambridge, 1975).

[39] NLW 423 D. I have discussed the volume and its reputed owner in 'The Grammar and Commonplace Book of John Edwards of Chirk', *BBCS* 34 (1987), pp. 179–82. See also D. Thomson, *A Descriptive Catalogue of Middle English Grammatical Texts* (New York, 1979), pp. 114–32.

brought Welsh speakers into contact with the English tongue and one must presume that the time spent abroad *in Anglia* must have left some permanent impact on the individual's language.[40] Lexical borrowings from English are increasingly reflected in the works of some fourteenth-century poets and in the case of one, Iolo Goch, a poet whose *opus* displays a large number of English loan-words, it has been plausibly suggested that he had learned English through contact with English settlers and was clearly conversant with contemporary English literary tastes. Conversely, Englishmen living in Wales may well have acquired some knowledge of Welsh. A Hereford witness at Cantilupe's canonisation proceedings in 1307 deemed it entirely possible that the bilingual skills so miraculously exhibited by a healed youth, who exclaimed in Welsh 'Arglwydd Dduw a Saint Thomas' (Lord God and St Thomas), could be explained by natural means since he had been exposed to a Welsh-language community since childhood. Simultaneous binomialism, a well-documented phenomenon, shows the easy passage of individuals between linguistic groups, just as the adoption of English names and naming practices by the Welsh and of Welsh ones by the English in Wales, betoken the mutual adaptation that might be achieved. Occupational labels such as *saer* or cooper, *eurych* or goldsmith, *cigydd* or flesh-ewer, *cribwraig* or kempster, were used interchangeably, and if this reflects collo-quial usage as well as scribal practice, a measure of bilingualism among artisans and town-dwellers is possible.[41]

What, therefore, were the main determinants of linguistic behaviour? Dominating the historiography of the Welsh language in Wales has been the theme of language proscription evinced by the 'language clause' of the Act of Union which provided that courts should be kept in the 'English tongue' and denied to those who used the Welsh speech or language 'all manner of offices within the realm of England, Wales or other the king's dominions'.[42] Yet, in so far as the fourteenth and fifteenth centu-ries are concerned, we search in vain for incontrovertible evidence that the use of Welsh was suppressed. True, it was then that the myth of linguistic proscription took root in many European communities. It was in the late-thirteenth century, for instance, that a Polish chronicler recorded how the Teutonic knights had intended to exterminate the Polish language. In England, as is well known, the Croyland chroni-cler expressed the belief that English had once been imperilled by the Normans who had been intent on its destruction and had ordained the use of French in all writings, charters and books and in the promulgation of law. In Ireland, alarmed at the progressive Gaelicisation of the English settler families, it was ordained that no one of English descent was to converse with other Englishmen in the Irish tongue, a measure which formed part of a broader, draconian attempt to curtail the adoption of Irish habits and customs by the *advenae* and to preserve a knowledge of English among them.[43] Measures of such severity and intensity, whatever their practical

---

[40] See the references cited in Smith, 'The Welsh Language', p. 37 n. 67.

[41] Ibid., n. 69.

[42] I. Bowen, *The Statutes of Wales* (London, 1908), p. 87.

[43] P. Knoll, 'Economic and Political Institutions on the Polish-German Frontier in the Middle Ages:

consequences may have been, were rarely encountered in Wales. Although intermarriage with Welshwomen, or the sending of children to be fostered among Welsh families was, occasionally, forbidden to Englishmen, evidence of a clearly articulated and persistent policy of language proscription, or, indeed, of a belief that one had existed, is elusive. Urban charters, such as that granted to Welshpool in 1406, might sometimes decree that pleading in the courts of the town should be allowed only in English or French, while Adam of Usk in his chronicle revealed how the common people of Cardigan, erstwhile adherents of Owain Glyndwr, deserted his cause and returned to their homes 'being permitted to use the Welsh tongue, although its destruction had been determined by the English'. His assertion, however, rests on doubtful authority and, indeed, by his own clear admission, the so-called 'decree' was revoked by Divine intervention and the prayer and cry of the oppressed.[44]

More important to the fortunes of the Welsh language than any explicit proscription were the silent influences at work within Welsh society. During the course of the fifteenth century, as was noted above, the steadily increasing prominence of English as a medium of documentary literacy in England was mirrored also in Wales, even though the Welsh language was itself fully capable of all the precision and technical rigour required of the formal documentary register. By contrast, the Welsh language, albeit extensively spoken at all social levels, a vibrant and resonant medium for creative literature and functional prose, a vehicle for private and public devotion, was not, in so far as can now be established, a normal medium of formal documentary literacy. Of the numerous property deeds of fourteenth- and fifteenth-century date which survive, not a single example was written in Welsh and although, as has also been noted, landowners might have recourse to the vernacular in recording particulars of their landed estates, such documents as we have bear the hallmarks of compilations intended for private, personal use rather than ones to be proffered as proofs of title in the public domain.[45] Likewise, of the wills so far discovered, although nearly a half were written partly or entirely in English, a few brief sentences interspersed in a Latin will of early-sixteenth-century date are all that survives in the native vernacular. The use of English was, quite clearly, proceeding apace in Wales several decades before the 'language clause' of the Act of Union ratified its enhanced primacy and prestige in the domain of royal administration and justice.

The burgeoning importance of English in fifteenth-century Wales need occasion little surprise. The language of literacy, so we are told, bears no necessary correla-

---

Action, Reaction, Interaction', in R. Bartlett and A. MacKay, eds, *Medieval Frontier Societies* (Oxford, 1989), p. 169; D. Burnley, 'Lexis and Semantics', *Cambridge History of the English Language*, II, pp. 409–99 (pp. 423–4); J. Lydon, 'The Middle Nation', in *English in Medieval Ireland*, pp. 1–26; R. Bartlett, *The Making of Europe: Conquest, Colonisation and Cultural Change, 950–1350* (London, 1993), pp. 203–4 and the sources cited there for Poland; S. Forde, L. Johnson and A. V. Murray, eds, *Concepts of National Identity in the Middle Ages* (Leeds, 1995).

44 M. C. Jones, 'The Feudal Barony of Powys', *Powysland Club* I (1868), p. 307: H. Ellis, ed., *Registrum Vulgariter Nuncupatum 'The Record of Caernarvon'* (London, 1838), p. 240; C. Given-Wilson, *The Chronicle of Adam of Usk* (Oxford, 1997), p. 146.

45 See above, p. 15.

tion to the speech used by the majority of the people.[46] Already redolent of authority and high social status, English was the language of lordship and power, of social aspiration and economic advancement. Itself enlarged and adorned for the services of national and civic bureaucracies, the English language, now increasingly standardised even before the advent of print, was likewise assuming its role as a vehicle for administrative procedures and processes in Wales. A class of professional scriveners, well versed in the conveyancing practices of Latin and English property deeds and linked with the urban milieux of royal and seignorial administrations, was emerging. At Caernarfon, to take one example, the Foxwist dynasty, whose skills may well have been passed down from father to son, possessed an extensive scribal practice at the turn of the fifteenth century, as is shown by the very considerable geographical range of the property deeds which they penned. If Richard Foxwist is, indeed, correctly identified as the legatee of the will of John Padyngton of London, then something is known of his training for the will directs that Richard should go to school for three years, for the first year to a chantry school, for the second to a grammar school and for the third to a writing school. Although much work remains to be done on the identities of these humble but indispensable practitioners, their role in the dissemination and enhancement of English as a language of documentary literacy in Wales seems clear.[47]

By the same token the low prestige of the Welsh language in the administrative and documentary domain may also be readily explained. For one thing, it is questionable whether the formal enrolment in writing of property transactions had ever formed part of the native legal tradition. George Owen of Henllys, once again an illuminating source for the practice and customs of earlier centuries, provides significant comment. Observing the remarkable absence of deeds of pre-Union date from the counties of Cardigan and Carmarthen, he maintained that before 1536 the practice was to pass all lands 'by surrender in the Lords Courte accordinge to the lawes of Howell dha', a custom confirmed also by later witnesses who likewise made note of how bond and free land was passed 'always in the lord's court by the rod, whereof a record was kept by the lord'.[48] Moreover, bereft of the stimulus to bureaucratic activity in Welsh which indigenous lordship might have provided in the post-conquest period, Welsh communities, on the contrary, were increasingly being exposed to the written registers of French and of English. Nor were the English rulers of Wales confronted with a clearly articulated demand for the use of Welsh in the spheres of administration and government as was the case in the lands of Brabant and Flanders, where a dominant Burgundian regime, for which French was the language of rule, nonetheless sanctioned the use of Flemish in several important

[46] M. T. Clanchy, *From Memory to Written Record: England 1066–1307* (Oxford, 2nd edn 1993), pp. 232–3.

[47] J. M. Lewis, *Welsh Monumental Brasses: A Guide* (Cardiff, 1974), pp. 40–1. Some of the issues raised in this paragraph are more fully discussed in Llinos Beverley Smith, 'Inkhorn and Spectacles: The Impact of Literacy in Late Medieval Wales', in H. Pryce, ed., *Literacy in Medieval Celtic Societies* (Cambridge, 1998).

[48] Owen, *Description*, I, pp. 169–70.

respects and where the use of Netherlandish was closely identified with the defence of urban and indigenous interests.[49] While the legislative intentions and the principles which informed the 'language clause' of the Act of Union may be open to continuing debate, it seems clear that the use and exercise of English had long exerted a formative influence on the role and prestige of the Welsh language in Wales.[50]

[49] C. A. J. Armstrong, 'The Language Question in the Low Countries: The Use of French and Dutch by the Dukes of Burgundy and their Administration', in J. R. Hale, J. R. L. Highfield and B. Smalley, eds, *Europe in the Late Middle Ages* (London, 1965), pp. 386–409.

[50] See P. R. Roberts, 'Tudor Legislation and the Political Status of "the British tongue" ', in *The Welsh Language before the Industrial Revolution*, pp. 123–153.

Historical Background of Multilingualism and its Impact on English

BEGOÑA CRESPO

Introduction

T HE AIM OF this paper is to outline, on a historical and linguistic basis, the multilingual situation in England during the late Middle Ages. Section one will deal with a preliminary presentation of the historical situation at that time, with special emphasis on the social questions of language contact, language conflict and language evolution towards uniformity. In section two we will analyse the concept of multilingualism and its different aspects, trying to apply the one most suitable for our purposes. Likewise, we will see the different foreign languages that exerted a certain influence on the development of English. The third section will tackle this foreign influence in the lexical field of 'trade', from a general perspective and via texts extracted from the *Helsinki Corpus*. Evidence of the introduction of these terms due to social exchange forms the basis of a sociolinguistic study. The final section will stress the importance of multilingualism in a time of change, and its contribution to the enrichment and further development of the English tongue.

A historical approach to language contact

Latin, French and English were the three languages that pervaded medieval England. Latin was the 'unifying European language' par excellence. It was the language of religion, hence of culture and power, and it was institutionalised throughout Europe, throughout the Middle Ages. French came to England as a consequence of a violent historical event that turned upside down the political structure of the country: the aristocratic invasion of the Normans made possible a bilingual situation among the people, running parallel to diglossia. English was finally ousted by the two prestigious languages, Latin and French, but never completely eradicated. It was the vernacular tongue of a subject people, yet crucial to their sense of being. Therefore, although England was certainly trilingual, the distribution of the languages used there was by no means uniform: see Table 1.

Table 1. Distribution of languages in contact

LANGUAGE	Register	Medium	Status
Latin	Formal-Official	Written	High
French	Formal-Official	Written/Spoken	High
English	Informal-Colloquial	Spoken	Low

This table shows the three main languages in contact at this period. It also exhibits the status, different registers and media in which they were used. As we can infer from these data, Latin was used for written purposes, but it was not normally used as a spoken language except (perhaps) in the highest ecclesiastical circles. The classical tongue 'was never actually spoken by more than a tiny minority of the English; as a result, its influence on our language has come mainly through theological and scholarly writings . . .'.[1] French was also used in a formal register for written purposes, but unlike Latin, French was a spoken language as well. It coexisted, together with Latin, as a language of record, the language of the court, of the institutions ruled by the Normans. But it never stopped being the language of the invaders and of successive waves of foreigners who occupied institutional and non-institutional posts: soldiers and, especially, traders and merchants went to England for other than political reasons. These groups spoke conversational French and intermingled with the natives. Nevertheless, they constituted a minority in contrast to the vast majority of the English-speaking population.[2] The lack of literacy and the fact of being the language of a conquered people limited English to the lower ranks of society. It was reduced to a conversational, everyday language that was transmitted orally.

The trilingual setting of medieval England was not destined to last for long. The course of politics, religion, economy and society was to foster an intricate system of relationships that would play a part in the particular development of the English language. The coexistence of several languages in different social contexts brought about a controversial linguistic situation. On the one hand, when, in the thirteenth century, French was used for the writing of official and semi-official documents, there arose an element of overlap in the high status languages: both were used for the same register, but the principle of economy, and the social environment of the times, was to cause one of them to disappear. Meanwhile, English, especially in the countryside, had just one point of convergence with French: the necessity which the members of the Anglophone speech community had to learn the prestige code for domestic or economic reasons.

Language conflict was for medieval England a collective phenomenon. It involved high and low social strata that would fight, together, to achieve a unique

---

[1] R. Claiborne, *English: Its Life and Times* (London, 1994), p. 110.
[2] R. Berndt, *A History of the English Language* (Leipzig, 1989), p. 378.

Table 2. Linguistic evolution

ENGLAND	*Languages*	*Linguistic situation*
Early Middle Ages	Latin–French–English	TRILINGUAL
14th–15th centuries	French–English	BILINGUAL
15th–16th c. onwards	English	MONOLINGUAL

culture and their own ethnic features. The chief bond was their common vernacular.[3] The Provisions of Oxford (1258) and the subsequent Barons' War (1258–1265/7) constitute a good example of this. A group of noblemen, headed by Simon de Montfort, decided to limit the king's power to prevent the coming of foreigners who 'ruled' the country, but the results did not fulfil the nobility's expectations and this in turn gave rise to the Barons' War. Two of the principles they backed were crucial for laymen: the expulsion of foreigners, defended by the Commons in Parliament,[4] and the use of the vernacular, the national tongue, so that the common people could understand the institutional system in which they were immersed. Patriotic ideology connecting society and language was to involve political operations and strategic devices that would promote the emergence of English. The initial trilingual situation (amongst at least certain groups) developed into oral bilingualism (though not universal) which in turn gradually resulted in vernacular monolingualism as table 2 shows.

Certain historical events or processes favoured the development of the original situation (trilingualism) and the shifts that came afterwards (bilingualism, then monolingualism): the military conquest and subsequent settlement by the Normans (1066) brought about bilingualism. The subsequent change towards monolingualism arose from the breakup of relationships with France and the separation from the French dukedom at the beginning of the thirteenth century, together with the effects this produced at a national level. Although the influence of French in England before the Conquest was not a minor one,[5] its role in the history of the English language from then on is undeniable. Many key social positions were transferred to the French aristocracy, and they remained in such positions for a century and a half. The beginning of the end of this period of linguistic dominance was marked by the secession from France in 1204. The loss of Normandy established an independent, incipient English nation as different from France and all things French. This feeling spread gradually and manifested itself through multiple confrontations with the 'mother' country and its language, and took the form of renewed wars (1213, 1215, 1242 . . .), and protests against the settlement of foreigners.[6] Political marriages among

---

3 For further information on the use of English as a nationalist tool in the Middle Ages, see B. Crespo, 'English and French as L1 and L2 in Renaissance England: A Consequence of Medieval Nationalism', *Sederi* 7 (A Coruña, 1996), pp. 107–14.

4 Petitions against foreigners were especially common in the fourteenth century (1346, 1377).

5 See C. Barber, *The English Language: A Historical Introduction* (Cambridge, 1994), p. 134.

6 In 1233 anger at Poitevin influence, notably that of Peter de Rivaux and Peter des Roches, provoked the Marshal rebellion.

Normans and Anglo-Saxons added a new element to the population of medieval England. The French-born mixed with the English-born. Hence, future generations living in the island would feel gradually more English. As time went on, the Norman ancestors were forgotten and young people formed part of a society which identified with the natural language of most inhabitants of the island. Migration imbued medieval English society with a more Norman character. This phenomenon began when people from the continent worked out the advantages which the new territory offered, and decided to profit from them. It was a land of opportunities for soldiers, craftsmen, even for merchants. Nevertheless, this relatively peaceful invasion of the vernacular speech community was a double-edged process: on the one hand, it helped emphasise the latter's national identity; on the other hand, it paved the way for still more linguistic consequences. Trade with other countries (especially the Netherlands) made possible language contact between English and other languages. This social activity together with the unavoidable presence of French speakers can be regarded as profitable, at least for the development of the lexis of English. Moreover, London became an important trade centre which allowed foreigners to be in touch with the natives. Even English merchants when travelling abroad could have played a part in the introduction of foreign terms into their mother tongue. A growing hatred towards invaders crystallised in the Hundred Years' War (1337–1453). This hostility towards foreigners paralleled the advance of the vernacular in the institutional and literary framework of English society.

The use of English probably did not elicit much support from the upper class, but it

> would seem a patriotic gesture to the middle class, who largely paid for the war
> and to whom the continued use of Latin and French was something of an incon-
> venience. The middle class had little love of anything foreign, and there was
> continued agitation to expel foreigners (including the Welsh) from English soil.[7]

As can be seen, social factors promoted a monolingual tendency which pushed for English to have the status of official language from the beginning of the fifteenth century. This is a process that encompassed three different stages:

1. *Normalisation* and *Standardisation.*   Normalisation consists in the conscious spread and establishment of a language as the L1 of a society at all levels. In the case of English, it took place at the end of the fourteenth and during the fifteenth century. This collective effort achieved its objectives when the common people, the nobility, government institutions and the king accepted and supported the use of English. Hence, once the normalisation process had been channelled in this way, the debate concentrated on 'the selection of optimal linguistic resources from those available',[8] that is, standardisation. At this stage, when written procedures started to be conducted in English, there were no norms for the written vernacular. The English

---

7   M. Richardson, 'Henry V, the English Chancery and Chancery English', *Speculum* 55 (1980), p. 740.
8   A. D. Svejcer and L. B. Nikolskij, *Introduction to Sociolinguistics* (Amsterdam/Philadelphia, 1986), p. 110.

population was not characterised by literacy. For these reasons, the written form was that of the most important of the national government offices besides the Exchequer: the Chancery. Chancery English developed as the new official language of administration that a body of professional clerks disseminated throughout the country.[9] Thus, the Royal Chancery fostered the regularity required to create a standard language. This generally accepted view is, however, disputed by others.[10] Caxton's printing press (1476) definitely consolidated the spread of Chancery English. The early decades of the sixteenth century were also a period when linguistic parameters were fixed, although the methods of teaching, which was carried out through translations of the classical tongues into English, slowed down the standardisation process.

2.   *Linguistic creation and codification.*   Renaissance scholars were conscious of the need for lexical enlargement of the mother tongue, and endeavoured to replenish it by creating new items or borrowing them from other languages. The most immediate corollary was the codification of this new material in dictionaries, grammars and other manuals.

3.   The next step implies the acceptance of prescribed or codified rules. Chronologically speaking, this extended far beyond the Middle Ages and the Renaissance.

If we analyse the way in which consolidation has evolved, i.e. how English became a national language, we may wonder in what sense we can tackle the phenomenon of multilingualism in England during the Middle Ages.

A multilingual setting

When more than two languages are involved, certain authors prefer to speak of multilingual situations. Charlotte Hoffmann's definition suggests that 'multilingualism comes about when speakers of different languages are brought together within the same political entity'.[11] According to her scheme we may be dealing with a multilingual situation instead of a trilingual one in the early Middle Ages. And it could be argued that multilingualism became extinct with the move towards monolingualism.[12]

However, Hoffmann's theory has broader implications. It applies to a state which

---

9   See J. H. Fisher, 'Chancery and the Emergence of Standard Written English in the Fifteenth Century', *Speculum* 52 (1977), pp. 870–99 and Berndt, *History*, pp. 34–8.

10 Contrary to this tendency, some scholars (namely Wright and Benskin) believe that the expansion of a uniform language was carried out by individual scribes. See L. Wright, *Essays in Honour of Eric Stanley*, ed. J. Toswell and E. Tyler (London and New York, 1996).

11 C. Hoffmann, *An Introduction to Bilingualism* (London, 1991), p. 157.

12 And this is so because the socio-historical context changes: '. . . an individual's abilities in his or her two, three or four languages will not be equal. On the contrary, we might predict that they will extend just about as far as circumstances demand' (J. Edwards, *Multilingualism* (London and New York, 1994), p. 34).

Table 3. Influence of other languages

LANGUAGES	*Direct Introduction*	*Indirect Introduction*
Latin	——	
French	——	
Scandinavian	——	
Low German	——	
High German	——	
Italian		through French
Spanish		through French
Irish	——	
Scottish Gaelic	——	
Welsh	——	
Cornish	——	
Other Celtic languages in Europe		through French
Portuguese		through French
Arabic		through French and Spanish
Persian		through French, Greek and Latin
Turkish		through French
Hebrew		through French and Latin
Greek		through French by way of Latin

covers a certain period of time and which may be studied from a synchronic or a diachronic standpoint. Such is the case of England whilst all three languages survived. Our conception of multilingualism involves the influence of several languages upon the development of another. In the first case we refer to 'territorial multilingualism' properly speaking[13] and in the second case we refer simply to 'multilingualism'. It is this second manifestation that we will analyse.

The stages of normalisation and codification imply a search for balance and regularity. It is then that all deficiencies and faults are unravelled. Speakers who use language as a living and constantly evolving entity take on loanwords consciously and unconsciously, finding them either useful or useless. The real awareness of this introduction of foreign terms takes place from the end of the fifteenth century onwards, although loanwords were also introduced through earlier contacts. At this point we can apply the term 'multilingualism' as one which embraces the influence several languages exert on another one. Serjeantson[14] puts forward a long list of languages that have left their marks on English: Scandinavian, French, Latin, Greek, Low and High German, Italian, Spanish, Celtic, Portuguese, Slavonic, Hungarian, Arabic, Indian dialects, Persian, Turkish dialects, Dravidian, Semitic dialects,

13 Hoffmann, *An Introduction to Bilingualism*, p. 165.
14 M. S. Serjeantson, *A History of Foreign Words in English* (London, 1962).

Tibeto-Chinese, Japanese, Polynesian, Indonesian, Australian, Bantu, Sudanese and other languages of Africa, American Indian, Eskimo . . . From this huge group not all had contact with English during the Middle Ages. Table 3 illustrates the impact of those languages that were in contact with English during the so-called Middle English period.

The languages that exercised the greatest influence on English in medieval times were Scandinavian, Latin and French. There are also traces of a large number of Dutch and German words. Latin in the Middle English period is mainly concerned with terms relating to religion and learning. From the eleventh century items of French origin advanced into English, but the impact of those which were acquired in the fourteenth century is still felt. The Scandinavian element made its way in before and during this time, with special emphasis on the fourteenth and fifteenth centuries. The Low German dialects exhibit a formal similarity to Middle English which makes it difficult to distinguish Dutch loans, for instance, from actual Middle English words. Nevertheless, history provides evidence of the commercial relationship between these countries. From this it can be gathered that English certainly acquired loanwords pertaining to commerce and industry. High German stands out in the field of mineralogy, particularly in the fifteenth century. The Celtic languages of the British Isles introduced lexical items directly into the vernacular, but their incidence was not of much importance. We can trace Irish influence as far back as the late fourteenth century. Words from Welsh are few. Scottish Gaelic supplied the most numerous group. There are also four words that probably came from Cornish.[15]

All the languages mentioned so far have directly impinged on English. There existed extralinguistic factors which favoured this phenomenon: loans are the result of trade and/or military relations. The following languages have supplied terms to English but mainly through French. English has borrowed from Arabic a great number of loan words thanks to French or, even, Spanish because of trade contact with the Mediterranean coast of Spain. During the fourteenth and fifteenth centuries scientific, religious and commercial words were abundant. Persian and Turkish usually follow the French route; Hebrew likewise, at least as far as trade terms are concerned, because biblical borrowings were taken from Latin. Classical Greek terms made their way first through Latin and then through French.

As can be deduced, there is a close connection between the incorporation of foreign terminology and the socio-historical context of language contact. This link forms the basic principle for a sociolinguistic study[16] of any lexical area of English. So far, we have posited a global overview of the effects of non-native tongues upon the vernacular. The next section will be devoted to an attempt to represent its more concrete counterpart, through a study of the semantic field of 'trade'.

[15] Ibid.

[16] The present study does not constitute a particular and detailed sociolinguistic analysis but it tries to approach this area from a more generic point of view.

English: A brief sociolinguistic study

Through the analysis of a particular semantic field, we will see how English has been enriched throughout the centuries due to constant contact with other tongues. 'Trade', as a social activity developed among speakers of different mother tongues, calls for linguistic intercomprehension. In a society that was getting more and more urbanised and money-based, the exchange of products and services was a major activity which could not hope to be fruitful if understanding failed. In order to illustrate the multilingual effects on English during the Middle Ages, we have selected the field of trade for two different reasons:

1.   It implies a wide selection of the most influential languages at this time, as Table 4 shows. It should be noted that, in this table, the 'original language' is not always the direct source of the English word, which is often acquired indirectly through an intermediary (typically, although not invariably, French).

During the late Middle Ages there was major social evolution, demonstrated by certain events. The devastating effects of the Black Death (1349–51) among the population led to the Peasants' Revolt (1381) which was the origin of a new socio-economic organisation. To this fact we must add that 'the woollen industry was the major industry of England in the Middle Ages'.[17] Exports and imports were an important part of national income. Thus, commerce with other countries promoted relations and exchanges which were reflected in the linguistic situation. Although the major enlargement of the lexis developed principally from the sixteenth century onwards, i.e. during the creation and codification stage, the unrest of the later Middle Ages triggered the process. At a linguistic level this multilingual influence encourages the distribution of words at particular levels, or, even, synonymy at different levels.

Contact with linguistic strata introduced from languages in a superior or inferior relationship with the vernacular will lead to the introduction of words that will finally acquire a low or high status. This is assumed to be the case for the Scandinavian and the French invasions respectively. Closely related to it is the fact that we can find synonyms at a popular, literary and learned level. As an example we can propose *rise-mount-ascend* or *ask-question-interrogate*.[18] If this can be said of the global evolution of language, there are certain processes that may affect the particular development of a word: for instance, the deterioration of *servile* or *obsequious*, which within the feudal system were neutral terms. However,

> It emerges that the breakdown of feudalism intensified the process of deterioration in words applied to those of lower station. Service, being no longer an obligation, became a disgrace.[19]

17   A. C. Baugh, and T. Cable, *A History of the English Language* (London and New York, 1991), p. 187.
18   Ibid., p. 187.
19   G. Hughes, *Words in Time: A Social History of the English Vocabulary* (Oxford, 1994), p. 46.

Table 4. Semantic field: Trade (objects and financial affairs)

ORIGINAL LANGUAGE	*14th c.*	*14th–15th c.*	*15th c.*
Scandinavian		mal (payment) coup (buy) scogh (wood) marc (money)	
French	payde marchande pore profyt ryche stor wage		
Dutch			mart (market) hop (plant) pickle guilder corf mechlin (lace) scone isinglass
Italian			artisan
Celtic			quay truant vassal
Arabic	saffron cotton amber lemon maravedi		
Indian dialects			pepper ginger
Semitic dialects			emerald coral cinnamon

The other side of the coin is that flourishing capitalism fostered the amelioration of terms such as *free, frank, liberal* and *generous*.[20] Then, isolated items also underwent semantic shifts. Languages develop internally because they are surrounded by the constant flux of events and collective movement. Since language is a continuum

[20] Other semantic shifts due to extralinguistic influence can be seen in words such as *ale*, which experiences a process of specialisation: until the growing of hops was introduced into England in the first half of the fourteenth century, ale and beer were synonymous terms in Middle English (according to the Middle English Dictionary). With the new crop, specialisation took place. The changing world of

Table 5. Samples from the Helsinki Corpus (1350–1500)

	1350-1500				1350-1420				1420-1500			
Total no. of words	61,558				35,014				26,544			
No. of selected items	150				40				110			
Percentage (%)	0.24				0.11				0.41			
Word category	N	V	A	A	N	V	A	A	N	V	A	A
No.	125	19	6	0	28	10	2	0	97	9	4	0
Percentage (%) (rounded to nearest 2 decimal places)	0.2	0.03	0.01	0	0.08	0.03	0.01	0	0.36	0.03	0.02	0

within society fed by its members, any process or change in a community may have its correlate in the language spoken, at a global or at a particular level. Linguistic phenomena are, in this sense, a corollary of social activity.

2.   The field of 'trade' has been analysed in a number of texts from the *Helsinki Corpus* ranging from 1350 to 1500. The texts selected contain 61,558 words. These texts are mainly legal documents and to a lesser extent sections of handbooks on astronomy, treatises on horses and other manuals.[21] It is important for our purposes to study the number of items belonging to the field of 'trade', the word category and the different etymological origin of the terms.

Table 5 collects information about the total amount of words related to our field, without considering the frequency of repetition of such items. Hence, in the first column we find that 61,558 words form our corpus of data and only 150 belong to the field of 'trade'. This quantity corresponds to 0.24% of the total. It is a very small percentage that can be justified by the type of texts analysed: only a few of them have any bearing on any sort of commercial relations. They are mostly parliamentary petitions and fragments of handbooks outside the financial world. All in all, if we included repeated items the number would increase to 1120, which would correspond to 1.82%, a higher although still small percentage. In the next two columns we see the data analysed by periods. In the first one (1350–1420) we have only traced 40 items, i.e. 0.11% of the total. This first period outnumbers by more than 10,000 words the second one, yet it exhibits 110 items (= 0.41%) related to our area of study. The reason lies in the greater number of texts having to do with economic life in the later Middle Ages. There is an increase in the number of legal documents concerning guilds, craftsmen, exchanges of money, products to sell and buy, and,

economy also expanded the meaning of *pay*, originally 'to please, satisfy', later, because of the influence of Latin PACARE 'to appease, pacify or satisfy, especially a creditor', it developed the present-day meaning and the first one became obsolete. It might be noted that this semantic development occurs also in Anglo-French, at an earlier date than it does in English: the ME change is likely to have been occasioned at least in part by Anglo-French.

21   Samples from the *Handbook of Medicine* have been discarded.

Table 6. Etymological origin

	Latin		Old French		Anglo-Norman		Old English		Others	
	T.A	%	T.A	%	T.A	%	T.A	%	T.A	%
1350–1420 40 words	1	2.5	20	50	1	2.5	17	42.5	1	2.5
1420–1500 110 words	2	1.8	46	41.8	14	12.7	45	40.9	3	2.8
1320–1500 **150 words**	3	**2**	**66**	**44**	**15**	**10**	**62**	**41.3**	**4**	**2.7**

there is, even, a document concerning the wool trade. The emergence of a new type of economy is felt in the way people live and establish their relations within their speech community. As for the word category that prevails, nouns are the most common, followed by verbs and adjectives. The total absence of adverbs obliterates the importance of the circumstantial element in trade connections, at least, at the beginning of their development. The area of naming objects is covered by the high percentage of nouns present. Although there are more verbs than adjectives, these two categories are limited to essential actions and essential characterisation, respectively. Still, this is not all. The field of trade is basically, and for the time being, composed of activities, relationships and products. Nouns constitute the most suitable category to name them.

The third part of our analysis deals with etymology. Table 6 reveals, both in general and by periods, the etymological origin of the items included in our semantic field as well as the corresponding percentage. The different etymologies proposed allow for four possibilities: Latin, Old French, Anglo-Norman and Old English. The fifth possibility covers the influence of other Germanic languages.

On the whole, there are hardly any words of purely Latin origin (the word *lucre* from L. LUCRUM 'illicit gain, profit' is an example). This is due to the fact that most of them were introduced later through Old French; hence, they are included in column 2. This phenomenon can be easily illustrated with terms such as *ducates/dokattis* or *tax*:[22]

> *Ducates/dokattis* (present-day English – henceforth PE – *ducat*) n. Gold or silver coin formerly used in Europe. About 1380 it was a Venetian coin, borrowed from OF *ducat* < Italian *ducato* < medieval L *ducatus* 'duchy, coin' from DUX-DUCIS 'duke', so-called because of the effigy or title of the duke who issued it, which was stamped on the coin.

---

[22] The etymology and meaning of the examples used have been taken from *The Barnhart Dictionary of Etymology*. Our classification follows the first proposal concerning origin that is put forward in the above-mentioned dictionary.

Tax (PE *tax*) v./n. 'To put taxes on'. Borrowed from OF *taxer* < L TAXARE, 'evaluate, estimate, assess'. The figurative sense of 'burden' is found in ME before 1327. The noun meaning 'assessment, levy' derives from the verb.

Certain items are traced as being just of Old French origin:

Quetans (PE *quittance*) n. < OF *quitance* 'payment'.

Bran (PE *bran*) n. 'Broken husks of grains'. < OF *bran, bren* from a Gaulish word.

Patent (PE *patent*) n. < OF *patente* 'a papal indulgence, a pardon'. The ordinary sense 'licence to make or sell an article to the exclusion of others, a government grant protecting someone's right to an invention' is first recorded about 1558, although as early as 1378 the sense of a licence is recorded in *Piers Plowman*.

In turn, most terms included in the Anglo-Norman group were originally Old French and/or Latin words:

Merchant (PE *merchant*) n. < A-N (Anglo-Norman) *marchaunt*, OF *marchëant* < Vulgar Latin MERCATANTEM, 'a buyer'.

Brokour (PE *broker*) n. 'Person who buys and sells stock'. About 1378 'commercial agent, middleman'. It was borrowed through A-N *abrokur, brocour*, from OF *brokeor*.

We have also traced an example of a word borrowed from Old French but of Arabic origin: OF *coton* < Arabic *qutun*. The Arabic is the source of similar forms in other Germanic languages.

The Old English (OE) group can be illustrated with the following examples:

Peny (PE *penny*) n. 'A silver coin equal to $^1/_{12}$ of a shilling'. < OE *pening, penig* 'penny'.

Sale (PE *sale*) n. It developed from late OE *sala*; it was borrowed from a Scandinavian source (compare Old Icelandic *sala, sal, sale*); it is related to OE *sellan* 'to sell'.

Finally, the column entitled 'Others' includes terms of Germanic origin such as *trade*: about 1375 'path, track, course of action' from Middle Dutch or Middle Low German *trade* 'track, course (probably of a trading ship)'; cognate with Old Saxon *trada* 'footstep, track', Old High German *trata* 'track, way, passage' and OE *tredan* 'to tread'.

Although on a very small scale and with very few examples, it can be inferred that English has incorporated, directly or through French, a great deal of Latin. French has also been a source from which to absorb new words, and it has acted as a vehicle for the incorporation of loans from other languages. Undoubtedly, the Latin branch of the Indo-European family has exerted an outstanding influence upon the vernacular. Nevertheless, our corpus can also provide evidence of the power of the Scandinavian linguistic substrata and their relatives in the Germanic branch as they contribute to the development of English.

Conclusion

By way of conclusion we may suggest two senses of 'multilingualism'. English in the late Middle Ages can be studied from two stances:

(a) the coexistence of French, Latin and English in an unbalanced functional distribution (territorial multilingualism);

(b) the analysis of the influence exerted on English by foreign languages as a consequence of expansion and contacts (multilingualism).

This second aspect, which in a way includes the first one, has been dealt with in more detail. There is the same historical background for the two, but this same history changed the course of English. The presentation of different loanwords in English, as a whole and through the analysis of certain texts, supports the suggestion of studying multilingual traces in the vernacular during the fourteenth and the fifteenth centuries. Many languages from all over the world have made their way into English. Taken together, they have introduced new realities, new conceptions, new words and, in some cases, they have even altered the evolution of the English lexicon. The structural transformation to which the English language was subjected by history, resulted in the emergence of a different language: a language of indisputable Saxon provenance, but also one which displays unquestionable multilingual influence.

L'Intellectuel «anglo-normand» face à la pluralité des langues: le témoignage implicite du MS Oxford, Magdalen Lat. 188

ANDRES M. KRISTOL

L'HISTORIEN de la langue qui étudie le fonctionnement du plurilinguisme en Grande-Bretagne médiévale se heurte à un problème constant: les informations disponibles sont en nombre limité; le corpus sur lequel nous travaillons est clos ou du moins ne s'enrichit que très lentement. Selon Short,[1] entre 1943 et 1978, un seul nouveau document[2] est venu alimenter le débat sur le bilinguisme dans l'Angleterre anglo-normande. Peu après, l'exploitation des actes du procès de canonisation de Thomas Cantilupe par Richter[3] a encore considérablement enrichi notre connaissance de la situation linguistique en Angleterre au début du XIVe siècle. Mais depuis, les sources ont l'air d'être taries: la recherche se voit plus ou moins réduite à repenser une documentation connue. La plupart des témoignages explicites sur les pratiques langagières en Grande-Bretagne médiévale ont d'ailleurs reçu des interprétations diamétralement opposées, en ce qui concerne le rôle, le statut et l'importance des différentes langues en présence. Le débat, faussé parfois par des *a priori* idéologiques, est loin d'être clos.

Dans cette situation, il m'a semblé que les manuscrits que j'ai consultés en préparant mon édition des *Manières de langage*[4] contenaient certaines informations inexploitées jusqu'ici. Je pense en effet que certains indices concernant le fonctionnement du plurilinguisme britannique médiéval peuvent se dégager non seulement de ce que les témoins *disent* de leurs pratiques linguistiques, mais encore de ce qu'ils *font*. Je serais même tenté de croire que le témoignage implicite est parfois plus fiable que les affirmations explicites, car il peut y avoir un abîme entre les affirmations métalinguistiques des auteurs et leurs choix linguistiques effectifs, surtout en ce qui concerne les variantes moins «prestigieuses» des langues qu'ils

1 I. Short, «On Bilingualism in Anglo-Norman England», *Romance Philology* 33 (1980), pp. 467–79.
2 Y. Lefèvre, «De l'usage du français en Grande-Bretagne à la fin du XIIe siècle», *Etudes de langue et de littérature offertes à Félix Lecoy* (Paris, 1973), pp. 301–5.
3 M. Richter, *Sprache und Gesellschaft im Mittelalter: Untersuchungen zur mündlichen Kommunikation in England von der Mitte des elften bis zum Beginn des vierzehnten Jahrhunderts* (Stuttgart, 1979).
4 A. Kristol, *Manières de langage (1396, 1399, 1415)* (London, 1995).

utilisent.[5] C'est en étudiant les pratiques réelles des différents rédacteurs qu'il devient d'ailleurs aussi possible de détecter en partie du moins les conceptions «théoriques» qui sous-tendent leur pratique.

Je ne suis évidemment pas le premier qui essaie d'exploiter le témoignage implicite des manuscrits conservés. Certaines tentatives de ce type ont déjà été entreprises par exemple par Suggett (1943, 1945)[6] ou par Fisher (1977),[7] qui ont cherché à mesurer l'importance respective du français, du latin et de l'anglais vers la fin du Moyen Age en dépouillant les *Rotuli Parliamentorum* ou d'autres collections de lettres et de pétitions.[8] Mais ce n'est pas sur cette voie quantitative que je désire m'engager ici. Le phénomène qui m'intéresse, c'est le travail concret du scribe dans son manuscrit, sur l'arrière-plan de l'enseignement orthographique et grammatical explicite qu'il a reçu. Je me concentrerai donc ici sur les petits indices qui illustrent de quelle manière le scribe plurilingue manie les différentes langues dont il dispose, et quelle est son attitude envers elles.

Je souligne que mon approche est très partielle; elle ne concerne que les usages *écrits*. Je ne dispose d'aucune nouvelle information sur le fonctionnement du multi-linguisme en Grande-Bretagne médiévale dans la communication *parlée*. J'insiste sur cette restriction: je suis persuadé qu'il est illégitime de tirer la moindre informa-tion au sujet des pratiques orales d'une analyse des pratiques écrites. Le non-respect de cette distinction est sans doute responsable en partie du moins du dialogue de sourds entre «francophiles» et «francophobes» dans la discussion sur l'importance du français en Angleterre médiévale. De tous temps, et dans de nombreuses sociétés humaines, la langue utilisée dans la communication écrite a été différente de celle des échanges oraux, et il en a été de même pendant une bonne partie du Moyen Age anglais. Même si certains témoignages, en particulier un passage de la *Manière de*

---

5   C'est la raison pour laquelle, en sociolinguistique, on a commencé à distinguer le prestige «ouvert» des variantes standard et le prestige «couvert» des variantes substandard: cf. P. Trudgill, «Sex, Covert Prestige and Linguistic Change in the Urban British English of Norwich», *Language and Sex: Differ-ence and Dominance*, éd. B. Thorne, N. Henley (Rowley, 1983), pp. 88–104.

6   H. Suggett, «An Anglo-Norman Return to the Inquest of Sheriffs», *Bulletin of the John Rylands Library* 27 (1943), pp. 179–82; et «The Use of French in England in the Later Middle Ages», *Trans-actions of the Royal Historical Society*, fourth series 28 (1945), pp. 61–83. Sa contribution est impor-tante, même si ses conclusions sont parfois problématiques. En particulier, H. Suggett tend à confondre usage écrit du français et vitalité de la langue dans la vie de tous les jours: «Every piece of information available seems to show that the French used in England was no mere accomplishment, but that it was a true vernacular whose roots had penetrated deeply into all classes of English society who could read and write» (p. 79). Par conséquent, elle s'étonne du changement de langue absolu-ment abrupt qui intervient vers la fin des années 1430: «[French] almost abruptly [. . .] ceased to be a living language [in England]» («An Anglo-Norman Return», p. 229, cité d'après D. A. Kibbee, *For to speke Frenche trewely, The French Language in England, 1000–1600: Its Status, Description and Instruction* (Amsterdam/Philadelphia, 1991), p. 58).

7   J. H. Fisher, «Chancery and the Emergence of Standard Written English in the Fifteenth Century», *Speculum* 52 (1977), pp. 870–99.

8   On pourrait être tenté d'entreprendre des explorations quantitatives d'une autre nature. Ainsi, dans la production didactique de William of Kingsmill (début XVe siècle), on constate que les textes en latin sont nettement plus nombreux que les textes en français. Mais aucune conclusion claire ne se dégage d'un tel constat: les textes en latin sont-ils plus nombreux parce que le latin est plus *important* que le français, ou parce qu'il est plus *difficile*?

langage de 1396, affirment que le français est toujours la langue de la conversation soignée dans certains milieux de la bonne société anglaise,[9] et que le maintien de la tradition orale anglo-normande est garanti par les transcriptions «phonétiques» du *Femina*,[10] la situation linguistique en Angleterre médiévale doit sans aucun doute être décrite comme une *diglossie codique*: l'oralité appartient essentiellement à l'anglais, alors que le français occupe une partie importante des usages écrits.[11] L'emploi important et suivi du français – et du latin – dans les documents écrits, qui est indéniable, ne nous apprend rien sur l'usage des langues dans le parlé quotidien.

Les langues présentes dans les manuscrits sur lesquels j'ai travaillé sont l'anglais, le français et le latin. Or, dire «le français» ou «l'anglais» est évidemment une simplification grossière. Ce qui caractérise la situation linguistique de l'époque concernée, c'est l'absence de formes standardisées des deux langues vernaculaires. La seule langue pour laquelle nous pouvons raisonnablement admettre l'existence d'une norme écrite pratiquement stable, c'est le latin. Dans les deux langues vernaculaires par contre, le scribe est confronté à une pluralité de traditions orthographiques dont certaines – pas forcément les siennes – jouissent d'un prestige apparemment supérieur aux autres. Concrètement, lorsque le scribe anglais médiéval rédige un texte, il le fait sur un arrière-plan de cinq traditions orthographiques concurrentes.

Deux de ces traditions sont spécifiquement «anglaises»:
— la longue tradition anglo-normande qui s'est fixée au cours du XIIe/XIIIe siècle et qui s'est perpétuée avec quelques aménagements jusqu'à la fin du Moyen Age, grâce à l'efficacité du système scolaire anglais,[12]
— les habitudes orthographiques du moyen anglais, avec leurs propres fluctuations internes, qui peuvent influencer l'écrit en français.

Deux courants orthographiques sont d'origine continentale et se manifestent surtout dans les textes rédigés en français:
— le modèle picard dont le prestige en Angleterre est dû sans doute au rayonnement des villes commerçantes du Nord de la France et au mariage d'Edouard III avec Philippa de Hainaut,[13]
— le modèle parisien et surtout orléanais dont le rayonnement est dû au grand nombre d'étudiants anglais qui ont fréquenté les Universités de ces deux villes.

Enfin, comme n'importe quel intellectuel en Europe occidentale, à cette époque, le scribe anglais est évidemment influencé par la tradition latine. Par conséquent, quelle que soit la langue qu'il écrit, il utilise certaines graphies latinisantes,

9 Cf. A. Kristol, *Manières de langage*, p. xxxi.
10 A. Kristol, «La prononciation du français en Angleterre au XVe siècle», *Mélanges Michel Burger*, éd. J. Cerquiglini et O. Collet (Genève, 1994), pp. 67-87.
11 C'est la conclusion à laquelle parvient déjà Serge Lusignan, *Parler vulgairement. Les intellectuels et la langue française aux XIIIe et XIVe siècles* (Paris/Montréal, 1986), p. 106, dans son analyse du prologue du *Donait* de John Barton.
12 A. Kristol, «La prononciation du français».
13 L'influence picarde est faible dans le manuscrit dont il sera question, mais elle est clairement perceptible dans d'autres manuscrits de la même époque.

«étymologiques» ou «savantes». Dans la mesure du possible, dans toutes les langues qu'il écrit, le scribe emploie d'ailleurs les mêmes abréviations conventionnelles qui proviennent de la tradition latine;[14] dans ce sens, il existe pour lui une réelle unité de l'écrit en tant que tel.

Face à cette diversité des traditions écrites, ce qui oriente sans doute les choix orthographiques du scribe, c'est la formation scolaire qu'il a reçue. A cet égard, la recherche sur l'anglo-normand se trouve dans une situation privilégiée, car – en dehors des grammaires occitanes qui ont été rédigées dans le Midi de la France, en Catalogne et en Italie – l'Angleterre médiévale est le seul pays européen, à ma connaissance, qui possède des ouvrages théoriques pour l'enseignement scolaire d'une langue vernaculaire. Nous sommes donc en mesure de comparer les pratiques réelles d'un scribe donné avec les informations théoriques que donnent les manuels scolaires.

Ce qui, à mon avis, est caractéristique pour l'enseignement orthographique dispensé en Angleterre, c'est la coexistence de deux tendances contradictoires, l'une *polylectale* et peu normative, l'autre *prescriptive*.

D'une part, ce qui frappe à bien des égards, c'est la faible normativité des manuels. Selon les traités d'orthographe conservés, l'*Orthographia gallica* et le *Tractatus orthographiae*, les professeurs de français en Angleterre étaient plutôt bien informés sur les différentes traditions dialectales et orthographiques en français continental et insulaire. Mais en général, ils énumèrent ces différences sans indiquer leurs préférences.

Ainsi, dans les deux manuels, différentes solutions orthographiques sont proposées pour les formes du pronom personnel *je* et du démonstratif *ce*:

(1) Item iste dicciones videlicet *je, jeo, jo, jou; ce, ceo, cou, chou* secundum modum et rectum sonum diversarum linguarum, prout hic evidenter patet, scribi debent et sonari.[15]

(2) Item ille sillabe *je ce, jeo, ceo* indifferenter possunt scribi cum *c.e.o.* vel cum *c.e.* sine *o.*[16]

De même, l'*Orthographia gallica* laisse le choix entre les formes anglo-normandes et franco-picardes pour *moi, toi, soi*:

(3) Item *moy, toy, soy* possunt scribi cum *i* vel cum *y*, cum *o* vel cum *e* indifferenter.[17]

Coyfurelly commente les différences entre le francien et le picard pour le traitement du *k*- latin prévocalique:[18]

---

[14] Ainsi, dans le manuscrit trilingue que nous allons étudier, la même abréviation est utilisée dans angl. *alle* «all», lat. *ille* ou frç. *ville*; angl. *spiritually* est abrégé de la même manière que lat. *spiritualiter*.

[15] Coyfurelly, *Tractatus ortografie* dans E. Stengel, «Die ältesten Anleitungsschriften zur Erlernung der französischen Sprache», *Zeitschrift für neufranzösische Sprache und Literatur* 1 (1879), p. 17.

[16] R. C. Johnston, *Orthographia Gallica* L8, ANTS Plain Text 5 (London, 1987), p. 11.

[17] *Orthographia Gallica* L26, p. 13.

[18] Kibbee, *For to speke Frenche* (p. 48), prétend que seul Coyfurelly (et son prédécesseur, le *Tractatus*

(4) *K* etiam in lingua romanica, non autem in lingua gallicana, nomine et loco *c* et *h* scribi debet et sonari, ut *kival* i. gallice *chival, kien* i. *chien, vake* i. *vache* et aliquando *q*, ut *quesne* i. *chesne*, necnon loco *c* debent scribi *c* et *h* secundum Romanicos, ut *pour chou* vel *pour cheu* i. gallice *pource* vel *pourceu, decha* i. *deca, tresdouche* i. *tresdoulce* et sic de aliis consimiliter.[19]

En dehors des traités d'orthographe, on trouve un reflet de cette même «permissivité» polylectale – qui correspond bien à la réalité de l'époque – dans d'autres manuels comme par exemple dans le glossaire du *Femina*, qu'on peut dater de 1415: dans celui-ci différentes formes régionales sont également mentionnées sur un pied d'égalité:

(5) Chien secundum pikardiam ⎤
                                ⎬ Cheen vel chaun An hound[20]
     Chaan secundum parisium ⎦

Dans l'exemple suivant, l'enseignement admet également l'existence de deux normes régionales, l'une insulaire, l'autre continentale; dans ce dernier cas, le manuel conseille au rédacteur de s'adapter au destinataire:

(6) Item pro *William* utuntur scribere *Gilliam*, si littera erit directa extra partes.[21]

Dans l'ensemble, cette «permissivité» orthographique contraste particulièrement avec les affirmations explicites de certains témoins anglo-normands depuis le XIIIe siècle, pour lesquels le prestige et la supériorité du français continental ne fait aucun doute:[22] dans la pratique, il est évident que les modèles continentaux ne sont pas adoptés de manière aveugle.

A ma connaissance, il y a un seul anglo-normandisme caractéristique qui est explicitement proscrit, selon l'*Orthographia gallica*: c'est la graphie *au* devant *n*+consonne.[23] Je mentionne ce cas parce qu'il me semble important pour la compréhension des stratégies «orthographiques» réelles que nous allons observer:

(7) Item iste sillabe seu dicciones *quant, grant, demandant, sachant* et huiusmodi debent scribi cum simplici *n* sine *u*, sed in pronunciacione debet *u* proferri.[24]

Voilà notre point de départ. Face à la multitude des traditions orthographiques et

---

orthographiae de T.H. publié par Pope 1910) s'intéresse à la variation dialectale. En réalité, il n'en est rien, comme le montrent les exemples de l'*Orthographia gallica* mentionnés sous (2), (3) et (6).

19 Coyfurelly, *Tractatus ortografie*, dans E. Stengel, «Die ältesten Anleitungsschriften», p. 17.

20 W. A. Wright, *Femina: Now first printed from a unique ms. in the Library of Trinity College, Cambridge* (Cambridge, 1909), p. 106.

21 *Orthographia Gallica* L20, p. 12.

22 Cf. Lusignan, *Parler vulgairement*, pp. 101–3.

23 Le même enseignement se reflète dans les transcriptions du *Femina*, qui insistent à de nombreuses reprises sur le fait que les mots comme *grant, quant*, etc. qui s'écrivent sans -*u*- maintiennent le -*u*- dans la prononciation (A. Kristol, «La prononciation du français en Angleterre», p. 75).

24 *Orthographia Gallica* L36, p. 14.

à la relative liberté que l'enseignement laisse aux étudiants, les questions qui se posent sont donc les suivantes:
— Comment le scribe anglais du XIVe–XVe siècle manie-t-il la pluralité des langues auxquelles il est confronté?
— Comment se comporte-t-il face à la variation interne à chacune des langues vernaculaires?
— Dans quelle mesure les différentes langues sont-elles traitées comme des entités distinctes, dans quelle mesure en respecte-t-il leur originalité?

Pour tenter de répondre en partie du moins à ces questions, je me limiterai à la documentation qui m'est familière, à savoir la production didactique consacrée à l'enseignement du français. Le principal témoignage sur lequel je m'appuierai, c'est le MS Lat. 188 de Magdalen College, Oxford.[25] C'est un manuscrit qui reflète sans doute l'activité didactique de Thomas Sampson, professeur de français à Oxford au dernier quart du XIVe siècle.[26]
— La première partie de ce MS (ff. 1–8v) contient des matériaux théoriques pour l'enseignement du français: la version longue (en latin) de l'*Orthographia gallica*, un *nominale* trilingue (latin-français-anglais), et une *Ars dictaminis* en français.
— La deuxième partie du manuscrit, beaucoup plus longue (elle se compose de 93 folios: f. 9r–102), est consacrée à la pratique. Ce très beau manuscrit (cf. illustration 1) contient un exercice de traduction qui s'appuie sur une collection de traités religieux, à savoir un commentaire des *Dix commandements*, un commentaire du *Credo*, et un commentaire allégorique sur la bête de l'Apocalypse, une *Vision de St-Jean*.[27] L'exercice linguistique consiste à traduire l'original français en latin et en anglais. C'est ce texte trilingue – que je n'ai pas encore entièrement dépouillé – qui me fournira la plupart des informations présentées ici. Je me garderai évidemment de tirer des conclusions trop générales de cet exemple individuel.

La forme du manuscrit et les trois versions parallèles permettent de reconstituer en détail la genèse de ce document:
— dans un premier temps, le scribe a calligraphié le texte français, d'un bout à l'autre du manuscrit, en réservant la place entre les lignes pour les deux traductions, latine et anglaise. Même si ce n'est que pour un exercice de langue, le texte est exécuté, relu et corrigé avec grand soin; je reviendrai à cette question. Il ne fait pas de doute que dans ce manuscrit, le français est la langue «noble», qui a droit à la

---

25 Depuis la parution de mon «recensement» des manuscrits contenant des matériaux pour l'enseignement du français en Angleterre médiévale (A. M. Kristol, «L'enseignement du français en Angleterre (XIIIe–XVe siècles): les sources manuscrites», *Romania* 111 (1990), pp. 289–330), ce manuscrit, déposé à la Bodleian Library au moment où je l'ai consulté, a été de nouveau transféré à la bibliothèque de Magdalen College. Je remercie Lisa Jefferson de m'avoir fourni cette information.

26 I. Arnold, «Thomas Sampson and the Orthographia Gallica», *Medium Ævum* 6 (1937), pp. 192–209.

27 Les deux premières parties ressemblent à certains égards aux chapitres correspondants du *Mirour de Seinte Eglyse* de Saint Edmond d'Abingdon (A. D. Wilshere, *Miroir de Seinte Eglyse* (London, 1982), pp. 28–32 et 34–7), mais semblent appartenir à une autre tradition; en particulier, le commentaire du *Credo* est beaucoup plus développé. La *Vision de Saint Jean* en est complètement indépendante.

ordineat a dieu esspenament Le quatir comandment

tho furste comandmente is ficke honoure thy

Quartir mandatu est tale . Honoza tuu

quatir comandment est nev . Honoine

fader & thy moder for thou shalt lyue more longe

patrem & tua matre. Dinn tu viues nuuct dun

ton pere & ta mere. Cay tu euuituyas plus longement

vapon thestho. his comanndmente . vo Putinest p° vo

Illustration 1. Detail of f. 12v, Magdalen MS Lat. 188.

By permission of The President and Fellows of Magdalen College, Oxford.

plus grande et à la plus belle écriture, ainsi qu'à des rubriques bien exécutées. Les deux autres versions ne sont que des outils de travail.

— dans un deuxième temps, l'auteur a rédigé une traduction latine absolument *littérale,* qui suit le texte français mot par mot, au mépris total de la syntaxe latine:

> (8) Non adorabis neque non seruies & neque pones non tuam spem principaliter nulli quam in me.
> Ne aoureras ne ne seruiras et ne metras pas t'esperance principaument fors a moy. (f. 9r, l. 1)

Le seul but de la version latine est donc d'expliquer le texte français; c'est le texte français qu'il s'agit d'étudier par le biais du latin. A quelques rares endroits, où le texte français est corrompu ou n'a pas été compris, la traduction latine présente d'ailleurs des lacunes.

— dans un troisième temps, une fois que l'«exégèse» en latin du texte français a été achevée, le rédacteur a abordé la troisième phase, à savoir une traduction en anglais. Le texte anglais est nettement plus idiomatique que la version latine, mais exploite à fond tous les emprunts que le moyen anglais a faits à l'anglo-normand, pour calquer de très près, souvent mot à mot aussi, le texte français:

> (9) But þe conscience is perilouse and it may be turnid to synne mortale that not hym kepith.
> Mes la conscience est perilleuse et puet l'en tourner a peche mortel qui ne s'en garde. (f. 10v, ll. 5–6).

Plusieurs indices permettent de déterminer que le texte anglais constitue effectivement la troisième phase du travail:

— quand la version latine est incomplète, le texte anglais est pratiquement toujours omis aussi;

— le texte anglais présente des lacunes supplémentaires par rapport au texte latin;

— parfois, le rédacteur a carrément omis des pages entières, quand il a ajouté la version anglaise.

— certains choix lexicaux de la version anglaise sont manifestement influencés par le texte intermédiaire en latin:

> (10) for eny nede that holy chirche **exceptith**.
> pro aliqua necessitate quam sancta ecclesia **exceptat**.
> pur aucune necessite que seint eglise **otroie**. (f. 12r, 8–9)

L'intérêt de ce document est évidemment multiple; c'est une véritable mine de renseignements que je serai incapable d'épuiser ici.

D'un point de vue grammatical, il est extrêmement instructif d'analyser de quelle manière certains phénomènes morphosyntaxiques du français sont rendus dans les versions latine et anglaise: la traduction permet d'entrevoir le genre de réflexions et de conceptions grammaticales qui sont véhiculées par l'enseignement du français en Angleterre. C'est un aspect que je suis obligé de négliger complètement ici. Les

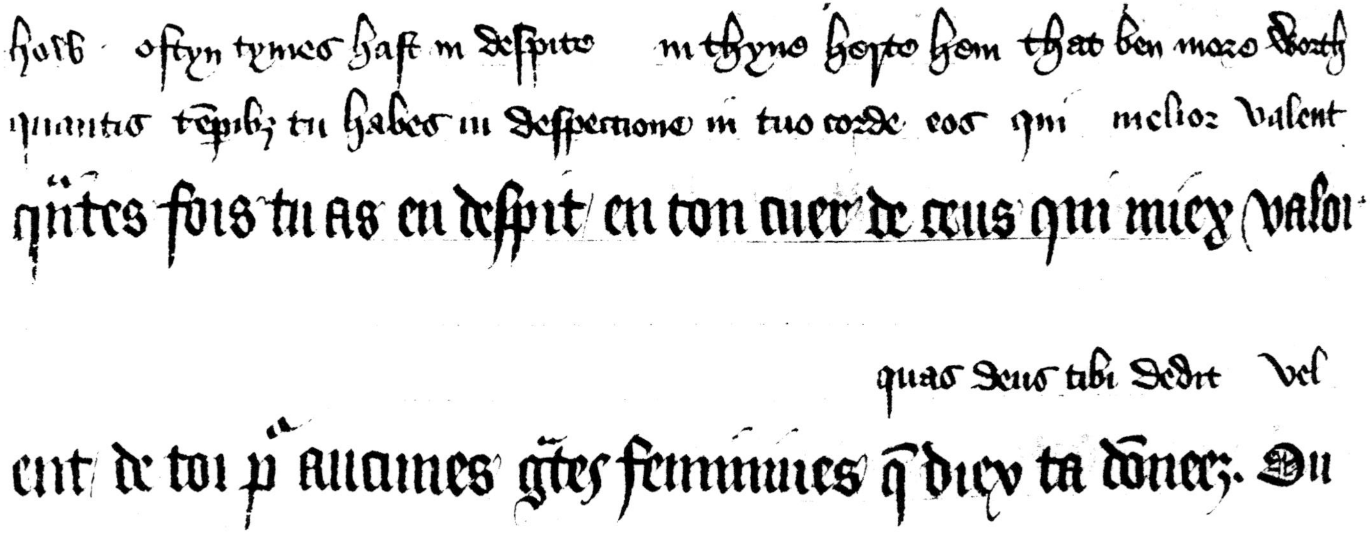

Illustration 2. Detail of f. 31v, Magdalen MS Lat. 188.
By permission of The President and Fellows of Magdalen College, Oxford.

exemples suivants doivent suffir pour indiquer le genre d'informations qu'on pourrait en tirer.

— L'article français est systématiquement identifié avec le démonstratif latin:

> (11) **le** premiers comandement: **hoc** primum mandatum, **the** ferst commaundement. (f. 9r, 1)

Mais même en anglais, on trouve l'emploi du démonstratif pour traduire l'article français:

> (12) **le** secunde commandement: **hoc** secundum mandatum, **this** secunde comaundement (f. 9v, 6)

— En latin et en anglais, la traduction cherche régulièrement à calquer la forme discontinue de la négation française (*ne . . . pas*):

> (13) tu **ne** prendras **pas**: tu **non** assumas **quovismodo**, thou shalt **not** take **in eniwyse** (f. 9v, 7)

Ce qui est particulièrement intéressant ici, c'est que ce manuscrit permet de découvrir une méthode concrète d'enseignement contrastif du français qui a été utilisée dans la deuxième moitié du XIVe siècle, mais qui est restée pratiquement inconnue jusqu'ici; on aimerait bien savoir depuis quand ce genre d'exercices existe dans l'enseignement du français en Angleterre. Ce qui est évident, c'est que cette méthode est axée sur l'acquisition de la langue écrite. Elle se trouve aux antipodes des *manières de langage* légèrement plus tardives, dont les dialogues modèles enseignaient la langue parlée quotidienne. C'est également une méthode très différente des traités d'orthographe théoriques qui – à mon avis – n'ont jamais pu servir dans l'acquisition concrète du français. Pour moi, la découverte de ce texte a été une véritable révélation, car je me suis souvent demandé comment le français écrit a été enseigné en Angleterre, en dehors des traités d'orthographe et des collections de lettres modèles, à une époque antérieure au développement d'un enseignement explicite de la syntaxe dans les manuels de grammaire: il me semblait exclu qu'on ait pu apprendre le maniement correct de la syntaxe française rien qu'avec ces manuels-là.

Dans ce type d'enseignement, le latin fonctionne comme une sorte d'«adjuvant», qui permet de mettre en relief, par le mépris même de la syntaxe latine, les particularités de la phrase française. Par ailleurs, cet emploi du latin constitue un élément de réponse à une question qui a souvent été débattue, à savoir si, dans l'histoire de l'enseignement des langues dans l'Angleterre médiévale, c'est le français, première langue de scolarisation, qui a servi pour enseigner le latin, ou si c'est le latin qui a servi à enseigner le français.[28] En ce qui concerne cet exercice précis, et pour ce moment précis de l'histoire de l'enseignement du français en Angleterre, aucun doute n'est possible: la traduction littérale en latin n'a de sens que pour un étudiant qui sait déjà le latin.

Mais la question la plus intéressante est sans doute de savoir pourquoi le texte a

---

[28] Pour un résumé de ce débat, cf. Kibbee, *For to speke Frenche*, pp. 55–6.

été traduit deux fois, et latin *et* en anglais. L'explication qui s'impose – et qui coïncide avec un témoignage explicite de Thomas Sampson[29] – c'est qu'une partie du public scolaire visé par cet enseignement n'avait pas de connaissances suffisantes de latin. On peut donc distinguer deux types d'étudiants: ceux qui apprennent d'abord le latin, et ensuite le français, et ceux qui n'ont pas besoin de savoir le latin, et abordent directement l'étude du français par le biais de l'anglais. Pour moi, cela signifie que – malgré la thématique religieuse des textes d'étude – l'enseignement du français tel qu'il est conçu ici ne s'adresse pas uniquement à des clercs ou à quelques rares intellectuels. A côté d'un public ecclésiastique qui manie les trois langues, il existe un public laïque qui a également besoin de maîtriser le français. C'est un indice parmi d'autres que dans la société anglaise de la fin du XIVe siècle, le français – écrit, en l'occurrence – conserve un attrait considérable.

Mais je reviens à la principale question qui m'intéresse ici. La coexistence des trois langues dans ce manuscrit permet d'étudier jusqu'à un certain point quelles sont les difficultés auxquelles un scribe anglais – qui doit manier trois systèmes d'écriture – est constamment confronté.

Une première observation est presque banale. Etant donné que le texte original est en français, que le texte français constitue la cible de l'enseignement, et qu'il n'a sans doute pas été composé par notre professeur de français lui-même, il n'a pas directement subi l'influence linguistique des deux autres versions présentes dans le manuscrit. Il illustre tout simplement le «bon français d'Angleterre» tel qu'il est pratiqué en cette fin du XIVe siècle, une langue qui fait depuis longtemps l'objet d'un enseignement scolaire systématique. Un tel texte permet de répondre en partie à la question de savoir *quel* genre de français a été enseigné dans les écoles anglaises;[30] il permet d'observer de quelle manière le rédacteur de ce manuscrit adopte et personnalise les enseignements de l'*Orthographia gallica*, qui se trouve justement dans la première partie du même manuscrit. Mais ce n'est pas tout, car en dehors des règles énoncées dans les traités d'orthographe, il existe évidemment une foule d'usages concrets qui ne sont pas mentionnés dans les ouvrages théoriques. Dans ces cas, il n'y a que l'observation des pratiques réelles qui nous permet d'appréhender les conceptions orthographiques d'un scribe donné.

Je serai bref en ce qui concerne les latinismes, dont la présence dans le manuscrit ne surprendra personne. Les exemples 14 à 16 regroupent des passages caractéristiques dans lesquels une même graphie apparaît dans deux ou même les trois langues:

---

29 Selon le prologue de son *Ars notaria* (MS BL Lansdowne 560, f. 30r), de nombreux étudiants ne savent pas assez bien le latin, de sorte qu'il se voit obligé d'enseigner en français: «A cause que je, Thomas S., enformer d'icel art, ay conceu que plusours enfantz [qui] sont si tenuement lettrez, je ferray la prologe devant en franceis» (cf. aussi Richardson, «Letters of the Oxford Dictatores», *Formularies which bear on the History of Oxford, c.1204-1420*, II, éd. H. E. Salter et al. (Oxford Historical Society, n.s., vol. 5), p. 335).

30 Je n'aborderai pas ici la question de la forme phonique de cette langue, lorsqu'elle est lue à haute voix (cf. A. Kristol, «La prononciation du français»). Les graphies inverses de notre texte laissent pourtant penser que son rédacteur maintenait dans sa prononciation les principales particularités du français régional d'Angleterre, qui remontent essentiellement à l'anglo-normand de la grande période (XIIe/XIIIe s.), et au-delà au normand continental.

(14) le **secunde** commau[n]dement, hoc **secundum** mandatum, this **secunde** comaundement (f. 9v, 6)

(15) son **creatore**, suum **creatorem** [mais: his **makere**] (f. 12r, 3)

(16) les autres festes **solempnes**, alia festa **solempnia**, othir feestis **solempne** (f. 12r, 5)

L'identité des trois graphies n'est pourtant pas toujours acquise. Ainsi, on rencontre trois graphies différentes pour un même mot dans l'exemple suivant:

(17) il enoublient leur **creature**, illi obliuiscuntur suum **creatorem**, thei forgeten her **creatour** (f. 9v, 2)

Il serait donc trop simpliste de postuler une sorte de syncrétisme orthographique généralisé; malgré les coïncidences ponctuelles, le scribe tend à considérer les trois systèmes orthographiques comme des entités indépendantes.

Qu'en est-il maintenant des interactions entre le français et l'anglais? D'une manière générale, dans l'ensemble des manuscrits didactiques sur lesquels j'ai travaillé jusqu'ici, les influences de l'orthographe anglaise dans les textes français sont plutôt rares. De ce point de vue, le MS Magdalen 188 n'est pas une exception. Comme je l'ai montré ailleurs,[31] les professeurs de français en Angleterre au Moyen Age faisaient des efforts considérables pour préserver la langue qu'ils enseignaient de certaines influences anglaises ressenties comme trop voyantes. Je pense que cette attitude «puriste» à l'égard des influences anglaises est due au prestige sociolinguistique relatif des deux langues pendant la plus grande partie de leur coexistence. Comme l'a montré Lusignan,[32] pendant très longtemps, dans le «concert» des langues qui se côtoyaient en Angleterre, le français a fonctionné comme langue haute (à côté du latin), et l'anglais comme langue basse. Or, en règle générale, dans des situations diglossiques et de contact linguistique de cette nature, la langue haute – et surtout sa graphie – est peu influencée par la langue basse.[33] Il est particulièrement significatif à cet égard que le texte latin ne subit pratiquement aucune influence des systèmes orthographiques «vulgaires». Par contre, la traduction anglaise foisonne de gallicismes.[34]

(18) For in erthe is noon so holy a man þat **parfitly** may **eschewe** alle **maneris**
Quia in terra non est tam sanctus homo qui perfecte potest evitare omnia genera
Car en terre n'i a si seint homme qui **parfitement** puit **eschiver** toutez les **maneris**

---

[31] A. Kristol, «La prononciation du français».

[32] Lusignan, *Parler vulgairement*, p. 118 et *passim*.

[33] Il est significatif à cet égard que les «transcriptions phonétiques» du *Femina* utilisent essentiellement les ressources orthographiques du système français pour indiquer la prononciation préconisée. C'est donc d'abord le système français qui s'est imposé à l'esprit du rédacteur. Ce n'est que dans les rares cas où le système français ne permettait pas de représenter un son donné qu'il a eu recours à certaines ressources orthographiques du système anglais.

[34] Leur densité est sans doute plus élevée que dans un texte anglais «normal» de cette époque, ce qui est dû à la nature de l'exercice.

of synnes that of thiise seven hedes **descendyn** withouten **especial privilege** of **grace**.

peccatorum que de hiis septem capitibus descendunt sine speciali privilegio gracie.

de pechiez qui des .vii. chefs **descendent** sans **especial privilege** de **grace**. (f. 25r, 1–4)

Même si l'essentiel des influences semble aller du français vers l'anglais, il serait évidemment naïf de croire que plusieurs siècles de contacts entre les deux langues – et le bilinguisme de tous les utilisateurs du français originaires d'Angleterre – n'aient pas laissé de profondes traces en anglo-normand tardif. Simplement, les influences anglaises ne se manifestent pas forcément là où on les attend.

Comme je l'ai souligné dans l'introduction, le texte français de notre manuscrit a été relu et corrigé avec beaucoup de soin. Or il est frappant de constater que ce sont souvent des graphies de type anglo-normand qui sont corrigées:

(19) c$\overset{i}{_\wedge}$el (f. 10r, 1), v$\overset{i}{_\wedge}$elle (f. 11v, 7)

Même si ces corrections sont le résultat d'une simple application mécanique de la première règle de l'*Orthographia gallica*[35] – ce qui provoque par ailleurs de nombreuses hypercorrections: *tiel* pour *tel* (f. 9v, 7), *quiex* pour *quels* (f. 11r, 7) – la tendance générale du scribe est donc de chercher la conformité avec les habitudes orthographiques continentales. Ces corrections vont dans le même sens que la règle citée sous (7) ci-dessus, qui proscrit les graphies anglo-normandes en -*aun*-.

On est donc surpris de constater que malgré tout, la graphie -*aun*- fait son apparition dans une série d'exemples du manuscrit:

(20) *devaunt* (f. 11r, 7), *ataunt* (f. 11v, 2), *graunt* (f. 24v, 4), *quaunt* (f. 26r, 2), *braunches* (f. 27v, 3); etc.

La question qui se pose ici est de savoir pourquoi notre scribe, qui a une graphie parfaitement soignée, qui se surveille et se corrige, qui est capable d'écrire le latin sans la moindre variation orthographique, qui applique les règles de l'*Orthographia gallica* de manière très disciplinée, laisse échapper ces graphies proscrites. Pourquoi ce maintien d'une particularité orthographique anglo-normande, malgré la pression du modèle continental et un enseignement totalement explicite?

Evidemment, une première hypothèse qui s'impose, c'est que notre scribe a copié un manuscrit antérieur à l'enseignement de l'*Orthographia gallica*, et qu'il se serait laissé influencer par la graphie de son modèle. Comme nous ne connaissons pas celui-ci, il est impossible de vérifier cette hypothèse, mais de toute façon, je ne crois pas que ce soit la meilleure interprétation possible. Pour moi, cette «irrégularité» dans la graphie de notre scribe est plutôt due à la coexistence des différentes langues et de leurs traditions orthographiques en Angleterre médiévale. Comme le montrent

---

[35] Diccio gallica dictata habens primam sillabam vel mediam in *e* stricto ore pronunciatam requirit hanc litteram *i* ante *e*, verbi gracia *bien, chien, rien, piere, miere*. (*Orth. Gall.* L1, p. 11).

les exemples sous (21), il y a une foule de mots que le moyen anglais a adoptés avec leur forme anglo-normande traditionnelle, et en anglais, aucune interdiction n'est venue frapper l'emploi des graphies en -*aun*-, qui se conserve encore en anglais moderne (*aunt, haunch, daunt, etc.*):

> (21) *commaundement* (f. 9r, 1), *commaundeth* (f. 9r, 1), *entendaunce* (f. 11r, 5) etc.

Par ricochet, le maintien des graphies anglo-normandes dans les emprunts en moyen anglais a sans doute pu consolider la tradition autochtone dans les textes en français aussi. Dans la mesure où la tradition orthographique anglo-normande a été interceptée par l'enseignement de l'*Orthographia gallica*, la réapparition de graphies anglo-normandes peut s'expliquer par l'existence parallèle de ces graphies en anglais. Le schéma ci-contre essaie de symboliser cette évolution.

Ce qui conforte cette interprétation, c'est que le cas du groupe -*aun*- n'est pas isolé. Ainsi, malgré les auto-corrections mentionnées sous (19), le scribe n'est pas entièrement conséquent non plus dans l'application de la règle n° 1 de l'*Orthographia gallica*:

> (22) so also the devel hath diverse **maners** of wrenchis to deceyve & to tempte the puple.
>
> ita eciam diabolus habet diuersos modos machinarum decipiendi et
>
> > gentres
>
> temptandi populos.
>
> aussi le diables a diverses **maners** d'enginz a decevoir et a tempter les gentz. (f. 24r, 8–9)

Dans ce cas aussi, il paraît évident que la graphie anglo-normande tardive a été consolidée par les formes anglo-normandes classiques qui ont «transité» par l'anglais. Je serais assez tenté de croire que c'est une des raisons qui explique pourquoi certains manuscrits anglo-normands très tardifs[36] sont marqués par un très net retour aux graphies autochtones, alors que certains textes antérieurs sont plus proches des modèles continentaux.

On sait depuis longtemps qu'une des caractéristiques de la graphie anglo-normande tardive, c'est son extrême instabilité qu'on a souvent voulu attribuer à une formation insuffisante des scribes, ou à leur ignorance du français. Je ne nierai pas que certains copistes aient pu avoir des connaissances plutôt limitées, mais c'est une explication trop courte des phénomènes qu'on observe dans un grand nombre de manuscrits de cette époque. Les intellectuels anglais du XIVe et du XVe siècle qui ont souvent rédigé des manuscrits trilingues, n'étaient pas des pauvres d'esprit, ignorants et mal formés, tout au contraire. Une fois de plus, je m'inscris en faux contre le préjugé très ancien au sujet du «mauvais français» qu'on aurait parlé et écrit en Angleterre, au Moyen Age. Pour moi, les jugements de valeur de ce type

---

36 P. ex. le fragment de Lincoln de la *Manière de langage* de 1399 ou la *Manière de langage* de 1415 (Kristol, *Manières de langage*).

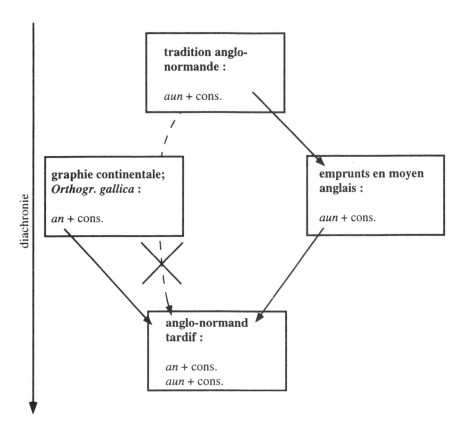

témoignent d'une incompréhension profonde de la réalité linguistique de l'époque et des capacités intellectuelles des copistes anglo-normands.

Il est vrai que l'orthographe anglo-normande tardive est souvent déconcertante à première vue. Lorsqu'on analyse de plus près ces aberrations apparentes, on se rend pourtant compte qu'elles sont moins absurdes qu'il n'y paraît.

— En règle générale, le scribe anglo-normand traite avec le plus grand respect les différentes langues de culture écrite dont il dispose. Même lorsqu'il emploie le latin de manière purement technique, comme dans notre manuscrit, il est parfaitement capable de l'écrire sans la moindre variation orthographique, et en ce qui concerne le français, il peut s'appuyer sur une tradition scolaire indigène explicite, qu'il s'applique à suivre fidèlement.

— Mais il serait évidemment anachronique de lui demander une graphie entièrement homogène. Tout d'abord, le français continental lui-même, à cette époque, est encore caractérisé par sa variation dialectale interne, et les professeurs de français en Angleterre en sont parfaitement conscients. Malgré le prestige croissant de la forme parisienne ou orléanaise à laquelle certains témoignages explicites font allusion, en réalité les différentes formes régionales coexistent encore de manière peu conflictuelle.[37] Etant donné que même les traités théoriques admettent la variation régionale, chaque scribe individuel est relativement libre et doit développer ses propres stratégies en ce qui concerne l'emploi de ces formes concurrencielles dont aucune n'a encore pu s'imposer. Chaque texte, chaque manuscrit sera donc caractérisé par le mélange spécifique des graphies qu'il présente, par les préférences qu'il accorde à telle ou telle forme régionale. L'enseignement est «polylectal», peu normatif, et comme le français est toujours une langue à usage interne de l'Angleterre, il n'y aurait aucun sens d'adopter aveuglément une quelconque «norme» continentale. De toute façon, parler de «norme», à la fin du XIVe siècle, fait encore peu de sens.[38]

Mais le principal résultat de l'examen de ce manuscrit trilingue, dans lequel les différentes traditions orthographiques coexistent, c'est le fait que le scribe est extrêmement sélectif. Les seules graphies «anglaises» qu'il maintient à l'encontre de l'enseignement explicite des traités d'orthographe, ce sont celles qui coïncident avec la tradition anglo-normande autochtone. A mes yeux, c'est une nouvelle évidence qui parle en faveur de la vitalité du français insulaire, jusqu'à la fin du Moyen Age.

---

[37] Dans un sens, si l'influence orthographique continentale n'était venue troubler la régularité de la tradition anglo-normande, les écrits en anglo-normand tardif pourraient se présenter de manière beaucoup plus homogène.

[38] Ce n'est qu'en 1529, sous la plume de l'humaniste et imprimeur Geoffroy Tory qu'on trouvera un premier appel à la création d'une norme du français qui, à ce moment-là, est encore parfaitement inexistante . . .

Collecting Miracles along the Anglo-Welsh Border in the Early Fourteenth Century

MICHAEL RICHTER

A NYBODY WHO has tried to investigate the state of the spoken languages in medieval England will be aware of the severe limitations of the sources available for this purpose. In what follows I will present some accounts which have specific strengths as well as weaknesses. I hope to make good use of the former and atone for the latter to some extent.

I will be dealing with a source which formed a major part of my book *Sprache und Gesellschaft im Mittelalter*[1] but which, to my knowledge, has not been investigated further. I will present aspects which are different from those which I investigated earlier.

Let me briefly introduce my source. In the year 1307 a delegation came to England from Rome in order to investigate miracles worked by Thomas Cantilupe, bishop of Hereford from 1275 to 1282. His successors had begun their efforts to have Cantilupe canonised quite soon after his death, but Rome moved slowly, and a quarter of a century had passed since his death before the practical steps were taken.

The Roman delegation consisted of several people, including notaries public, whose task it was to collect the evidence presented and to write an account of it in Latin. Their main partner on the other side was the procurator of Hereford Cathedral. There is evidence that he had prepared the encounter carefully, and so he presented, first in London, later in Hereford, groups of people who each gave evidence concerning a specific miracle allegedly worked by the intercession of Thomas Cantilupe.

The task that lay ahead had to come up to certain expectations on the part of the investigating delegation. A fixed number of questions were put to the witnesses in the course of their depositions, including the independence of their statements from each other as well as their relationship or otherwise to Thomas Cantilupe. Finally, all were obliged not to talk about their deposition until the miracle was made public.

The result of the work of the commission is a dossier of 245 folios containing the depositions of altogether 203 witnesses.[2] The work had taken almost exactly four

[1] Michael Richter, *Sprache und Gesellschaft im Mittelalter: Untersuchungen zur mündlichen Kommunikation in England von der Mitte des elften bis zum Beginn des vierzehnten Jahrhunderts* (Stuttgart, 1979).
[2] MS Vat. Lat. 4015.

months, and it can be estimated that more than 90% of the depositions were made in languages other than Latin, the principal language of our source. On the other hand, the present text contains no more than perhaps a dozen sentences in languages other than Latin. One gets the impression that in the course of their work the commission gradually lost their patience, for the examinations got increasingly shorter the more time passed.

I will present two cases, recounting miracles IX and XIII. These cases show the variety contained in the source, but they also illuminate each other in certain ways. The cases involve altogether eighteen witnesses; for each miracle there are nine witnesses. Quite apart from the miracle involved in each case, the strength of our source is the information it provides concerning each deposition. The witness is named, the essential social details are given concerning age, social status, and, for our purpose most relevant, the language in which the deposition was made.[3] From the source as a whole one can gather that the commmission preferred the evidence to be given in Latin. The other languages that figure are clearly presented in a hierarchical order. This was, in a descending scale, French, English and Welsh.

Miracle IX: The story of John de Burton

From the depositions of nine witnesses who were questioned for three days (21, 30 and 31 October), a quite detailed account can be reconstructed of a young man called John de Burton which is of interest to us for various reasons. John de Burton, so called after his alleged place of birth, had been born without a tongue. He received a good and functioning tongue through the intercession of St Thomas Cantilupe in May 1288 when he was aged about sixteen. All the witnesses more or less agreed that with this tongue he was able to speak English and Welsh. Soon after the miracle had happened, John vowed to make a pilgrimage to the Holy Land with a priest called William[4] and was not seen thereafter.

By the time the depositions concerning this miracle were given, nineteen years had passed since the event, and the accounts show that this miracle had become part of the collective memory of the citizens of Hereford. There are many parallels and similarities of phrasing in the accounts available, but there are also significant variances which give the story considerable depth.

John de Burton, cured at the age of about sixteen in Hereford Cathedral, had earned his livelihood beforehand by begging. In fact, before going to Hereford, persuaded to do so by the gardener of the Franciscan convent of Hereford, he had spent a number of years begging in the town of Ludlow. For this we have two witnesses altogether, both of whom had lived there before they moved to Hereford. Symon, called in our account 'burger of Hereford' (131), but still known as Symon of Ludlow, aged fifty, according to his own statement had moved from Ludlow to

3   See Richter, *Sprache und Gesellschaft im Mittelalter*, Appendix, pp. 205–17.
4   132, f. 205v.

Hereford c.1281. By that time John de Burton would have been only nine years old. Before his move to Hereford, Simon had seen John begging frequently, and the witness had apparently frequently inspected John's mouth and had seen that there was no tongue in it. John could only utter unintelligible sounds.

The other person who had known John from Ludlow was Margeria Thurgrym. In 1307 she gave her age as twenty-eight years, and she was the wife of a rich Hereford burgher, Walter Thurgrym. She had seen John de Burton when he called at her parental home in Ludlow and, in her own words, had frequently given him alms at the door. At that time she was only nine years old; no wonder that she estimated John de Burton to be much older than the others, twenty instead of sixteen. She said that she often had the opportunity to look into his mouth; she saw no tongue, large or small, and the beggar used two fingers to introduce food into his throat (134, f. 207r: cum ipsa in domo paterna moraretur in villa de Lodelaw vidit ibi frequenter per unum annum ut estimat predictum Johannem mendicantem et sepe manu propria elemosinam ministravit eidem et aperto ore ipsius Johannis vidit sepius ad hostium domus sue paterne et in aliis locis quod . . . habebat linguam nec magnam nec parvam nec aliqui loco linguae et os eius erat totum vacuum interius et cibum sibi ministratum cum duobus digitis impingebat).

She claimed that her mother had persuaded the beggar to go to Hereford for help. Margeria de Thurgrym thus had not experienced John in Hereford. She moved there later and married a rich man. This shows that the story of John de Burton had become part of the collective memory of Hereford which Margeria could join and enrich when she moved there.

It is not quite clear how it came about that Hugh de Brompton, the gardener of the Franciscan convent of Hereford, came across John de Burton, but he persuaded him to come to Hereford and pray to St Thomas Cantilupe to help him in his affliction. There is also some more uncertainty. There are versions according to which John stayed for a while at Hereford, and that he received a small tongue with which he could speak even though fairly poorly,[5] that he then left Hereford and came a second time when the actual miracle took place.

However, before this happened, John had a brief begging career, if one may use this term, in Hereford also after several years as a beggar in Ludlow. He encountered at least six burghers of Hereford, one woman, the rest men, who in 1307 were aged between forty and fifty-five, thus considerably older than Margeria de Thurgrym. The woman among these was also married to a Thurgrym, Richard, who was like-wise described as being well-off (*dives*). Whether or not the two Thurgrym families were related is not known. On the other hand, it would appear that it was no coincidence that affluent people were involved in this case. John seems to have chosen rich people as his clientele, and he seems to have been somewhat successful.

Here again one learns that the beggar, claiming to have no tongue, had to allow

---

5   121, f. 186v: parva lingua cum qua lingua loquebatur sed non aperte anglicum et walense. . . . et audiebat eum loquentem anglicum non bene quia repetebat bis vel ter verba priusquam intellegeretur et audivit etiam eum loquentem alium linguagium quod videbatur sibi esse Walense.

his mouth to be scrutinised closely. He must have been well used to the procedure and perhaps even volunteered it. This would make good sense in view of the fact that there are two reports that John was beaten up in order to find out whether he could speak after all. In one case it was said that other beggars were set upon John and beat him with his own staff; this happened outside the church of St Nicholas and was inititiated by Thomas Sandi (132, f. 205r: quia mendicando non proferebat dictus Johannes vocem articulatam sed emittebat quosdam rugitus volens probare idem testis si fingeret se mutum vel non esse fecit eum in dicta civitate Hereford prope ecclesiam sancti Nicolai bis vapulare per alios mendicantes cum baculo quem ipse Johannes portabat et non dedit aliquod vocem sed rugitum predictum ad instar latrans canis et fecit aperiri os eius et probaret et videret si haberet linguam et dictus Johannes vidente ipso teste inmittens digitum suum in os suum proprium apertum ostendit sibi dictum defectum lingue . . .).

The noise made by John was likened there to the whining of a dog. Subsequently, John had to open his mouth once more and show that there was no tongue. This rough handling of the young invalid is told quite factually; it may have been a rather common experience. Another witness who said that John had called at his house hundreds of times freely admitted that the beggar was beaten up frequently in his presence (133, f. 206v: et venerat idem Johannes ad domum ipsius testis centum vicibus et ultra pro elemosina habenda, et interdum in eius domo fuerat hospitatus . . . illis temporibus dictus Johannes mendicando nec etiam cum frequenter presente ipso teste fuisset verberatus ullam reddebat vocem articulatam et distinctam . . .). It is not said whether after this brutal procedure John was given alms.

We now come to the miracle itself. This is told, as if in a slow motion sequence in a film, in quite some detail by a witness no less respectable than Gilbert, procurator of the chapter of Hereford cathedral. His fellow-friar Hugh had brought John de Burton back to Hereford and asked Gilbert to keep an eye on him.[6] By that time John did not speak anything that Gilbert could understand. John spent three days near the tomb of St Thomas. John was not the only pilgrim around. On 9 May about the hour of prime, John sat in front of the tomb. Gilbert saw him kissing the tomb three times, and then laying his head on the tomb. He had fallen asleep, and as he would recount later, St Thomas appeared to him and slightly touched his throat (135, f. 208r: et cum dicta lingua narravit eis predictum sanctum Thomam apparuisse sibi illa nocte in sompniis in ecclesia Hereford. et videbatur . . . Johanni quod cum manu strinxerat sibi guttur et evigilans post dictam strictionem invenerat se habere linguam predictam cum qua laudabat et glorificabat deum et dictum sanctum Thomam loquendo ydioma anglicum et intelligibiliter quod ydioma retrahebat ad ydioma Walense ex quo ipse frater et alii estimabant fuisse ortum et nutritum ex Walensibus nescit tamen bene et ex quibus parentibus traxit originem).

He slept as long as it would have taken a man to walk for one mile (136, f. 209r). Next Gilbert heard someone shout: 'Argluth deu e seint Thomas', shouting it time and again. The shout came from John de Burton. Gilbert hastened to the spot. 'Can

---

6   Witness 131 alleged that Hugh was actually present at the miracle which is not confirmed by 136.

you speak, John?', he asked somewhat sheepishly, and John answered that he could (dictus testis predicta audiens peciit ab eo potes loqui Johannes et ille respondit quod sic (209r); it is not stated in which language this exchange was carried out). And then John showed to the witness and all the others who were around a long and beautiful and huge tongue which he had, he stuck it out of his mouth, and he spoke with this tongue Welsh and English.

After what has been said before it is little wonder that John de Burton showed his beautiful immaculate tongue to whoever happened to be near, pulling the tongue out as far as it would go. He could also speak properly with that tongue, apparently instantaneously (131, f. 204v: qui exibebat omnibus volentibus videre cum lingua pulcra, magna et perfecta absque aliquo defectu absque apparens divisione quam linguam sepissime idem Johannes tunc aperiendo os suum et protrahendo summitatem lingue extra dentes et os monstravit publice ipsi testi et omnibus aliis videre volentibus et eadem hora ipso teste audiente eo loquebatur anglicum et intelligibile et Walense).

As to the quality of his speech, this is not assessed unanimously. According to some, he spoke English and Welsh intelligibly.[7] According to others, their statements can be understood to mean that he spoke English in the Welsh manner (?with a Welsh intonation?).[8]

This account requires a closer look. John de Burton himself is simply said to have come from Burton, his father's birthplace; nothing is known about his mother. He would appear to have grown up in a bilingual, English-Welsh, environment and to have acquired a sound enough passive knowledge of the two languages so as to be able to speak them both as soon as he obtained a tongue. While John would have heard English in Hereford during his existence there as a beggar, Welsh would not have been equally present. The same applies to Ludlow where he had spent at least seven years before going to Hereford.

Now to the languages of the nine witnesses. Most of these were aged between forty and fifty-five in 1307; only one, Margeria Thurgrym, was twenty-eight and thus had been a child when John received his tongue. The languages in which the witnesses testified are impressive: only one of them, Thomas Sandi, gave his evidence in English, four of them did so in French, two, both apparently lay people, spoke partly in French, partly in Latin, and the two clerics, a Franciscan John of Brompton, and the procurator of the chapter of Hereford, Gilbert, gave their evidence in Latin. Both women who appear in the record gave their evidence in French. Both are said to have been wives of affluent Hereford citizens; it is possible that their linguistic competence was a factor of their social status as well. Their husbands bear the same name, and so it is not far-fetched to think that they were related to one another. The younger of the two women was a native of Ludlow who

---

7   131: anglicum et intelligibile et Walense (f. 204v; cf. 116, f. 206r; 133, f. 206v).
8   121, f. 187r: set dictum Anglicum aliquantulum miscebat cum linguagio Walentium. 132, f. 205v: audivit ipsum cum dicta lingua loquentem idioma anglicum trahens se ad ydioma Walense. 135, f. 208r: loquendo ydioma anglicum et intelligibiliter quod ydioma retrahebat ad ydioma Walense ex quo ipse frater et alii estimabant fuisse ortum et nutritum ex Walensibus.

had married outside the parish. There are indications at least that she came from an affluent family herself. It is implied in this case that the witnesses had no difficulty in identifying the Welsh language. On the other hand, there is little enough evidence for the presence of Welsh in Hereford; some evidence is provided by our other story, miracle XIII.

On the other hand, French, the language in which the majority of the witnesses of John's tongue gave evidence, was to all appearances not their mother tongue but instead a language of education and an indication of a higher social status.

The one institution which we encounter in our source is the Friary of Hereford. This appears as a meeting place of the various regional languages. There were two friars who could act as interpreters between Welsh and Latin; another member, John of Brompton, translated from English into Latin on a medium-term basis.

Miracle XIII: The story of William ap Rees

Our next case study refers to a miracle which happened about eighteen months after the miracle of John de Burton. It took place in Swansea. Its main character is William ap Rees, who was hanged in the first week in November 1289 but who, apparently dead as an effect of the hanging, came back to life and was alive and well when he himself gave evidence in Hereford in the autumn of 1307.[9] Again we have nine people to give evidence, but this case provides richer information concerning the linguistic interaction between the inhabitants of Swansea and the surrounding area. This is also caused by the wider social range of the personalities involved.

The wide social and linguistic range in this case is represented at one end by the main character of the case, William ap Rees, also known as William Cragh, a monoglot Welsh speaker, and at the other end by Maria de Braose, widow of William de Braose the elder and step-mother of William de Braose the younger.[10] Maria was of Norman descent, and she gave her deposition in French. The commission were discreet enough not to ask the lady's age, for none is given. In her company were her stepson and the chaplain. In between the representatives of the castle, the Marcher lord and his circle, and the victim William ap Rees, there were four burghers of Swansea as well as a priest. These all were not sympathetic to William ap Rees, and one would like to know how they got on together in Hereford, and whether any of the Swansea burghers knew enough Welsh to communicate with William ap Rees. This we do not know.

Let us first look at the three people from Swansea Castle. They all made their deposition in French, *in vulgari Gallico*, as the record states for them all, and this

9   Cf. M. Richter, 'Waliser und Wundermänner um 1300', in *Spannungen und Widersprüche, Gedenk-schrift für František Graus*, ed. S. Burghartz et al. (Sigmaringen, 1992), pp. 23–36, for an elaboration of the social dimensions of this account. I hope to provide an edition of the complete Latin text of this case in the near future.

10 For the wider political context see J. B. Smith and T. B. Pugh, 'The Lordship of Gower and Kilvey in the Middle Ages', in T. B. Pugh, ed., *Glamorgan County History*, vol. III (Cardiff, 1971), pp. 218–43.

shows that this was the language which they shared. The chaplain, even though apparently unable to give his statements in Latin, nevertheless showed language competence in a second acquired language. For in the course of his deposition he said that William ap Rees had intended to make his confession to him before his execution: 'the said William Cragh did not know English, and the said witness, who is English himself, did not speak nor understand Welsh, the language of the said William Cragh' (f. 13r).

We will look next at the language competence of the burghers of Swansea. Of the four laymen, only one was able to testify in French, the other three gave their evidence in English. Furthermore, the Swansea priest gave his evidence in French as well. Unlike the clerics from Hereford, he was unable to do so in Latin. We have seen that among the Hereford lay witnesses two had had some competence in Latin. The distance between the people in Swansea Castle and the town of Swansea was not just a linguistic barrier. It seems almost symptomatic that William de Braose, interviewed in London in mid-July, was not aware that William ap Rees was still alive then whereas the Swansea burghers who gave their evidence three months later in Hereford, all knew it, and not just because he was among their party.

At the other end of the scale was William ap Rees, monoglot Welsh as is stated explicitly in more than one place. In order to get his evidence, the commission drew on Welsh speakers from the convent of Friars Minor of Hereford. These are named as Johannes iuvenis and Maurice de Pencoyt. They administered the oath of William ap Rees in Welsh, whereas the others in the party gave their oath in English:

quia supradictus Willelmus ap Rees nesciebat loqui litteraliter nec ydioma Anglicum nec Gallicum set dumtaxat Walense, ut dicebatur, iidem domini commissarii ad exponendum eidem Willelmo capitula iuramenti per eundem prestandi et interpretandum deposicionem faciendam per eum adhibuerunt fratres Johannem iuvenem et Mauricium de Pencoyt convencionales in domo fratrum minorum de Hereford' qui dicebantur de Wallia fuisse oriundi et intelligere et scire loqui ydioma Walense, qui fratres tactis sacrosanctis evangeliis presente dicto procuratore iuraverunt fideliter exponere dicto Willelmo illa que per dictos dominos commissarios dicerentur eisdem et fideliter eis referre et interpretari responsionem et deposicionem eiusdem et eam tenere secretam quousque fuerit legitime publicatum. (ff. 219v–220r)

Our dossier shows that the restricted language competence of William ap Rees had its effect upon the deposition which is much briefer than the case would merit since his evidence was truly of crucial importance, particularly relating to the dream which he had had before his execution, in which Mary mother of God and St Thomas Cantilupe appeared to him and promised to rescue him (f. 220v). William did not say that he had intended to make his confession to the castle chaplain. But he did say that he made his confession, in Welsh, to a priest called Madoc, said to have been a rural dean (f. 221v).

The two Swansea burghers who gave their evidence in French are said to have done so *in Gallico*. The language is not qualified the way it was concerning the three people from the castle. This should not be taken as evidence that their competence in

French was higher than that of the party from the castle but would appear rather to indicate that over the three months' period of collecting evidence the commission had become somewhat more lax in their assessment of linguistic competence.

One of these Swansea burghers, John de Laggeham, *deposuit in Gallico quia nesciebat loqui litteraliter sicut dixit* (f. 225r). He had been one of ten men on horseback who had been around at the time of the execution at the command of William de Braose to ensure that the candidates for the hanging would not be freed by friends or relatives. His language competence was the same as that of William de Braose.

The two cases that I have presented here give welcome insights into the plurilingual situation in England and Wales before and after the year 1300. I have attempted here to exploit the evidence provided by the Vatican dossier as fully as possible. In one form or another the four languages, Latin, French, English and Welsh were present in everyday affairs. The different kind of evidence from Hereford as compared to Swansea should be taken as a warning against generalisations as regards language competence in an urban as against a rural environment. Also, the apparently limited knowledge of Latin by some clerics, including the court chaplain of the de Braoses, should be noted alongside the rather surprising familiarity of two Hereford laymen with Latin where there is no indication of how this can be accounted for.

This linguistically quite mixed community is accessed here through a source which is written almost exclusively in Latin. The information about the language competence of the participants is provided for the purpose of the exercise as a whole, the rather scrupulous pursuit of truth for the greater glory of God and St Thomas Cantilupe. It is heartening for the historian that this situation works in favour of the reliability of the information provided, fragmentary as it may well be.

Appendix

Languages of deposition

2 Maria de Breuse: deposuit in Gallico vulgariter, f. 10r

3 Willelmus de Breuse: deposuit in vulgari Gallico, f. 13r

4 Willelmus de Codineston: simpliciter litteratus deposuit vulgariter lingua Gallica, f. 13r

145 Willelmus ap Rees, alias dictus Cragh: deposuit in ydiomate Walensi, f. 222r

146 Thomas Marescalc, presbiter: deposuit in Gallico, f. 223r

147 Johannes de Laggeham: deposuit in Gallico quia nesciebat loqui litteraliter sicut dixit, f. 225r

148 Henricus Pelliparius: deposuit in Anglico quia nesciebat loqui litteraliter nec Gallicum sicut dixit, f. 226r

149 Adam de Loghorne: deposuit in Anglico quia nesciebat loqui litteraliter nec Gallicum sicut dixit, f. 226v

150 Johannes ap Howel: deposuit in Anglico quia nesciebat loqui litteraliter nec Gallicum sicut dixit, f. 227v

121 Ysolda Thorgrume: deposuit in gallico, f. 187v

122 Johannes Moniword: deposuit in gallico, f. 188r

131 Symon de Lodelawe: deposuit in gallico et intelligebat et loquebatur latinum, f. 205r

132 Thomas Sandi: deposuit in anglico quia nesciebat loqui gallicum nec literaliter sicut dixit. f. 205v

116 Johannes Alkyn: deposuit in Gallico et intelligebat Latinum f. 206r

133 Rogerus de Hampton: deposuit in Gallico f. 207r

134 Margeria Thurgrym: deposuit in Gallico f. 207v

135 Fr. Johannes de Brompton: deposuit litteraliter f. 208v

136 Gilbertus procurator capituli Herefordensis: deposuit litteraliter f. 209v

Translating for the commission from English

Johannes de Brompton: 135 f. 207v: frater Johannes de Brompton de ordine fratrum minorum propter interpretationem lingue anglicane ab eis supra dudum assumptus ut assisteret in examinatione testium fuerat socius dicti fratris Hugonis et quod sciebat veritatem de dicto miraculo . . .

The Languages of the Law
in Later Medieval England

PAUL BRAND

IN 1295 the prior of Lewes was suing Richard of Gravesend, the bishop of London, in the Common Bench in an action of *quare non admisit* for refusing to admit his candidate to the Essex church of Little Canfield after the prior had succeeded in establishing his right to present to the church against Drew Barentyn in an assize of darrein presentment. The bishop's defence was that on receiving the prior's letters of presentation he had followed the proper procedure. He had instructed the local rural dean to make the appropriate enquiry. The dean had then reported back to him that the prior's candidate was not a suitable candidate to receive a benefice. We know about this case only from the formal, official Latin enrolment of it made for the court's plea roll.[1] The plea rolls do not normally tell us anything about the serjeants who did the actual speaking in court on behalf of litigants, but this case is one of the relatively rare exceptions. It does not tell us who made the prior's opening count but it does inform us that this defence was made by Henry Spigurnel, who was one of the court's leading serjeants.[2] The enrolment also tells us that the justices then asked Henry Spigurnel to be more specific about the grounds for the rejection of the prior's candidate and that he refused to do so. They then recited his answer to the bishop's attorney, as the roll informs us, in English 'because he said that he did not understand French'.[3] They asked him whether or not he 'avowed' this answer on his client's behalf: that is to say, whether or not he wished Henry's answer to be binding on his client.[4] The clear implication is that whatever had been said in the defence, and almost certainly more generally in the pleading of the case as well, had been said in French (*gallicum*). It also incidentally shows us that the court was quite capable, if necessary, of translating what was said in court into English.[5] It is less clear whether we can legitimately also conclude that

---

[1] PRO, CP 40/110, m. 239.

[2] For an outline of his career see *The Earliest English Law Reports*, vol. II, ed. Paul Brand (Selden Society 112, 1996), pp. civ–cviii.

[3] 'super hoc responsione facta per predictum Henricum pro predicto episcopo etc. recitata anglice per justiciarios et dicta attornato ipsius episcopi, qui se dixit gallicum non intelligere . . .'.

[4] On the avowal of serjeants see Paul Brand, *The Origins of the English Legal Profession* (Oxford, 1992), pp. 98–100.

[5] For another almost contemporary case where this occurred see PRO, CP 40/125, m. 278.

the bishop's attorney really did not understand French. It is not impossible that he was simply trying to buy time for his client by playing dumb.

This case illustrates some of the linguistic complexities of the conduct and recording of litigation in royal courts in England in the later thirteenth century. The formal records of proceedings in the royal courts (the plea rolls) were in Latin, as they had been ever since the first surviving plea rolls of the royal courts were compiled in the mid-1190s and almost certainly ever since the first plea rolls were compiled during the reign of Henry II from c.1176 onwards.[6] I have described these plea rolls as being in Latin and that is, broadly speaking, an accurate characterisation. But there are also occasional words or phrases in English. In a plea roll of 1290 there is, for example, a reference to a 'custom' allegedly established with the consent of all the free tenants of a Lincolnshire village 'que vocatur byrlaghe' about the enclosure of a particular pasture during Lent;[7] and in a plea roll of 1305 with a *postea* recording a jury verdict of the following year a reference to an assault conducted by men lying in wait, each with a 'washbeetle' (though on a second occasion the clerk uses the proper Latin word for this, 'baterelli').[8] There are also occasional words and phrases in Anglo-Norman French. In the same 1305 case the men lying in wait to make an assault on a monk are said to have been wearing the form of woman's clothing known as the 'rochet', what we would now call a smock;[9] and among the defendants sued in a case of 1294 was a man and 'Laurencium son fiz en lay'.[10] More curiously for a period in the early fourteenth century beginning in 1301 we sometimes find the whole of the accusations made in individual criminal appeals (private prosecutions for felony) being recorded on the plea rolls in French but the rest of these cases continuing to be recorded in Latin.[11]

Michael Clanchy has suggested that even if the initial formal pleadings in royal courts in Edward I's reign were spoken in French, the subsequent forensic dialogue might well have been in English and certainly cannot be proved to have been spoken in French.[12] Our 1295 case, however, is not the only direct evidence that the language actually used in English royal courts for forensic dialogue in the later thirteenth century was indeed French, rather than English. Even more convincing is the evidence of a 1291 case in King's Bench in which Roger of Somerton was claiming the Norfolk manor of West Somerton on behalf of the king against the prior of Butley. This manor had been given by Ranulph de Glanvill to a leper hospital at West Somerton controlled by the priory. In the course of the pleadings Roger challenged the words the defendant had used in placing himself on the verdict of a grand

6   Paul Brand, *The Making of the Common Law* (London, 1992), pp. 95–6.
7   PRO, CP 40/86, m. 243.
8   PRO, CP 40/154, m. 92.
9   'veste muliebri que vocatur "Rochet" '.
10   PRO, CP 40/103, m. 89.
11   The earliest examples I have noted are the multiple appeals made by Margery the widow of Adam of Silkeston against her husband's alleged killers in Hilary term 1301: PRO, CP 40/136, mm. 190–190d. I am not certain how long the phenomenon continued.
12   M. T. Clanchy, *From Memory to Written Record, England 1066–1307* (2nd edn, Oxford, 1993), p. 209.

assize for describing the manor as the right of his church (the priory of Butley) rather than as the right of the lepers. The prior said he had not avowed what his serjeants had previously said about the manor having been given to the lepers rather than to the priory on behalf of the lepers and so he had not been inconsistent in the form of words he had used in putting himself on the grand assize. Roger said that even if he had not explicitly avowed his serjeants he had done so implicitly because his attorney 'who understood French' (*romanum intelligens*) had sat listening to the case being pleaded for two days without specifically disavowing them. The clear implication is that the pleadings had indeed been wholly conducted in French.[13]

In a famous article of 1943 George Woodbine suggested that English had been the language of the English royal courts up until the middle of the thirteenth century and that it was only subsequently that their proceedings began to be conducted in French.[14] He himself admitted that there was no direct evidence for his hypothesis but thought that it was made plausible both by the English technical vocabulary used in *Bracton* and by the use of phrases in English on the plea rolls of the reign of Henry III. Although the direct evidence either way is slight there is, I think, just enough of it to indicate that Woodbine was wrong. The probable use of French in the king's courts can certainly be taken back without too much difficulty to the 1250s. The so-called *Hengham Magna* was probably the work of John Blundel and reflects his experience as the keeper of writs and rolls in the Common Bench between 1257 and 1262.[15] Most of the treatise is in Latin but on almost every occasion when the author wants to represent what is actually said in the king's court he puts the dialogue into French.[16] There is also indirect evidence at least for a much earlier date. One of the major differences between the wording of the oath taken by the jurors of the knightly grand assize and the wording of the oath taken by members of other kinds of jury was that the latter took an oath to 'tell the truth to the best of their knowledge (or understanding)' whereas the former had merely and unconditionally to take an oath 'to tell the truth'. The Latin version of the qualifying phrase which the jurors of the grand assize had to omit was 'secundum intellectum [meum]';[17] the French version of the same phrase 'a [mon] ascient'.[18] When a register of writs was copied for transmission to Ireland in 1210 one of the writs it contained was the writ for summoning the four electors of the grand assize who were to choose its twelve knights. Its rubric discussed various related matters. One noted in Latin that 'they ought to take an oath that they will tell the truth without adding those words that are

---

13 PRO, KB 27/127, m. 9.
14 George E. Woodbine, 'The Language of English Law', *Speculum* 18 (1943), pp. 395–436.
15 Brand, *Making of the Common Law*, pp. 369–91.
16 *Radulphi de Hengham Summae*, ed. W. H. Dunham, jr (Cambridge, 1932), pp. 15, 20, 25–6, 29, 34, 35, 38, 39, 41. The only exception is for the making of an essoin when the dialogue is given in Latin: ibid., p. 16.
17 *Four Thirteenth Century Law Tracts*, ed. G. E. Woodbine (New Haven, 1910), pp. 120–1.
18 *Brevia Placitata*, ed. G. J. Turner and T. F. T. Plucknett (Selden Society 66, 1951), pp. 3, 44, 156; BL MSS Additional 31826, f. 323v, and Additional 37657, f. 48v.

said in other jury verdicts, that is (and this phrase is in French) "a son ascient" '.[19] The phrase can only be in French because it was already the current English practice for this oath to be taken in French. It is difficult to believe that this would have been the case if the rest of the court's proceedings were being conducted in English. As for Woodbine's positive evidence, it does not seem to me that the number of English words found on the plea rolls of the reign of Henry III is that significant: it is probably no greater than that found in the reign of his son. A re-examination of the English words found in *Bracton* indicates that they are either everyday, non-technical terms or technical terms confined to one particular area of English law, the criminal law (and particularly the tithing system). Since the lower levels of the criminal justice system were one area of substantial continuity from the Anglo-Saxon legal past it is hardly surprising that some of the technical legal vocabulary of Anglo-Saxon survived here. The absence of any technical terms derived from English in other areas of English law after the middle of the thirteenth century is quite marked. This alone would suggest how unlikely it is that proceedings had been conducted in English in the major royal courts up to the middle of the thirteenth century and thus long enough for the legal system to have developed the need for a relatively sophisticated technical vocabulary. It seems much more likely that French had been the language of the royal courts from the very beginning of the system of central royal courts established by Henry II and that French was their language because in that period it was the first language of the men appointed as royal justices and of many of the litigants. French seems then to have remained the language of the courts in part because of cultural conservatism, the absence of any really compelling reason for changing accepted practice; in part because there were advantages to the professional elite who came to dominate legal practice in using a language which needed to be learned and mastered by outsiders and which enhanced their mystique; in part also because the courts had developed a technical French vocabulary that was not easily translatable into English.

It is unfortunate that our 1295 case is not one of those for which there also survives a law report, though there are surviving identifiable law reports for at least fifteen other cases heard during that same term.[20] These reports, unlike plea roll enrolments, were wholly unofficial in character and survive in legal manuscripts which were originally in private ownership, though most are now in public or quasi-public collections such as the British Library and the University Library in Cambridge. The earliest surviving law reports date from the very end of the reign of Henry III but down to 1291 they survive only in relatively small quantities (only around three hundred reports for the whole period) and only as part of miscellaneous

---

[19] 'et debent jurare precise quod veritatem dicent, non audito illo verbo quod in aliis recongnicionibus dicitur, scilicet "a son ascient" ': *Early Registers of Writs*, ed. E. de Haas and G. D. G. Hall (Selden Society 87, 1970), p. 7. For the dating and context of this register see Brand, *Making of the Common Law*, pp. 450–6.

[20] I am engaged on a long-term project to edit and publish all the unprinted reports of the reign of Edward I. These are the cases I have transcribed and identified as belonging to this term; they remain as yet unpublished.

collections of reports of various dates.[21] From 1291 onwards reports survive in much larger quantities and often as part of collections of reports from a single term (or pair of terms) or a single session of the General Eyre. For Michaelmas term 1291, for example, there still survives a collection of eighty-two reported cases;[22] and there is a collection of one hundred and thirty-nine cases from the 1292 Herefordshire eyre.[23] In general, the reports tell us much more about cases than the enrolled official version. They tell us which particular serjeants participated in pleading in the case and what part in proceedings was played by individual royal justices and clerks. They also tell us much more of the ultimately unsuccessful or abortive arguments advanced in court. All is typically reported in direct, rather than indirect, speech.[24]

For the first two decades of law reporting and perhaps even longer, it was evidently not absolutely fixed what language was appropriate for this purpose. Most law reports were in what soon became the conventional language of law reporting, Anglo-Norman French, but a significant minority was in Latin. That Latin is in general less flowing than the Latin of the plea rolls and often reads as though it is a translation of a text first written in French.[25] The general adoption of French as the conventional language of law reporting is hardly surprising. It was the 'natural' language for this purpose as it allowed the apprentices and others who were sitting in court to record at least part of what they actually heard there without having to go through the bother of translating what they heard in French into Latin.[26] The reports do indeed supply additional reasons for supposing that what was said in court was indeed spoken in French rather than English. It is difficult to see why if pleading had been in English and law reports were initially made by law students and others for their own use they should have bothered to translate what they heard into French. It is even more difficult to understand why, if that was indeed what they were doing, they should have translated everything other than proverbial phrases from English into French. English proverbs seem to have been left in the original precisely because this was indeed the language in which they were spoken, used by the justices from time to time for its very pithiness or its quaintness. In an early-

21 Paul Brand, 'The Beginnings of English Law Reporting', in *Law Reporting in England*, ed. Chantal Stebbings (London, 1995), pp. 1–14. For the original manuscript context of these early reports see also *The Earliest English Law Reports*, vol. I, ed. Paul Brand (Selden Society 111, 1996), pp. xxvi–cxv.

22 *YBB 21 & 22 Edward I*, ed. A. J. Horwood (London, 1873), pp. 453–577, 587–605. The editor wrongly attributed these reports to the 1294 Middlesex eyre, but most can easily be identified as belonging to the Common Bench and to this term.

23 *YBB 20 & 21 Edward I*, ed. A. J. Horwood (London, 1866), pp. 3–207.

24 I discuss these differences at greater length in a paper 'Inside the Courtroom: Lawyers, Litigants and Justices in England in the Later Middle Ages' given at the 1996 Birmingham Past and Present Conference on 'The Moral World of the Law' which will appear in a published volume of the conference proceedings.

25 For a fairly clear example of a French report with a matching Latin translation see *The Earliest English Law Reports*, vol. I, pp. 120–2.

26 For the identities of the earliest law reporters see Brand, 'The Beginnings of English Law Reporting', pp. 7–8, 12–13.

fourteenth-century land case, for example, the defendant denied that he held the land claimed and the plaintiff wanted to traverse this and prove to a jury that the defendant had held the land on the day the writ initiating the litigation was purchased. The defendant and the court were hostile. Willoughby for the claimant said that if he was not allowed to prove his allegation and recover the land if he could prove it, exactly the same could be done by the current tenant when he brought a new writ against him. Justice Bereford's response was 'Ne his tha no other asse bote malle' which the reporter glosses 'sestasaver nul autre voye de remedie qe cele, quasi diceret sic (dentdelyoun)'.[27] But it was not only English that provided proverbial or humorous phrases for in another speech just before this Bereford, commenting on the plaintiff's refusal to accept the disclaimer, said 'Il vus donne bon payn e vus le refusez e volez plus payn de cayllowe'. The reporter again glosses this, though here by revealing what he thought to be the implication of Bereford's remark: that if the defendant really had been the tenant of the land on the day of the purchase of the writ the demandant could safely exercise his right to enter and take possession of the land.

For courts other than the king's our evidence is much less good. Latin is certainly the language of the few surviving fragments of county court rolls from the fourteenth and early fifteenth centuries.[28] It is also the language used in the (exceptional) plea rolls of the county palatine of Chester of which the earliest to survive comes from 1260;[29] and in the rare surviving cartulary transcripts of other county court enrolments from the second half of the thirteenth century.[30] It seems likely that it was the language of these rolls from the time they first began to be compiled at the beginning of the thirteenth century (if not before).[31] Latin was also the language of the formal records of the city courts of London from at least the third quarter of the thirteenth century,[32] as also of the Oxford city court from at least the 1290s onwards.[33] It was probably also the language of record of other city courts as well. It was also the language used for hundred court rolls from the time of the earliest known surviving hundred court roll (of 1261–2);[34] and also of all known surviving

27 BL MS Harley 572, f. 180v.
28 R. C. Palmer, *The County Courts of Medieval England, 1150–1350* (Princeton, 1982), p. 225; BL Egerton Roll 2092 (Rutland county court roll 1386-87). See also BL Sloane Roll XXXI.4, m. 3 (copy of entry from Staffordshire county court for April 1383).
29 PRO, CHES 29/1. There are also transcripts from now lost rolls of the Chester county court in BL MS Harley 2148, of which one goes back as early as 1240 (ibid., f. 22r).
30 For examples of entries which seem to be straight transcripts of enrolments from county court rolls see for example *Sibton Abbey Cartularies and Charters*, part four, ed. Philippa Brown (Suffolk Records Society, Suffolk Charters X, 1988), pp. 25-6, no. 971 (calendar of entry from Suffolk county court of 1298); BL MS Cotton Vespasian E. XVIII, f. 124 schedule (entry from Lincolnshire county court roll for 1290). The surviving original returns to writs of *recordari facias* in the surviving Common Bench plea rolls are also often direct copies of entries on the county court's plea roll.
31 For the beginnings of county court rolls see Palmer, *County Courts of Medieval England*, pp. 38–40.
32 The earliest surviving Husting Rolls of Common Pleas and Pleas of Land in the Corporation of London Records Office date from 1273.
33 The earliest surviving roll is now Oxford City Archives D.17.1 (b).
34 For a list of pre-1307 hundred court rolls see H. M. Cam, *The Hundred and the Hundred Rolls*

manorial court rolls (of which the earliest known surviving original roll comes from 1246 and the earliest known example surviving only in a later copy from 1237).[35]

It is much more difficult to know for certain what the language of pleading and proceedings in these courts was. For the county court we do have the evidence of surviving early fourteenth century reports from the Warwickshire county court and of two reports from the Cambridgeshire county court of about the same date, all of which are in French and which read as though they are indeed reporting proceedings that had been taking place in that language.[36] There is also some indirect evidence from earlier in the century. A British Library manuscript contains a collection of notes in Latin, for the most part summarising the outcome of litigation in the Common Bench between 1252 and 1256. It was printed by Dunham under the title *Casus et Judicia*.[37] This collection includes a note on the necessary elements for inclusion in the plaintiff's count and defendant's defence in an action of replevin heard in the county court, perhaps sparked off by an action brought in the Common Bench in 1250 to review a judgment in the county court of Rutland dismissing a case because of omissions of necessary elements in the count.[38] Both are given in Latin but the Latin of the defence in particular sounds like very lightly disguised French and clearly hints at the French verbal formula which lies behind it. There also survive at least two reports of pleadings in the London city courts from the last quarter of the thirteenth century and from the city courts of York and of Worcester from around the same period, again in a French which sounds like the language actually being used in the cases reported.[39] Although at least one report of case heard in a hundred court has been identified and this is indeed in French the report is essentially only a narrative of what happened in the hundred court and does not purport to record what was said there.[40] Only at the manorial court level do we find any real evidence for the use of English in legal proceedings during the thirteenth or early fourteenth centuries. An inquisition *ad quod damnum* of 1270 inquiring into any possible loss to the Crown from the confirmation of a grant made by Richard of Havering to the master and brothers of the hospital at Hornchurch in Essex which

(London, 1930), p. 286. Since Cam wrote, the rolls of Highworth hundred for the period 1275–87 have been edited by Brenda Farr for the Wiltshire Archaeological and Natural History Society, Records Branch, as vols XXI and XXII in 1966 and 1968.

35   Zvi Razi and Richard M. Smith, 'The Origins of the English Manorial Court Rolls as a Written Record: A Puzzle', in *Medieval Society and the Manor Court*, ed. Zvi Razi and Richard M. Smith (Oxford, 1996), pp. 36–68 (pp. 39–40).

36   R. C. Palmer, 'County Year Book Reports: The Professional Lawyer in the Medieval County Court', *English Historical Review* 91 (1971), pp. 776–801; Brand, *Origins of the English Legal Profession*, p. 194, note 58. For other reports of the same period which appear to report proceedings in county courts and are also in French see CUL MS Dd.7.14, f. 383r, BL MS Additional 31826, ff. 131v–132r, and CUL MS Mm.5.23, ff. 12r–v (apparently reports of the same case).

37   See appendix I to *Casus Placitorum and Reports of Cases in the King's Courts, 1272–1278*, ed. W. H. Dunham, jr (Selden Society 69, 1952), pp. lxxv–lxxxiv.

38   *Casus Placitorum*, p. lxxv. The case is PRO, KB 26/143, m. 15d.

39   BL MS Harley 2183, ff. 5r–v; LI MS Miscellaneous 738, f. 69r; R. C. Palmer, 'The Origins of the Legal Profession in England', *Irish Jurist*, (new series) 11 (1976), pp. 126–146 (p. 127, note 7); CUL MS Dd.7.14, ff. 378r–v.

40   Trinity College, Cambridge, MS 0.3.45, f. 54v.

was a dependency of the alien house of Montjoux in Savoy found that there was no damage to the king or others from remitting the suit the brothers owed to the ancient demesne court of Havering because the Savoyard brothers were of no use in the rendering of judgments as they did not know the language of the court.[41] Savoyards would have known French and presumably been able to follow proceedings and participate in judgments if they were rendered in that language; the difficulty must have been that they did not know enough English to participate in proceedings in that language. There is also early fourteenth-century evidence suggesting that proceedings at a manorial view of frankpledge may have been conducted in English, a form of oath to be used by a manorial juror making presentments in that language

> This you herest sire Stiward yat ic W. schal soot seyen ant no soot forhelen for lef ne for loth, for sille ne for freinde, for huyre ne for biyete ne for non oyer yinge, of yat you schalt asken me on ye kynges halve an on sire R., so helpe me God and ye halidom.[42]

However, evidence that even at this level of the legal system English may have had to encounter rivalry from French is suggested by the presence of another oath of about the same date entered into the same manuscript for use by a man entering into a frankpledge group for the first time.

> Ceo oyez ws, bone genz, ke jeo serrai leaus e ke jeo ne rien ne emberay ne larun ne larcin ne celeray e ke jeo serray justisable a mon frauncplegg.[43]

Woodbine also argued that Latin was the only written language of English law until after the royalist triumph at the battle of Evesham and that it was only after 1265 that French began to offer it any competition.[44] It is, however, clear that at least three surviving works of legal literature in French were compiled prior to 1265. There is no good reason to date the compilation of the miscellaneous collection of notes on cases and general rules edited under the title *Casus Placitorum* as Woodbine did as late as the reign of Edward I; it is much more plausibly dated at least in part as its editor Dunham subsequently suggested to the 1250s.[45] Woodbine also postdated the compilation of two other treatises, *Fet Asaver* and *Brevia Placitata*. He ascribed them to the final years of the reign of Henry III.[46] But the original version of *Brevia Placitata* seems clearly to belong to the year 1260 and *Fet Asaver* must have been written before 1263 and may have been written before 1259.[47]

All three works have plausibly been seen as by-products of the process of legal

---

41 'eo quod nichil prosunt in judiciis reddendis . . . eo quod ignorant idioma': PRO C 143/3, no. 17.
42 BL MS Lansdowne 564, f. 109v.
43 BL MS Lansdowne 564, f. 110r (specifically said to be for an 'anilepman').
44 Woodbine, 'The Language of English Law', p. 425.
45 *Casus Placitorum*, pp. xx–xxiv; Woodbine, 'The Language of English Law', pp. 432–3.
46 Woodbine, 'The Language of English Law', p. 401, note 3.
47 Paul Brand, 'Legal Education in England before the Inns of Court', in *Learning the Law: Teaching and the Transmission of Law in England, 1150–1900*, ed. Jonathan A. Bush and Alain Wijffels (London, 1999), pp. 51–84 (pp. 59–61).

education, as recording the teaching of anonymous instructors in the common law. The first indubitable evidence of oral instruction in the Common Law comes from two manuscripts (BL MS Lansdowne 467 and CUL MS Hh.3.11) which record the lectures of an anonymous lecturer probably given at Westminster and in or shortly before the year 1278.[48] These lectures provide an elementary introduction to common law litigation and are (like the three treatises) in Anglo-Norman French. But French may not have been the only language used in oral legal education and was certainly not the only language used for educational treatises during the last quarter of the thirteenth century. *Modus Componendi Brevia* is a short treatise composed in Latin c.1285. It provides a brief analysis of the various kinds of action about title to land and to advowsons, explaining the different circumstances in which each was appropriate. It discusses the differing uses of the three different kinds of remedy available in the case of disputes about liability to feudal services. It also gives an account of the different remedies available in pasture right disputes and concludes with a brief introduction to the different kinds of exception.[49] It is possible that it is derived from what was originally a lecture or lectures but it is perhaps more likely that it only ever existed as a written treatise. It certainly went into general circulation as a fairly basic treatise containing information that was useful to law students at a very early stage in their career and perhaps to non-experts too. A second treatise also in Latin and apparently composed around the same time is *Hengham Parva*.[50] This covers four separate topics: the different kinds of essoin; the different kinds of dower action; the rules about the viewing of land in land actions; and the working of the assize of novel disseisin. All are discussed with particular reference to the relevant statutes relating to each topic. In its final version *Hengham Parva* was evidently completed between 1285 and 1290. There, is, however, also an earlier version of what is evidently the same work in a Bodleian MS (Douce 139) with a number of significant differences. This must have been written between 1278 and 1285.[51] This work may well derive from lectures given by chief justice Hengham, perhaps a set first given before 1285 and then revised and given again after that date. Hengham's lectures might, of course, have been given in French and then been translated into Latin but this seems unnecessarily complicated. It is perhaps more plausible that the lectures too were given in Latin. Latin was also the language of two other works originally compiled earlier in the thirteenth century but evidently still considered valuable introductions to English law and widely copied in legal manuscripts compiled during the last quarter of the thirteenth century and first quarter of the fourteenth century, *Judicium Essoniorum* and *Hengham Magna*.[52] Latin was, of course also the language of the major treatise of English law,

---

48 Ibid., pp. 76–7. For an earlier discussion of one of these manuscripts see Brand, *Making of the Common Law*, pp. 61–2.
49 *Modus Componendi Brevia* was edited by Woodbine in *Four Thirteenth Century Law Tracts* at pp. 143–62. He discusses its date in footnote 1 to p. 38.
50 This is edited by Dunham in *Radulphi de Hengham Summae* at pp. 51–71.
51 Bodleian MS Douce 139, ff. 175v–177r.
52 On the dating and content of *Judicium Essoniorum* see Paul Brand, ' "Nothing which is new or

Bracton, originally written in the 1220s and 1230s and sporadically revised down to the 1250s but not available for copying until after the death of its last reviser, Henry of Bratton, in 1268.[53] Most of the fifty surviving manuscripts of this treatise belong to the late thirteenth or early fourteenth centuries.[54]

But French was the language of the future in 1300 for English legal instruction. From shortly after 1300 come the first surviving fragments from what look to have been lectures or readings on a statute: here on the statute of Westminster II, c.1: *de Donis conditionalibus*.[55] These preserve the language of the original statute (Latin) for quoting sections of its text but the commentary on that text is given entirely in French. This is also the practice in the first more extensive set of notes on a lecture given on the whole of a statute (again Westminster II) dating from c.1344 and found in BL MS Additional 22552 (at ff. 51v–54v) and became the norm in all later readings on the statutes. French was also the language of the *quaestiones disputate*, some of which may derive from teaching but others perhaps from actual academic disputations, and later of the moot cases used for exercises in the inns of court and for the discussions and arguments to which they gave rise.[56]

As Woodbine correctly noted, the first legislation to be officially enacted and published in French was the statute of Westminster I of 1275, the first major piece of legislation of the reign of Edward I. The statute of Jewry and the statutes of the Exchequer enacted later that same year were also in French. But this did not mark a permanent change in the language of English official legislative texts.[57] There exist both French and Latin texts of the statute of Gloucester of 1278 and it is not entirely clear which represents the 'official' published text but the statute of Mortmain of 1279 was published in Latin and Latin was the language of the second great statute of the reign of Edward I, the statute of Westminster II of 1285.[58] Over the reign as a whole, Latin and French seem to have been used in similar amounts for legislative texts and with no clear line of demarcation between the contexts in which they were used. With the reign of Edward II, French becomes the predominant, but by no

unique"? A Reappraisal of *Judicium Essoniorum*', in *The Life of the Law: Proceedings of the Tenth British Legal History Conference, Oxford 1991*, ed. Peter Birks (London, 1993), pp. 1–7 and for texts of it see J. H. Baker, *A Catalogue of English Legal Manuscripts in Cambridge University Library* (Woodbridge, 1996), pp. 78–9; on the dating, content and texts of *Hengham Magna* see Brand, *Making of the Common Law*, pp. 369–91 and Baker, *Catalogue of English Legal MSS*, pp. 64–5.

53 Paul Brand, 'The Age of Bracton', in *The History of English Law: Centenary Essays on 'Pollock and Maitland'*, ed. John Hudson (*Proceedings of the British Academy* 89, 1996), pp. 65–89.

54 George E. Woodbine in *Bracton on the Laws and Customs of England*, edited by G. E. Woodbine and translated with revisions and notes by Samuel E. Thorne (4 vols, Cambridge, Mass., 1968–77), vol. I, pp. 5–20, 24; vol. III, pp. v, liii.

55 Brand, 'Legal Education in England before the Inns of Court', pp. 66–7.

56 Brand, 'Legal Education in England before the Inns of Court', pp. 67–9; *Readings and Moots at the Inns of Court in the Fifteenth Century*, vol. II, ed. Samuel E. Thorne and J. H. Baker (Selden Society 105, 1990).

57 *Statutes of the Realm*, i. 26–39, 197–8, 221–221a. For the dating of these two statutes see T. F. T. Plucknett, *Legislation of Edward I* (Oxford, 1962), p. 60 and note 2; *Select Pleas, Starrs and Other Records from the Rolls of the Exchequer of the Jews, AD 1220–1284*, ed. J. M. Rigg (joint publication of the Jewish Historical Society of England and the Selden Society, 1902), pp. xl–xlii.

58 *Statutes of the Realm*, i. 45–50, 51, 71–95.

means the exclusive, language of legislation but it was to be more than a century before the last legislation was enacted in Latin during the reign of Henry VI.[59] The eventual triumph of French for legislative purposes (short-lived though it was) is less surprising than the slowness with which total victory was achieved. As we have seen, French was the working language of judges and lawyers and it made a great deal of sense to enact legislation in their professional language. But that triumph also probably owed much to the fact that French was, in the thirteenth century at least, and probably also for part if not all of the fourteenth century, the language in which legislation was first drafted and also the language in which it was discussed.

That French was the language of legislative drafting can first be demonstrated in 1259 where there survives a penultimate French draft text of the whole of the Provisions of Westminster and also a French draft of an earlier version of part of that text as well as a Latin draft text apparently prepared for publication.[60] It is also apparent from a surviving draft French text of the statute of Acton Burnel of 1283 with a series of erasures and interlined amendments. The fact that these are also in French strongly suggests that the discussion was also in that language.[61]

French was also as early as 1215 the language into which Magna Carta was translated, apparently unofficially, for local publication in at least one English county, as we know from a surviving copy of that translation now in Rouen to which Professor Holt drew attention in 1974.[62] The next clear evidence for the translation of a Latin legislative (or quasi-legislative) text into the vernacular (in this case both French and English) comes from 1255, when the Dean of Lincoln ordered publication in both languages whenever expedient of the *Sentencia Lata* against those infringing the provisions of Magna Carta (which is in Latin). It is less clear whether or not other (and less significant) legislation was regularly translated into French and even into English for local proclamation in this way. Professor Holt suggests that it may have been and that local clerks may normally have made *viva voce* translations of the Latin texts they were sent.[63] English and French appear as the languages for communication between the baronial council and local communities in October 1258 when the council issued a document in the king's name confirming the transfer of responsibility for reform of the *status regni* from the committee of twenty-four to which the king had agreed in May 1258 to the new king's council and requiring all his subjects to take an oath to observe and maintain all the provisions already made and all future provisions made by the council. It has generally been assumed that there was a Latin original text of this document, though the only evidence for this is the statement of the Burton Annalist. It seems more likely that the document was drafted in French and then translated into English and texts in both languages sent out to the localities for publication and that no Latin text was ever needed. Both texts appear to have

59 *Statutes of the Realm*, i, p. xli.
60 Brand, *Making of the Common Law*, pp. 325–67.
61 PRO, E 175/11/4.
62 J. C. Holt, 'A Vernacular-French Text of Magna Carta, 1215', reprinted in his *Magna Carta and Medieval Government* (London, 1985), pp. 239–57.
63 Holt, *Magna Carta and Medieval Government*, p. 239.

been composed and written by an exchequer official, Robert of Fulham.[64] It is dubious, however, whether even on a generous definition this text can be described as 'legislative'. More obviously legislative is the so-called 'Ordinance of the Sheriffs' of the same month. Again, modern historians seem generally to have accepted the word of the Burton Annalist that texts were prepared in Latin, French and English, but the only texts to survive are in French and it seems quite likely that this legislation was enacted and sent out for proclamation only in French.[65] The first evidence to suggest that when legislation was proclaimed in Westminster Hall it might be proclaimed initially in Latin and then in English (though it might be in French) comes, as Holt notes, from 1300 when the St Alban's chronicler Rishanger notes that Edward I ordered that Magna Carta be read out *prius litteraliter, deinde patria lingua.*[66] But we cannot assume that what was done for the politically charged Magna Carta was the normal practice for more routine legislative texts.

It seems likely that the archives of the royal government preserved somewhere copies of virtually all, if not quite all, of the legislation enacted during the course of the thirteenth century.[67] Much of the legislation of the period prior to 1260 was copied onto one of the two main series of chancery rolls. Less of the legislation enacted after 1260 was entered there, perhaps because separate copies were retained of much of the legislation enacted during this period. Neither practice can have made legislation easy to find. Copies of some of the more important thirteenth-century statutes were also entered into the Red Book of the Exchequer and were available there for the use of the Exchequer but they were scattered through the volume in the middle of a quantity of quite different material and the collection was certainly radically incomplete. There was thus no readily available and easily accessible official repository of legislative enactments in force even by 1300; indeed, as Richardson and Sayles demonstrated long ago, it was only during the course of the fourteenth century that the 'Statute Roll' or 'Great Roll of Statutes' became for the first time just such an official and authoritative archive. All these official texts preserved the legislation in the original language of their enactment. There were also private collections of thirteenth-century legislative texts. The first was probably put together c.1240. It seems to have contained no more than Magna Carta and the Forest Charter of 1225 plus various pieces of legislation of the 1230s and it formed only a subordinate part of a larger volume whose main contents were a text of the later twelfth-century legal treatise *Glanvill* and a copy of a pre-Mertonian register of writs. A similar collection of material but with less of the legislation of the 1230s and with the addition of copies of a number of pieces of supposed, as well as actual,

---

64 R. F. Treharne and I. J. Sanders, *Documents of the Baronial Movement of Reform and Rebellion* (Oxford, 1973), pp. 116–17.

65 Treharne and Sanders, *Documents*, pp. 118–22; Holt, *Magna Carta and Medieval Government*, p. 242.

66 Holt, *Magna Carta and Medieval Government*, p. 239.

67 Paul Brand, 'English Thirteenth Century Legislation', in *'Colendo iustitiam et iura condendo': Federico II Legislatore del Regno di Sicilia nell' Europa del Duecento*, ed. A. Romano (Rome, 1997), pp. 325–44.

eleventh- and twelfth-century legislation plus copies of the statute of Marlborough (1267), the statute of Westminster I (1275) and the statute of Jewry (1275) is to be found in BL MS Harley 746. Although Liebermann was misled by later material added at the beginning and end of the volume into thinking that it was copied as late as 1325 its true date is probably as early as 1275x1278. The evidence of the surviving manuscripts suggests, however, that it was only during the 1280s and still more during the 1290s that the tradition of making and copying private collections of statutes really gathered strength in England.[68] Most were copied into books which contained other legal materials such as registers of writs and legal treatises, though at least one early-fourteenth-century roll of statutes also survives. The main purchasers of such collections were probably professional lawyers. In some of the very small volumes which seem in the main to date from after 1300 we may see volumes intended for lawyers to carry round the country with them while they were on professional business. Most of these collections of statutes preserved the language of the original texts as enacted (whether Latin or French) for the actual original wording of the text might be important to lawyers if there was any kind of dispute about the interpretation of the statute. But the lawyer's greater familarity with French was perhaps responsible for the phenomenon of collections of statutes in which all the statutes (whether originally in Latin or in French) are given in French;[69] and also the appearance of at least one attempt to turn one of the major Edwardian statutes (Westminster II) into Anglo-Norman doggerel verse.[70]

The languages of English law in the thirteenth and fourteenth century were primarily Latin and French. Latin was and remained the language of formal record at all levels of the court hierarchy. It was also the language of some of the thirteenth-century instructional literature of English law and even perhaps of some of the actual instruction. Its status as the language of formal legislation appears to have gone unchallenged prior to the last quarter of the thirteenth century but thereafter was increasingly challenged by the Anglo-Norman French of the common lawyers. Anglo-Norman French was the language actually used in pleading not just in the royal courts but also in county and city courts and came to be the invariable language of the law reports which recorded such pleading and which were also used to teach the following generation of law students.[71] Anglo-Norman was also the language of oral legal instruction and of the legal literature which grew out of such instruction and of some other instructional literature as well. Anglo-Norman may always have been the language for the drafting and discussion of legislation but was also from 1275 onwards one of the two languages used for the formal enactment of

---

[68] Don C. Skemer, 'Reading the Law: Statute Books and the Private Transmission of Legal Knowledge in Late Medieval England', in *Learning the Law*, ed. Bush and Wijffels, pp. 113–31.

[69] The examples which are known to me are CUL MS Hh.4.6; Harvard Law Library MS 12 and Folger Shakespeare Library MS V.a. 256. There may well be others.

[70] Bodleian MS Douce 139, ff. 117r–124v and 130r–139r. There is also a doggerel French version of a treatise on the Court Baron which survives in at least four different manuscripts: Baker, *English Legal MSS in CUL*, p. 589.

[71] Brand, 'The Beginnings of English Law Reporting', pp. 7, 12.

legislation as well. The third language used in thirteenth- and early-fourteenth-century England, English, is little in evidence here. It may have been used in some proceedings in local manorial courts and may sometimes have been used in the local proclamation of legislation, but it was not for the most part one of the written languages used in legal contexts. But there is one rather surprising exception to this. This is a manuscript now in the Bodleian Library in Oxford (Rawlinson B520) which appears to belong to the early years of the fourteenth century and contains translations into English of many of the main thirteenth-century statutes, some of the short legal memoranda often found in close association with such tracts and some of the shorter legal treatises of the period (including *Luttle Hengham* and *Muchele Hengham*). It was known to the editors of *Statutes of the Realm* but seems not to have received any real attention from legal historians or scholars specialising in Middle English, though it has recently received at least passing mention from Professor J. H. Baker.[72] It is of particular interest as by far the earliest known attempt to translate much of the technical vocabulary of English law (almost exclusively Romance in derivation) into English; its existence also provides a warning against drawing too firm conclusions about the status and function of our three languages in thirteenth- or early-fourteenth-century England, for if this one manuscript did not survive we would have no idea that anyone in early-fourteenth-century England would have thought it useful to have these statutes and treatises translated into English and would have no idea that the effort had ever been made.

---

[72] *Statutes of the Realm*, i, p. xliii; Baker, *Catalogue of English Legal MSS in CUL*, pp. xxxvi–xxxvii.

Linguistic Aspects of Code-Switching in Medieval English Texts

HERBERT SCHENDL

Historical Background

CODE-SWITCHING (CS), i.e. the change from one language (or variety) to another within one act of communication, was most likely an important discourse strategy throughout the history of many European nations including Britain. The complex multilingual situation in medieval Britain must have been especially favourable for this sociolinguistic phenomenon, though the coexistence of different languages and language varieties within Britain certainly did not mean universal individual bi- or multilingualism: on the one hand, there were a number of predominantly monolingual areas, such as much of the Celtic territories and the greater part of the rural English-speaking country; on the other hand, monolingualism was clearly also a social phenomenon, with widespread English monolingualism at least among the lower social ranks, and French monolingualism as a feature of the highest nobility particularly in the early Middle English (ME) period. However, with many members of the higher and the educated middle ranks of society, bilingualism – or even trilingualism – seems to have been no unusual phenomenon in both oral and written communication,[1] involving either two vernacular languages (English, French) or Latin as the High variety with one or two vernaculars.[2]

The relative status of the different languages and their functional range, especially those of English and French, clearly changed over the centuries, especially in regard to their main functions and domains.[3] While the role of French became increasingly restricted to a small number of functions such as law in the late ME

---

[1] Cf. M. Richter, *Sprache und Gesellschaft im Mittelalter: Untersuchungen zur mündlichen Kommunikation in England von der Mitte des elften bis zum Beginn des vierzehnten Jahrhunderts* (Stuttgart, 1979) and I. Short, 'On Bilingualism in Anglo-Norman England', *Romance Philology* 33 (1980), pp. 467–79.

[2] In this paper I will disregard the various Celtic languages, the pockets of Low German immigrants, especially in parts of the Eastern Midlands, and the Scandinavian language(s) in the early Middle English period; equally, the different varieties of French, English and Latin will not be considered.

[3] Cf. R. Berndt, 'The Linguistic Situation in England from the Norman Conquest to the Loss of Normandy (1066–1204)', *Philologica Pragensia* 8 (1965), pp. 145–63; Short, 'Bilingualism in Anglo-Norman England'; and D. A. Kibbee, *For to speke Frenche trewely: The French Language in England, 1000–1600: Its Status, Description and Instruction* (Amsterdam/Philadelphia, 1991).

period, and English at the same time extended its functional range, Latin maintained its status as the High variety in most functions throughout the ME period (and well into Early Modern English, EModE).

Quite a number of English medieval sources explicitly or implicitly point to bilingualism and the use of different languages according to communicative situation and participants, i.e. to a kind of diglossic or even multiglossic situation.[4] Of particular interest is Richter's detailed study of the languages used by the more than 200 witnesses in the canonisation procedure of Thomas Cantilupe, bishop of Hereford, in 1307, many of whom used a more prestigious language than their L1 on this occasion.[5] These are clear cases of the type of 'situational CS' typical of a diglossic situation.[6] A different kind of evidence is the fact that many medieval manuscripts contain texts in Latin, French and/or English in no apparent order, which points to the multilingualism of the scribes and of the users of these manuscripts.[7]

The co-existence of and contact between these different languages and varieties have evidently left traces in the structure of modern English. English historical linguistics has extensively studied the *results* of language contact on the English linguistic system. Lexical borrowing, which led to a partial relexification of English from French and Latin sources, has been studied in particular detail, and so have the morphological and syntactic influences from Scandinavian, French and Latin. But more performance-related aspects, such as language mixing (or 'code-switching'),[8] in specific texts, the syntactic types of and possible constraints on switching, as well as the communicative functions of such textual switching, have so far been neglected by most historical linguists. Though the existence of these texts has sometimes been acknowledged in passing, their linguistic significance has been largely ignored.[9]

---

4   Cf. Short, 'Bilingualism in Anglo-Norman England', pp. 474, 478f, and Richter, *Sprache und Gesellschaft*, pp. 55f, 61ff, 69, 73, 83.

5   Richter, *Sprache und Gesellschaft*, Part 4, esp. section 3; cf. also C. Krötzl, '*Vulgariter sibi exposito*: Zu Übersetzung und Sprachbeherrschung im Spätmittelalter am Beispiel von Kanonisationsprozessen', *Das Mittelalter* 2 (1997), pp. 111–18. See also Richter, this volume.

6   In 'situational' CS, the change of codes coincides with situational changes (e.g. new topics or participants), while in 'metaphorical' (or 'conversational') CS, switches fulfil different discourse functions, occur within the 'same minimal speech act', and stand in a complex relation with social variables: see J. J. Gumperz, *Discourse Strategies* (Cambridge, 1982), pp. 60f, and S. Romaine, *Bilingualism*, 2nd edn (Oxford, 1995), pp. 161–5.

7   Cf. T. Hunt, *Teaching and Learning Latin in Thirteenth-Century England*, 3 vols (Cambridge, 1991), pp. 16, 434f, and L. E. Voigts, 'Medical Prose', in *Middle English Prose: A Critical Guide to Major Authors and Genres*, ed. A. S. G. Edwards (New Brunswick, 1984), p. 316.

8   The terms '(code-)switching' and '(code-)mixing' will not be differentiated in this paper; for a discussion of these terms see C. W. Pfaff, 'Constraints on Language Mixing: Intrasentential Code-Switching and Borrowing in Spanish/English', *Language* 55 (1979), p. 295; Romaine, *Bilingualism*, p. 124.

9   However, literary scholars and medievalists have long been aware of the existence of these 'macaronic' texts and have studied various non-linguistic aspects, including the literary and textual functions of language mixing – though this has never been a 'mainstream' concern; cf., e.g., E. Archibald, 'Tradition and Innovation in the Macaronic Poetry of Dunbar and Skelton', *Modern Language Quarterly* 53 (1992), pp. 126–49; P. E. Nolan, 'Beyond Macaronic: Embedded Latin in Dante and Langland', in *Conventus Neo-Latini Bononiensis*, ed. R. J. Schoeck (Binghamton, NY, 1985), pp. 539–48; Sister C. Sullivan, 'The Latin Insertions and the Macaronic Verse in Piers Plowman' (Ph.D. disserta-

This neglect is not so much due to a lack of data, but rather to a generally negative attitude towards language mixing, which was widespread even in modern sociolinguistics until some decades ago. However, such older mixed texts should certainly not be taken as the result of imperfect language competence or as random idiosyncrasies of use, nor should the languages involved be regarded as 'debased' forms of Latin, French or English. The mixing of languages in medieval written texts represents, rather, in most cases a specific discourse strategy, similar to the one found in modern CS. Thus these texts constitute an important category of their own and deserve to be studied in their own right.

There is a considerable number of mixed-language texts from the ME and the EModE periods, many of which show CS in mid-sentence. The phenomenon occurs across genres and text types, both literary and non-literary, verse and prose; and the languages involved mirror the above-mentioned multilingual situation. In most cases Latin as the 'High' language is one of the languages, with one or both of the vernaculars English and French as the second partner, though switching between the two vernaculars is also attested.

One aim of this paper is to show that the linguistic study of such mixed texts should be of major interest for historical linguistics, in particular as written testimony of early English bilingualism and language contact; furthermore, these texts are an important – otherwise 'missing' – link for the actual process of lexical borrowing; finally, their analysis provides the still lacking diachronic dimension to modern studies of code-switching, which makes them of major importance for general linguistics and sociolinguistics alike.

Domains – Genres – Text Types

Unfortunately, there is still no inventory of ME and EModE mixed-language texts and text types available. The following section, which in no way aims at completeness, will provide samples of mixed language texts in a number of different domains, genres and text types, from the ME and EModE periods, to show the textual and temporal diversity and range of this phenomenon (the more detailed linguistic discussion of CS below will, however, concentrate on late ME and on two specific genres, sermons and poems). Furthermore, the examples will illustrate different types of syntactic switching as well as some functional aspects of CS. The material studied so far seems to indicate that some of the syntactic and functional differences in the switching strategies of these texts may be typical of certain genres or text types, though this hypothesis will have to be substantiated by further research on a much larger corpus.

tion, Catholic University of America: Washington, DC, 1932); P. Zumthor, 'Un problème d'esthétique médiévale: l'utilisation poétique du bilinguisme', *Le Moyen Age* 66 (1960), pp. 301–36, 561–94, etc.; of particular interest is S. Wenzel, *Macaronic Sermons: Bilingualism and Preaching in Late-Medieval England* (Ann Arbor, 1994), who has edited a number of mixed sermons and has also discussed syntactic and pragmatic aspects of his text corpus.

(a)   Among the *non-literary* mixed texts we find: (i) sermons; (ii) other religious prose texts; (iii) letters; (iv) business accounts; (v) legal texts; (vi) medical texts.

(b)   The main *literary* sources are (i) mixed or 'macaronic' poems; (ii) longer verse pieces; (iii) drama; (iv) various prose texts.

Non-literary texts

The religious prose text from the early ME *Ancrene Wisse* illustrates a simple and very common pattern, which is also widespread in other domains and text types: a Latin (in this case biblical) quotation is followed by a more or less close English translation, a free paraphrase, an explanation, etc.[10] Syntactically, the Latin switches in this type tend to be 'intersentential', i.e. they occur between sentences or independent clauses.[11]

(1)   *Ancrene Wisse* (early thirteenth century)

> Schirnesse of heorte is Godes luue ane. I þis is al þe strengðe of alle religiuns, þe ende of alle ordres. *Plenitudo legis est dilectio.* 'Luue fulleð þe lahe,' seið seinte Pawel. *Quicquid precipitur, in sola caritate solidatur.* 'Alle Godes heastes,' as sein Gregoire seið, 'beoð i luue irotet.'

The same pattern of intersentential switching is typically found in medieval English sermons, such as the one under (2) from the early twelfth century. The Latin quotations provide the general structure of the sermon and thus have a clear discourse function.[12]

(2)   *In diebus dominicis* (twelfth century)

> [. . .] þe mare to haligen and to wurðien þenne dei, þe is icleped sunnedei; for of þam deie ure lauerd seolf seið: *'dies dominicus est dies leticie et requiei* sunnedei is dei of blisse and of alle ireste. *non facietur in ea aliquid, nisi deum orare, manducare et bibere cum pace et leticia* ne beo in hire naþing iwrat bute chirche bisocnie and beode to Criste and eoten and drinken mid griðe and mid gledscipe.' *sicut dicitur: 'pax in terra, pax in celo, pax inter homines'* for swa is iset: 'grið on eorðe and grið on hefene and grið bitwenen uwilc cristene monne.'

While (2) is an English sermon with some Latin insertions, the late fifteenth century piece under (3) is a Latin sermon with numerous English insertions of varying length,[13] which do not serve any obvious function. This type of mixed

---

[10]   The switches in the 'embedded language' (see note 13) will be printed in italics.

[11]   C. M. Myers-Scotton, *Duelling Languages: Grammatical Structure in Codeswitching* (Oxford, 1993), p. 4 and Romaine, *Bilingualism*, pp. 122f.

[12]   Cf. also Wenzel, *Macaronic Sermons*, pp. 74f.

[13]   The classification of a text as Latin or English will be based on purely quantitative criteria, and not on additional linguistic ones.

sermon is quite widespread in the late ME period, from about 1350 to 1450.[14] Syntactically, most of these switches are 'intrasentential', i.e. they occur within the sentence and involve all kinds of major and minor sentence constituents. Such patterns are similar to those used in CS in modern speech and will be discussed further below, in particular in regard to switching points and switched constituents.

(3) *De celo querebant* (early fifteenth century)[15]

> Set quia secundum doctores crudelis punicio sine misericordia cicius dicetur rigor quam iusticia, ideo necessario ramus misericordie debet eciam crescere super vitem. Domini *gouernouris most* eciam *be merciful in punchyng.* Oportet ipsos attendere quod *of stakis and stodis* qui deberent stare in ista vinea quedam sunt *smoþe and lightlich wul boo,* quedam sunt *so stif and so ful of warris* quod homo *schal to-cleue hom* cicius quam planare. Quidam subditi sunt humiles *and buxum,* et de facili volunt corigi; quidam sunt *as stiburne* et duri cordis quod mallent frangi quam flecti [. . .] Prima res intellecta in celo Ecclesie est corpus perfectum, *þe nurchinge* sol curatorum *with his bemis al brennyng.* Ex quo magnus philosophus Eraclitus vocat solem fontem celestis luminis, [. . .] racionabiliter possum huic comparare prelatos, curatos, et *men* Ecclesie, qui pre omnibus aliis statibus *most schyne* in firmamento Ecclesie *in holy lyuynge,* . . .

The following letter from Richard Kingston, Dean of Windsor, to King Henry IV, provides one example of English–French CS, with both inter- and intrasentential switches. Switching may have been due to the great haste in which the letter was written ('Escript . . . en tresgraunte haste'), but the fact that CS is found in a letter to the king seems to point to the basic social acceptability of this linguistic strategy.

(4) Letter from R. Kingston to King Henry IV (1403)

> *Please* a vostre tresgraciouse Seignourie entendre que a-jourduy apres *noone* . . . qu'ils furent venuz deinz nostre *countie* pluis de .cccc. des les rebelz de Owyne, Glyn, Talgard, et pluseours autres rebelz des voz marches de Galys . . . *Warfore, for goddesake, thinketh on your beste frende, god, and thanke hym as he hath deserued to yowe! And leueth nought that ye ne come for no man that may counsaille yowe the contrarie* . . . Tresexcellent, trespuissant, et tresredouté Seignour, autrement say a present nieez. Jeo prie a la benoit trinité que vous ottroie bone vie ove tresentier sauntee a treslonge durré, *and sende yowe sone to ows in help and prosperitee; for in god fey, I hope to almighty god that, yef ye come youre owne persone, ye schulle haue the victorie of alle youre enemyes.* . . . Escript a Hereford, en tresgraunte haste, a trois de la *clocke* apres *noone,* le tierce jour de Septembre.

Yet the attempt to determine the language of elements is problematic even here, since a number of the items designated as examples of CS (*please, countie, noone,*

---

14 Cf. Wenzel, *Macaronic Sermons,* pp. 31ff.
15 Ibid., pp. 274ff.

clocke) could also be interpreted as legitimate Anglo-Norman forms (cf. AND sub **plaisir, cunté², none¹, clokke¹**).

A rather different type of mixing is found in some Subsidy Rolls[16] and in the various business accounts extensively studied by Laura Wright.[17] Wright suggests[18] that 'macaronic business writing was . . . invented to serve a particular need' and that it was 'a written, formal, business register'. A feature of such texts is their extensive use of abbreviations, and corresponding lack of morphological information,[19] which often neutralises the languages involved and thus blurs the switch sites. The generally problematic distinction between switching and loan words[20] is almost impossible to make in such cases. Wright's material also illustrates the diachronic changes between the ME business texts, with predominantly isolated English noun phrases, mainly single nouns, in an otherwise Latin text, and the EModE ones, where Latin has become restricted to function words such as numbers, prepositions, conjunctions, etc., while English language material is no longer restricted to noun phrases and single nouns.[21] For a sample of such texts see Wright, this volume.

The sixteenth-century English legal text under (5), a deposition, uses Latin mainly in formulae and fixed expressions. It starts with the formulaic *Ad primam excepcionem*, then continues in English; the switch to a Latin relative clause in mid-text may have euphemistic reasons (*vbi eam carnalliter cognouerit*; cf., however the preceding equivalent English clause *that he had carnall act with her*!). Towards the end, Latin starts again in a passage of typical legal character, with another final switch to English in mid-sentence. The two Latin phrases *ad primam excepcionem* and *ad reliquos articulos* structure the text by introducing new pleas or topics, and thus again clearly fulfil a discourse function.

(5) Deposition in trial: Affiliation (Bishop's Court, Chester, 1562/63)

> *Ad primam excepcionem* / This deponent saies, for any thinge that this deponent knowes, Mary Haselwall is an honest damoysell. and further, this Deponent saies, That he, this deponent, and George Garrat, were sent by Henry Monelay, brother vnto Margaret Monelay, to John Cotgreve, to knowe the certenty and truth of hym, whether that he wold deny or confesse the Act. and at the first, he did stoutly deny it; but afterward he confessid that he had carnall act with her ons; and shewid them the place *vbi eam carnalliter cognouerit* / And further he saies, the said Cotgreve said he neuer had to do with her but ons carnally /

---

16 Cf. E. Ekwall, *Two Early London Subsidy Rolls*, edited with an introduction, commentaries, and indices of taxpayers (Lund, 1951).

17 Cf. L. Wright, 'Macaronic Writing in a London Archive, 1380–1480', in *History of Englishes: New Methods and Interpretations in Historical Linguistics*, ed. M. Rissanen, O. Ihalainen and T. Nevalainen (Berlin, 1992), pp. 762–70; L. Wright, 'Early Modern London Business English', in *Studies in Early Modern English*, ed. D. Kastovsky (Berlin, 1994), pp. 449–65; and her contribution to this volume.

18 L. Wright, *Sources of London English: Medieval Thames Vocabulary* (Oxford, 1996), p. 12.

19 Cf. L. Wright, 'Early Modern London Business English', pp. 455f.

20 Cf. Romaine, *Bilingualism*, pp. 142–61, for a critical survey.

21 L. Wright, 'Early Modern London Business English', p. 452.

*Ad reliquos articulos, Dicit se nihill scire, nec potest excipere contra testes;
sed de fama, ait,* that she is taken for an honest wenche, but for that one
Dede. and forther, this Deponent hearith it comenly reportid that the said
Cotgreve is father of the Child.

That CS was still actively used in seventeenth century scientific writing is documented by William Harvey's famous anatomical lectures, *Prelectiones Anatomie
Universalis* (cf. (6)). The predominantly Latin medical text shows quite a number of
short intrasentential switches into English, quite similar to the switches in the
sermon under (3) and to those in modern speech. In some instances, the graphemic
(and phonemic) similarity or identity of a lexeme in English and Latin blurs the
switch site (cf. *cley color contracti*), i.e., there is a transition zone between the two
languages, a fact which frequently triggers switches in modern speech.[22]

(6)   William Harvey, *Prelectiones Anatomie Universalis* (1616)

   Observatio: 1. in prima conformatione albi ut nix; 2. embrione ante aeris
   haustum eodem quo iecur colore ut pueris ante partum *and in two whelpes
   the one borne ded,* unde Avicenna albificat ipsos aer, ex accidente ideo
   color; 3. morbosis *swarty purple blewish* ut peripneumonia, sanguine refer-
   tissimi; *a duskey ash color, a durty greye, ledish* in apostemate absque et
   cum venis livescentibus; *more white and yellow, cley* **color** contracti.
   Hecticis ut tam homine tam simea mea *seacol* absque potu.

Literary texts

Language mixing in literary texts has been commented upon by literary scholars and
medievalists for a long time, but has again been rather neglected by historical
linguists. Purely literary aspects of mixing will not be discussed here, though there
is often no clear-cut border between a literary and a pragmatic/functional analysis of
mixing.

Perhaps the best-known instances of literary CS are the so-called 'macaronic
poems'.[23] The short passage from a trilingual Latin–French–English poem under (7)
illustrates the sometimes highly artistic mixing of the languages. In each of the first
two lines, the first half line is in French, the second in Latin. In the next two lines,
Latin comes first, followed by English. In lines 5 and 6 the three languages alternate
in every half line (F–L–E–L). Every single half line is connected by rhyme, with
both the internal and the end rhymes showing the rhyme scheme aa bb cc. These
poetic means establish a harmonious integration of the three disparate languages.

---

[22] Cf. M. Clyne, 'Constraints on Code-Switching: How Universal are they?' *Linguistics* 25 (1987), pp.
   739–64; Romaine, *Bilingualism*, pp. 149f.
[23] For a discussion of this literary genre and its supposed origin and history see O. Delepierre, *Maca-
   ronéa ou mélange de littérature macaronique des différents peuples de l'Europe* (Paris, 1852); J. A.
   Morgan, *Macaronic Poetry* (New York, 1872); L. Lazzarini, 'Aux origines du macaronique', *Revue
   des Langues Romanes* 86 (1982), pp. 11–33; for an account of English macaronic poetry see W. O.
   Wehrle, *The Macaronic Hymn Tradition in Medieval English Literature* (Washington DC, 1933).

(7) *On the times* (London, BL Royal 12 C xii ('R'), first half of fourteenth century)

Quant houme deit parleir, *videat que verba loquatur;*
Sen covent aver, *ne stulcior inveniatur.*
Quando quis loquitur, bote resoun reste þerynne,
Derisum patitur, and lutel so shall he wynne.
En seynt' eglise *sunt multi sepe priores;*
Summe beoþ wyse, *multi sunt inferiores.*

But even in macaronic poems, the switching patterns may be less regular and also independent of the metrical structure, i.e. closer to the pattern found in modern speech, cf. the example under (8):

(8) *Ballade set on the gates of Canterbury* (J. Speed Davies MS, mid-fifteenth century)

Regnum Anglorum regnum Dei est,
As the Aungelle to seynt Edward dede wyttenesse.
Now *regnum Sathane*, it semethe, *reputat* best.
For *filii scelerati* haue broughte it in dystresse.

Piers Plowman, a long alliterative ME religious verse piece, is known for its great number of Latin passages, mainly biblical quotations; many of these are fully integrated in the text and often switch in mid-sentence.[24] Apart from the great number of verbatim quotations, the author sometimes changes and adapts the quotations to the particular context, as in the passage under (9). Here the Vulgate reading of Matthew 4.4 *Non in solo pane vivit homo* ('Not in bread alone doth man live') is changed by adding *et in pabulo* ('and in food') and by reinterpreting *solo* as an ablative form of *solum* 'soil' (in another context, however, the original, verbatim quotation is given). Another change occurs in the quotation from the *Pater Noster* (*voluntas tua* into *voluntas dei*).[25]

(9) *Piers Plowman* (c.1394)

For in my consience y knowe what Crist wolde y wrouhte:
Preyeres of a parfit man and penaunce discret
Is the levest labour þat oure lord pleseth.
'*Non de solo*' y sayde, 'for sothe *vivit homo,*
Nec in pane et in pabulo; the pater-noster witnesseth,
Fiat voluntas dei þat fynt us alle thynges.'

In medieval drama, switching involves mainly English and Latin, less frequently

---

24 For a detailed discussion of Latin elements in *Piers Plowman* see Sullivan, *Latin Insertions*; J. A. Alford, *Piers Plowman: A Guide to the Quotations* (Binghamton, NY, 1992); T. W. Machan, 'Language Contact in Piers Plowman', *Speculum* 69 (1994), pp. 359–85.
25 For a discussion of the passage cf. J. A. Burrow and T. Turville-Petre, *A Book of Middle English* (Oxford, 1992), p. 145, note.

French and Hebrew.[26] Since dramatic texts are addressed both to an audience and to one or more dramatis personae, the functional range of switching is considerable. In general, Latin is used as the 'divine' language in the religious sphere, though exceptions do occur.[27] In the exchange between Mary and Elizabeth from the *Mary Play* of the N-Town Cycle (cf. (10)), Mary switches from her normal use of English to Latin when she quotes the texts of the *Magnificat* and the *Gloria*; after every second line spoken in Latin by Mary, Elizabeth provides an English version of the Latin text. According to Diller this dialogue-like presentation in two languages is 'a convenient device to differentiate the women's status, but by rhyming the English with the Latin the latter is made less distant from the former than it usually is'.[28] Syntactically, intersentential switches involving quotation of full sentences predominate in medieval drama, though intrasentential switching does occur.

(10) *Mary Play* (ll. 1492–1539)

> *Maria*:   For þis holy psalme I begynne here þis day:
> *Magnificat: anima mea dominum*
> *Et exultauit spiritus meus: in deo salutari meo*
> *Elizabeth*:   Be þe Holy Gost with joye Goddys son is in þe cum,
> þat þi spyryte so injouyid þe helth of þi God so.
> *M.*:   *Quia respexit humilitatem ancille sue*
> *Ecce enim ex hoc beatam me dicent omnes generaciones*
> *E.*:   For he beheld þe lownes of hese hand-maydeȝe,
> So ferforthe for þat all generacyonys blysse ȝou in pes. [. . .]
> *M.*:   This psalme of prophesye seyd betwen vs tweyn,
> In hefne it is wretyn with aungellys hond;

Even this rather sketchy survey of mixed-language texts from almost five centuries should have illustrated that switching is evidently a common phenomenon in the history of written English texts and occurs in a variety of domains, text types and/or genres. The examples also illustrate some of the different syntactic switching patterns and strategies in certain texts (possibly even genres and/or text types), such as single-word switches, inter- and intrasentential switching. In addition, some functional aspects of CS also become apparent. These linguistic aspects of CS will be looked at in more detail in the next section.

---

[26] In making these remarks on medieval drama I am much indebted to H. J. Diller after his recently published article, 'Code-Switching in Medieval English Drama', *Comparative Drama* 31 (1997/98), pp. 506–37, which provides excellent information on language mixing in medieval drama, particularly from a functional point of view.

[27] Cf. ibid., pp. 516f.

[28] Cf. ibid., p. 525.

Linguistic Aspects of CS

The enormous number of linguistically-oriented studies of modern CS have mainly centred on three areas: (i) the distinction between CS and borrowing, (ii) the syntactic patterns, switch sites and possible universal syntactic constraints on CS, (iii) the functional/pragmatic aspects of CS. Some of the theoretical insights gained from these modern studies can be profitably applied to the analysis of older mixed texts, even though there are a number of difficulties due to the nature of diachronic linguistic data. The present paper will, however, only look at the first two areas listed above.

Borrowing or switching

Bilingualism and CS must have played a major role in the process of lexical borrowing[29] and mixed-language texts can thus provide interesting information on the process of widespread relexification of English in the ME period. As Rothwell has pointed out 'generations of educated Englishmen passed daily from English into French and back again in the course of their work',[30] a process which must have led to specific lexical transfers both in the field of technical and of general vocabulary.[31] As pointed out above, the widespread use of abbreviations and the graphemic (and phonetic) identity or similarity of French, Latin and English words make the clear assignment to a particular language (and thus the decision between switching and borrowing) often difficult or even impossible in written texts. Even partial phonological or morphological integration is no longer seen as a sufficient criterion for such a distinction in modern studies of CS, while frequency criteria often do not yield satisfactory results with older corpus languages. The problem of switching vs. borrowing[32] also has important consequences for the organisation of the bilingual brain, e.g. in regard to the storage of and access to the mental lexicon.[33]

More practical questions include the lexicographer's dilemma concerning the inclusion or exclusion of specific lexical items into language-specific dictionaries, when the linguistic status of a specific single lexical item is ambiguous.[34] Even the most comprehensive ME dictionary, the MED, is not always consistent in this respect, as the following example will illustrate. The lexemes *advertaunt, collaudaunt*, and *scandaunt* are given in the MED as ME hapax legomena, with their only

---

[29] Cf. W. Rothwell, 'Stratford atte Bowe and Paris', *Modern Language Review* 80 (1985), pp. 39–54.

[30] W. Rothwell, 'The Missing Link in English Etymology: Anglo-French', *Medium Aevum* 60 (1991), quoted in Wright, *Sources of London English*, p. 7.

[31] Cf. W. Rothwell, 'The Missing Link', and Wright, *Sources of London English*, pp. 6f.

[32] For a survey see Romaine, *Bilingualism*, ch. 4.6; cf. also S. Poplack and D. Sankoff, 'Borrowing: The Synchrony of Integration', *Linguistics* 22 (1984), pp. 99–135; C. M. Myers-Scotton, 'Comparing Code-Switching and Borrowing', in *Codeswitching*, ed. C. M. Eastman (Clevedon, 1992), pp. 19–37.

[33] Cf. Romaine, *Bilingualism*, pp. 87–107.

[34] Cf. also the discussion of different types of 'foreign' lexical material in medieval texts in Rothwell's contribution to this volume.

occurrence in the macaronic poem *The Coronation of the Virgin II*, cf. (11); *exaltant*, on the other hand, which occurs in the same syntactic environment in the same poem is not included in the MED, i.e. it is evidently considered a switch into Latin (L *exaltare* 'raise (voice), exalt'). However, it is more than doubtful whether the spelling difference (<au> vs. <a>) alone can justify such a distinction.

(11) *The Coronation of the Virgin II*, Harley MS 2255 (c.1460)

> Vndir a park ful prudently pyght
> A perillous path men passyd by,
> There herd I a melodye of myght,
> **Scandaunt** on skalys aboue the sky,
> Aungellys **exaltant**, bothe lowde and hih,
> Tenours, trebelys, many a meene ther was:
> They sett ther song ful sapiently,
> *'Benedicta sit sancta trinitas.'*
>
> A melodious myrthe it was to me,
> fful pure and precious be poyntes passaunt,
> So shynyng vpward the excelcite,
> With obediaunt beemys bryghtly abundaunt.
> Angellys, archangellys, froom vicis **advertaunt**,
> Moore gloryous than euere was gleem or glas,
> Thronys, dominaciouns, thus Crist **collaudaunt**,
> With *'Benedicta sit sancta trinitas.'*

Collaudaunt could, however, equally be interpreted as another Latin switch (cf. L *collaudare* 'to praise'), and so could – though less convincingly – even be *advertaunt* (L *avertere*, with a form *avertant* from 1197 quoted in DMLBS[35]). Since such an interpretation is not possible with *scandaunt* (L *scandens*, from *scandere*), one might prefer to classify all the above lexemes (i.e. including *exaltant*) on the basis of their syntactic distribution as ME borrowings from Latin.

Syntactic patterns and constraints

The establishment of relative frequencies of switched constituents and switch sites as well as the formulation of possible (language specific and – more important – universal) syntactic constraints on CS have been a major research topic for many years.[36] These attempts reflect the view that CS is basically rule-governed, and thus,

---

[35] R. E. Latham and D. R. Howlett, *Dictionary of Medieval Latin from British Sources* (Oxford, 1975–).

[36] Cf. L. A. Timm, 'Spanish–English Code-Switching: El porqué y how-not-to', *Romance Philology* 18 (1975), pp. 473–82; C. W. Pfaff, 'Constraints on Language Mixing'; S. Poplack, 'Sometimes I'll start a sentence in English y termino en español: Toward a Typology of Code-Switching', *Linguistics* 18 (1980), pp. 581–618; S. Berk-Seligson, 'Linguistic Constraints on Intrasentential Code-Switching: A Study of Spanish/Hebrew Bilingualism', *Language in Society* 15 (1986), pp. 313–48; M. Clyne, 'Constraints on Code-Switching'; J. L. Jake, 'Intrasentential Code Switching and Pronouns: On the Categorical Status of Functional Elements', *Linguistics* 32 (1994), pp. 271–98; S. Mahootian,

to a certain extent, 'predictable'. According to the syntactic nature of the switched units, three types of switching have generally been distinguished, though their definitions are not always consistent: (i) intersentential switches, (ii) tag-switches, (iii) intrasentential switches. Intersentential switches will be defined here as switches between sentences or independent clauses, whose integration into a text in a different language does not present any particular difficulties for the bilingual speaker. Intrasentential switches are switches between or within the constituents of a sentence, including dependent clauses.[37] They involve the matching of the syntactic rules of different languages, and are therefore linguistically more complex than the other two types – though it is controversial whether they are typical of or restricted to fluent bilinguals.[38]

Detailed (ideally quantitative) studies of the syntactic patterns of CS in a variety of older mixed texts and text types are important in a number of respects: they evidently provide information about the major switching strategies at particular periods, and possibly about differences between specific texts, text types or genres; the comparison of these results with modern CS data on the one hand and with the predictions of theoretical models on the other should provide an insight into the diachronic stability and changes of CS patterns and could also test the validity of theoretical models of CS.

But there are a number of general and methodological problems in the study of historical CS. For one, the number of mixed texts is considerably smaller than that of monolingual texts.[39] Secondly, the medieval systems of the languages involved are less clearly definable and less well described (classical vs. different types of medieval Latin; various ME dialects; different types of medieval French). Further problems are due to the specific nature of the texts, whose authors, audience, genesis and function are not always known, though these factors have an influence on the language of the texts. Let me restrict myself to two genres, which will be used below to illustrate this aspect in more detail, namely (i) 'macaronic' poetry and (ii) 'macaronic' sermons.[40] With the sermons there is, for example, disagreement about the origin and function of these mixed texts, i.e. whether the manuscripts represent the linguistic form in which they were delivered. With the poems, the artistic function of language switching and metrical considerations may have influenced the switching patterns – though it is unlikely that metrical constraints would have completely over-

---

'Codeswitching and Universal Constraints: Evidence from Farsi/English', *World Englishes* 15 (1996), pp. 377–84, etc.; for recent surveys see P. Muysken, 'Code-Switching and Grammatical Theory', in *One Speaker, Two Languages: Cross-Disciplinary Perspectives on Code-Switching*, ed. L. Milroy and P. Muysken (Cambridge, 1995), pp. 177–98; Romaine, *Bilingualism*, pp. 125–30.

37   Cf. Myers-Scotton, *Duelling Languages*, p. 4 and Romaine, *Bilingualism*, pp. 122f.

38   Cf. Poplack, 'Sometimes I'll start a sentence in English', p. 581; M. Pütz, *Sprachökologie und Sprachwechsel: Die deutsch-australische Sprechergemeinschaft in Canberra* (Frankfurt, 1994), pp. 279ff.

39   This does not apply to all text types or all periods; cf. Wright, *Sources of London English* (p. 6): 'it is easier today to find macaronic documents from the late Medieval period in Record Offices than it is to find monolingual texts'.

40   Cf. Wenzel, *Macaronic Sermons*.

ridden linguistic ones. A crucial problem for any statistical analysis is the differentiation between switching and borrowing discussed above.

The present data consist of a total of about 500 switches from an early fifteenth-century mixed sermon[41] and a number of fifteenth-century mixed poems and carols. The choice of text samples, especially of the poems, was based on syntactic and semantic considerations about switching strategies, i.e. only texts which also show intra-sentential switching have been chosen. In the poems English can be considered as the base or 'matrix' language by quantitative criteria, while Latin is the matrix language of the sermon, with frequent English insertions of various length. Although many poetic switches involve quotations from hymns, the Bible and other religious texts, and thus involve quasi-'prefabricated chunks' (which may be found in more than one text), the linguistic integration of these chunks into the English text often shows a high degree of flexibility and competence. (It is worth noting that even present-day monolingual spoken discourse shows a high frequency of such ready-made chunks.)

Although the data on which the following observations are based are still rather small, a number of interesting tendencies emerge, which will be compared with findings from some studies on modern CS, in particular Berk-Seligson (Spanish/ Hebrew),[42] Pütz (English/German),[43] and Poplack (Spanish/English).[44]

With regard to the type of switched constituents, there is a clear predominance of switching between major constituents (NP, VP, PP) over switching within major constituents in both poems and sermon, a tendency also attested in modern speech. With regard to the categories of switched constituents, the two sub-corpora show an amazing variety, as the examples under (12) illustrate:

(12) Syntactic types of switching[45]

i.   S(indep): Mercyfulle God, it ys tyme thow for vs awake! *'Mercenarius fugit,'* ne wylle make resistence, He fereth the wolf that wolde hys bonys crake. (*Ballade set on the gates of Canterbury,* John Speed Davies MS)
     In erthe be peas to man also / *Et gaudium sit angelis.* (J. Ryman, *Now the Most High,* Cambridge University Library Ee. 1.12)

ii. S(gover): Now be the Juys fallyn in fyghte Of Seynt Stevyn, that nobull knyghte; Because he sayde he saw a syghte, *Lapidauerunt Stephanum.* (Huntington Library MS HM. 147)

---

41 *De celo querebant,* in ibid.
42 S. Berk-Seligson, 'Linguistic Constraints'.
43 Pütz, *Sprachökologie.*
44 Poplack, 'Sometimes I'll start a sentence in English'.
45 The following examples are ordered by switched constituents, i.e. those in the embedded language. In order of apppearance, the following abbreviations are used: S 'sentence'. (in)dep '(in)dependent', gover 'governing', postmod 'postmodifying', adv 'adverbial', N(P) 'noun (phrase)', V(P) 'verb (phrase)', subj 'subject', obj 'object', Det 'determiner', PP 'prepositional phrase', Aux 'auxiliary', inf 'infinitive', adj 'adjective'.

iii. S(dep) postmod: He hus all to heuyn bryng *Qui mortem cruce voluit.* (National Library of Scotland MS Advocates 19. 3. l)

iv.   S(dep) adv: Sette hym *ut sedeat in principibus*, as he dyd before. (*Ballade set on the gates of Canterbury*, John Speed Davies MS)

v.   S(dep) non-finite: Knytes kemyn fro Henry Kyng, Wykkyd men, withoute lesyng; Ther they deyn a wonder thing, *Feruentes insania.* (BL MS Sloane 2593)

vi.   NP+VP / (other constituent): Fro heyuyn to erthe to saue monkynd *Pater misit Filium.* (National Library of Scotland MS Advocates 19. 3. l)

vii. NPsubj: *Puer natus* to vs was sent (Bodleian Library MS Arch. Selden B. 26)

viii. NPobj: 'Thou shalt conseyve this sam day *Saluatorem mundi.*' (Bodleian Library MS Engl. poet. e.i)

ix.   NPadv: The gretest clerk of al this lond, Of Cauntyrbery, ye vnderstond, Slawyn he was with wykkyd hond, *Demonis potencia.* (BL MS Sloane 2593)

x.   PPadv: He brynge vs alle to good ende *In die nouissima.* (BL MS Sloane 2593)

xi.   VP: Vpon a nyght an aungell bright *Pastoribus apparuit* (Cambridge University Library MS Ee. 1.12, J. Ryman)
      Exortum est in loue and lysse: (Bodleian Library MS Arch. Selden B. 26)

xii. Aux / Vinf: *þei most* habere eciam fistulam ad os. (*De celo*, 337)

xiii. NP+Gerund: *Tempus* ys come falshede to dystroy, *Tempus eradicandi* the wedes fro the corne, *Tempus cremandi* the breres that trees noye (*Ballade set on the gates of Canterbury*, John Speed Davies MS)

xiv. Single lexemes:
      N: possum huic comparare prelatos, curatos, et *men* Ecclesie (*De celo*, 170)
      Det: Sic *þis* florens vinea *faded* indies (*De celo*, 113)
      V: quia sicut materialis sol *goth* suum cursum per omnia duodecim signa in zodiaco (*De celo*, 180)
      Adj: oportet vt abscidas omnes ramos *vnthrifti*, ramos superbie et gule (*De celo*, 16)
      Adv: non *wrongfulich* perdidit suam terram. (*De celo*, 58)

Some of the above patterns are rare, such as the switched determiner *þis* or single verbs, while others show middle to high frequencies (cf. below). Furthermore, there is a surprising degree of correlation between the ME patterns and those found in the modern studies, though there are some clear differences as well. Two points in which the older data differ from the modern ones are: (i) The almost complete absence of so-called 'emblematic switches' (tags, interjections, negative and affirmative particles) in the old texts, while 'emblematic switches' account for a large amount of switches in spoken data. This is clearly due to pragmatic factors (written register, topic, level of formality). (ii) The relatively high frequency of non-finite switched clauses (between 5% and 9%, cf. example (12.v) above), a pattern which does not occur in the modern studies. This seems again to be due to differences in register and not to the structure of the embedded languages, since the pattern occurs with both Latin and English.

In a number of points only one of the two sub-corpora differs from the modern ones: (i) The poems show less than 3% of single-word switches, which result from the extensive use of 'prefabricated chunks' (i.e. quotations) in this text type, while single-word switches constitute a major part of most speech-based switching (between 19% and more than 50%) and of switching in the sermons (about 20%). (ii) The poems show a high frequency of switched NPs (about 30%), while the sermons (about 9%) again behave more like modern speech (between 2.5% and about 11%). This high frequency in the poems seems due to two factors: on the one hand to the structure of the embedded language Latin, with frequent adverbial NPs in the ablative case, e.g. (12.ix); on the other hand to a stylistic factor, namely the great number of Latin NP appositions (e.g. *sol de stella* as an apposition to *Mary*).

In two features the sermon differs from both the poems and the modern data: (i) The number of intersentential switches is very low in the sermon (less than 1.5%), while the poems with more than 20% are closer to the frequency in modern speech (about 15%–34%); (ii) A stylistic feature typical of the sermons is their frequent use of coordinate constituents (about 12%), such as 'de misericordia *and comfort*'; 'vult misereri nobis *and send vs comfort* de celo'. Since such coordinate, often synonymous NPs, AdjPs and VPs are also a well-known stylistic feature of ME and EModE monolingual texts, their use in the sermons is most likely also stylistically motivated.

So much for switching patterns and frequency hierarchies. What about the much discussed universal syntactic constraints, which would also apply to older data? Contrary to earlier models, syntactic constraints are now increasingly understood as probable rather than categorical[46] so that variation is to be expected with CS patterns as with any other linguistic phenomenon. CS involves a range of speakers with different degrees of competence in the languages used, so that absolute regularity would be a surprise. While the 'ideal competent native speaker' is a valuable theoretical construct and can form the basis of grammatical description and judgements on grammaticality, I can see no room for an 'ideal competent bilingual speaker' in any theory of CS; therefore, judgements by bilingual speakers on the grammaticality and/or acceptability of specific switches are both theoretically and methodologically problematic. On the basis of the data analysed, it seems that – as so often in comparing two diachronically related linguistic systems – the main difference between switching strategies in the medieval written and the modern spoken data lies less in the presence or absence of specific features or types, but rather in their relative frequencies. These different frequencies seem to be at least partly due to

---

[46] Cf. Muysken, 'Code-Switching and Grammatical Theory'.

pragmatic and stylistic factors, partly to the different structures of the languages involved. This does not apply to certain specific cases, such as the macaronic business accounts, and to features of formal text types which no longer show CS today.

Conclusion

CS in written texts was clearly not an exception but a widespread specific *mode of discourse* over much of the attested history of English. It occurs across domains, genres and text types – business, religious, legal and scientific texts, as well as literary ones. These texts provide important information on early bilingualism and specific modes of discourse, which can be seen in a new light, if we apply the theoretical frameworks developed by modern research on CS. Many of the features of modern CS can be traced back to older periods, and even though they may not be proof of categorical universals, they attest to a diachronic continuum of a phenomenon which has developed into one of the most exciting branches of modern (socio)linguistics. The study of older texts is as profitable and exciting as that of modern speech.

French Phrasal Power in Late Middle English: Some Evidence Concerning the Verb *nime(n)/take(n)*

LUIS IGLESIAS-RÁBADE

IT HAS BEEN STATED repeatedly that the Norman Conquest had far-reaching consequences for the English language. There is no doubt about two direct effects of this historical event on the English language: on the one hand, Romance words and phraseology replaced an important part of Germanic English vocabulary; and, on the other hand, the enormous diversity of Old English inflectional systems advanced towards simplification. Most discussion about French influence upon the English language has predominantly concentrated upon the scope and the character of the Romance words that made their way into Middle English, yet few modern scholars have accounted for the semantic connotations of these French words. Furthermore, the controversy about the use and status of English and French in the post-Conquest period is still raging.[1] Thus, there are still at least four fundamental questions to be solved:

(a)   in which domains and to what extent did French displace English in oral communication?

(b)   to what extent did French loan-words change or restrict the meaning of native words? Certainly, scholars have indexed almost all the French words which made

---

[1]   Conflicting views have been put forward by B. Clover, *The Mastery of the French Language in England from the 11th to the 14th century* (New York, 1888); J. A. Derocquigny, *A Contribution to the Study of the French Element in English* (Lille, 1904); O. F. Emerson, 'English and French in the Time of Edward III', *Romanic Review* 7 (1916), pp. 127–43; R. M. Wilson, 'English and French in England 1100–1300', *History* 28 (1943), pp. 37–60; H. Suggett, 'The Use of French in England in the Later Middle Ages', *Transactions of the Royal Historical Society* 28 (1945), pp. 61–83; A. C. Baugh, *A History of the English Language* (London, 1951); C. Cottle, *The Triumph of English, 1350–1400* (London, 1969); R. Berndt, 'The Linguistic Situation in England from the Norman Conquest to the Loss of Normandy (1066–1204)', in *Approaches to English Historical Linguistics*, ed. R. Lass (New York, 1969), pp. 369–91; R. Berndt, 'The Period of the Final Decline of French in Medieval England (Fourteenth and Early Fifteenth Centuries)', *Zeitschrift für Anglistik und Amerikanistik* 20 (1972), pp. 341–69; W. Rothwell, 'The Role of French in 13th Century England', *Bulletin of the John Rylands University Library* 58 (1976), pp. 445–66; W. Rothwell, 'A quelle époque a-t-on cessé de parler français en Angleterre?' in *Mélanges Ch. Camproux* (Montpellier, 1979), pp. 1075–89; I. Short, 'On Bilingualism in Anglo-Norman England', *Romance Philology* 33 (1980), pp. 467–79; D. A. Kibbee, *For to speke French trewely: The French Language in England 1000–1600* (Amsterdam/Philadelphia, 1991); L. Iglesias-Rábade, *El uso del inglés y francés en la Inglaterra normanda y plantagenet 1066–1399* (Santiago, 1992).

their way into ME texts, but there does not appear to have been any systematic research into their denotational and connotational meanings. As Sykes[2] has pointed out, to what extent, for instance, were OE words such as *þing* or *sum* ('some') affected by the French words *cause, affaire, matter* or *certain*, respectively?

(c)   how far can French loan-words be judged fundamental necessities for the expression of the contemporary socio-cultural setting?

(d)   in macro-socio-linguistic terms, are we sufficiently trained to interpret the medieval writer's and medieval audience's attitude towards wording? Inexperienced modern readers of medieval texts tend to regard medieval words as if they were written by modern writers. Thus, when we come across an unusual word we tend to infer its denotational meaning, that is, the dictionary definition of that word. However, in the Middle Ages there were no dictionaries to look up the meaning of words. Most of the population received no education that enabled them to read a text. So when a person heard an unusual word he associated it with a varied range of meaningful connotations. Furthermore, most words used in poetic diction were subject to some constraints such as alliteration, rhyme, etc. Thus for the purpose of rhythmic composition authors used to incorporate words which had no stable concurrent evocative associations for the audience. Apart from that, the correct interpretation of a medieval text is hindered by two historical facts: on the one hand, the small amount of medieval literary output and the 'absence of a coherent and consistent tradition' inhibit 'the development of literary connotation as we understand it now'; and, on the other hand, the 'distance of the medieval period from our own prevents us from acquiring any idea of what the colloquial or at least the less literary associations of words were.' Thus, medieval words did not have 'the same clear-cut significance or connotative associations' which modern words have.[3]

But, if this holds true for words, we cannot state the same for phrases, turns of speech, proverbial sayings and idioms. In fact, this type of composition was much more stable because unlearned people have an enduring tendency to use phraseology and proverbial sayings to describe a particular situation, a given event or their own experience. These sayings were always present in daily talk and were easily transmitted from older to rising generations. However, the origin of many phrasal structures colloquially used in late ME is still a matter of conjecture. In my own view, and in this I concur with Sykes,[4] ME phrasal systems underwent a massive process of Romanisation which occurred 'as early as the romanisation of its vocabulary'.

This paper, then, retraces Sykes's, Sypherd's and Prins's steps by calling attention to the role of French in the formative phrasal system of English, particularly in the fourteenth and fifteenth centuries.[5] In so doing I will concentrate on two types of

2   F. H. Sykes, *French Elements in Middle English* (Oxford, 1899), p. 5.
3   Cf. N. F. Blake, *The English Language in Medieval Literature* (London and New York, 1977), pp. 80–1.
4   Sykes, *French Elements*, p. 7.
5   Sykes, *French Elements*; O. Sypherd, 'Old French Influence on Middle English Phraseology',

phrasal patterns with the verb *nime(n)/take(n)*: (a) verbal idiomatic phrases made of the 'light verb' *nime(n)/take(n)* + a deverbal noun ('Wortverbindungen') such as *taken ende* 'to come to an end; achieve an outcome'; and (b) verb + 'prepositional deverbal' such as 'take bi hond', 'take in cure'.

1. Verbal phrasals made of a 'light' V(erb) + deverbal noun

Scholars[6] usually agree in describing such constructions as *taken ende, beren armes,* etc. as a verbal phrasal splitting into two parts: the first element (e.g. *taken*) is a 'light verb' or an 'operator' that functions like an auxiliary verb and bears all the grammatical features such as the inflections to mark tense, number and person, whereas the second deverbal element (*ende, armes*) functions like a true verb because it expresses the action and carries the lexical meaning.

The use of these phrasals dates from OE, although it was basically restricted to the verbs *habban* 'to have' and *niman* 'to take', e.g. *habban cyþþe* 'to know' or *geleafan niman* 'to believe'. However, this syntactic pattern was extensively used in late ME. There remains a fundamental question to which there is no definite answer: were phrasals such as *bear arms, make war, take advantage* rooted in the parallel French pattern, *porter les armes, faire la guerre, prendre avantage,* or were they positively English phrasal structures enriched with French vocabulary?

The enormous number of phrasals of this type obliges me to restrict my research to the ME 'light verb' *nime(n)/take(n)*. Let us consider, as an example, the ME phrasal (a) **take(n) dai** 'set a day (for doing sth.)'. The earliest record in the MED[7] is in **c1440 (c1350)** *Octav. (1)* 159/1330: *The parties ere withdrawen awaye, And taken there es anoþir daye, That the batelle sulde be.* We may posit that this phrasal is a native English structure because OE records a similar phrasal form, **dæg settan**, *Ps,* Th., lxxv, 7 (B-T). However, Old French also had the phrasal **prendre jo(u)r** [*a uitave jor en pris, En.* 10010. (TL)]. The question to be solved is why *nime(n)/take(n) dai* does not occur in ME until the second half of the fourteenth century. Was it, then, a recuperation of an older similar form *dæg settan* or the direct

---

Modern Philology 5 (1907–8), pp. 85–96; A. A. Prins, 'French Influence in English Phrasing', *Neophilologus* 32 (1948), pp. 28–39 and 73–83; A. A. Prins, *French Influence in English Phrasing* (Leiden, 1952).

6 Cf. T. F. Mitchell, 'Some English Phrasal Types', in *In Memory of J. R. Firth*, ed. C. E. Bazell, J. C. Catford, M. A. K. Halliday and R. H. Robins (London, 1966), pp. 335–58; G. Nickel, 'Complex Verbal Structures in English', *International Review of Applied Linguistics* 6 (1968), 1. p. 21; D. Bolinger, *The Phrasal Verb in English* (Cambridge, Mass., 1971); A. H. Live, 'The Take-Have Phrasal in English', *Linguistics* 95 (1973), pp. 31–50; A. Wierzbicka, 'Why can you *have a drink* when you can't **have an eat*?' *Language* 58 (1982), pp. 753–99.

7 Abbreviations used in this article (other than those listed above, p. x):
Lit: E. Littré, *Dictionnaire de la langue française* (Paris, 1873)
BT: Bosworth-Toller, *An Anglo-Saxon Dictionary* (Oxford, 1882–98)
BT-S: Supplement to Bosworth-Toller, *An Anglo-Saxon Dictionary* (Oxford, 1921)
NED: *A New English Dictionary on Historical Principles* (Oxford, 1888–1933)
TOWN: The Towneley Plays.

translation of the OF form *prendre jour*? The latter seems to be favoured by similar meaningful contexts and by the fact that the verb *nime(n)/take(n)* (counterpart of the French verb *prendre*) is substituted for the old verb *settan* in such a phrasal and thus becomes parallel with the French phrasal form.

The data drawn from the MED seem to prove that the emergence and preponderance of these verbal idiomatic constructions in late ME was at least favoured by Anglo-Norman, though the structure was already productive in OE. In fact, the majority of these ME structures had no prototype in OE, and when they occurred in English they tended to follow the French pattern. Thus, OF expressions such as *faire cause commune, prendre corone* occur in late ME as *maken comun cause* ('to make common cause') and *taken coroune* ('assume the sovereignty over a country'). There is a tendency to translate the OF 'light' verbs (*faire, prendre, porter*) and the function words (articles, prepositions and conjunctions) into English, whereas nouns, adjectives and adverbs maintained their French form adapted to English spelling.

Sykes[8] and, particularly, Prins[9] have found about 623 phrases, which had no prototype in OE, and which English at some time or other might have adopted from French. For instance, *take lond* ('disembark') does not occur in OE, but it does in Old French as *prendre terre*. Prins[10] has listed 31 verbal idiomatic phrases of French provenance with the verb *taken* (OF. *prendre*) + a deverbal noun: *taken + advice, (the) air, battle, breath, care, conge, counseil, cure, delight, (an) end, entent, example, guard, harbour, haven, heed, ill, keep, land, leave, occasion, pains, part, pity, pleasure, rest, truce, vengeance, (one's) venia, (the) waters, (the) word.* However, I have counted 306 constructions with the verb *taken* + a deverbal noun. I have also found that 49 phrasals are OF calques, whereas 156 had a similar pattern in OF.

Patterns and occurrences of *nimen/taken*-phrasals in ME are listed below.

Type A: The first occurrence of *nimen/taken* phrasals[11]

Two occurrences of phrasal-*nimen* are recorded in the twelfth century. There is, however, a remarkable growth of these phrasals in the thirteenth century, most of them with *nimen*; thus 40 new phrasals are indicated for this period in the MED, almost all of them dating from in the first half of the century. But the flourishing of *nimen/taken*-phrasal occurs in the fourteenth century. The MED records 148 new phrasals (52 phrasals in the first half of the century and 96 in the second half). The increasing usage of this phrasal system in the second half of the fourteenth century coincided with the ascendancy of French elements in the English language. It is worth noting that most of these phrasals had an equivalent French pattern. However, some phrasals are purely English, enriched with French deverbal nouns. The number

---

8   Sykes, *French Elements*.
9   Prins, 'French Influence', and *French Influence*.
10   Prins, *French Influence*.
11   I will only consider the first record dated in the MED.

of new phrasals declines in the fifteenth century. Thus the MED records 74 phrasals in the first half and 50 in the second half of the century. This decay also accords with the decrease in the number of French words which made their way into English.

Type B: Origin (English/French) of the deverbal noun

1100–1200: The two new records found in the twelfth century include a deverbal noun of English provenance (for fuller accounts of these and following observations see Appendix A).

1200–1300: The thirteenth century records 30 *nimen*-phrasal and 6 phrasal-*taken* followed by a deverbal noun of English origin, whereas only 4 phrasals (3 with *nimen* and 1 with *taken*) are followed by a deverbal noun of French provenance.

1300–1350: In the first half of the fourteenth century there are 9 phrasal-*nimen* and 16 phrasal-*taken* which are followed by a deverbal noun of English origin, whereas 27 phrasals (15 with *nimen* and 12 with *taken*) are followed by a deverbal noun of French provenance.

1350–1400: The second half of the fourteenth century includes 4 phrasal-*nimen* and 37 phrasal-*taken* followed by a deverbal noun of English origin, whereas 59 phrasals (5 with *nimen* and 56 with *taken*) are followed by a deverbal noun of French provenance.

1400–1450: In the first half of the fifteenth century 31 phrasals are followed by a deverbal noun of English origin, whereas 45 phrasals are followed by a deverbal noun of French provenance. Phrasal *nimen* is not found, except *nimen licence* (**a1420** Lidg. *TB* 12139).

1450–1500: Finally, the second half of the fifteenth century records 14 phrasals followed by a deverbal noun of English origin, whereas 35 phrasals are followed by a deverbal noun of French provenance. Phrasal *nimen* is not found, except *nimen sted* (**a1450** *Parton (1)*, 2968), *nimen cristendom* (**a1450** *St. Editha*, 23) and *nimen priorie* (**?c1450** *St Cuth.* 2056).

Dates of new phrasals	English deverbal nouns	French nouns deverbal	Total
1100–1200	2	0	2
1200–1300	36	4	40
1300–1350	25	27	52
1350–1400	41	59	100
1400–1450	31	45	76
1450–1500	14	35	49
ME period	149	170	319

The above table shows conclusively that the rates of occurrence of deverbal nouns of English or French provenance are not strikingly different, and that the increasing number of French deverbal nouns in the second half of the fourteenth century and throughout the fifteenth century coincided with the incorporation of French vocabulary into English.

Type C: The ME *nime(n)/take(n)*-phrasal has an OE counterpart, e.g. *token ensaumple wele to don* (*Arth. & M.*7964). This phrasal, *token ensaumple*, had a parallel *niman*-phrasal in OE, *bysne niman*.

1200–1300: 5 phrasals have a parallel form in OE: *niman graman and andan, frið niman, eard niman, leaf niman, weg niman.*
1300–1350: (4): *ware niman, fon to rice, niman to ræde, lare niman*).
1350–1400: (10): *dæg settan, mod niman, feorh beniman, flæsc under-feng, wæpna niman, gemæccan niman*).
1400–1450: Only one phrasal has a parallel form in OE: *lufe niman.*
1450–1500: No parallel OE phrasal is found.
There are 16 parallel OE phrasals which represent 5.01% of the total number of new phrasals found in ME in the MED.

Type D: The ME *nimen/taken*-phrasal is an OF calque, e.g. *Vter Pendragon coroun nam And king of Inglond bicam* (*Arth. & M.* 2049). Cf. OF: *prendre corone*, e.g. *Heraut prist corone a Nöel* (*Rou* III 5965).

1200–1300: 2 phrasals are OF calques: *nimen* (*prendre* in French) *discipline, ~ venie.*
1300–1350: (18): *take/(nime) (prendre* in French) *assaut, ~ bataille, ~ bapteme, ~ coroune, ~ counseil, ~ crois, ~ discipline, ~ ensaumple, ~ ese, ~ fin, ~ forme, ~ habit, ~ hostel, ~ ordre, ~ pas, ~ sojourn, ~ vengeaunce, ~ viage.*
1350–1400: (15): *nime/take (prendre* in French) *air, ~ amendise, ~ arivage, ~ armur, ~ avantage, ~ avis, ~ confort, ~ congé, ~ curs, ~ entente, ~ ire, ~ joie, ~ lessoun, ~ part, ~ pes.*
1400–1450: (6): *taken (prendre* in French) *armes, ~ avis, ~ garde, ~ plait, ~ penitence, ~ tor.*
1450–1500: (8): *taken (prendre* in French) *corage, ~ crestendom, ~ force, ~ hardement, ~ justice, ~ pleit, ~ plasure, ~ respit.*
There are 49 phrasals which are a calque from French, that is, 15.36% of all the phrasals.

Type E: The *nimen/taken*-phrasal has a similar OF counterpart, e.g. *Whene þey had made vp hyr offeryng . . . they lay a-downe & toke restyng* (**a1475** *Ihesu was born* (Prk) 19). Cf. OF: *prendre repos*, e.g. *Amors, qui les fins cuers esveille . . . La nuit, quant repos doivent prendre* (*Clef d'Am.* 3).

1200–1300: 30 phrasals had the corresponding structural phrase in Old French (cf. Appendix A); **1300–1350:** 36; **1350–1400:** 55; **1400–1450:** 18; **1450–1500:** 17.

About 156 phrasals had, then, a similar structure in Old French; these represent 48.9% of the phrasals recorded in the MED.

To summarise, this syntactic pattern acquired great popularity in lME with extensive use and a varied typology. I do not claim that this construction is a French imprint, because it occurred in OE, but in my opinion French contributed decisively to the use of this type of structure consisting of a light verb translated from French + a deverbal element which bears the action and the lexical meaning and which usually kept the French form and content. However, there are also dissenting opinions about this type of structure. Thus Owen Sypherd[12] considers that this phrasal type is deeply rooted in the English language and supports his theory by an analysis of the *Ormulum*, a text which is supposed to maintain the English oral tradition and is therefore unlikely to have been contaminated by French wording and phraseology. And, as Sypherd points, out we can read in the *Ormulum* phrases like the following: 'take example', 'take death', 'take heed', 'take wife', 'take order', 'take witness', etc. Unfortunately, Sypherd does not prove that they were necessarily native English phrases, he only asserts that they occur in the *Ormulum*. It could be argued that Sypherd thereby shows that the purity of the English diction of *Ormulum* might also be challenged.

2. The 'light' verb *nime(e)/take(n)* + a 'prepositional' deverbal

My concern now is the treatment of the following phrasal combination: a 'light' verb (e.g. *bere(n)*, *haue(n)*, *make(n)*, *nime(e)/take(n)*, etc. + a 'prepositional deverbal' such as *take(n) in gree*, *take(n) to herte*, etc. It is noteworthy that these structures are not made of a predicator (for example, *take(n)*) + prepositional phrase (**in gree*). In fact, the verb *take(n)* and the preposition *in* form a verbal phrasal unit because the preposition is closely attached to the verb producing a single semasiological assemblage.

This pattern, too, dates from OE, though it was restricted to the verb *niman* + an object preceded by *on*, e.g. *on gemynd niman* ('to bear in mind'). However, this construction came to be much more frequent in lME, particularly with sequences which had no prototype in OE, and, more intriguingly, most of them were a calque in both form and content from French and/or Latin.

The controversy about the route of the transmission of these Latin-French phrasals into late ME is still lively. We may suppose that they came to be used in written texts as a result of a bilingual context in the post-Conquest period, particularly in the thirteenth century, but it is still difficult to determine whether and to what extent thirteenth-century England was socially bilingual or not. I believe that they might have made their way into English following the common route of other

---

[12] Sypherd, 'Old French Influence'.

phrasal structures: namely, they tend to occur first in English translations from French and Latin texts. A subsequent step was for scholars and students to become familiarised with them at school via their reading of these English versions. Later on they became part of the daily talk of educated people and eventually in the course of time they were adopted by lower strata of society. Take, as an example, 'light' *nime(n)/take(n)* + a 'prepositional deverbal' introduced by:

(a) *bi*:

Take bi (the) bodi (32) 'seize (sb.) bodily'. **(1426–7)** *Paston* 1.8.

Take bi the bridel (30) 'get control of a horse by grasping its bridle'. **c1450** *Alph.Tales*.409/11.

Take bi the helm (30) 'grab (sb.) by the helmet'. **c1450** *Ponthus* 54/20.

Take bi the honde (30) 'take (sb.) by the hand or hands'. **c1350** *A child is boren* 1.

Take bi the kne (30) 'clasp (sb.) by the knee'. **(a1393)** Chaucer, *CA* 5.6566.

Take bi the nose (30) 'clasp (sb.) by the nose', also 'interrupt (sb.)'. **(1451)** *Paston* (Gairdner) 2.239.

Take bi the rein (30) 'get control of a horse by grasping its reins'.**(a1470)** Malory *Wks*. 29/9.

Take bi the sleve (30) 'hold (sb.) by the sleeve'. **(a1393)** Chaucer, *CA* 5.77669.

Take bi the tail (30) 'grab (sb.) by the tail'. **a1500 (?a1425)** *Chester Pl. Antichr.* 515/697.

Take bi the temples (30) 'grab (sb.) about the temples'. **c1250** **St. Marg.(2)* 187.

Take bi the top (30) 'grab (sb., oneself) by the hair'. **C1225 (?c1200)** *St. Juliana* 63/683.

Cf. in OF:

Prendre par la barbe (TL) *Florimont* 12093.

Prendre par la main (TL) *Ferg*. 44, 36.

Prendre par la mamele (TL) *Mont. Fabl.* I.263.

Prendre par la poitrine (TL). *Mont. Fabl.* VI 184.

Prendre par le braz (TL) *Ch. Rol.* 2552.

Prendre par le frain/frein (TL) *Auc.* 32.9.

Prendre par le regne/rein (TL) *FCand. Sch.-G.* 662.

Prendre par les dois (TL) *Ferg*. 1.25.

The use of the 'light' verb *nime(n)/take(n)* + a 'prepositional deverbal' introduced by **bi** appears in the first half of the thirteenth century when the phrasal is used to convey the idea of 'laying hands on a part of the body of a person or an animal' as in *take sb. bi the temples/the top*. However, it came to be extensively used in the fifteenth century, particularly in the second half.

It is also worth noting that this construction in unsupported by analogous OE phrasals and therefore its occurrence in late ME must be interpreted as French influence of parallel phrasal usage of *prendre* and *tenir*.

(b) *to*:

Take to baille (32) 'take (sb.) into (one's) custody by putting up bail, go bail for (sb)'. **(1457)** *Let.BK.Lond.K* 390.

Take to counseil (54) 'to take (sb.) to counsel with, consult with (sb.)'. **a1500 (?a1400)** *Morte Arth.(2)* 956.

Take to covenaunt (39) 'receive (sb.) into (one's) service'. **(c1475)** *LRed Bk.Bristol* 2.156.

Take to felaushipe (39) 'accept (sb) as an associate'. **?a1425** **Chauliac(1)* Oa/b.

Take to gest (39) 'receive (sb.) as a guest'. **1400 (a1325)** *Cursor* 5404.

Take to grace (39) 'have a mercy on (sb.), be merciful to (sb.)'. **(1428)** *Doc in Sur. Soc.* 85.5.

Take to heart (39) 'take (sb.) to one's heart, hold (sb.) dear'.

Take to hevinesse (57) 'regard (sth.) with vexation, be vexed at'. **a1500 (1422)** Yonge *SSecr.* 172/6.

Take to honour (45) 'select (sb.) for an honor or a high position'. **c1440 (a1401)** *Life Bridlington* in *NM 71* p. 143.

Take to hostage (32) 'take (sb.) into (one's) custody by putting up bail, go bail for (sb)'. **a1400–a1500** *Rich.* (b-version: Brunner) 261/7.

Take to ill (Sykes, 21) 'take agrief'. *Sir Deg.*, 442.

Take to lef (39) 'take (sb.) as (one's) lover'. **?a1350** *Guy(3)* 137.

Take to mercy (39) 'have a mercy on (sb.), be merciful to (sb.)'. **c1390** *I wolde witen* 118.

Take to plegge (32) 'take (sb.) into custody as a hostage.**?a1475 (?a1425)** *Higd.(2)* 7.179.

Take to purpose (Sykes, 21) 'to take (sb.) to counsel with, consult with (sb.)'. *Bruce*, xii. 389.

Take to rede (Sykes, 21) 'to take (sb.) to counsel with, consult with (sb.)'. *St. Nicolas* (Delius), p. 92.

Take to seruice (39) 'receive (sb.) into (one's) service'. **a1425 (?a1400)** *RRose* (Htrn) 6062.

Take to thank (57) 'be gratified by'. **a1400 (c1303)** Mannyng *HS* 12530.

Take to wife (Sykes, 21) 'take (sb.) as (one's) wife'. *Horn*, 536.

Take to the verrei valeu (40) 'buy at a fair price' **(1423)** *RParl.* 4. 257b.

Take to wrath (57) 'be angry at (sth.)'. **a1400 (c1303)** Mannyng *HS* 780.

Cf. in OF:
Prendre a (bon) greit. (TL) *Poème mor* 298[a].
Prendre a avoé (TL) *SThom. W.* 476.
Prendre a conseil. (TL) *Villeh.* 20.
Prendre a gré (TL) *TL.* 414.
Prendre a ire (TL) *Joufr.* 2455.
Prendre a merci (TL) *Enf. Og.* 197.
Prendre a moiller (TL) *Chr. Ben. Fahlin* 40389.

Prendre a parole (TL) *Ch. lyon* 6398.
Prendre a pris (TL) *Atre per.* 4337.

Some of these phrasals made their way into ME, e.g.:
Take to heart (< OF *prendre a coeur*).
Take to ill (< OF *prendre a mal, prendre a tort*).
Take to mercy (< OF *prendre a merci*).
Take to purpose (< OF *prendre a conseil*).
Take to ransom (< OF *prendre a rançon*).
Take to rede (< OF *prendre a conseil*).
Take to wrath (< OF *prendre a ire*).

There are also French calques such as:
Take agref (amis) (57) 'take amiss' (*King Alis.*3785) from OF *prendre/tenir a grief*; *take agame* (57) 'to consider (sth.) as a joke' (h., C. *Mars*, 277) from OF *prendre a jeu*.
Take to also occurs as a calque from Latin **ad+prehendere** and **ad+sumo**. Consider: 'thou shalt take to' (L. adprehendes) **(c1384)** *WBible(1)* Mic.6.14; 'I shal take to the tree' (L. adsuman lignum) **(c1384)** *WBible(1)* Ezek. 37.19; 'The spirit took me to' (L. adsumpsit) **(c1384)** *WBible(1)* Ezek. 3.12.

The use of the 'light' verb *nime(n)/take(n)* + a 'prepositional deverbal' introduced by **to** began to appear in the second half of the fourteenth century, though most phrasals are not recorded until the fifteenth century.

It is important to emphasise that the preposition *to* is not used to indicate 'direction' or 'motion', but forms a single semasiological unit with the preceding verb. It should be noted that OE had no parallel patterns, but OF had. Thus, I conclude that the extensive use of this construction is rooted in the phrasal usage of *prendre*.

(c) *in*:

Take in (good) intent (Sykes, 20) 'accept with good grace'. *Alex* (Laud, 622) 336.
Take in (gret) worshipe (56) 'hold (sb.) in great esteem'. **a1500** *Chartier Treat. Hope* 90/26.
Take in a conseil (38) 'bring (sb.) before a council'. **c1425** *Bible SNT(1)* Deeds 5.27.
Take in a scorn (57) 'take (sth.) as an insult or as a mockery'. **c1440 (a1400)** *Eglam.* 68.
Take in bourde/game (57) 'take (sth.) as a jest'. **a1400** *Wycl.MPL.* 43.
Take in charge (66) 'undertake (sth.)'. **a1500 (?c1450)** *Merlin* 28.
Take in cure (39) 'take (sb.) under one's care or protection'. **?1425 (1380)** Chaucer, *Bo.* 2. pr. 3.29.
Take in despit (57) 'be disdainful of (sth.)'. **a1400** *Cursor* (Frf) 4619.
Take in disdeine (57) 'be disdainful of (sth.)'. **(c1387–95)** Chaucer, *CT.Prol.*A.789.

Take in displesaunce (57) 'be displeased with'. **(c1422)**. Hoccl. *Dial.* 270.

Take in ernest (57) 'take (sth.) seriously'. **c1440 (c1380)** Chaucer *HF* 822.

Take in felaushipe (39) 'take (sb.) for a fellow'.**c1475 (c1445)** Pecock *Donet* 61/15.

Take in frenshipe (39) 'take (sb.) for a friend'. **c1475 (c1445)** Pecock *Donet* 61/15.

Take in gre (43) 'accept with good grace'. **a1425 (?a1400)** *RRose* (Htrn) 4349.

Take in gref/grevinge (57) 'take (sth.) amiss'. **c1390** *In a Chirche* 35.

Take in hond (63) 'deliver (sb.); deliver (animals, goods, . .) into the possession of (sb.)'. **(a1382)** *WBible(1)* 30.35.

Take in hostage (32) 'take (sb.) into (one's) custody by putting up bail, go bail for (sb)'. **(c1384)** *WBible(1)* 1 Mac.11.62.

Take in kepinge (39) 'take (sb.) under one's care or protection'. **a1400** *Cursor* 20105.

Take in mercy (Sykes 20)) 'have a mercy on (sb.), be merciful to (sb.)'. *Bruce* xiv. 414.

Take in mirthe (48) 'bear (sth.) cheerfully'. **a1500 (?a1400)** *Firumb.(2)*856.

Take in pacience/tholemodnesse (48) 'bear (sth.) patiently'. **(c1385)** Chaucer, *CT.Kn.* A. 1084./ **c1400 (?c1308)** Davy *Dreams*, 157.

Take in pite (39) 'to be merciful to (sb.)'. **c1400 (?a1300)** *KAlex.*1896.

Take in pleie (57) 'take (sth.) as a jest'. **a1400** *Wycl.MPL.* 43.

Take in privete (38) 'take (sb.) aside privately'. **a1450** *SLeg.MPChr.* (StJ-C) 983.

Take in reputacioun (57) 'hold (sb.) or (sth.) in esteem'. **c1475** *Why Nun* 216.

Take in servise (39) 'receive (sb.) into one's service' **?a1425** *Chauliac (1)* Oa/b.

Take in thank (Sykes, 21) 'be gratified by'. *Bruce* xx. 176.

Take in vein (57) 'take (sth.) lightly'. **c1450 (a1400)** *Titus & V.*3103.

Take in ward (39) 'take (sb.) under one's care or protection'. **a1500** *Cursor* (Vsp) 16762.

Take in worth (43) 'accept with good grace'. **c1450 (1410)** Walton *Boeth.* p. 64.

Cf. in OF:

Prendre en (bon) gré (TL) *Gace de la Buigne*, 2802.

Prendre en (tel) haor/haur (TL) *SThom.W.*739.

Prendre en conduit (TL); *H Val* 682.

Prendre en corage (TL) *Rou*, III, 2932.

Prendre en cure (Sykes, 20) *Bu.de C.*, 1411.

Prendre en desdein (Sykes, 20) *St. Brandan*, 531.

Prendre en felonie (TL) *Escan.* 12800.

Prendre en garde (TL) *Mousk.* 27253.

Prendre en grief (TL) *Blancandin* 762.

Prendre en hé (TL) Godefr. de Bouillon, 857.

Prendre en het (TL) *GMuis* II. 146.

Prendre en mains (TL) *Rou*, III, 5357.

Prendre en mal (TL) *Erec.* 2471.

Prendre en pacience (Sykes, 21) *Juven. Ch.,* vi. 1380 (L).

Prendre en purpens (TL) *Benedeit St. Brendan* 39.
Prendre en vein (Sykes) Rubric, *Man. Pech.*f. 1311.

The flood of these phrasals consisting of the 'light' *nime(n)/take(n)* + a 'prepositional deverbal' introduced by **in** is first recorded by the close of the fourteenth century and early in the next century. This seems to prove that OE phrasal patterns such as *on gemynd niman* ('to bear in mind'), *on ýdel niman* ('take in vain') are not the immediate source of this late ME phrasal influx. In my opinion this process of forming new phrasals throughout the fifteenth century must be interpreted as French influence rather than a recuperation of OE constructions. My assertion is based on two main grounds: firstly, OE combinations such as *on gemynd* or *on ýdel* were freely used and were not limited to the verb *niman*, and when it occurred *niman* had true lexical meaning. Secondly, it is far too difficult to explain the discontinuity of their usage in the course of early ME. Furthermore, these phrasals began to appear in English just half a century after the great influx of French loan-words. Many of the expressions listed above include nouns which are clearly loan-words. It seems plausible that the introduction of foreign single words precedes the incorporation of foreign phrases, turns of speech, proverbial sayings and idioms.

To conclude, I believe that English had borrowed from French an important bulk of phrases and turns of speech which today are considered to be part of daily speech. In my opinion phrasal structures of this type must have been rather artificial and removed from everyday speech when they first appeared in late ME works. I base this conclusion on the fact that such phrases were not common in a contemporary specimen of colloquial speech, the *Towneley Plays* (cf. Appendix B). I thus suggest that most of them made their way into English via literature and the translation process, rather than through the natural process of social bilingual speech. It is worth noting that most ME literature is based on French patterns or French matter. Most of this phrasal borrowing was the natural product of translation and composition. I agree with Prins[13] when he asserts that 'many of the terms taken over by English were taken over in a certain context, in phrases and constructions which lent themselves either to complete or partial translation into English or complete transposition into English in the Romance form in which they were couched'.

---

13 Prins, 'French Influence', p. 39.

Appendix A:
('light' *nime(n)/take(n)* + a deverbal noun)[14]

Twelfth century

Nimen frume (MED 987[15]) 'take one's beginning, begin (at a place)'. **c1150 (?OE)** *PDidax.* 5/9.
F: *prendre comencement.*
TL: *Brut. Arn.* 3873.
Nimen geld/yeld/gyld (MED 987) 'levy a tax'. **a1121** *Peterb. Chron.*an. 1110
F: No example.

Thirteenth century

(a) Phrasal *Nimen/taken* + an English deverbal
Taken bisne at (bi, o,of); bisning bi (o); fore-bisne of (MED 54) 'learn a lesson from (sb. or sth.), take example from'. **?c1200** *Orm.* 14470:
F: *prendre essemple.*
TL: *MFce Fa.* 14.
BT: **Bysne niman be** 'to take example by, from', *Homl. Th.* i. 148, 5.
Nimen bote (MED 994) 'to make amends for one's sin'. **a1225 (?OE)** *Lamb. Hom.* 31.
F: *prendre amendise.*
TL: *Poème mor,* 105c.
Nimen deth (MED 990) 'die'. **a1200** *Body & S.(2)* 6/44.
F: *prendre decès/definement.*
TL: *Wace Vie SNicolas,* 73.
TOWN: 5/681; 10/4.
Nimen ende/endinge (MED 992) of happiness: 'to come to an end'. **c1225 (?c1200)** *SWard* 38/354.
F: *prendre cesse/fin/definement.*
TL: *Ph. Thaon Comp.* 2172.
TOWN: endying 7/299; 7/403.
Nimen fight (MED 992) 'to engage in battle'. **a1225 (?a1200) Lay.** *Brut* 172.

---

14 The corpus is based on the data provided by the medieval English and French dictionaries available (MED, Lit, G, TL, BT, BT-S, NED) and the works of Sykes and Prins. The first record is chronologically classified to show the dates at which new phrasal patterns made their way into English. A further classification includes the English or the Anglo-Norman provenance of the deverbal form. [Editor's note: this corpus does not include Anglo-Norman as a separate variety, nor does it draw on AND. It would be interesting to know whether the findings would have been modified by the incorporation of (or indeed exclusive use of) Anglo-Norman.]

15 The page number of the phrasal in the MED is included in brackets after the abbreviation as shown in the text (MED 987).

F: *prendre guerre, prendre strif.*
TL: *SThom. W* 2574.
Taken gete (MED 58) 'take notice of (sb. or sth.), pay attention to, observe'. **c1250** *Serm. St. Nich.* 65/86.
F: *prendre garde.*
TL: *Rose L* 13089.
Nimen geme/yeme (of) (MED 993) 'pay attention, take notice'. **a1225 (?OE)** *Lam. Hom.*
F: *prendre garde.*
TL: *Rose L* 13089.
Nimen gome/gume (MED 989) 'take a husband'. **c1225 (?c1200)** *HMaid.* 12/159.
F: *prendre mariage.*
TL: *Brut Arn.* 1579.
Nimen gram and onde (MED 990) 'become angry (toward sb.)'. **a1225 (OE)** *Ves. A. Hom. Init. Creat.* 223.
F: *prendre ire/tençon/haïne.*
TL: *Clig.* 4144. (Cf. F: *take ire* in Ch., *C. Mars,* 132).
This structure also occurs in OE as **graman niman** 'take offence, feel angry'.
BT: *Homl. Th.* i. 16.30.
Nimen frith (MED 992) 'make peace'. **a1225 (?a1200)** Lay. *Brut.* 6202.
F: *prendre pais.*
TL: *Ch. lyon* 5632.
This phrasal dates from OE: **frið niman wið** 'to make peace with'.
 BT: *Chr.* 867; Erl. 72, 17:868; Erl. 72, 29.
Nimen haven (MED 992) 'enter a harbor, reach port'. **a1225 (?a1200)** Lay. *Brut.* 17264.
F: *prendre port (et) terre.*
TL: *Alex.* 16e.
Taken hele / helthe / stat of helthe (MED40) 'regain health, be cured'. **?c1200** *Orm.* 5378.
F: no example.
Taken herberwe (MED 76) a) 'reach a haven (harbor); enter a harbor, put in at a haven'; b) of an army or a commander: 'make camp'; also refl.; c) 'take up lodging; also, in *fig.* context, of the devil: take up residence (in sb.)'; d) (MED 63) 'offer shelter, provide lodgings' a) **c1275 (?a1200)** Lay. *Brut* 14411; b) **1275 (?a1200)** Lay. *Brut* 3977; c) **c1330** *Orfeo* 41/484; d) **a1325 (c1250)** *Gen. & Ex.* 1391.
F: *prendre herbergement/herbergerie.*
TL: *MFce Lais Chv* 34.
OE also records **Eard niman** 'to take up one's abode'.
BT: *P. Th.* 131. 15.
Nimen hethenshipe (MED 991) 'accept paganism'. **a1225 (?a1200)** Lay. *Brut.* 29190.
F: no example.

Nimen kinedom/kinehelm (the) (MED 988) 'assume the sovereignty over a country'. **a1225 (?a1200)** Lay. *Brut* 18158.

F: *Prendre corone.*

TL: *Rou* III 5965.

Cf. OE: *fon to rice.*

Nimen leve (at, of) (MED 991) 'to ask for and obtain permission (from sb.) to go'; 'take leave (of sb.)'. **a1225 (?a1200)** Lay. *Brut* 1271.

F: *prendre congé.*

TL: *Alex.* 120c.

Cf. OE **læaf niman**.

Nimen lond (MED 992) 'arrive, disembark'. **a1225 (?a1200)** Lay. *Brut* 9737.

F: *prendre terre.*

TL: *Alex.* 16e.

Nimen lord (MED 989) 'take a husband'. **a1225 (?a1200)** Lay. *Brut* 3021.

F: no example.

Taken lust of (toward) (MED 50) 'be filled with desire for (sth.), take pleasure in (sth.)'. **c1230 (?a1200)** *Ancr.* 31/17.

F: *prendre plaisance.*

TL: *BSeb.* XVI 773.

Nimen mede (MED 987) 'exact a fee (from sb)'. **a1225 (c1200)** *Vices & V.(1)* 79/6.

F: no example.

TOWN: 15/3.

Nimen mot (MED 994) 'to intercede (for sb.)'. **a1250** *Lofsong Lefdi* (Nero) 205.

F: no example.

Nimen name (MED 987) 'take a name'. **a1225** *Lamb.Hom. Pater N* 59/69.

F: no example.

Nimen pride (MED 990) 'become proud or arrogant'. **c1200** *Wor. Serm.* in *EGSt. 7* 29.

F: *prendre orgueil.*

TL: *Florimont* 4812.

Take rath bitwene (MED 54) 'take counsel among (themselves)'. **?c1200** *Orm.* 2368.

F: *prendre conseil.*

TL: *Troie* 24705.

Nimen red (MED 993) 'take counsel; also, give advice'; (994) 'make an agreement'. **a1225 (?a1200)** Lay. *Brut* 5345.

F: *prendre conseil.*

TL: *Troie* 24705.

Taken reste/restinge (MED 74) 'take (one's) rest, go to bed'. **?c1200** *Orm.* 6492.

F: *prendre repos.*

TL: *Clef d'Am.* 3.

TOWN: 5/580; 14/328; 16/24; 18/12.

Nimen right (MED 994) 'do justice to oneself through penance'. **a1225 (c1200)** *Vices & V.1* 125/29,30.

F: *prendre justise.*

TL: *Perc. H.* 8960.

Nimen (the) se (MED 992) 'embark on a sea voyage'. **a1225 (?a1200)** Lay. *Brut* 1281.

F: Fr. *prendre passage.*

TL: *Troie* 1804.

Nimen shrift (MED 994) 'confess one's sins, receive penance from a confessor'. **a1225 (? OE)** *Lamb. Hom.* 17.

F: *prendre penitence/confesse.*

TL: *Reimpr.* I 64.

Nimen warde (MED 993) 'keep watch'. **c1225 (?c1200)** *SWard* 6/54.

F: *prendre garde.*

TL: *Rose L* 13089.

Taken wei (MED 77) 'travel a road or path, go, set out on the way; proceed to go'; with inf.: **wei to wenden**, 'depart'. **a1325 (c1250)** *Gen. & Ex.* 1300.

Cf. F: *Prendre voiage.*

TL: *FCand. Sch.-G.* 13212.

BT: *Weg niman* 'to take, go one's way', *Cd. Th.* 80, 16; *Gen.* 1329.

TOWN: way 16/21.

Nimen wif (MED 989) 'take a woman in marriage'. **c1325 (c1250)** *Gen. & Ex.* 453.

F: *prendre feme.*

Sykes: Wace, *Brut*, 1489.

Sykes: Cf. OE, *niman wif.*, *Luke*, xx. 29.

BT: to gemæccan niman, *Cd. Th*, 76, 17; *Gen.* 1258.

Nimen wikinge (MED 987) 'settle, take up residence'. **a1225 (?a1200)** Lay. *Brut* 31861.

F: *prendre herbergement/herbergerie.*

TL: *MFce Lais Chv* 34.

Taken witnesse (MED 71) 'call someone (or sth., earth and heaven) to witness'. **a1325 (c1250)** *Gen. & Ex.* 4123

Cf. F: *traire a tesmoin.*

Sykes: *Aiol*, 10.

Nimen wrak (MED 992) 'take vengeance, inflict punishment'. **a1225 (?c1175)** *P. Mor.* (Lamb) 205.

F: *prendre venjance/vengement.*

TL: *Ch. Rol.* 1459.

TOWN: wreke (wrake) 'avenge' 10/195; 15/602.

wrath til (yen) (MED 50) 'be hostile toward (sb.), be resentful of'. **c1200** *Orm.* 19558.

F: *prendre ire.*

TL: *Clig.* 4144.

(b) Phrasal *nimen/taken* + a French deverbal

Nimen discipline (MED 994) 'undertake penitential exercises'. **a1225 (c1200)** *Vices & V.(1)* 125/29,30.
F: *prendre desipline.*
Sykes: Wace, *Brut* 14904.

Nimen mark (the cristes godes) (MED 994) 'receive the tonsure', enter a religious order'. **a1225 (c1200)** *Vices & V.(1)* 57/31.
F: no example.

Taken rites (MED 40) 'receive the last rites of the church'. **?c1200** *Orm* 9544.
F: no example.

Nimen venie (one's) (MED 994) 'make a penitential prostration'. **c1230 (?a1200)** *Ancr.* 29/20.
F: *prendre (sa) venie.*
Prins: *prendre sa venie.*
TOWN: *veniance* 4/393; 4/439.

Fourteenth century (1300–1350)

(a) Phrasal *nime/take* + an English deverbal:

Take ded (47) 'suffer death, die'. **a1400 (a1325)** *Cursor*(Frf) 21008.
F: *prendre decés/definement.*
TL: *Wace Vie SNicolas*, 73.
TOWN: *dede* 17/181.

Nime flight (992) of a dragon 'fly, take off'. **c1300 (?c1300)** *Bevis* 124/2641.
F: Fr. *prendre fuie.*
TL: *Benedeit S Brendan*, 1166.

Nime gestening/gestinge (987) 'take lodging'. **a1400 (a1325)** *Cursor* 11456.
F: *prendre herbergement/herbergerie.*
TL: *MFce Lais Chv* 34.

Take hed (58) 'take heed, take note, notice'. **c1325** *Lytel wotyt* 27.
F: *prendre cure/garde.*
TL: *Benedeit S Brendan*, 162.
Cf. *OE ware niman.*
BT: *Swt.* 52,16.
TOWN: 1/233; 2/174; 2/290; 3/75; 5/128; 5/603; 6/625; 7/157; 11/173; 15/290, 17/180–1.

Take herte to (unto) (63) 'give (one's) heart to (sb.), be devoted to; also, become an adherent of (Jesus, a personified vice)'. **a1325** *SLeg. Magd.(1)* (Corp-C) 52.
F: *prendre cuer.*
TL: *Jourd. Bl.* 2721.

Take husbonde (45) 'take (sb.) as a husband'. **c1300 (?c1225)** *Horn* 43/735.
French includes *prendre mariage, prendre espus.*
TL: *Brut Arn.* 1579.

Nime kep (993) 'pay attention, take notice'. **(a1333)** Shoreham *Poems* 100/72.

F: *prendre garde.*

TL: *Rose L* 13098. (TL).

TOWN: *kepe* (= 'prendre garde') 16/19.

Take kithinge with (54) 'recognise (sb.)'. **a1400 (?a1325)** *Cursor* 4817.

F: no example.

Nime lordshipe (988) 'assume rule (over a country)'. **?a1400 (a1338)** Mannyng *Chron. Pt.1* (Petyt) 36.

F: *prendre maistrie.*

Sykes: Wace, *Rou* i. 236.

Nime manreden (991) 'receive a pledge of fealty'. **(c1300)** *Havelok* 2265.

F: no example.

Take minde of (54) 'turn (one's) mind to (sb.), be mindful of'. **c1330 (?c1300)** *Spec.Guy* 619.

F: *prendre porpens.*

TL: *Benedeit S Brendan* 1093.

12) **Nime oth** (992) 'swear an (one's) oath'. **c1325 (c1300)** *Glo. Chron. A* 4795.

F: no example.

13) **Take pite of** (50) 'take pity on (sb. or sth.)'. **c1330 (?c1300)** *Guy(1)* 4656.

F: *prendre pitié.*

Prins: qu'il vous pregne pitié de (cf. *prendre mercie* = take mercy on).

14) **Take siknesse with** (47) 'catch a sikness from (sth.)'. **c1330 (?a1300)** *Arth. & M.* 64.

F: *prendre mal.*

TL: *Florimont* 8919.

Take skil (52) 'follow reason, act reasonably'. **?a1400 (a1338)** Mannyng *Chron. Pt. 2.* p. 184.

F: no example

Nime sorwe (990) 'experience sorrow'. **a1325 (c1250)** *Gen. & Ex.* 368.

F: *prendre nul confort.*

Sykes: *Couci* ix.

Take stede (75) 'have an effect on (sb.)'. **a1400 (a1325)** *Cursor* 29274.

F: no example.

Take stie (a) (77) 'take a path or road, go by a path, road'. **?a1400 (a1338)** Mannyng *Chron. Pt. 2* p. 319.

F: *prendre chemin/curs.*

Prins: *R. u. P.,* 5, 27.

Cf. OE: *weg niman* 'to take, go one's way'.

BT: *Cd. Th.* 80, 16; *Gen.* 1329.

Take strete (77) 'go on the way'; also with inf.: 'go forth (to do sth.)'. **a1400 (a1325)** *Cursor* 17643.

F: *prendre chemin/curs.*

Prins: *R. u. P.,* 5, 27.

Cf. OE: *weg niman* 'to take, go one's way'.

BT: *Cd. Th.* 80, 16; *Gen.* 1329.

Nime treues (992) 'make a truce'. **c1325 (c1300)** *Glo. Chron.A* 10005.
F: *prendre trieue(s)*.
TL: *Clig.* 3653.
Take trewth (43) 'accept (a woman's consent to marriage)'. **a1400 (c1303)**
Mannyng *HS* 8403.
F: no example.
Nime wei (992) 'make one's way'. **c1300** *SLeg. Becket* (Ld) 1980.
F: *prendre chemin/curs*.
Prins: *R. u. P.*, 5, 27.
OE: *weg niman* 'to take, go one's way'.
BT: *Cd. Th.* 80, 16; *Gen.* 1329.
Take wind (49) 'catch (one's) breath, take a breath'. **c1330 (?a1300)** *Arth. & M.*
9226.
F: *prendre l'air*.
Sykes: *God. de P.* 308.
Take wreche (74) 'to execute vengeance, take vengeance'. **c1300** *Evang.* 469.
F: *prendre venjance/vengement*.
TL: *Ch. Rol.* 1459.

(b) Phrasal *nime/take* + a French deverbal.
Take assaut (*MED* 66) 'make an attack'. **c1330 (?a1300)** *Tristrem* 1443
F: *prendre envaïe, prendre assalt*.
TL: *Troie* 9271.
Nime bataille (MED 992) 'join battle, engage in combat, make war'. **c1300**
SLeg.Mich. (LD) 46.
F: *prendre bataille*.
TL: *Gorm.* 157.
Nime bapteme/baptist (MED 994) 'receive or accept baptism'. **a1400 (a1325)**
Cursor 12831.
F: *prendre batesme*.
TL: *FCand. Sch.-G.* 968.
Take cark (53) 'assume an obligation or a responsibility, vouch'. **a1400 (a1325)**
Cursor 20790.
F: no example.
Take chastiinge (47) 'suffer castigation (penitential, chastisement)'. **a1400 (a1325)**
Cursor 28974.
F: *prendre penitence*.
TL: *Reimpr.* 1. 64.
Take chaunce (48) 'submit to (one's) fate, accept (one's) lot'. **c1330** *Le Freine* 113.
F: no example.
Nime coroune (988) 'assume the sovereignty over a country'. **c1330 (?a1300)** *Arth.*
& M. 2049
F: *prendre corone*.
TL: *Rou* III 5965.

Cf. OE: *fon to rice.*

Nime counseil (994) 'make an agreement'. **c1300** *Otuel* 335.

F: *prendre conseil.*

TL: *Troie* 24705.

OE: *niman to ræde.*

Nime crois (the) (992) 'go on a crusade'. **c1300** *SLeg. Becket* (Hrl) p. 1.

F: *prendre (la) croiz.*

TL: *Rou* III 9693.

Take cross, cross on honde (29) ' become a bishop or an archbishop'. **c1300** *SLeg. Becket* (Ld) 292.

F: no example.

Nime discipline (994) 'undertake penitential exercises'. **a1225 (c1200)** *Vices & V.(1)* 125/29,30.

F: *prendre desipline.*

Sykes: Wace, *Brut* 14904.

Nime dol (990) 'to cause suffering (to sb., to oneself)'. **c1300** *SLeg.* (Ld) 369/86.

F: no example.

Nime ensaumple at (bi, of) (993) 'imitate (sb.) as model of virtue; also, learn a lesson from sb. **c1300** *SLeg. Becket* (Ld) 2363.

F: *prendre essemple.*

TL: *MFce Fa.* 14.

OE: **Lare niman** 'to accept teaching'.

BT: *Salm. Kmbl.* 926; *Sal.* 462.

TOWN: *ensampyll* 4/718.

Take ese (74) 'take (one's) rest, rest oneself'. **c1330 (?a1300)** *Arth.& M.* 8209.

F: *prendre aise.*

G: Al. Char., *Con. trois v.*

Take feute (40) 'exact a public acknowledgment of fealty'. **?1400 (a1338)** Mannyng *Chron.Pt.* 2.3.

F: no example.

Take fin (47) 'suffer death, die'. **a1400 (a1325)** *Cursor* 21102.

F: *prendre decés/definement.*

TL: *Benedeit S Brendan* 738; TL: *Wace Vie SNicolas*, 73.

Nime forme (991) of a fetus: 'take on human shape or appearance'. **c1300** *SLeg.Mich.* (Ld) 716.

F: no example.

Nime habit (the) (994) a) 'put on a religious habit'. **c1300** *SLeg. Becket* (Ld) 1153.

F: *prendre dras/abit.*

Sykes: *Josaph.*, 114.

Nime hostage(s) (990) 'take (sb.) into custody as a hostage'. **c1330** *SMChron.* (Auch) 980.

F: no example.

Take hostel (76) 'take (one's) lodging, lodge'. **c1330 (?a1300)** *Guy(2)* p. 524.

F: *prendre ostel.*

TL: *Ch. lyon* 5148.

Take ordre(s) a) (53) 'take holy orders, be ordained'; **b)** of knight, **ordre and degre** of knighthode (53) 'become a knight'; **c) ordre** of prest, **ordre (testament)** of prest(hede) (53) 'be ordained priest'. **a)** c1330 *Otuel* 184. **b) (a1420)** Lydg. *TB* 3.2100. **c) (1357)** Gaytr. *LFCatech.* 68/339.

F: *prendre ordre.*

TL: *Rou* II 1756.

Nime pas (992) 'make one's way'. **c1330 (?a1300)** *Arth. & M.* 2526.

F: *prendre chemin/curs.*

Prins: *R. u. P.*, 5, 27.

OE: *weg niman* 'to take, go one's way'.

BT: *Cd. Th.* 80, 16; *Gen.* 1329.

Nime sojourninge (987) 'stop, stay in a place'. **c1400 (? a1300)** *KAlex.* 125.

F: *prendre sejor.*

TL: *Ch. Rol.* 3696.

Nime taillage (991) 'receive tallage'. **c1300** *SLeg. Becket* (Ld) 389.

F: no example.

Take talent (54) 'take a notion (to do sth.), form a desire (to do sth.)'. **a1400 (a1325)** *Cursor* 3913.

F: no example.

Take vengeaunce (74) 'to execute vengeance, take vengeance'. **a1400 (c1303)** Mannyng *HS* 5488.

F: *prendre venjance/vengement.*

TL: *Ch. Rol.* 1459.

Nime viage (992) 'make one's way'. **?a1400 (a1338)** Mannyng *Chron. Pt.1* (Petyt: Hearne) p. cxciii.

F: *prendre (son) voiage.*

TL: *FCand. Sch.-G.* 13212.

OE: *weg niman* 'to take, go one's way'.

BT: *Cd. Th.* 80, 16; *Gen.* 1329.

Fourteenth century (1350–1400)

(a) Phrasal *nime/take* + an English deverbal

Take amis (wrong) (MED 55) 'understand (sth.) wrongly, misinterpret'. **a1425 (?1384)** *Wycl. Church* 343.

F: no example.

Take beginninge (MED 75) 'take beginning, originate, begin'. **(c1385)** Chaucer *CT.Kn* A.3007.

F: *prendre comencement.*

TL: *Brut. Arn.* 3873.

Take birthe (MED 40) 'to receive (one's) birth, be born'. **(c1390)** Chaucer *CT.ML.* B. 192.

F: *prendre naissance.*

TL: *Barb. u. M.* III 140, 388.

Take bite (MED 36) of a spear: 'to strike a blow, hit'. **a1425 (?c1350)** *Ywain* 2444.

F: no example.

Take bolhede to (MED 50) 'to take boldness (corage) to (oneself), be emboldened, take heart'. **a1400 (a1325)** *Cursor* 27136.

F: *prendre corage.*

TL: *Florimont* 7725.

Take borwing (MED 43) 'to take a loan, borrow'. **(a1382)** *WBible (1)* (Bod 959) Prov.22.7.

F: no example.

Take breth (MED 49) 'catch (one's) breath, take a breath'. **(a1398)** *Trev.Barth.* 70b/b.

F: *prendre l'air.*

Sykes: *God. de P.* 308.

TOWN: *brede* ('breath') 12/346.

Take dai; day of accord (love), love-day (72) a) 'set a day (for doing sth.); b) 'appoint a day for reconciliation'.a) **c1440 (c1350)** *Octav. (1)* 159/1330. b) **?a1400 (a1338)** Mannyng *Chron.Pt 2* p. 51.

F: *prendre jo(u)r/terme.*

TL: *En.* 10010.

OE: *dæg settan.*

BT: *Ps*, Th., lxxv, 7.

Take dom (47) 'receive a sentence'. **(?1387)** Wimbledon *Serm.* 85/384.

F: *prendre jugement.*

TL: *Benedeit SBrendan*, 1254.

Take frendshipe to (63) 'to bestow friendship on (sb.)'. **c1380** *Firumb.(1)* 279.

F: no example.

Take gladnesse of (50) 'derive (one's) happiness from (sth.)'. **(a1393)** Gower *CA* 2.223.

F: *prendre confort/solaz/plaisance/déduis.*

Sykes: *Machault*, 135; 137.

Take halt (65) 'prevent (sb) from going'. **c1400 (?1380)** *Pearl* 1158.

F: no example.

Take hert (50) a) 'take heart, gain or regain courage, pluck up one's courage'; b) (43) 'accept (someone's love, amorous advances). a) **a1425 (c1385)** Chaucer *CT* 4.617. b) **(c1395)** Chaucer *CT.Sq.F.* 535.

F: *prendre corage.*

TL: *Florimont* 7725.

OE: *mod niman.*

BT: *Bd.* i. 16; S. 484, 15.

Take heven (49) 'behold the heavens'; – used in *fig.* context. **?a1425 (c1380)** Chaucer *Bo.* 1. pr.3.2.

F: no example.

Take hevinesse (50) 'take offence; also, feel sorrow'. **(a1393)** Gower *CA* 4.2937.

F: cf. *take sorrow.*

Take house (76) 'take up lodgings, lodge'. **c1390** *Evang.* (Vrn) 355.

F: cf. *prendre herbergerie/ostel.*

Take lif (40) **a)** 'be born'. **?a1425 (?c1350)** *NHom.(3) Pass.*2120. **b) lif** to (63) 'entrust (one's) life to (sb.)'. **a1400** *Cursor* (Trin-C) 7213.

F: *prendre (la) vie.*

Sykes: *Bu. de. C.,* 3792.

Cf. OE: *feorh beniman.*

Take logginge: a) (76) of an army or a commander, 'make camp'; also refl. **a1450 (c1410)** Lovel.*Merlin* 19814. **b)** (76) 'take up a defensive position'. **1448** *Glo.Chron.C* p. 451. **c)** (76) 'take (one's) lodging, lodge'. **(c1390)** Chaucer *CT.NP.*B.4185.

F: cf. *prendre herbergerie/ostel.*

Nime manhede (994) 'become incarnate' (cf. Sykes: *take humanity, take flesh*). **c1390** *Castle Love(1)* 919.

F: *prendre cors/humaine figure.*

Sykes: *Eneas,* 2886.

Cf. OE: *flæsc under-feng.*

Sykes: *Lives,* xxx. 64.

TOWN: *cors* 11/487/ *Take flesh & blode* (TOWN) 13/236/ *Take blode* (TOWN) 13/236.

Take sete (76) *refl* 'proceed to occupy a seat, seat oneself'. **a1375** *WPal.* 753.

F: *prendre estal.*

Sykes: *Ch. de R.,* 2139.

Take sight of (49) 'get view of (sth.)'. **(a1382)** *WBible(1)* (Bod 959) TL. 7.13.

F: no example.

Take skil (52) 'follow reason, act reasonably'. **?a1400 (a1338)** Mannyng *Chron. Pt. 2.* p. 184.

F: no example.

Take slep/slepinge (74) 'sleep, fall asleep'. **(c1385)** Chaucer *CT. Kn.* A. 1390.

F: *prendre som(e), someil.*

TL: *Ch. lyon* 2757.

Take speche on honde (69) 'use (one's) faculty of speech, use (one's) voice'. **(a1393)** Gower *CA* 5.3976.

F: *prendre parole.*

TL: *Rose L* 3255.

Take stede (75) 'have an effect on (sb.)' **a1400 (a1325)** *Cursor* 29274.

F: no example.

Take stie a) (77) 'take a path or road, go by a path road'. **?a1400 (a1338)** Mannyng *Chron. Pt. 2* p. 319.

F: *prendre chemin/curs.*

Prins: *R. u. P.,* 5, 27.

OE: *weg niman* 'to take, go one's way'.

BT: *Cd. Th.* 80, 16; *Gen.* 1329.

Nime strengthe (991) 'gain or regain one's strength'. **(a1382)** *WBible (1)* (Bod 959) Judg. 19.8.

F: *prendre corage.*

TL: *Florimont* 7725.

Take strife (66) 'join battle, engage in combat, make war'. **c1430 (c1386)** Chaucer *LGW* 595.

F: *prendre meslee.*

TL: *Narbon.* 4614.

Take strithe (77) *refle.* with in inf.: 'poise oneself (to do sth.)'. **c1400 (?c1390)** *Gawain* 2305.

F: no example.

Take thought (50) 'feel sorrow, be sad'. **(a1393)** Gower *CA* 4.2937.

F: cf. *prendre confort/solaz.*

Take tonge (69) 'use (one's) tongue'. **(a1382)** *WBible(1)* (Bod. 959) Jer. 23.31.

F: *prendre parole.*

TL: *Rose L* 3255.

Take trust of (50) 'trust (sb.)'. **(a1382)** *WBible(1)* (Bod 959).

F.cf. *prendre foi.*

TL: *Ch. lyon* 3290.

Nime wedes (994) 'put on apparel'. **c1390** *Castle Love(1)* 547.

Take wepenes (29) 'to take up weapons, join battle'. **(a1387)** Trev.*Higd.* 7301.

F: *prendre armes.*

Sykes: *Cligés*, 121.

OE: *wæpna niman.*

TB: *Swt.*, 44, 32.

Take wonder of (50) 'be shocked or surprised at (sth.)'. **c1400 (?a1350)** *Bytwene a pousend* p. 72.

F: no example.

Take woning (76) 'take (one's) lodging, lodge'. **c1390** *Evang.* (Vrn) 351.

F: *prendre herbergement/herbergerie.*

TL: *MFce Lais Chv* 34.

OE also records **Eard niman** 'to take up one's abode'.

BT: *P. Th.* 131. 15.

(b) Phrasal *nime/take* + a French deverbal

Take air (the) of a person 'to take in the fresh air, expose oneself to the fresh air, go outdoors for refreshment or recreation; of an object: be exposed to the air'. **(a1393)** Gower *CA* 3.1215.

F: *prendre l'air.*

Sykes: *God. de P.* 308.

Take amends (Sykes, 14) 'to amend'. *Bruce* XII, 382.

F: *prendre amendise.*

TL: *Poème mor*, 105c.

Nime arrai upon (MED 994) 'dress (oneself), put clothes on (oneself)'. **(a1393)** Gower *CA* 1.901.

F: *prendre draz*

Sykes: Gaimar, 1566.

Take aryvage / arivail(l)e (MED 76) 'land from the sea, come ashore'. **c1450 (c1380)** Chacer *HF* 223.

F: *prendre arivage/arivement.*

TL: *Barl. u. Jos.* 7402.

Take armure (MED 29) 'take up arms, join battle'. **(a1398)** Trev.*Barth.* 127 a/b.

F: *prendre armes/armur.*

Sykes: *Cligés*, 121.

OE: *wæpna niman.*

TB: *Swt.*, 44, 32.

Take avauntage (MED 40) 'receive a benefit (an advantage)'. **(a1393)** Gower *CA* 5.4425.

F: *prendre avantage.*

Sykes: *Yr.-Bk. Ed. I., p. 119 (anno 1292)*].

Take aventure (MED 48) 'take (one's) chances, accept (one') fate'. **(c1385)** Chaucer *CT Kn* A. 1186.

F: no example.

Take avys (MED 36) 'to take thought, ponder'. **(c1390)** Chaucer *CT.Mel.* B. 2916.

F: Fr. *prendre avis.*

G: Gen., *Best.*, B. M.

Take avisemente (MED 54) 'to take thought, ponder, reflect'. **(c1390)** Chaucer *CT.Mel.* B. 2941.

F: *prendre porpens.*

TL: *Benedeit S Brendan* 1093.

Take charge (53) 'assume an obligation or a responsibility, vouch'. **(1389)** *Lond. Gild. Ret.* in *Bk. Lond. E.* 47/87.

F: cf. *prendre foi.*

TL: *Ch. lyon* 3290.

Take chaumbre (76) 'take up residence in a chamber' **a1425 (?a1350)** *7 Sages (2)* 1521.

Cf. F: *prendre herbergement/herbergerie.*

TL: *MFce Lais Chv* 34.

Take chauninge of (47) 'be subject to alteration by (sth.), be altered by'. **(a1398)** *Trev.*Barth.* 106b/a.

F: no example.

Take chere on hond (50) 'become cheerful'. **(a1393)** Gower *CA* 1.1767.

F: no example.

Take comfort (50) 'take comfort, be comforted'. **(a1382)** *WBible (1)* (Bod 959) Josh. 18.

F: *prendre confort.*

Sykes: *Ch. d. N.*, ii. 25892.

Take conclusion (52) with **that** clause: decide (that one will do sth.). **(c1385)** Chaucer *CT.Kn.*A 2857.

F: no example.

Take conge of (to), – **conge and licence** of (36) 'request permission to go from (sb.); take (one's) leave of (sb.)'. **(c1378)** *PPl.B* (Ld) 13.202.

F: *prendre congié.*

TL: *Alex.* 120 c.

Take consolidacioun (40) of a wound: 'close up, heal'. **c1475 (1392)** *MS Wel.* 564 101a/a.

F: no example.

Take corrupcion (47) 'become infected'. **(a1398)** Trev.*Barth.* 64b/b.

F: no example.

Take cours(es) (77) 'to go on (one's) way'. **(a1387)** Trev. *Hidg.*2143.

F: *prendre curs.*

Sykes: *St. Brandan* 234.

OE: *weg niman* 'to take, go one's way'.

BT *Cd. Th.* 80, 16; *Gen.* 1329.

Take cure of (58) 'take note of (sb. or sth.), pay attention to (sb. or sth.). **(c1387–95)** Chaucer *CT. Prol.* A. 303.

F: *prendre cure (de..).*

TL: *Benedeit S Brendan* 162.

Take damage (47) 'suffer injury, be damaged; suffer a loss'. **(a1398)** *Trev.Barth.* 106b/b.

F: no example.

Take deliberacioun (54) 'confer together, consult with others, take counsel, deliberate together'. **(c1390)** Chaucer *CT. Mel* B.2977.

F: *prendre conseil.*

TL: *Troie* 24705.

Cf. OE *niman to ræde.*

Take displesaunce (of) (50) 'take offence at (sb. or sth.), feel rancor toward, be offended by'. **(c1390)** Chaucer *CT.Ph.* C.74.

F: no example.

OE: *Andan niman* 'to take umbrage, offence'.

TB: *Homl. Th.*i. 26, 21.

Take disport (74) 'take (one's) amusement, amuse oneself'. **(c1390)** Chaucer *CT.WB.*D.319.

F: *prendre plaisance/solaz.*

Sykes: *Machault*, 135; 137.

Take effect (75) 'produce an effect, have a result; *law.* come into force, become operative'. **(c1390)** Chaucer *CT.Pars.* I.607.

F: no example.

Take entente to (58) 'pay attention to (sb. or sth.)'. **(c1384)** *WBible(1)* Zech.1.4.

F: *prendre entente/cure/garde.*

TL: *Rose L* 13089.

TOWN: *intent* 4/10.

Take feute (40) 'exact a public acknowledgment of fealty'. **?1400 (a1338)** Mannyng *Chron.Pt.* 2.3.

F: no example.

Nime homage (991) 'receive a pledge of fealty'. **a1375** *WPal.* 1309.

F: no example.

Take impressioun (49) of a person: 'receive a mental image or an emotional impression'. **(c1390)** Chaucer *Ct.Mil.* A.3613.

F: no example.

Take ire for (50) 'be angered by (sth.)'. **c1450 (c1385)** Chaucer *Mars* 132.

F: *prendre ire.*

TL: *Clig.* 4144.

Take joie (50) 'be delighted, take pleasure; also, take (one's) pleasure'. **c1390** *NHom.Narrat.* 17.273/52.

F: *prendre plaisance/solaz.*

Sykes: *Machault*, 135; 137.

Tajen journei (77) 'set out on (one's) journey, make a journey'. **c1380** *Firumb.(1)* 4029.

F: *prendre (son) voiage.*

TL: *FCand. Sch.-G.* 13212.

OE: *Weg niman* 'to take, go one's way'.

BT: *Cd. Th.* 80, 16; *Gen.* 1329.

Take lessoun (40) 'receive a lesson, be taught a lesson'. **(a1398)** *Trev. Barth. 8a/a.*

F: *prendre leçon.*

TL: *Rose L* 4276.4277.

OE: **Lare niman** 'to accept teaching'.

TB: *Salm. Kmbl.* 926; *Sal.* 462.

Take meassure (72) 'take measurement, measure'. **?a1425 (?c1350)** *NHom.(3) Pass.* 2387.

F: no example.

Take morality (the) (54) 'draw the moral, elicit the spiritual significance (of sth.)'. **(c1390)** Chaucer *CT.NP.*B. 4630.

F: no example.

Take offense of (50) 'take offense at, (sth.), be offended by'. **(a1393)** Gower *CA* 1.2073.

F: no example.

OE: *Andan niman* 'to take umbrage, offence'.

TB: *Homl. Th.*i. 26, 21.

Take partie to (71) 'to refer one's cause to'. **?a1425 (?c1350)** *NHom.(3) Pass:* 1580.

F: no example.

Take part of (37) **a)** 'have a share in (sth.), partake of'. **b) part** (with) (47) 'suffer a fortune (with sb.), share (someone's lot)'. **a) (c1384)** *WBible(1)* Heb.2.14. **b) (1470)** Malory *Wks.* 1203/17–19.

F: *prendre part.*

Sykes: *A. N. Ch.*, i. 16.

TOWN: *(one's) parte* 8/559.

Take persoune (a) (65) 'be a respecter of persons, exhibit partiality'. **(a1382)** *WBible(1)* (Bod 959) Is.42.2.

F: no example.

Nime pes (992) 'attain peace'. **(a1393)** Gower *CA* prol. 982.

F: *prendre pais.*

TL: *Ch. lyon* 5632.

OE: *frið niman wið* 'to make peace with'.

BT: Chr. 867; Erl. 72, 17: 868; Erl. 72, 29.

Take possession (34) 'acquire territory, get control of a piece of property; gain a kingdom; also, gain possession of (sth.)'. **(a1393)** Gower *CA* prol.813.

F: no example.

Take pouere/power (53) 'assume authority'. **(1397)** *RParl*.3.379[a].

F: *prendre maistrie.*

Sykes: Wace, *Rou*, i. 236.

Take prei (34) 'seize booty, steal an object'. **(a1387)** Trev.*Higd.* 3.187.

F: no example.

Take prisoner (32) 'take a prisoner; also, take (sb.) prisoner'. **a1375** *WPal.* 1289.

F: no example.

Take purpos (52) 'resolve on a course of action, make a plan, adopt a course of action'. **(a1393)** Gower *CA* 5.7534.

F: no example.

Take querele: a) (66) 'undertake a battle'. **c1380** *Firumb.(1)* 668. b) **querele** ayenes (67) 'bring a lawsuit against (sb.), take legal action against'. **(a1393)** Gower *CA* 2.2702.

Cf. in F: *prendre estrif.*

TL: *Guil. d'A.* 593.

Take recet (76) 'take refuge, take shelter'. **c1400 (?c1380)** *Pearl* 1067.

Cf. in F: *prendre estage, prendre herbergerie.*

Take recorde at (of) a) (71) 'to call (Jesus, the sun, moon, heaven) to witness; also, cite (Jesus) as proof'. **c1400 (c1378)** *PPl.B* (Ld) 15.85. b) **recorde** on (71) 'cite the case of (a nation) as proof'. **(a1420)** Lydg. *TB* 4.4526.

F: *traire a tesmoin.*

Sykes: *Aiol*, 10.

Take remembraunce of (58) 'to take notice of (sb. or sth.), pay attention to, observe'. **(a1393)** Gower *CA* 1.1060.

Cf. *prendre entente/garde.*

Nime rent (991) 'receive rent (from a tenement)'. **a1400** *Usages Win.* p. 94.

F: no example.

Take repentaunce (50) 'feel remorse, be contrite'. **(1393)** Gower *CA* 3.803.

F: no example.

Take resoun (52) 'follow reason, act reasonably'. **(a1393)** Gower *CA* 5.7387.

F: no example.

Take savour in (50) 'take delight in (sth.)'. **(a1392)** Clanvowe *2 Ways* 68/457.

F: no example.

Take seisine/seisinge (34) 'take seizin, take possession or control; establish (one's) authority'. **(a1393)** Gower *CA* 7.564.

F: no example.

Take spouse/spousesse (45) *fig.* 'take as a spouse, espouse'. **(a1382)** *WBible(1)* (Bod 959) Wisd. 8.2.

F: *prendre feme.*

Sykes: Wace, *Brut*, 1489.

OE: *niman wif.*

BT: *Luke*, xx. 29.

See also OE *to gemæccan niman* 'to take to wife'.

BT: *Cd. Th*, 76, 17; *Gen.* 1258.

Take tenour in (71) 'draw the tenor of one's text from (another writer or text)'. **c1430 (c1386)** Chaucer *LGW* 928.

F: no example.

Take tente (58) 'to take notice of (sb. or sth.), pay attention to, observe'. **(a1382)** *WBible(1)* (Bod 959) Gen. 2 Par. 31.4.

Cf. in F: *prendre entente/cure/ garde.*

TOWN: *tent* 1/482; 1/587; 3/595; 6/400; 8/28; 10/180; 11/560; 12/224; 13/439; 14/251; 15/560; 17/60; 12/340.

Take torvaile (67) 'make an effort, take trouble; with inf.: take the trouble (to do sth.)'. **c1400 (?c1390)** *Gawain* 1540.

F: no example.

Take traine (66) 'undertake a trick'. **a1425 (?a1350)** *7 Sages(2)* 526.

F: no example.

Fifteenth century (1400–1450)

(a) Phrasal *nime/take* + an English deverbal:

Take answere (MED 65) 'to give an answer (to sb.). **c1450 (?c1400)** *3 KCol.(1)* 82/1.

F: no example.

Take aue of (MED 50) 'be respectful of (God)'. **(a1415)** *Wycl. Lantern* 95/15.

F: no example.

Take bilde (MED 76) 'to take (one's) abode, make (one's) residence'. **c1450 (a1425)** *MOTest.* 12219.

F: *prendre herbergement/herbergerie.*

TL: *MFce Lais Chv* 34.

Cf. OE **Eard niman** 'to take up one's abode'.

BT: *P. Th.* 131. 15.

Take bodi to religion (MED 38) 'to take (one's) body to the religious life, enter a religious order'. **(?a1439)** Lydg. *FP* 9.1596.

F: no example.

Take bourde for (MED 50) 'be amused at (sth.), be entertained by'. **(c1449)** Pecock *Repr.* 156.

F: no example.

Take brinke (MED 76) 'land from the sea, come ashore'. **c1425 (c1400)** *Ld.Troy* 4227.

F: *prendre saut.*

TL: *MFce Fa.* 74, 31.

Take cast (69) with inf.: 'to take (one's) opportunity (to do sth.), take occasion (to do sth.)'. **a1500 (?c1400)** *EToulouse* 455.

F: no example.

Take cold (a) (47) 'catch a chill, become pathologically cold or chilled'. **a1425** **Treat.Uroscopy* 125/141.

F: no example.

Take drede in (of) (50) 'feel apprehension about (sth.), be worried about'. **a1400** *Lanfranc* 173/15.

F: *prendre pëor.*

TL: *Clef. d'Am.* 947.

Take dwellinge (76) 'take (one's) abode, make (one's) residence'. **(a1420)** Lydg. *TB* 1.62.

F: *prendre herbergement/herbergerie.*

TL: *MFce Lais Chv* 34.

Cf. OE **Eard niman** 'to take up one's abode'.

BT: *P. Th.* 131. 15.

Take feith (51) 'to have faith'. **a1425** *Here begynnes a new* 37.

F: *prendre foi.*

TL: *Ch. lyon* 3290.

Take feld (a, the) (76) 'move onto the battlefield; also, engage in battle'. **(1425)** *Doc. Conspir: Hen.V* in *D.K.R.43* 591.

F: no example.

Take fir (44) 'to catch fire; also *fig.*' **(a1440)** Scrope *Othea* 34/14.

F: no example.

Take harm (47) 'sustain an injury, be injured or damaged, suffer harm'. **a1400** *Cursor* (Göt) 23089.

F: no example.

Take heuen to mede (40) 'receive heaven as (one's) reward, be rewarded with salvation'. **c1450 (c1415)** *Roy.Serm.* 202/20.

F: no example.

Take hold (78) 'occupy a temporary seat in a sign of the zodiac'. **(a1420)** Lydg. *TB* 2. 2380.

F: no example.

Take knouleche of (onto) (54) 'recognise (sb. or sth.); also, remember (sb.or sth.)'. **c1440 (?a1400)** *Perceval* 1052.

F: no example.

Take laughter (a) (74) 'laugh'. **a1450 (c1412)** Hoccl.*RP* 3400.
F: no example.
Take logginge: a) (76) of an army or a commander, 'make camp'; also refl. **a1450 (c1410)** Lovel.*Merlin* 19814. **b)** (76) 'take up a defensive position'. **1448** *Glo.Chron.C* p. 451.
F: no example.
Take love of (to) (50) 'fall in love with (sb.)'. **(c1440)** Scrope *Othea* 66/24.
F: no example.
OE: *Lufe niman* 'take an affection for'.
BT: *Homl. Th.* i. 342. 2.
Take meknesse (51) 'to take meekness to (oneself), practice in (one's) life'. **(?1439)** Lydg. *FP* 1.41.
F: no example.
Take nap (74) 'take a nap'. **a1425 (?a1400)** *RRose* (Htrn) 4005.
F: no example.
Take nedes (in place) (66) 'take action, undertake affairs'. **a1400** *Cursor* (Trin-C) 4795.
F: no example.
Take pul (66) 'make an attack'. **a1500 (?a1400)** *SLChrist* 5167.
F: no example.
Take reward (58) 'take heed, pay attention'. **a1475 (?a1430)** Lydg. *Pilgr.*1000.
F: no example. Cf., however, *prendre garde/cure/entente*.
Take stroke (a) (36) 'deal (sb.) a blow'. **(1448)** *Paston* 2.28.
F: no example.
Take water (76) 'put to sea; also, of an animal: plunge into water, take to the water'. **a1450 (c1410)** Lovel. *Grail* 50.63.
Cf. F: *prendre les eaux*.
Prins: prendre les eaux.
Take worshipe to (63) 'give worship to (sb.)'. **c1400** *Bk. Mother* 35/22.
F: no example.
Take wound (47) *fig.* 'suffer a wound of love'. **a1425 (?a1400)** *RRose* (Htrn) 1966.
F: no example.

(b) Phrasal *nime/take* + a French deverbal:
Take accioun ayenes (of, upon) (MED 67) 'bring a lawsuit against (sb.)'. **(1443)** *Doc. Trade* in *BRS 7* 77.
F: no example with *accioun*, cf., however, *prendre plait*.
Take armes (MED 29) 'take up arms, join battle'. **a1425 (?a1400)** *RRose* (Htrn) 7131.
F: *prendre armes*.
Sykes: Que d'autrui ne uuel armes prendre; *Cligés*, 121.
OE: *wǽpna niman*.
TB: Swt., 44, 32.

Take assai(e) (MED 66) 'undertake an examination of (sth.), consider (sth.)'. **c1475 (c1445)** Pecock *Donet* 54/14.

F: no example.

Take assuraunce (MED 40) 'to exact or receive a pledge'. **(a1420)** Lydg. *TB* 5.2288.

F: no example.

Take attendaunce/attente (MED 58) 'to take notice of (sb. or sth.), pay attention to'. **(c1443)** Pecock *Rule* 428.

F: *prendre escout.*

TL: *Barb, u. M.* III 394, 46.

Take availe (MED 40) 'receive a benefit (an advantage)'. **(1449)** *RParl.* 5.169ª.

F: no example. Cf., however, *prendre avantage.*

Take avys (MED 36) a) 'to obtain advice, get counsel; (52) b) follow the discretion or judgment (of sb.); (54) c) to take thought, ponder; (54) d) deliberate together, consult with others'. a). **(1428)** *Doc.* in *Sur. Soc.* 85 8. b). **a1500 (?a1400)** *Firumb.(2)* 360. c) **(c1390)** Chaucer *CT.Mel.* B. 2916. d) *ibid.* 2977.

F: *prendre avis.*

G: Gen., *Best.*, B. M.

Take banke (MED 76) 'land from the sea, come ashore'. **c1425 (c1400)** *Ld.Troy* 4227.

F: no example. Cf., however, *prendre terre.*

Take benefice (MED 40) 'receive a benefit (an advantage)'. **(1449)** *RParl.* 5.169a.

F: no example. Cf., however, *prendre avantage.*

Take cause (67) 'bring a lawsuit against (sb.), take legal action against'. **(1425)** *RParl.* 4. 298ª.

F: no example. Cf., however, *prendre jugement.*

Take compassioun (51) 'take upon (oneself) compassion, be compassionate'. **?a1425** *Orch.Syon* 233/25.

F: F: no example.

Take delectacioun of (50) 'take pleasure from (sth.)'. **a1500 (?c1425** *Spec.Sacer.* 91/27.

F: no example.

Take devoucioun (54) 'desire (to do sth.)'. **(c1440)** Scrope *Othea* 96/14.

F: no example.

Take disese (50) 'be unhappy, feel upset'. **a1450 (c1410)** Lovel. *Grail* 12.459.

F: no example. Cf., however, *prendre mal.*

Take distresse (74) 'to take the legal action of seizing goods, chattels, etc. as satisfaction for arrearage, damages, etc.'. **(1411)** *EEWills* 20/19.

F: no example.

Take eclipse (47) 'undergo eclipse; also *fig.* **a1425 (?a1400)** *RRose* (Htrn) 5334.

F: no example.

Take estat (65) 'give (to sb.) legal right or title to property'. **(1436)** *Paston* 2.5.

F: no example.

Take examinacioun of (67) 'conduct a formal investigation or interrogation of (sb.)'. **(1435)** *RParl.* 4.487a.
F: no example.

Take gage (65) 'provide (sb.) security for an agreement'. **c1460 (?c1400)** *Beryn* 3567.
F: no example.

Take garde (58) 'take notice of (sb. or sth.), pay attention to, observe'. **c1450 (c1400)** *Sultan Bab.* 2957.
F: *prendre garde.*
TL: *Rose L* 13089.

Take honour (53) 'assume an exalted position'. **c1450 (?a1400)** *SLChrist* 36.
F: no example.

Take juwise (65) 'pass sentence, give judgment'. **?a1450 (c1400)** *Siege Jerus.(1).*
F: *prendre jugement.*
TL: *Benedeit SBrendan* 1254.

Nime licence of (991) 'to ask for and obtain permission (from sb.) to go'. **(a1420)** Lydg. *TB* 1.2139.
F: no example.

Take mansioun (78) 'occupy a temporary seat in a sign of the zodiac'. **(?c1421)** Lydg. *ST* 11.
F: no example.

Take matere (79) with inf.: 'to have cause (to do sth.)'. **a1500 (c1410)** *Dives & P.* 1.239.
F: no example.

Take merci of (63) 'have mercy on (someone's soul)'. **(1439)** *RParl.* 5.29b.
F: *prendre grace, pitié.*
Sykes: *Ch. d. N.*, 568; Wace, *Nicholas*, 98.

Take obedience (51) 'take upon (oneself) obedience, be obedient'. **?a1425** *Orch.Syon* 385/23.
F: no example.

Take occasioun for (of) (69) 'take the opportunity for (sth., doing sth.)'. **a1500 (c1410)** *Dives & P.* 1.239.
F: no example.

Take palais (78) 'occupy a temporary seat in a sign of the zodiac'. **(?c1421)** Lydg.*ST* 11.
F: no example.

Take passage (77) 'go, make (one's) way'. **(a1420)** Lydg.*TB* 1.2843.
F: no example. Cf. *prendre passage* 'embark'.

Take plaine (the) (76) 'move onto the battlefield; also, engage in battle'.**c1450 (?c1400)** *Siege Milan* 1162.
F: no example.

Take ple (67) 'bring a suit'. **(1430–31)** *RParl.* 4.376a.
F: *prendre plait.*

Take pointe (72) *surg.* 'to make (a stitch to close a wound)'. **?a1425** **MS Htrn.95* 89a/b.
F: no example.

Take preve/proof of (66) 'undertake an examination of (sth.), consider (sth.)'. **c1475 (c1445)** Pecock *Donet* 54/14.
F: no example.

Take process ayenes (67) 'bring a lawsuit against (sb.), take legal action against'. **(1423)** *Pet.Sutton* in *Fenland NQ* 7 308.
F: no example. Cf. *prendre plait.*

Take proof (MED 66) 'undertake an examination of (sth.), consider (sth.)'. **c1475 (c1445)** Pecock *Donet* 54/14.
F: no example.

Take religioun (53) 'join a religious order'. **a1450 (1410)** *This holy tyme make* 121.
F: no example.

Take sacrament (40) 'receive the sacrament of baptism or matrimony'. **a1400** *Cursor* (Frf) 19531.
F: no example.

Take sojoure (78) 'occupy a temporary seat in a sign of the zodiac'. **(a1420)** Lydg. *TB* prol. 146.
F: no example.

Take souringe (47) 'of dough: to undergo leavening, be leavened'. **a1400** *Ancr.* (Pep) 2/25.
F: no example.

Take stat of penance (40) 'be penitent' **(c1440)** Scrope *Othea* 84/27.
Cf. in F: *prendre penitence.*
TL: *Reimpr.* I. 64.

Take sute ayen(s, (upon) (67) 'bring a lawsuit against (sb.), take legal action against'. **(1448)** *Shillingford* 68.
F: no example. Cf. *prendre plait.*

Take tirannie (51) 'take upon (oneself) sternness, be unmerciful'. **a1425** *Ben.Rule(1)* 43/13.
F: no example.

Take turn (77) 'depart'. **c1400** *St.Alex.(3)* 33/343.
F: *prendre tor.*
TL: *Gorm* 296.

Fifteenth century (1450–1500)

(a) Phrasal *nime/take* + an English deverbal:
Take abidinges (MED 76) *fig.* of the hearts: 'to dwell on (sth'). **a1450** *12 PTrib. (3)* 87/15.
Cf. in F: *prendre estage, prendre herbergerie.*
TL: *FCand. Sch.-G.* 9620.
Take bath (MED 74) *refl.* 'take a bath'. **a1450** *Rev. HWoman* 68/304.

F: no example.

Take bere (MED 44) 'to take (one's) manner, conduct oneself'. **(a1470)** Malory *Wks*.323/13.

F: no example.

Take boldnesse (MED 50) 'be emboldened'. **c1475** *Chartier Quad. (1)*.181/5.

F: no example. Cf., however, *prendre corage*.

Take gladinge (50) 'enjoy oneself'. **a1450** *SLeg.Suppl.Bod.* 407/65.

F: no example. Cf, however, *prendre plaisance*.

Take ground upon (54) 'base (sth.) on (sth.), base an argument upon (certain words); also, of an undertaking: be based upon (sth.)'. **a1500 (c1477)** Norton *OAlch.* 1219.

F: *prendre fonz.*

TL: *Mon. Guill.* 6617.

Take hope (50) 'have hope, be hopeful'. **c1475** *Chartier Quad (1)* 215/14.

F: no example.

Take met (72) 'take measurement, measure'. **c1450** **Vegetius (1)* (Dgb) p. 516.

F: no example.

Nime sted (992) 'take to horse'. **a1450** *Parton.(1)* 2968.

F: no example.

Take sword (29) 'take up a sword, join battle'. **a1500** *Sidrak & B.* 5518.

F: no example.

Take taste to (58) 'to take notice of (sb. or sth.), pay attention to, observe'. **a1450** *Castle Persev.* 1640.

F: no example. Cf., however, *prendre garde/cure/entente.*

Take tene to (58) 'to take notice of (sb. or sth.), pay attention to, observe'. **1592** *Chester Pl.* (Add) 2.154.

F: no example. Cf., however, *prendre garde/cure/entente.*

Take tripet (47) 'be tripped up'. **c1475** *Mankind* 113.

F: no example.

Take world to entente (50) 'embrace the world, be well disposed to wordly things'. **a1450** *Castle Persev.* 389.

F: no example.

(b) Phrasal *nime/take* + a French deverbal:

Take abstinence (MED 51) [Fr. *prendre abstinence*] 'to take abstinence to (oneself), practice in (one's) life'. **a1500** **Sidrak & B.*3605.

F: no example.

Take aggregacioun (MED 72) 'to add' [Fr. *prendre agregation**]. **c1450** *Art Number.*45/22.

F: no example.

Take carping (47) 'suffer (someone's) rebuke'. **a1450** *Castle Persev.* 201.

F: no example.

Take charite (51) 'take charity to (oneself), practice in (one's) life'. **a1500** **Sidrak & B.* 3605.

F: no example.

Take circumcisioun (40) 'be circumcised'. **a1500 (a1460)** *Towneley Pl.* 88/96.

F: no example.

Take corage upon (50) 'to take boldness (courage) to (oneself), be emboldened, take heart'. **a1500** *Chartier Treat.Hope* 101/28.

F: *prendre corage, reconfort.*

TL: *Florimont* 7725.

OE: *mōd niman.*

BT: *Bd.* i. 16; S. 484, 15.

Take credence (51) 'to have feith'. **?a1525 (?a1475)** *Play Sacr.*

F: no example.

Nime cristendom (994) 'receive or accept baptism'. **a1450** *St. Editha.*

F: *prendre crestïenté.*

TL: *Gaimar Estoire,* 1052. 1056.

Take delite (50) 'take pleasure from (sth.)'. **a1500** *Lo here is* 22.

F: no example. Cf., however, *prendre plaisance.*

Take discrecioun (52) 'follow the discretion or judgment (of sb.)'. **a1500 (a1475)** Ashby *Dicta* 726.

F: no example.

Take displesir with (50) 'be angry with (sb.)'. **c1460** *Lydg. TB Chapt.Headings* (Roy) p. 43.

F: no example.

Take doute (no) (54) 'have no doubt, rest assured'. **a1500 (c1477)** Norton *OAlch.* 878.

F: no example.

Take enquere / inquisicioun (67) 'make an official investigation, take evidence or depositions'. **(1460)** *RParl* 6. 5a.

F: no example.

Take enterprise (66) 'undertake a task or a military enterprise'. **a1500 (?c1450)** *Merlin* 3.

F: no example.

Take feith (40) 'exact or receive a formal pledge of fealty'. **a1450** *Gener.(1)* 9969.

F: no example.

Take force (no) (73) 'be indifferent, be unconcerned'. **(a1470)** Malory *Wks.* 65/25.

F: *prendre force.*

TL: *Lyon. Ys* 167.

Take hardiment (50) 'be emboldened'. **c1475** *Chartier Quad. (1).*181/5.

F: *prendre hardement.*

TL: *Ch. Lyon* 3172.

Take justice (65) 'administer justice'. **a1500** *Chartier Treat.Hope* 45/10.

F: *prendre justise.*

TL: *Perc. H.* 8960.

Take language (69) 'begin to talk', also, with adverbs. **c1475** *Chartier Quad.(1)* 175/12.

F: no example. Cf., however, *prendre (la) parole*.

Take memory (40) 'receive (good) memory'. **a1500** **Sidrak & B*.6069.

F: no example.

Take onde (49) 'catch (one's) breath, take a breath'. **a1500** *Add.37075 Gloss* 104/345a.

F: no example. Cf., however, *prendre l'air*.

Take pacience to (51) 'take patience to (oneself), practice in (one's) life'. **a1500** **Sidrak & B*. 3605.

F: no example.

Take parcialte ayen (50) 'be prejudiced against (sb.)'. **a1500 (?1451)** *Poem Waynflete* 94.

F: no example.

Take pleinte (67) 'bring a lawsuit against (sb.), take legal action against'. **(1455)** *RParl.FA* (Walbran) 58.

F: *prendre plait*.

TL: *Clig.* 4183.

Take plesire/plasure in (of) (50) 'take pleasure from (sth.)'. **c1475** *Abbrev.Trip.SSecr.* 338/21.

F: *prendre plasier/plaisance*

TL: *BSeb.* XVI 773.

Nime priorie (the) (994) 'take the rule of a priory (on oneself)'. **?c1450** *St. Cuth.* 2056.

F: no example.

Take recreacioun (74) 'relax, amuse oneself; also, of a nun: take a formal period of recreation'. **c1460** *Tree & Fruits HG* 15/5.

F: no example. Cf. *prendre plaisir*.

Take respecte unto a) (58) 'to take notice of (sb. or sth.), pay attention to, observe'. **(c1472)** *Grant Arms* in *Antiq.49* 289. b) **respect** (74) 'take a respite, make a pause, hold off action'. **c1450** *Alph.Tales* 155/9.

F: no example.

Take respite (74) 'take a respite, make a pause, hold off action'. **a1500** **Sidrak & B*. 10850.

F: *prendre respit*.

TL: *FCand. Sch.-G* 8660.

Take seintuarie (76) 'flee to sanctuary (in a church), claim sanctuary by fleeing to a church'. **(1454)** *RParl.5.* 248a.

F: no example.

Take sentence (47) 'receive a sentence'. **?c1450** in Aungier *Syon Mon.* 264.

F: no example.

Take serche (67) 'make an official investigation, take evidence or depositions'. **(1472–3)** *RParl.6.5a.*

F: no example.

Take spirit onto (50) 'get hold of oneself, control one's emotions, take one's courage in hand'. **c1450** *Alph. Tales* 57/26.

F: no example.

Take terme unto (40) 'be granted time until (a certain date)'. **c1450** *Ponthus* 90/32.
F: no example.

Take tonsure (43) 'receive the tonsure, be tonsured'. **(?c1450)** *St. Cuth.* 6412.
F: no example.

Appendix B:
Take-phrasals in the *Towneley Cycle*[16]

All the occurrences of a phrasal are also given.

Take blode: 13.236; **Take brede**: 12.346; **Take cors**: 11.487; **Take dede**: 17.181;
Take deth: 5.681; 10.4; **Take endying**: 7.299; 7.403; **Take ensampyll**: 4.718; **Take
flesh & blode**: 13.236; **Take a foyn**: 4.552; **Take gere**: 11.210; **Take hede**: 1.233;
2.174; 2.290; 3.75; 5.128; 5.603; 6.625; 7.157; 11.173; 15.290, 17.180–1;**Take
intent**: 4.10; **Take kepe**: 16.19; **Take mede**: 15.3; **Take pace**: 12.370; **Take (one's)
parte**: 8.559; **Take penance**: 12.252; **Take rest**: 5.580; 14.328; 16.24; 18.12; **Take
tent**:1.482; 1.587; 3.595; 6.400; 8.28; 10.180; 11.560; 12.224; 13.439; 14.251;
15.560; 17.60; 12.340; **Take the bore**: 8.150; 8.196; **Take the grace**: 5.373; **Take
veniance**: 4.393; 4.439; **Take wage**: 15.334; **Take way**: 16.21; **Take wreke**: 10.195;
15.602; **Take wyrk**: 2.238.

---

[16] M. Stevens and A. C. Cawley, eds, *The Towneley Plays*, I (Oxford, 1994).
   The plays are represented by a number in this Appendix: **1**. First Shepherds' Play; **2**. Second Shepherds' Play; **3**. Offering of the Magi; **4**. Herod; **5**. Conspiracy and Capture; **6**. Buffeting; **7**. Scourging;
   8. Crucifixion; **9**. Play of the Dice; **10**. Harrowing of Hell; **11**. Resurrection; **12**. Pilgrims; **13**. Ascen-
   sion; **14**. Murder of Abel; **15**. Judgment; **16**. Lazarus; **17**. Abraham; **18**. Jacob.

Code-Switching in Medical Texts

TONY HUNT

IT IS A COMMON, but erroneous, assumption that first language acquisition is principally, and most naturally, located in a monolingual community with a well-defined image of its language. The facts, however, suggest that, outside a few western societies with a strong sense of language identity and near-universal literacy, conditions which obviously did not obtain in medieval Britain, *multi*lingualism is the norm. Hence the linguistic description of medieval England, made by scholars tied to an exceptional, West European, viewpoint, has rarely been satisfactory and has been undertaken in almost complete ignorance of socio-linguistics. If language acquisition does takes place in a context of competing codes in a multilingual situation in which individuals accommodate their linguistic behaviour to that of groups with which they wish to be identified, or contrariwise, then the situation is inevitably one of great complexity, which will not surprise anyone familiar with contact linguistics and the world of bi-dialectalism, bilingualism, diglossia, borrowing, transfers, interference, shift, relexicalisation, pidginisation, and creolisation. Linguists have frequently sought to identify borrowings in the languages of medieval Britain, but in the context of multilingual societies it can be unrealistic to attempt to distinguish code-switching from borrowing. It is not, of course, to be expected that from the residue of the manuscript page one can penetrate the internal dynamics of the true linguistic situation any more than historians can readily obtain answers from documents to the questions which sociology bids them ask. But a sharper awareness of the problems and greater conceptual refinement can certainly prevent us from making crass errors, such as the belief that Anglo-Norman held sway for at least two centuries after the Conquest as the true vernacular of these isles.[1] As part of the study of multilingualism in medieval Britain the purpose of the present paper is to facilitate access to a new corpus of material and to a specific phenomenon characteristic of that material, namely to popular medical texts and the question of code-switching/-mixing. By 'popular' medicine I understand a medicine exclusively concerned with the therapeutic application of naturally occurring *materia medica* without recourse to theory or the

---

[1] W. Rothwell has done his best to combat this view in a long series of studies, for which see the bibliography in S. Gregory and D. A. Trotter, eds, *'De mot en mot': Aspects of Medieval Linguistics. Essays in honour of William Rothwell* (Cardiff, 1997), pp. xi–xiv.

written transmission of scientific learning[2] – in other words medicine which could never find a home in the university. Code-switching/-mixing is sometimes studied in terms of **contrast** and the specific effects intended by that contrast, especially when used as a rhetorical strategy, as in macaronic poetry.[3] On the other hand it is also possible to examine code-switching in terms of *lack* of language demarcation. Certainly, code-switching/-mixing may be used either to maintain or else to undermine language boundaries. It may conveniently be analysed into tag-switching (exclamations, interjections), *inter*sentential switching (where the switch occurs at a clause or sentence boundary) and *intra*sentential switching (where the switch occurs within the clause or sentence boundary). Full descriptive analysis will also cover the flagging or non-flagging of switch sites. In the Appendix this is indicated by the expressions 'marked' and 'unmarked' (i.e. for language). Consideration of possible morpho-syntactic constraints on code-switching, studied at length by Myers-Scotton,[4] is beyond the scope of the present contribution, as are numerous problems examined by recent linguistic investigators.[5]

Of course, the materials I am studying display only very simple examples of code-switching. It may be that the unmarked lexical items will be seen simply as loanwords, though Carol Eastman has suggested that 'efforts to distinguish code-switching, code-mixing and borrowing are doomed' and that 'in addition the study of loanwords *per se* out of context is a relic of the past'.[6] The debate concerning whether there is a system for distinguishing borrowed and code-switched lexemes is a continuing one. More extensive mixing may appear to retain a glossing function, but Romaine points out that whilst code-switching is frequently imagined to serve the purpose of filling lexical gaps, a belief often shared by bilingual speakers themselves, it is in fact very often used by speakers for terms which they know perfectly well in both languages, and, indeed, has as one of its commonest discourse functions that of repeating the same thing in both languages. Romaine concludes that 'Mixing and switching for fluent bilinguals is thus, in principle, no different from style-shifting to the monolingual.'[7] Another problem in relation to language marking is the question of naturalisation and, particularly, encysts, that is words naturalised as to use, but not as to form, inflexion or pronunciation e.g. *artetica passio*.

There has been little study of code-switching in a medieval context. In English the best studied area has been that of sermons and Siegfried Wenzel published in 1994 a study of 43 sermons in a mixture of English and Latin from the period

2   See Tony Hunt, *Popular Medicine in Thirteenth-Century England: Introduction and Texts* (Cambridge, 1990), p. ix.
3   See the strikingly virtuoso poem by Alexander Nequam printed in T. Hunt, 'Anecdota Anglo-Normannica', *The Yearbook of English Studies* 15 (1985) [1–17], pp. 13–14.
4   C. Myers-Scotton, *Duelling Languages: Grammatical Structure in Codeswitching* (Oxford, 1997).
5   See L. Milroy and P. Muysken, eds, *One Speaker, Two Languages: Cross-Disciplinary Perspectives on Code-Switching* (Cambridge, 1995); H. Giesbers, *Codeswitching: tussen dialect en standaardtaal* (Amsterdam, 1989); M. Heller, ed., *Codeswitching: Anthropological and Sociolinguistic Perspectives* (Berlin etc., 1988).
6   In C. M. Eastman, ed., *Codeswitching* (Clevedon etc., 1992), p. 1.
7   S. Romaine, *Bilingualism* (Oxford, 1989), p. 132.

1350–1450, in which the English element ranges from 2.28% of the whole sermon to 33.36%.[8] But even this expert scholar finds it difficult to identify a coherent system behind the phenomenon he is examining.

The principal corpus of medical receipt collections on which the present study is based comprises three unpublished compendia.[9]

1.   MS Oxford, Bodleian Library, Rawlinson C 814 (s.xiv[1]) ff. 33v–73v (index on ff. 9ra–11rb). This compendium contains 632 receipts of which 217 (34.3%) are in Latin, the rest in Anglo-Norman. Many of the receipts are extremely short (one line), a few extend to about one third of a page. The index is not included in the present enquiry.

2.   MS Cambridge, Corpus Christi College 388 (s.xiv) ff. 1ra–35vb. A compendium of 702 receipts of which 223 (31.5%) are in Latin, 226 (32.2%) in English, and 253 (36%) in French (a few are mixed) – an extraordinarily equal proportion. The languages tend to be represented in blocks or sequences. The range extends from a single line to half a page. Again, I have not included the index, but have cited the examples from the treatise on urines which precedes the receipt collection.

3.   MS Cambridge, Corpus Christi College 388 (s.xiv) ff. 36ra–48vb. A collection of 186 receipts: 185 in English, 1 in French. Once more I have not included the index.

For purposes of comparison I have drawn on two printed collections from MS London, British Library, Add. 15236 (c.1300).[10] The first collection, ff. 29r–39v (= A in Appendix) is mainly in Latin: 107 receipts in Latin against 13 in French (= 12.1%). The second collection, ff. 41r–90v (= B in Appendix), also mainly in Latin, contains, as printed by me (some exclusively Latin receipts *in a later hand* are omitted), and excluding the index, 176 receipts, of which 10 (5.6%) are in French.

The aim of the selection is to obtain evidence from different matrix languages, with some language mixing within the collections. On this occasion I leave aside translations: they involve special problems and tend to illustrate a specific function, the filling of a lexical gap in the vernacular by taking over the Latin, with or without morphological adaptation.[11]

There is, of course, the important qualification that the texts are essentially compilations and do not represent a single, continuous communicative exchange. Nevertheless, each corpus displays relatively consistent characteristics.

In seeking to sketch a simple taxonomy of switching I have identified three categories of material. The first category 'Synonyma' is referential, wholly content-related, in which the discourse function is plant identification. Within this category

---

8   *Macaronic Sermons: Bilingualism and Preaching in Late-Medieval England* (Ann Arbor, 1994).
9   I have an edition of all three in preparation.
10 Hunt, *Popular Medicine*, pp. 217–63.
11 See for examples the ME translation of Platearius's *Practica brevis* cited in T. Hunt, *Anglo-Norman Medicine*, vol. 1 (Cambridge, 1994), pp. 157f.

of botanical nomenclature may be distinguished four subsections. The first of these (1a), which I call compositorial, represents formulas which are the work of an author/compiler and which offer explicit, discursive explanations or guidance to plant identification, rather than possible scribal substitutions or synonymic glosses: the formulas follow the pattern 'une herbe que nus apelum . . .', 'une herbe ke est apelé . . .', 'une herbe qui ad (a) nun . . .', 'herba que dicitur . . .' – with or without a language marker, such as 'anglice', 'romanice', 'gallice', 'latine', 'en angleis'. As the next sub-category (1b) come interlinear glosses in the second language: these are, of course, commonplace in Latin herbals like that of Macer and in receipt collections are likely to be scribal, since they are not integrated in the text. The third subcategory (1c) comprises glosses, both unmarked and marked for language, which are integrated in the text. The distinction between marked and unmarked raises the difficult question of whether the appearance of the language marker is largely arbitrary or, on the contrary, significant in separating loan words (in the matrix text) from second language words. In particular, what are we to make of flagged 'switches' which are actually monolingual as in MS Corpus Christi 388 f. 19rb 'Tack þe modurwrt anglice "mougwed" ' (these are listed as alternatives in my *Plant Names*,[12] so that it is the 'anglice' that surprises); see also f. 19va 'Tac þe jus of maydeil anglice "heyhove" ', f. 22va and 'tack þe herdez, eie rose [?. . .] anglice "pisse" ', f. 24ra 'fri hem in seym anglice "gres" ', f. 32ra 'ȝif him to drincken serfoyl anglice "red hertistunge" ' and cf. BL Add. 15236 no. 52 'wodbynd .i. "wethwynd" '. The fourth category (1d) represents individual lexical items figuring as constituents in lists of ingredients, almost all of them plant names, unmarked for language, most of which might be considered loanwords (rather than as unflagged switches) with no suggestion of language boundaries.

The second major category is intersentential switching involving the rubric and text as switch sites.

The third category is represented by code-mixing, often intrasentential, which either extends beyond the single-word switch or involves words which are not the names of ingredients.

Before summarising the results of my investigation of each medical collection, I should like to illustrate a few questions concerning glossing which present problems. One question for investigation is consistency. How often are the same words glossed, are they glossed with the same equivalents, and are they marked or unmarked for language? This can be simply illustrated from a medical compilation I published some years ago, MS London, Wellcome Historical Medical Library 544 (s.xiv in) pp. 254–69 (hereafter W).[13] In W12 (see Appendix) the French words for Elecampane, Mugwort, Ground Ivy and an uncertain species have been glossed in English; in W16 three of these French names appear without glossing and again in W22, whilst in W28 one of them is glossed again. Determining the status of indi-

---

[12] T. Hunt, *Plant Names of Medieval England* (Cambridge, 1989) e.g. sub *artemisia* and *regina*.

[13] T. Hunt, 'Anglo-Norman Medical Receipts' in I. Short, ed., *Anglo-Norman Anniversary Essays* (London, 1993) [179–233], pp. 200–21.

vidual words as loans, transfers etc. is not easy. Thus, 'ambrosie' occurs six times, but is glossed only once ('ço est sauge sauvage'). 'Regal', otherwise unknown, is glossed 'id est cucukesmete' in one receipt, so when it recurs unglossed in the immediately following receipt we are not surprised. On the other hand, other, to us unfamilar words, e.g. 'okulescunse', seem never to be glossed at all despite the fact that in *Plant Names*[14] the vernacular equivalents provided by four synonyma lists were all different – evidently people just *thought* they knew what the plant was. Similarly 'gaudine' occurs no fewer than eight times unglossed, though none of the dictionaries have it, and once (W12) it is glossed 'ço est hove': 'hove' denotes Ground Ivy and the similarity of the form at least suggests the possibility that 'gaudine', except in its standard OF acceptation of wood, is a ghost word, a corruption of the English *grund ive* (in W21 it is next to 'ere arbrine'!).

Another question is the function of multiple glossing involving a switch, where we might consider the intention to be didactic, namely to teach other equivalents. Thus we have the occasional remark like (W61) 'triblé of "porniwort" [corr. peniwort] e cele herbe resemble herbe Robert' or (W95) 'prenge une herbe que hem apele synphoine / vel sinphele/' (identification very insecure), or in W12 'haune .i. "scabwort'" u "horselne" '.

A third question is the possible correlation between date and incidence of glossing. The earliest mixing I find is in a twelfth-century set of receipts (BL Royal 12 C XIX): 'Pernez la racine de l'amorosche, ço est "melden" en engleis', and (unmarked mixing) 'des ciuns de la runce e des cherlokes'. By the fifteenth century, of course, Anglo-Norman had lost its Special Language Status and hence ability to inhibit language shift and most receipt collections are monolingual and English. But in the fourteenth century everything is more complex and fluid and it is for this reason that I have based the present study on this 'hinge' period which is much less well represented in textual editions than the thirteenth or fifteenth centuries and offers particularly interesting evidence of language mixing.

The Appendix is designed to provide material for analysis, investigation and commentary. The present brief study can do no more than make a few general observations concerning the use of code-switching in the documents that I have transcribed.

1.   The first compendium is entirely in French and Latin, with no receipts in English, which is surprising considering the date of the compendium (or at least of the copy). What few English words there are are mostly unmarked for language. Code-mixing is very rare. Even the use of synonyms occurs only very sporadically. The Latin receipts tend to come in 'runs' or blocks. The languages are largely kept apart, that is there is not much in the way of transfers, assimilation etc. (though the fact that many of the synonymic glosses are not marked for language suggests a degree of assimilation).

[14]   P. 189 sub *oculus consulis.*

2. The second compendium is trilingual and displays a significantly greater incidence of marking for language. No mixing occurs in receipts written in English.

3. The third compendium is completely in English except for one receipt, which is in French with a Latin rubric.

4. MS Add. 15236 (A) There is little in French. The receipts are mostly Latin with notable free use of unmarked English vernacular terms, as if without language boundaries. There is only one marked gloss! Indeed, overall there is very little marking for language and almost no mixing apart from the straight plant lists.

5. MS Add. 15236 (B) Although the index covers both collections indiscriminately, what I identified as an originally independent collection emerges as clearly distinguished from (A) by a higher number of *marked* glosses, though the tendency to mix unmarked items in lists is still very strong. This second collection offers the most examples of code-mixing outside simple lists and provision of synonyma. It also, uniquely, provides three examples of the use of French as the glossing language in recipes in English.

Appendix

MS London, Wellcome Historical Medical Library 544 (ed. Hunt)

12. *Bon Beyvre*
Bon beivre a dertre e a gut[e] auere e a roine: Pernez moleine, avence, *haune .i. scabwort u horselne, e gaudine, ço est hove, hermoise, ço est mugwort*, roge ameroske, fenuil, luvesche, ruge parele, celidoine, cerfoil, milfoil, cheverefoil, *lumbre de fosse, ço est flectrit*, feverefui, fumetere, penewi[t], wimauve, bburguns de seu e de runce e de coddre e de tuiz oelement. Tribler of seu de mutun u de beste savage e bure. E faire quire en vin u en eysil e metre oile de olive e cire e encens bastard e franc encens e code e faire [en] mesmes la manere quire e aturner sicom est escrit en oygnement de plae.

16. *Pur r[oine]*
Pur roine e pur dertre e pur gut[e] auere e pur decratture [sic]: Pernez *la racine de haune* et la racine de la ruge parele e celidonie e *gaudine* e *lumbre de fosse* e luvesche e fenuil de deus maneres des racines – de(s) chascune une poignee – e del *lumbre* cinc poygnees et une pognee de savine. E (de) tribler of gresse de geline e seu de mutun et quire en eisil vermeil. E metez oile de olive e sufre vif e vif argent, e faites quire un petit.

22. *A dertre e a roygne*
[A] dertre, a roine e a teine: Pernez moleine, *haune, flectriz, gaudine*, la racine de la

ruge parele, tunmelde, rue, feverefoil, fumetere, ameroske, lovesche, fenuil, savine, burguns de coudre, l'enterus del neir pruner, coperuns de siu e de runce e cheverefoil.

28. [B]on beivre pur roine: Pernez moleine, avence, *haune, ço est horselne, gaudine*, hermoise – de chescon oelement – e quire en bel ewe of un poi de licoris deque la meité seit quit hors. E beivre el seir chaud e al matin freid.

MS Oxford, Bodl. Libr. Rawlinson C 814

1. Synonyma

1a Compositorial:

[Cf. monolingual pattern: accipe herbam que vocatur dens leonis (f. 36v)]
Accipe herbam vocatam anglice 'ravenesfot' .i. pes corvi . . . (f. 35v); Pernez une herbe que est apelé confirie (f. 40v); le felun que ad colour de saphir que est apelé noli me tangere (f. 45v); arthemesie que mater herbarum dicitur (f. 50r); Pernez un herbe que est apelé palma Christi (f. 52v); Pernez un herbe que est apelé nimpha aquatica (f. 53r); Pernez un herbe que ad nun muge dé bois (f. 55r).

1b Interlinear glosses: ——

1c Integrated glosses:

[Cf. monolingual pattern: Pernez fugerole .i. polipodie de chene (f. 41v); Ad idem valet herba sancti Cristofori .i. oculus Cristi (f. 44v); Arthemesia .i. mater herbarum (f. 56v); solitariam herbam .i. luciam (f. 59v); dragaunce que est apelé serpentine (f. 62v); le coperun de rounce que est apelé englenter (f. 64v); matecicle (?), ceo est cheverefoile (f. 67r).]

unmarked: folia persice .i. pecher tere et impone ut emplastrum (f. 39r); Quilez une bone partye de pruneles dé bois .i. slon . . . (f. 39v); Pernez la osmunde .i. horsehove . . . (f. 40r); Bevez la racine de fugere .i. farn (f. 41r); distempera cum berziza .i. wort (f. 42r); Triblez tresben l'ameroche .i. maithe (f. 42v); Item iacea nigra .i. martefelun (f. 44r); Superpone salem et vitellum .i. le moeal (f. 44v); . . . pone saponem .i. savun (f. 44v); Pernez maroil e seim .i. sope (f. 45v); Pernez chiverefoil, ceo est wodebinde (f. 47r); Ici comence medicine pur jauniz, contra ictericiam .i. jauniz: (f. 49v); Pernez la racine de yreos .i. glajol (f. 53r); Pernez archaungele .i. blinde nettle (f. 53v); Pernez chardon .i. souethistel (f. 54r); folia sambuci .i. ellerne (f. 56r); morele od sa baye .i. niȝteschode (f. 58r); Triblez la polipodie .i. evervarn de chene (f. 58r); Pernez sigillatam, ceo est seele, e frotez (f. 62r); launcelé .i. lanceolata vel quinquenervia (f. 68r); Aqua tartari sic fit .i. ewe de argoil (f. 71r); De signis lupi et cura .i. le lou (f. 71v).

marked: si le medlez ensemble od les pruneles anglice 'slon' (f. 39v); Ad lumbricos .i. vermes in ventre, anglice voca[n]t[ur] 'ffiches' (f. 42r); succus maricii .i. 'maithe' anglice (f. 44v); Pernez un herbe que ad nun muge dé bois .i. 'woderove' en engleis (f. 53r); seminis eruce .i. alba sinapis anglice 'hwit mustard-sed' (f. 55r); l'ulmentel que est apelé 'elm' en engleis (f. 57v).

1d   mixed lists (unmarked):
superpone et interim bibat oculescunse e morele (f. 38v); . . . de lange de chien e de heihove (f. 39r); Pernez thunderdokke e malve e les quisez en leit de vache (f. 42v); Pernez paritorie, horhune, grund-ivi, wormod e boilez ensemble (f. 43r); Pernetz sowthistel e triblez . . . (f. 44r); Pernez herbe beneite, ache e chikenemete (f. 46r); e le jus de sperewort . . . stoncrop e herbe Water (f. 49r); Pernez grecam urticam od planteine, si le destemprez (f. 50r); E chervile, hennebane ensement (verse, f. 52r); Pernez archaungele .i. blinde nettle, stonore [MS stomere], e lorele, betoine, turmen-tille, herbe beneite, saxifragie, gamalie, feliure, foile de coudre, þe rode [MS re rode] de honi-pere-tre, hayrive, violete grant, gyngivere, plaunteine, weybrode, launcelé, egremoine (f. 53v); escorche de ellerne . . . jubarbe .ii. unces, wort douce un galun (f. 54r); . . . la racine de gladene (f. 54r); . . . metre en le bain lemke e walwort (f. 56r); Recipe ache multum, fencresses multum, consoude, senchun, hove, crop de rouge urtye e de rouge cholet, herneles cum butiro recenti et sepo ovino conmisceantur (f. 56r/v); Accipe linguam canis, radicem gletonie et cerlange (f. 56v); Fac eam portare mugwort (f. 58v); Pernez turmentille, horoune, houndestonge e les triblez ensemble ben (f. 59r); Pernez malve e grundeswilie (f. 63r); primerole, cousloppe, avence, camamille, calketrappe, heyhove (f. 68r); de la parele de ewe e de la wilde clote e de la grant clote e de grundeswelie e braez ensemble (f. 68v); tanesie savage, wilde tasel, milfoile . . . celidoine, stichewort . . . urtie . . . (f. 69v); alum de glas (f. 71v).

2.   Rubrics

Ad oculos lacrimantes: Pernez un foile de cholet (f. 34v); Item contra tussim siccam: Pernez la semence de ache (f. 40r); Item a rancle: Marubium cum vino coque . . . (f. 46r); Item pro allopicia: Pernez la fente de chat e mel (f. 55r); Medicine encuntre la goute kaÿve: Mox ut ceciderit occide canem et extrahe fel eius (f. 59v); Pur suffrer de estre tranché ou ars sans grant grevance: Accipe radicem pionie et tere fortiter (f. 59v); Pur oster dens de la bouche sauns dolour: Si dentes canino lacte tetigeris, sine dolore cadent (f. 59v); Pur conustre quant l'em ne deit seyner ne pociun prendre par phisike: Tres sunt dies in quibus nulla necessitatis occasione liceat homini vel pecori sanguinem minuere (f. 60r); Unguentum pro salso fleumate: Recipe racine de fenoil, de peresil, de wymawe, de alisaundre (f. 62v); Ad faciendum claretum: Ewe de mel serra distillé par un alembic (f. 71r); Aqua lac virginis dicta pro scabie et salso fleumate: Pernez litarge e fetez pudre (f. 71v).

3. Mixing

Pro quibuscumque brisuris (f. 9rb); Ad occidend[um] feloun (f. 9va); Propter unum wenne (f. 9va/56v); si les destemprés od vin ou servoise; u ewe vive seit mis a quatre herbes desus ové la warence et ex liquido bibat paciens bis in die, et curabitur. Vel fiant pillule et custodiantur per annum. E si sur la playe viegne nule legere char . . . (f. 64v); Sume betoyne e selfhele, plantayne e eble e herbe Roberd e bugle e sanicle e pimpernele e menu ache e columbine e avence e quintefoile e sauge e averoigne e mel et omnia ista terantur simul in mortariolo (f. 64v); Pernez colofonie .ii. unces, piz e piz liquide ana unciam unam, olibanum, orpiment, aloum, terebentine ana uncias .ii. (f. 66r/v); Pernez oile de olive libram unam et semis, cire rouge uncias quatuor . . . (f. 67r); alum e mirre, armoniac ana unciam .i. (f. 67r).

Latinisations of vernacular terms: gromilium (f. 50v); plauntago (f. 56v); radix wimalve (f. 56v).

MS Cambridge, Corpus Christi College 388 ff. 1ra–35vb

1. Synonyma

1a Compositorial:
[Cf. monolingual pattern: le erbe ke est apellé orpyn (f. 10ra); Cape erbam que vocatur pes leonis (f. 10vb/11ra); pernez un herbe que est appelé symphonie (f. 14vb); pernés un erbe que est appellé ficoral (f. 15va); Pernés un herbe que crest en checun bruere que est appellé tormentine que porte un petyt flour jaune ow .iiii. foylez (f. 21ra); un herbe que est appellé burnette (f. 21rb); Pernez pessoun que est appellé roche (f. 33va).]

here te[re]estre, þat is heyhowe, e .viii. unces de puliole, þat ys hulwrt (f. 3ra); primeveyre ov tut le racine, ce este cowesloppez (f. 3rb); erbam Jovis que dicitur humlock (f. 4va); pernés aloyne, þat is wermod (ff. 13vb/14ra); contra illam infirmitatem que dicitur vulgariter 'ȝeskyngus' (f. 18rb); de le herbe que est apellé 'notisoda-berien' anglice (f. 21vb); un pere que est appellé 'flynt' (f. 22vb); hermoyse est en englez 'mogwed' (f. 24va) [Note: tack þe modurwrt anglice mougwed! (f. 19rb)]; ambrose, þat is wilde tanse (f. 27ra); cape erbam que vocatur walwrt (f. 29ra); cape erbam que vocatur mushere (f. 29rb).

1b Interlinear glosses:
launcelé [corr. l'aune]/anglice rue/(f. 8rb); un herbe que est appellé burnette/a. tunhove/ (f. 21rb).

1c Integrated glosses:
unmarked: [Treatise on urines: admisse vaccas lauri .i. coesloppes (f. 1vb).]

marked: accipe apium anglice 'ache' (f. 2rb); pernez wy de pomere anglice 'winballez' (f. 3rb); semense de cenevé anglice 'carloc-seid'; farine fabarum anglice 'flour-ben' [corr. ben-flour] (f. 3vb); radicem feniculi et levestici anglice 'þouþistele' (f. 4va); lessive de lis anglice 'lilie' (f. 6va); succum mente campestris anglice 'hormynte' (f. 6va); accipe viperam anglice 'lokechestre' qui cum multis pedibus vadit (f. 7rb); Item pur macle dé oys anglice 'howe' (f. 8rb); Item a le teye anglice 'pyn' medicine eprové (f. 8va); A l'oscureté dé oys anglice 'gluskynge' (f. 8vb); layvendulam anglice 'bynde' (f. 9vb); pevre anglice 'pepur' (f. 9vb); spigurnellam tritam anglice 'spurge' (f. 10rb); le feye de bef anglice 'galle' (f. 11vb); le seu de buck anglice 'gres' (f. 13rb); a veruis oster anglice 'wrottus' (f. 13rb); lavenenam [corr. lavendulam] anglice 'bynd' (f. 13va); Pernez erbe benet anglice 'humelock' (f. 13vb); accipe elenam campanam anglice 'horsheline' (f. 14rb); pernés de pé de puleyn anglice 'fole-foit' (f. 15rb); foyle de cabaline terrestre anglice 'ivi' (f. 15rb); doce de aly anglice 'garlek' (f. 15va); de mylueyne etscorché anglice 'hulwr[t]' (f. 16vb); sicudam viridem anglice 'humeloc' (f. 17va); succum vervenie anglice 'verveyne' (f. 17va); Item a clouus anglice 'biles' que levunt desure le corps de humme (f. 17vb); le umbryl anglice 'novele' (f. 18ra); Item pur culivures que sunt entur [corr. entré] le cors de humme anglice 'wirmus' (f. 18ra); contra nauseam anglice 'caste' (f. 18rb); semen cauli anglice 'wrte' (f. 19ra); radicem de paradella anglice 'docke' (f. 20ra); si garr[e]z le feye anglice 'galle' (f. 21rb); Pernez se que lé chaminnus(?) reunt de lour quiscine anglice 'squot' (f. 21vb); pur trenchivesouns anglice 'freit in þe wombe' (f. 22ra); feel de thor anglice 'galle' (f. 22rb); aly anglice 'garlec' (f. 23ra); cum sanguine vulpis anglice 'fox' (f. 23ra); semen tritum cum vino anglice 'senevey' bibat (f. 23va); ut penna viri erigatur anglice 'pyntul' (f. 24ra); in vadora anglice 'gravel' (f. 24rb); pernés jubarbe anglice 'husse-leck' (f. 28rb); viridem pinguedinem anglice 'vertegres' . . . picem anglice 'pick' (f. 29va); jus apii anglice 'hache' (f. 31rb); accipe stercus anseris anglice 'gander' (f. 31va); radices arundinis anglice 'reed' (f. 31va); Item valerianum, hoc est anglice 'wilde sethewale' (f. 32vb); Querez ambrose anglice 'wilde sauge' (f. 33va); pone in aqua anglice 'wyn-soppe' (f. 35rb).

1d   Mixed lists (unmarked):
[Treatise on urines: Cape succum de hellerne-beriun . . . succum de mousere (f. 1vb); liquiriciam et hertestunge (f. 2ra); postea accipe humlock (f. 2rb)]; Tac rose floures and fenkel and filago (f. 7va); le jus de wermod (f. 12ra); feniculum et walwrt (f. 14rb); succum de ache et de endive (f. 17va); radicem de glatenere (f. 20ra); succum de morel (f. 20ra); foyle de clote (f. 22vb); lyngua avis e cressoun de ewe (f. 23rb); succum de morel (f. 24ra); Pernez hayhove od sou de mutoun (f. 26ra); Pernés ribwrt e la foyle de cheverfoyle (f. 27va); faverolez que cressunt entur cressen (f. 27vb); pernez un yolke de oif crue (f. 28vb); solcicle e mariegolde (f. 28vb); e[st] bon pur feloun e pur brock (f. 28vb); Pernez smalache e folefot e treblés ben ensemble (f. 28vb); cape welwrt et semen lyn[i] (29rb).

2. Rubrics

Item pur le chef espurger: Tac pellestre and schou þe rote (f. 4vb); For bledyngge at te nese: Fac pulverem de ruta (f. 12rb); Item for wertes: Accipe sanguinem de pullis columbarum (f. 13va); Item pro manibus et ali[i]is menbris endormés: Fettez quire en veli serveyse (f. 14rb); Item pur le tusse: Gere super te spumam maris (f. 15vb); Item contra morbum cordis qui aufert ab homine affectum comestionis: Tac centurie and scith it wel (f. 16rb); Pro morbo cardialy: Tack unioun (f. 6va); Item pro appostamatibus infra corpus hominis vel foris quamvis sint dura: Tack webrede and erbe Johan and mushere (f. 20rb); Item for brusyng of lendes, ut si quis ab alto precipitetur: Millefolium cum aceto bibat et curabitur (f. 24vb); Item pur feloun garer: Accipe farinam frumenti (f. 28rb); Item for þe felun: Accipe solsequium et albumen ovi (f. 29ra); Item pro carne mortua: Tac þe curnele of þe walnote (f. 29ra); Item for þe felun: Accipe stercus porci (f. 31va); Item [pro] dolore ventris: Tac suþernewode and tansey et comede cum sale et exiet (f. 32vb); Item contra guttam ossis: Querez ambrose (f. 33va); Item ad guttam festinandam: Pernez pessoun (f. 33va).

3. Mixing

Hoc facto lokechestre vivens coque (f. 6va); un poyn de hawes (f. 6vb); alun de glas (f. 9va); vel infunde succum in naribus tuis de humelock (f. 11ra); folia de alisaunder (f. 13ra); Item pur etstancher sang: Ditez 'God was born in Beedlem and ifulled in þe flum Jurdan; as wis as þe floid witstoid, also stancche .N. þi blod' (f. 13ra); Pernez quit uyn e seym de pork marle (f. 13ra); pernez primerole e primeveyre ut supra in capitulo 'Pur dolour de chief' (f. 13vb); foyle de wilw (f. 13vb); Accipe hulwrt et tere, cum aqua misse et bibe (f. 16va); Tack rounceval anglice 'burre' (f. 17vb); succum de horune (f. 19vb); Asimus panis, wastel oþer simnel pissi et ponite in dulcedine (f. 19vb/20ra); Item a lez emeraudes: Pernés mulene-gras and stamp it weel wit freis schepus-talw e metez desure un launge a fundement, e il gara (f. 24rb); A comensement fettes spelkez de arbre ben acordans a les os brusés . . . desure lez spelkes (f. 25rb); Item a lé pees emflés ut superius habetur (f. 25va); pernés jubarbe anglice 'husse-leck', crowesipe, fane, tunhove, walwrt les treblez ensemble (f. 28rb); Item contractus que valent a le festre (f. 29rb); Sciendum est þer be tweie guttus festrez, þe ton cold, þe thoþer brennande hot (f. 30vb); Item [pro] dolore ventris: Tac suþernewode and tansey et comede cum sale et exiet (f. 32vb)

Mixed forms: smalagium (f. 14rb); emplaystrum (f. 24rb); respelkés (f. 25rb); serfolium (f. 28ra); plaistrum (f. 29rb); emplaystrum (f. 31rb).

MS Cambridge, Corpus Christi College 388 ff. 36ra–48vb

1. Synonyma

2. Rubrics

Contra maculas faciei: Pernés oyle que vent de porck (f. 48rb/va).

3. Mixing

E pus pernez la ruse de cherfoyle and wodebynde and vinegre e sape d'Etspayne (f. 48va).

MS London, British Library Add. 15236 ff. 29r–39v = A

1. Synonyma

1a Compositorial ——

1b Interlinear glosses:
consolidam minorem /.i. briswort/(18); pelusel /.i. mouser vel capillos Veneris .i. maydynher/ (25).

1c Integrated glosses:
unmarked: pentafilon .i. quintefoil, millefolium, linguam avis .i. bridistunge vel stichewrt . . . waranciam .i. madir (1); oint de jars .i. gandirsmere (3); semence de cressun du jardyn .i. tuncars (13); jus de ache .i. merche (13) de foliis lauri .i. lorer et origani .i. puliol real . . . de centaurea .i. cristisladdir . . . de ebulo .i. wallewrt . . . de peretro .i. peletre . . . de rafano .i. radich (37); cinerem radicum et foliorum ebuli .i. wallewrt (42); marubium .i. horhunne (52); edere terrestri .i. heyhove (62); Aloyn .i. warmot distempera cum aqua (73); succum marubii .i. horehunne (91).

marked: in dulcidrio anglice 'wrt' (78).

1d Mixed lists:
Persil-rote, fenoil-rote, radich-rote manipulum unum, violette, dayse, strowbery-wise, bugle, scabiose, musere, hertistunge, cetrac, pollitricum, adiantos manipulos duos, wallewrt-rote, fumetere, corticis sambuce manipulum semis. Terantur et coquantur (0); Accipe semen vel summitates canabi, summitates veprium rubeorum, summitates oleris rubei, summitates urtice rubee, tenesye, avence, herbe Johan, herbam Roberti, herbam Walteri, sanicle, plantaginem, consolidam minorem, pentafilon .i. quintefoil, millefolium, linguam avis .i. bridistunge vel stichewrt, bugle et ad pondus omnium istarum herbarum waranciam .i. madir (1); Flewrt,

herbe Robert, heyhove simul terantur et fiat emplastrum (2); Recipe egremoyn, columbinam et pinguedinem apri (6); Recipe de madir manipulos duos, ribbewrt manipulum unum, mugwrt manipulum unum, warmot unum, wodesur manipulos duos et bene terantur (17); corticis ebuli, mediam corticem sambuci, manipulos duos; violete, hertistunge, strouberywyse, mousere, herbe Jon, bugle, sanicle, maydenhere, cetrac, adiantos, de qualibet manipulum unum (30); Recipe fenyl-rote, persil-rote, violette, dayse, weybrede, hertistunge, musere, liverwrt, centorie, linary, bugle, sanicle, strowberywyse, warmot, cetrac, maydenhere, adiantos, de qualibet manipulum unum (31); Recipe de peniwrt manipulum unum et manipulos duos de watercars et simul terantur (32); Recipe mugwrt-rote, matefelum-rote, hertistunge, herbe Jon, musere, bugle, de qualibet manipulum unum (33); Recipe burnettam maiorem et southrinwde (35); Accipe dok-rote et rue et simul terantur (36); unam [libram] de foliis lauri .i. lorer et origani .i. puliol real, unam de cristisladdir, unam de bissopwrt, unam de gasir . . . (37); capiatur una libra de fumetere, alia libra de musere, tertia libra de spinacle (61); cum gromille et coque bene (71); Recipe mugwrt-rote, matefelun-rote, hertistunge, herbe Jon, rathele, bugle, de qualibet manipulum unum, wodesure manipulos tres (77); Recipe alisaundir-rote, persil-rote, fenil-rote, columbine-rote vel semen betonie, rue, ysop, eufrase, simul terantur (78); Recipe warmot et ova formicarum (80); Recipe summitatem matefelun (81); sume pedelyun et tere et pone super vulnus (83).

2.   Rubrics

Collirium electum pro occulis et pro albedine occulorum: Pernez une poigné de eufrase (10).

3.   Mixing

Pur fundure seu contra ydropisim qui accidit ex fundacione (0); Pur goute: Egremoyne, weybrede, musere, scabiose, carsin, warmot, pimpirnel .i. flewrt, heyhove, alisaundre, wodethunge, spinacle, herbe Jon, bremilcrop, red-cowilcrop. De hiis et butiro de mayo fit optimum unguentum pro gutta (4); U pernez greyn de centirgalle et metez chescun jour en l'eoil un greyn u deus u treis. Prescripta medicina valet contra albuginem occulorum (19).

MS London, British Library, Add. 15236 ff. 41r–90v = B

1.   Synonyma

1a   Compositorial:
non autem attirlobery quia attirloue dicitur ipsa herba seu folia, attirloubery dicitur ipse fructus (12); wodeþong sive yekesters quod idem est (64); folia illius herbe que vocatur walwort (112); Recipe herbam que vocatur mousgras vel horwey, quod idem

est (117); folia illius herbe que vocatur wallewort (121); cum succo illius herbe que vocatur walwort anglice (144); recipe herbam que vocatur violet (156); herbam que vocatur seynte Mary wort (158).

1b   Interlinear glosses:
siccorie /.i. roddis/ (39); recipe lymyk /.i.senekyl/ (64).

1c   Integrated glosses:
unmarked: umbilici Veneris .i. peniwort . . . occulorum populi .i. bourjuns de pepeler (3); urtidegres .i. brounewort maior (7); acetosum lac .i. sour milk (14); Item pro antrace .i. feloun (21); absinthium .i. warmot, morel .i. attirlouebery, apium .i. merche (29); succum ebule .i. walwort (32); lingua cervina .i. hertistong, violaria .i. violet, radices artamesie .i. mogwort-rotis, capillus Veneris .i. maydynher, centaurea .i. centory, solsequium .i. roddis (34); testudinem .i. snayl (37); petrosillini .i. persel-rotis manipulum semis . . . maratrum .i. fenyl-rotis . . . in dulcidruo .i. wort (39); pilocellam .i. lathyve vel mouser (46); mentastrum .i. horsmyntis . . . scolopendria .i. hertistong . . . scarioli .i. hyndhal . . . marol .i. horhound . . . epatik .i. livyrwort . . . enule campane .i. horsel, mater herbarum .i. mogwort . . . rubei tinctoris .i. madir (48); clavyr .i. samrock vel trifolium portans florem rubeum (52); sperge .i. pé de colum . . . warence .i. madir . . . caumbre .i. hennpe . . . rounce .i. bremmyl . . . urtye .i. netyl . . . hevyrferne .i. polipody (52); farinam de siligine .i. ry-mele (53); scero .i. wey vel pireta .i. puree (54); folia solsequii .i. roddis (57); alteam .i. wymawe (60); micas .i. miis (61); Contra albuginem occulorum .i. wyte et lipitudinem occulorum .i. bleriyne[s] et galyrsoul (79); pinguedo caponis .i. chappounysgres (79); croci .i. safran (80) de burnete .i. moderwort (82); malvam minorem .i. lityl hook (82) pro omnibus pistulis .i. bilis (82); teratur bene red may .i. huundefenyl (85); purnelys dé boys .i. slou (93); vers .s. anguiltwychis (95); apium .i. merche (108); ad uvam pendentem .i. strichil (109) super verticem capitis .i. mold (110); radicem [. . .] .i. poukspere (111); herbam grani solis .i. gromly (111); truncus quod est in medio radice .i. spir (112); potagium .i. hymmerolys (117); lé graundes formies .i. emotis (126); recipe archam angelicam .i. blyndenetil, agrymoniam .i. egyrmoyn, ditonia .i. dyttaundyr, peluseta .i. mouser (128); eruce .i. skyrwyttys (132); baucias crudas .i. pestirnepis (136); subscriptas herbas videlicet sourdokkys (138); pinguedo lactis .i. [c]reeme (138); e stipitibus fabarum combustis .i. de benhelme combustis (141); illud qod est grossum .i. ballis vel cnappis (141); fistulis et pistulis .i. bylys (142); auxugia porcina .i. wyt saym (142); una scutella .i. plateyn (142); pistulas .i. bylys (142); ad umbilicum .i. navyl (148); mentastrum .i. horsmyntis (151), herba Johannis .i. herbe Jon (151); subfumigatio .i. unum stu cum hiis herbis (152); malvam agrestis .i. smal-hokkys (153); in sepo porcino .i. wyt seym vel wyt gres (153); radicem altee recentem .i. rot of þe wymaw vel radicem accori .i. gladyn (153); cavilla pedis .i. ancle (153); febrifugam .i. fethirvoy (155); fistulam .i. festyr (156); radices flagris .i. seggys (157); assensum matricis .i. rakynggys (158); illiacam passionem .i. jaundiz (159); Recipe ysopum .i. ysop (160); pultes .i. potagium sive gruellum vel pappe (161); concussa .i. ystoneyd

(163); semen jusquiami .i. heneban (164); contra antracem .i. feloun (167); Recipe mussourounys .i. poukisthes qui crescit super sterquilinium .i. miskyn (170); cum sanguine vulpino .i. foxsis blode (171).

marked: Item pro malis casuris anglice .i. 'lithyr fallingys' (4); muel de buef anglice 'couhismarch' (7); si quisét ben en 'wort' anglice (9); lus crey, hibernicum nomen est (13); bursam pastoris anglice 'porswort' (14); rutam anglice 'ru' (15); sit inter duas scapulas anglice 'yhornid' (16); similam avenaticam anglice 'grittis' (18); capias anglice 'þe rede mosse of þe mor' cum aqua (19); pernez la racine de gletener graunt anglice 'muche clit' (23); pannum azorii coloris anglice 'blu cloth' (26); alveariam anglice 'a be off hive' (47); farinam de vermibus anglice 'wrmele' (53); omne genus prandii guttosum anglice 'goutouse' (55); cane anglice 'yhorydde' (57); *succum de heyrive gallice* 'glavelye' (82); *villis* 'cerfoyle' *gallice* (100); succus herbe qui vocatur 'walwort' anglice; de succo senecii sive cardui benedicti anglice 'groundyswyly' (145); aliquem motum ad modum vermiculi repentis anglice 'any stiryng as a crepinde worme' (156).

1d   Mixed lists (unmarked):

Recipe yeke[sters] sive wodeþong, heneban, ramnus, ysop, camamyl in equali proporcione (1); de subscriptis herbis, walwort, alizaundir, hockys, heyhove (6); Recipe mouser et bene teratur (8); Pernez linory, polipodi, racine de gladyne, violet, livyrwort, persoyl, fynoyl (9) Coquantur bene et diu helryn-rindis . . . betyn-rotis in equali proporcione sumantur, item hokkys quantum de duabus aliis (10); terentur herbe subscripte bene videlicet ribwort, weybred, attirloue (12); Recipe subscriptas herbas videlicet weybred, yarou, streberiwyse (13); non commedat carnes bovinas nec congruum nec anguillas nec lang nec ray (14); terentur herbe videlicet pervenk, stichewort (16); succum herbarum videlicet mouser, matfeloun, yarou, houndefenyl temperatarum cum vino (20); succum herbarum videlicet mouser, matfeloun (21); Recipe endive manipulum semis, violet manipulum unum, borage manipulum unum, maydynher manipulum semis, lyvyrwort manipulum unum . . . bugyl manipulum semis, polipody manipulum semis . . . linory manipulum unum (39); mentam rubeam manipulum unum, puliol real manipulum unum, tyme manipulum unum, puliol montan manipulum unum, ysopum manipulum unum, camamyl manipulum unum (49) Pernez bugyl, senekyl, pigyl, verveyne, betoyne, pimpirnol, herbe Water, herbe Johan, herbe Robert, herbe ive, flur of brome, spinakyl, wodsour, percepere, filago, turmentille, quintefoyl, burnet, croysry, fymter, hyndehale, pulleol montayne, plantayne, clavyr .i. samrok vel trifolium portans florem rubeum . . . mouser, milefoyl, valerian, eskeban, egremoyn, madefeloun, nepte, scabios, streberiwyse, sauge, ragwort, ribwort, wodbynd .i. wethwynd, dayce, primrol, croploeswort, dittoundir, tansey, sperge .i. pé de colum, horshunde, solsekyl, horpyn, violet, columbyn, wildnetil, le tendrun de warence .i. madir, le tendrun de caumbre .i. hennpe, le tendrun de rounce .i. bremmyl, le tendrun de urtye .i. netyl, le tendrun de ruge cholet, groundeswyly, hevyrferne .i. polipody, wodrove, filis, conferry, herbe coppi, dauke, dente de lyoun, lavandir, suthirnwodde, puleol real, avance – summa omnium herbarum 66. Item de istis omnibus herbis sit equalis proporcio . . . (52) Recipe hyndehale, merche de qualibet equaliter, folia solsequii .i. roddis in quarta proporcione respectu unius predictorum, ragydwort eodem modo, weybreed eodem modo, glassyn kylle eodem modo, bremylcroppis eodem modo, ribwort eodem modo, iste herbe terentur (57); teratur ru et minutatim (63); item vertgrys (64); manipulum unum de lorel, item manipulum unum de violet (66); folia de violet, horhound, ana (69); succum de heyreve et de burnete (77); Recipe croppis offe þe red netyl et heyreve in equali proporcione (78); ribwort manipulum unum, ben-levis manipulum unum (79); et etiam barchys-gres (79); Recipe warmot, red may, reed mynt, reed netlys, sage, halfwodde, fymeter (83); Accipe burnetam maiorem, southrinwode et herbam Roberti (88); Recipe salgiam, hindehale, watircars, primerole, piper, avencia, wythewynde, butirum de maii (89); radix matefeloun (96); Recipe warmot, centoyre, fumtere etc . . . ex hiis quatuor herbis videlicet mercuriali, luvache, fenil et celidoyn (98); petrocillum, gromyl ana (106); Recipe hundefenyl et medwort ana (110); urticam, mentam, warmot, hundefenyl (113); Recipe endive, maydynher ana (114); Recipe horsmynt, herb Jon ana (115); Recipe cropleswort vel brounwort, quod idem est (120); Recipe bremmylcrop, reed-coulcrop, hempcrop, reed-netilcrop, fenylcrop, tansy ana, maddyrcrop ad quantitatem omnium aliorum (122); recipe pimpirnol, bugyl, senekyl ana (123); aliis crescentibus in ortis vel pratis, smal-hokkys, roddis, warmot, weybred (138); Recipe warmot et teratur (139); de cineribus de wyche-hasil . . . de woodeactyn duas libras (141); cineres de wodacsyn (141); item de salpetyr (141); sumatur de eddyrgomme (141); nisi quod eddyrgomme fit artificiose de predicta arbore (141); sine turbentyn . . . sicut cum turbentyn (142); sumantur subscripte herbe videlicet goutfan, walwort, hokkys, heyhove, chikynmet (144); cum syndyr (144); cum hiis herbis .s. fenyl, smal-hokkys, holyhokkys, chikkynmette, heyhove (148); Recipe urticas, weybred, waterca[r]s (150); Recipe neptam, salgeam, pulliol real, ysopum, mentastrum .i. horsmyntis, verveyn, mogwort, askeban, herba Johannis .i. herbe Jon, maddyr (151); recipe camamyl et calamynt (152); in qua herbe bone sint cocte videlicet feniculum, heyove, lovage, chikynmet, walwort (153); Recipe rybwort (158); Recipe selvegren . . . teratur selvegren . . . .v. coclearia succi selvegren (159); Recipe askeban, ysop, briswort, confory . . . coquantur in aqua merche, hokkys, chikynmet, heyhove . . . recipe merche, lymyk, ana (163); Recipe yarou, feltwort, radices wymau, weybrede, sepum porcinum vel wyt sayme (165); sepum porcinum vel wyt sayme (166); Recipe betoyn, maddyr, roddis, bugyl, halfewodde ana (167); Recipe weybrede, wylde sage ana (169).

2. Rubrics

Item ut pili non crescant: Pernés lé graundes formies (126);
Ad idem: Pernez les eofs des formies (127).

3. Mixing

sic mixtas in diversis parvis sacculis galice en diverse peti pouchis pointe a la maner de un actoun . . . et cum fuerint cocti galice mettez un pouche apré un autir ausi chaute cum ele pust suffrire sur tote sa membre et sur la greynnour parti de sun quiis et sic semper utatur mulier talibus sacculis parvis calidis (13); Item pro morsu canis and lithir prikkyngys de ferro vel de aliis (15); Item pro omni genere inflationum anglice 'for al maner swolling and wreching' optimum emplastrum (18); minuat . . . usque 'ad swownyng' anglice (21); per cribra expulsa, hoc est 'ysiftyte' anglice (50); Item ad delendum morfeam sive lepram cutis anglice 'mool þat is oppe þe velle of manis body' (62); une poigné de merche et .i. de rathele et .i. de violet et .i. de bugle et .i. de conseude la petite et une de mouser et une de bugyl savage et .i. de celidone et .iii. poygnés de wodesour (92); Contra calculum, pur le gravel (93); Item contra jaundis (114); Item contra fluxum ventris et nedynggys quod est magna pena (117); cessabit fluxus et nedynggys (117); Item pro subbito assensu matricis, hoc est aþye þe verliche rakynggys off þe modyr to wommanhis hert (120); Pro gravi infirmitate . . . et similiter pro brook (138); de seminibus ipsius gladyn (140); habeat tres vel quatuor walmys (141); ab uno hypebon usque ad aliud hypebon (148); et illi cnappis frangantur bene (141); item de salpetyr dragme due, item de alym dragme due (141); pannus lineus ad modum blodebende (148); ita quod saculus extendat se a navyl usque ad os claustri pudoris et de uno hyppebon ad aliud hyppebon (153); de predicta herba þre croppis (155); et non solum cessabit rakynggys (158); Contra bottouns exeuntes sive etiam currentes sanguine sive etiam non currentes, precipue tamen contra bottouns sanguine fluentes et vocantur alio nomine etiam emoroide (164); Item contra brok (170).

Bills, Accounts, Inventories:
Everyday Trilingual Activities in the Business World of Later Medieval England

LAURA WRIGHT

A S THIS VOLUME is a celebration of multilingualism in later medieval Britain, the present paper is about a text type where a mixing of two or more languages is the norm: the text type of accounts and inventories. I will discuss the linguistic make-up of this mix of languages, concentrating on variation between two or more languages, and also language-internal variation. My purpose is to claim that variation is in itself a characteristic of the text-type. Of course, most medieval British text-types show some kind of written variation, such as spelling a given word in more than one way, or writing one section in one language and the next section in another. What is of particular interest about mixed-language business texts is that they used a rule-governed mixture of two or more languages, as I shall demonstrate.

I use a font that replicates the later medieval orthographic system[1] used in Britain, partly because this helps to demonstrate visually the amount of multilingual material there was in business writing in later medieval Britain; and partly so as to avoid imposing my own modern notions of what 'correct' medieval Latin or Anglo-Norman might have been like, and thus miss what is actually there. I will conclude that an appreciation of the multilingual content of business records leads to the perception of Britain not as a monolingual island, but as a multilingual part of the European trading area.

Business documents written in Britain in the later Middle Ages commonly make use of the medieval abbreviation and suspension system. The abbreviation and suspension system was used, to a greater or lesser extent, in all text types, but is particularly prevalent in accounts and inventories. An obvious function was to save

---

[1] A font replicating this, known as 'Record Type', used to be available but has fallen into disuse. By and large, it makes little difference to historians or literature students whether a medieval document is transcribed and published precisely as it appears on the page, or whether the process of editing tidies up the abbreviation and suspension signs found in most medieval manuscripts. Such readers are mainly interested in the sum of the meaning of the words contained in the manuscript. However, the historical linguist is interested in the form that those words take as well as their meaning, and to tidy up the form for publication, however easy that may be on the eye of the reader, does tamper with the historical evidence. The medieval abbreviation and suspension font used here was created by Stephen Miller, who at the time was working for the National Academic Typesetting Service, since disbanded, at the Oxford University Computing Service. The copyright is owned by Monotype.

parchment space, ink, time, and to facilitate line-justification, but there were further linguistic and interpretive advantages, as detailed below. Example 1 represents both the letters on the page and the abbreviation and suspension signs:

Example 1.
London, Corporation of London Records Office MS Bridge House Rental volume 3, (17D). 29 Sept 1460 x 29 Sept 1461, fo 34v.[2]

Eî p j vyle p acuacôe de leȝ Tide sawes empt' & remañ xij^d. Eî p j noua serra empt' p le Tidemañ & remañ in stauro pont' iijs iiijd. Eî pro quinque pailes & iiij^or scovpes empt' xxd Eî p j skeyne de Pakthrede empt' per Custoɗ batellaȝ vijd. Eî p j shodeshouell empt' iiijd. Eî p iij shouell treis empt' vjd. Eî p xiiij^a polles de fraxiû empt' p bedehokes inde fact' xijd. Et' p vj doß ix ℔ candelaȝ hoc anno empî & expñ tam in domo Compî q^a m inter Carpentar' & laboratores tempore yemali hoc anno p̃c cuiuslt ℔ jd. vjs ixd Eî p viriɗ Candel empt' & expñ ad festum Natiuitatis scī Johis Baptiste hoc anno iijd.

(And for 1 file for the sharpening of the tide saws bought and remaining 12d. And for 1 new saw bought for the tideman and remaining in the bridge store 3s 4d. And for 5 pails and 4 scoops bought 20d. And for 1 skein of packthread bought by the keeper of the boats 7d. And for 1 shod shovel bought 4d. And for 3 shovel trays bought 6d. And for 14 ash poles bought for manufacturing beadhooks 12d. And for 6 dozen 9 pound candle allowance this year bought and used both in the counting house and among the carpenters and labourers in winter time this year, price of each pound 1d – 6s 9d. And for green candles bought and used at the feast of the nativity of St John the Baptist this year 3d.)

This is an extract from the accounts of London Bridge. The bridge infrastructure required considerable maintainance and the tidemen were the employees who worked at low tide to repair the cutwaters (known as 'starlings') and piers, and clear them of debris. As is typical of accounts at this time, this extract was written in a mixture of medieval Latin and English. Medieval Latin was used for the closed-class function words and all other parts of speech, whereas English was optionally used for nouns, adjectives and deverbal nouns only (see *vyle, Tide sawes, Tidemân, pailes, scovpes, skeyne, Pakthrede, shodeshouell, shouell treis, polles, bedehokes, Candel*). Accounts clerks frequently used both languages for the same referent in close proximity, which happens here in the first line where both English *sawes* and Latin *serra* occur. Although the base language of accounts-keeping was either medieval Latin (as in the extract above) or Anglo-Norman, the abbreviation and suspension system served to background the Romance morphology and foreground the English, and Latin/English, stems. Thus it is not entirely essential that the reader should know how to decline the genitive plural of a noun like 'candela', as the symbol ȝ represented this morpheme, and it could easily be ignored in the sequence of graphs *candelaȝ*. The reader could interpret it as 'candle' or 'candelarum',

---

2   Note: translation in V. A. Harding and L. C. Wright, eds, *London Bridge: Selected Accounts and Rentals, 1381–1538*, London Record Society 31 (London, 1995), for the year 1994, p. 132.

according to competence and choice. As this text type obligatorily contained much English vocabulary, it is not only easy to read an English word like *Tidemân* as English, it is also easy to visually map the English words 'remain, custodian, carpenter, candle' onto *reman̄, Custoḍ, Carpentar̄, Candel̄*, and thus they are simultaneously interpretable as both Latin and English.

Some commentators have, in the past, condemned this kind of accounts-keeping Latin as 'degenerate' and linguistically inadequate.[3] I have elsewhere argued that far from being inadequate, it was a functional register, with its own internally-consistent grammar. An advantage of the abbreviation and suspension system was to facilitate the accurate reading and comprehending of business documents such as accounts and inventories, regardless of one's mother tongue or precise competence in Latin syntax and morphology. The phenomenon cannot fully be subsumed under the many kinds of codeswitching discussed by synchronic linguists,[4] because switching is compulsory in this text type, and regulated, although not predictable. That is, any noun, adjective or *-ing* form could surface in either English or a Romance language (Latin or French), but closed-class function words and finite verbs had to be in Romance, and Romance/English calques in close proximity were part of the makeup. Further, the switchpoints are not always identifiable, as clerks frequently used the abbreviation and suspension system to obscure the status of a word (as for example in *Carpentar̄*) above, which although morphologically explicit in that the abbreviation sign indicates a plural morpheme, is graphically both good medieval Latin and good late Middle English simultaneously). The best way, it seems to me, to deal with this regular and systematic enmeshing of medieval Latin or Anglo-Norman and English by means of the abbreviation and suspension system, is to regard it as a functional variety in its own right.[5]

---

3 For a summary, see L. C. Wright, 'The Records of Hanseatic Merchants: Ignorant, Sleepy or Degenerate?' in *Multilingua* 16/4, ed. E. H. Jahr and L. C. Wright (Berlin, 1997), pp. 337–49.

4 For a summary see L. C. Wright, 'Mixed-Language Business Writing: Five Hundred Years of Codeswitching', in *Language Change: Advances in Historical Sociolinguistics. Trends in Linguistics Studies and Monographs*, ed. E. H. Jahr (Berlin, 1998), pp. 99–117.

5 For further discussion of the morphological rules in medieval mixed-language writing, see H. Schendl, 'Text Types and Code-Switching in Medieval and Early Modern English', *Vienna English Working Papers* 5:1 and 2 (1996), pp. 50–62; H. Schendl, 'To London fro Kent/Sunt predia depopulantes: Code-Switching and Medieval English Macaronic Poems', *Vienna English Working Papers* 6:1 (1997), pp. 52–66; L. E. Voigts, 'What's the Word? Bilingualism in Late-Medieval England', *Speculum* 71 (1996), pp. 813–26; a series of studies by L. C. Wright: 'Macaronic Writing in a London Archive, 1380–1480', in *History of Englishes: New Methods and Interpretations in Historical Linguistics*, ed. M. Rissanen, O. Ihalainen, T. Nevalainen and I. Taavitsainen (Berlin, 1992), pp. 762–70; 'Early Modern London Business English', in *Studies in Early Modern English*, ed. D. Kastovsky (Berlin, 1994), pp. 449–65; 'A Hypothesis on the Structure of Macaronic Business Writing', in *Medieval Dialectology*, ed. J. Fisiak (Berlin, 1995), pp. 309–21; 'Trade between England and the Low Countries: Evidence from Historical Linguistics', in *England and the Low Countries in the Late Middle Ages*, ed. C. Barron and N. Saul (Woodbridge, 1995), pp. 169–79; 'Middle English *-ende* and *-ing*: A Possible Route to Grammaticalisation', in *Linguistic Change under Contact Conditions*, ed. J. Fisiak (Berlin, 1995). pp. 365–82; *Sources of London English: Medieval Thames Vocabulary* (Oxford, 1996); 'Medieval Latin, Anglo-Norman and Middle English in a London Text: An Inquisition of the River Thames, 1421', in *De Mot en Mot: Aspects of Medieval Linguistics. Essays in Honour of William Rothwell*, ed. S. Gregory and D. A. Trotter (Cardiff, 1997), pp. 223–60; 'The

If a modern editor were to expand all the abbreviation and suspension signs into 'correct' Classical Latin morphology, it would prevent the interpretation of the fused Latin/English as either English or medieval Latin according to choice, and it would also force a decision on expansion of signs which may be otiose, from an expander's point of view. For example, *Tidemañ* would presumably have to be rendered something like 'tidemann', yet word-final nasal consonants were frequently written with some kind of superscript flourish and it is not certain whether the flourish represented anything other than the end of a word. Belonging as we now do to societies that favour a single, correct orthography, any expansion of signs is likely to be consistent (that is, a sign like *p* is likely to be expanded by a modern editor to 'pro' each time it occurs, unless it occurs as a word-initial morpheme where 'por' might be preferred) regardless of the fact that medieval languages did not observe regular spelling conventions. This may not seem important with a sign like *p*, which cannot admit of too much variation, but a form like *doß* 'dozen' could have been spelled in full in numerous ways at the time. Most of all, it serves to obscure the fundamental variation of medieval texts. Almost every word would have at least a majority spelling and a minority spelling in a given hand, and the abbreviation and suspension system quickly multiplies the possibilies. A short word like *anno* could appear spelled in full, as here, or abbreviated to *año* or *a°*, whereas a long word like *bedehokes* could be spelled in several ways, even before considering abbreviations signs (such as the plural marker *-hokę*, for example). To represent all of these forms by a single modern rendition is to falsify the data for the historical linguist.

Languages are not 'pure' and distinct, but stem from historical systems which were partially shared with other languages. There is much overlap between medieval Latin and English on a lexical, morphological and syntactic level, because they are cognate languages which, theoretically, stemmed from the same protolanguage, or variants thereof. Subsequently, there has always been the potential for borrowing from the various dialects of one language to the other, and this has occurred in both directions to a greater or lesser extent at different points in time. Thus there are two kinds of overlap between the two languages for speakers at any point along the time continuum; those which are simply felt to be similarities, and those which are perceived to be recent borrowings.

Similarly, the mixed Latin/English of medieval accounts and inventories shows varying degrees of assimilation of English to Latin. Sometimes there is a full translation from English to Latin, sometimes there is a morphological addition of a Latin suffix by letter graphs to an English root, sometimes there is a morphological addition of a Latin suffix by an abbreviation or suspension sign, and sometimes there is no attempt to 'fit' the English word into the Latin background at all.[6] All of these

Records of Hanseatic Merchants' (n. 3, above); 'Mixed-Language Business Writing' (n. 4, above); 'Medieval Latin and Middle English Accounts: The Scandinavian Semicommunication Model', in *Language Contact in the History of English*, ed. D. Kastovsky (Berlin, forthcoming).

6   See Wright, 'Medieval Latin, Anglo-Norman and Middle English in a London Text' for a further discussion.

methods are an integral part of the linguistic makeup of the business account text type. Example 2 occurs overleaf from Example 1:

Example 2. [fo 36][7]

Eî ꝑ calibic' iiijᵒʳ tideaxes viijd. Eî ꝑ vylyng ij sarraꝯ nouaꝯ ꝑ le tidemañ xd. Eî Radulpho Reynold pictori ꝑ pictura signi Capitis Saraʒeni in Est Chepe xiijs iiijd. Eî eidm̄ ꝑ pictura signi Corone in teñ bras in Suthwerk xxs Eî Johi Copyñ founder ꝑ emend̦ vnius Cawdroñ de eneo ꝑ calefaccôe Cementi pro opib̦ʒ Cementar' viijs viijd. Eî ꝑ emendacôe de la Millespyndell molend̦ grani iuxta Stratford iiijs. Eî Rogero yoñ ꝑ euacuacôe xij doliat' st̄coꝯ de latrina in teñ ad macella scī Nichi capient' ꝑ qualt doliat' ijs viijd xxxijs

(And for steeling 4 tideaxes 8d. And for filing 2 new saws for the tideman 10d. And to Ralph Reynold, painter, for painting the sign of the Saracen's Head in East Cheap 13s 4d. And to the same for painting the sign of the Crown in the brewhouse in Southwark 20s. And to John Copyn, founder, for mending a cauldron of brass for heating cement for the masons' works 8s 8d. And for mending the mill spindle of the grain mill by Stratford 4s. And to Roger Yon for emptying 12 tuns of ordure from the latrine in the tenement at St Nicholas Shambles, taking for each tun 2s 8d – 32d.)

A full translation from English to Latin can be seen not only in the function words, verbs, nouns and adjectives such as *calibic'* 'steeling', *pictori* 'painter', *eneo* 'brass', and such inflexions as are rendered in full by letter graphs, but also in the tenement names *Capitis Saraʒeni* 'Saracen's Head', *Corone* 'Crown', and *macella scī Nichi* 'St Nicholas Shambles'. Business texts did not just interpolate English proper names and English words which were too technical to be translated into half-understood medieval Latin, as has sometimes been thought, as otherwise the clerk would not have bothered to translate such proper names (nor would Romance/English calques have been a typical feature).[8]

The adaptation of English to Latin by means of a suffix spelled out in full occurs in the words *signi* 'sign' and *Cementi* 'cement', and with a prefix in *emend̦* 'mend'. The technique was to choose the Latin word closest visually to the English form, so that the English reader merely has to concentrate on the root. The same principle is at work in *teñ* 'tenement', but instead of letter graphs, the word is assimilated to both languages by means of a suspension sign, which obscures the morphological information which would assign it to one or other language. And many of the words are not assimilated to Latin at all: *tideaxes, vylyng, tidemañ, founder, Cawdrôn, Millespyndell.* The first element of *Millespyndell* is calqued in the following stem *molend̦* 'mill-', and this is another common technique of this text type: to render compound nouns in English, but one of the elements of that compound nearby in Romance. It would have been perfectly possible to write a medieval Latin text that

---

[7] For translation see Harding and Wright, eds, *London Bridge*, pp. 134–5.
[8] Such calques are also a feature of pidgin languages, which typically evolve under the same circumstances as these trade accounts.

looked utterly unlike English, but it was the convention of this text type to have a close visual affinity with both languages.

I have tried to show that the expansion of medieval abbreviation and suspension signs may hide a linguistically salient feature of a text, and in particular, in the text type of business accounts and inventories, it would hide the syntactic underpinning of the text itself. There are many reasons as to why editors, even editors preparing texts for linguists, might fight shy of representation of such signs. We are taught, when learning Latin, that there is a correct Latin morphology. I have occasionally found scholars asserting that Ango-Norman scribes have got their grammar wrong, presumably on the basis of a knowledge of Anglo-Norman literature (which is not in itself morphologically uniform). So when confronted with Anglo-Norman and medieval Latin with abbreviated inflexions, the temptation is to replace the abbreviation with the 'correct' suffix – that is, it is part of the job of editing, and not to do so would somehow be cheating. But expansion of the abbreviation and suspension signs allows the modern editor to impose a spurious *uniformity* on a medieval text, because it is rare for an editor to choose to expand such signs in different ways on different occasions. The usual technique is for the editor to scan the text to see how a given abbreviation looks when it is spelled out in full (for example, to look through a hand to see how the scribe spells words with the sequence <pre-> or <prae-> or <per-> or <par-> when confronted with the *p* symbol in word-initial position, and to repeat that same expanded form each time the *p* symbol occurs). Yet medieval scribes did not adhere to spelling uniformity. Just because a scribe wrote <per-> on one line, was no reason for him not to write <par-> on the next.

To pursue the scenario of the modern editor who has decided to be inconsistent: such an editor would want to know what the rule for variable expansion was. What was it that caused a scribe to write <bedehokes> on one line and <beedhokys> on the next? Recently,[9] I analysed some Middle English morphological variation within a group of ten London documents, written for the same purpose and within three months of each other by seven scribes. I found that whilst the documents all showed differing amounts of variability, individual scribes had internally consistent morphological habits. That is, those scribes who wrote more than one document had stable ratios of variation across several documents. Thus, in the four documents written by Scribe A, Scribe A put an *-n* suffix on his verb infinitives [2%, 0%, 0%, 10%] of the time, whereas Scribe B put an *-n* suffix on his infinitives in the two documents that he wrote [54%, 57%] of the time. In the four documents written by Scribe A, past participles were prefixed [0%, 8%, 3%, 8%] of the time, whereas Scribe B put prefixes on his past participles [24%, 25%] of the time.

Traditionally, the dialectologist, upon seeing these results, might then seek to find out where the two scribes learned to write, and thus to explain the difference in morphological habit by means of geolinguistics. The difficulty with this approach is that it works best for dialects that admit of small amounts of variation (if there were

---

9   L. C. Wright, 'Middle English Variation: The London English Guild Certificates of 1388/9', in *Language Change: Advances in Historical Sociolinguistics*, ed. E. H. Jahr (Berlin, 1998), pp. 169–96.

any), and for text types that don't show dialect contact – obviously, this is not applicable to traders. One has to be careful, for example, not to end up claiming that all the London scribes originated from outside London, because of the large amount of variation found in their texts. The sociolinguist, on the other hand, is expecting to see variation within a dialect, however stable. Traditionally, the sociolinguist then tries to account for the variation as being determined by some kind of social grouping; for example, by age, class, or gender.[10] This approach is very hard to implement, because we don't usually have sufficient social information over such a historic time depth. Nonetheless, it may be that social groupings do explain why one scribe preferred a 5% ratio of -*n* suffixes on infinitives, and another scribe writing at the same place, time, and for the same purpose, preferred a 55% ratio. Only if the modern editor were master of such information could s/he begin to understand the rationale behind an individual's variability, and I suspect that if a modern editor *were* to have access to such information, the desire to suppress the variability would evaporate.

Finally, it is very difficult to assess the degree of assimilation of a borrowed word to a given language at a given point in time, whether that time be now or in the past. It is theoretically difficult to account for just how assimilated borrowings such as 'restaurant', 'palaver', 'kimono' are to present-day London English speakers, not least because the words belong to different fields – 'kimono' being restricted to Japanese-like garments, 'restaurant' being unmarked as to register but marked for some speakers as to pronunciation,[11] and 'palaver' belonging to an informal register and rarely seen in print outside journalism. Speakers may regard one, two or three as English, or one, two or three as borrowed, if they think about the matter at all. The unmarked term for older multiple-occupancy dwellings in Scottish cities is still 'tenement', but in English cities such buildings go by other names ('mansion block' in London, for example – another latinate term, if it is private, and 'council block' or just 'block' if not). Thus this word is now restricted for the English reader, but unmarked for the Scottish urban reader. Just how current or marked the word 'tenement' was to the medieval London speaker is not easy to assess, so when the abbreviation and suspension system allows the visual mapping of one language onto another, the reader has difficulty in deciding whether this is mere professional exploitation of cognate forms, or whether it tells us something about the vernacular of the time. The expansion of the abbreviations and suspensions in the mixed-language business text will always serve to 'latinise' the text, thereby possibly overlooking the fact that one medieval Latin term, with diachronic currency in English, has been preferred over another. In Example 1 the form *batellaꝫ* 'of the boats' contains the root *batel* 'boat', which is of Anglo-Norman, rather than medieval Latin, etymology. Does this mean that medieval Latin as constructed in London in

---

[10] See T. Nevalainen and H. Raumolin-Brunberg, eds, *Sociolinguistics and Language History: Studies Based on the Corpus of Early English Correspondence* (Amsterdam/Georgia, 1996) for a bold application of this theory to historical data.

[11] For some speakers, the Frenchness of 'restaurant' may still be marked by a word-final nasal vowel, as opposed to the more prevalent anglified version, realised either with an aspirated /t/ or a glottal stop.

1460 had borrowed and fully assimilated this Anglo-Norman term, or does it tell us that, like so many words of Anglo-Norman etymology, 'batel' had become part of the English vocabulary? Turning to contemporary documents to check the frequency of occurrence of the term in all three languages, we can verify that 'batel' was a word in medieval Latin, Anglo-Norman, and late Middle English. However, to what extent it was current in late Middle English, and in how many dialects and registers, is less easily recovered as a very large amount of data is needed before confident deductions can be made. I am not suggesting that limitation to one technical register somehow makes a word less important. Nobody speaks all the registers of English, but all the speakers speak several registers. Linguistically it is not justifiable to marginalise say, building terms, as historical dictionaries have tended to do in the past.

In sum, my suggestion that the abbreviation and suspension system be taken into account by the historical linguist is not a new point of departure, merely a reworking of what was already understood in the late nineteenth and early twentieth centuries. And I certainly don't insist upon it for users other than linguists. However, whilst it cannot resolve difficulties such as that just outlined, it may enable the linguist to rethink modern assumptions about the distinctions between these three medieval languages. There are dangers in ignoring variation (be it graphic, morphological, or between two or more languages). The main change from writing in later medieval Britain to Early Modern Britain is the development of Standard English, and the main feature of Standard English as compared to what went before is its comparative lack of variants. To ignore variation in business records is to risk losing sight of one of the pragmatic functions of business writing, that is, engagement in the activity of trade with speakers who did not necessarily have English as their mother tongue. 'Once established as a crossing point of the Thames, and as the focus of a road system, London was exceptionally well situated as a trading centre, with communications inland and, downstream, ready access to the trading networks of the North Sea and Channel coasts and to the river systems leading off them. The Rhine and the Seine were almost as important as the Thames to the early trading prosperity of London'.[12] So in this functional variety, the presence of medieval Latin, Anglo-Norman, and words derived from Middle Low German, Old Norse and other European languages, gives us information about the *social* circumstances of the skilled and professional person who was doing the writing.

---

12 D. Keene, 'Medieval London and its Region', *The London Journal* 14 (1989), p. 100.

Onefold Lexicography for a Manifold Problem?

FRANKWALT MÖHREN

SOME TIME AGO, during a couple of stormy days over the Channel, the front-page headline of an English newspaper read *Continent cut off*. To a continental this seems to be typical British humour: what is cut off is not the smaller part, but the lesser part. Everything depends on the point of view.

Let us see if we can transfer the observation to our field of investigation. The *Atlas of Forms and Constructions Drawn from French Charters* by Dees[1] includes the Walloon part of Belgium, but cuts out the British Isles and Ireland.[2] The *Revised Medieval Latin Word-List*, edited by Latham, registers and duly marks material from Gascony, but the Heidelberg *Dictionnaire onomasiologique de l'ancien gascon* omits these precious materials,[3] even though they are easily recognisable. Generally speaking, scholars from the British Isles cut the Continent off less readily than vice versa.

We could shift from the geographical sphere to the higher sphere of philology: and here too there are shortcuts. Studies of French neglect medieval Latin and Anglo-Norman, studies of English fail to include Anglo-Norman and medieval Latin, and so on. One example will suffice: Burgess, in an otherwise fine survey of Anglo-Norman in *Lexikon der romanistischen Linguistik* 2,2, 337–346, names desiderata like the study of the influence of English on Anglo-Norman, but fails to draw proper attention to medieval Latin.

If it is easy to observe deficiencies, it is difficult to advance an explanation. Our science, we hope, has been brought to maturity over the centuries. It started with Isidore, attained some peaks, for instance with Du Cange, whose *Glossarium* is nowadays believed to be a dictionary, but which, in fact, is an encyclopaedic glossary,[4] and our science reached summits with the OED and the FEW, for instance. These modern summae, especially the FEW, may give us a deceptive feeling of security, as we believe that they did really integrate all the knowledge obtainable at their time. In reality, the use made of the OED or of Du Cange in the FEW, for example, is

---

[1] A. Dees, *Atlas des formes et des constructions des chartes françaises*, 1980.
[2] DeesAtlas[2] – literary sources – includes Anglo-Norman.
[3] See D. A. Trotter, *De Mot en mot*, pp. 199–222, and 'Some Lexical Gleanings from Anglo-French Gascony', ZrP 114 (1998), pp. 53–72. The OED and the MED furnish Old French materials which have not been exploited fully, see for instance OF *haraz*, DEAF: Britt in OED, BibbF in MED, not known before AND.
[4] See Sharpe's article cited below, n. 8.

casual. Consequently, our own research has to go beyond these works, and this requires painstaking investigation. I am not sure that these times are fit for that challenge, times where serious labour is much less honoured than 'science-management' and showy events.

Yet, there are positive signs, especially in Great Britain. It is not just politeness that inspires me to say that recent works from British scholars show again and again the paths through the British multilingual jungle. We have all read from Rothwell's pen about Latin *clamare*, Anglo-Norman *clamer* and English *to claim*, about its semantic developments to be checked against Anglo-Latin,[5] and we have all learnt the lesson that Middle English borrowing from French is in fact borrowing from Anglo-Norman and that direct influence from the Continent is scarce.[6] On the other hand, there has been no isolation: potentially each and every continental French or Latin word may occur in Anglo-Norman or in Anglo-Latin or in English. All this has been said before on the British Isles and on the Continent, but the severe criticism advanced by Rothwell, Trotter and others provides sufficient proof that the easy, broad way, guaranteeing quick results, is far too attractive for most modern scholars.[7] Instead of arguing theoretically on behalf of scientific self-containment and the advantage of blinkers for effectiveness in output, let us examine together one simple example – just as medieval scholars did. We all know that it is easy to *behold* the *mote that is in thy brother's eye*, so, instead, I will try to *consider the beame that is in* mine *owne eye* (Mt 7,3, Auth. V.), by choosing a tiny article of the DEAF for a quick analysis.

Again, we will start on this side of the Channel. The British Latin loan-word *garillum*, meaning an outer barricade in castle fortifications, can nicely illustrate the wattle enclosing the different philologies. The word is Richard Sharpe's 'favourite example' of a functional borrowing 'formed by a clerk who needs to refer in Latin to something for which he knows no Latin word'.[8] Using the materials of the DMLBS,

---

5   Rothwell, *Journal of French Language Studies* 6 (1996) 198; 206. Cf. AN *abscission* – AL *abscisio* – ME *abscisioun* in D. A. Trotter, 'Les néologismes de l'anglo-normand et le FEW', in *Le Moyen Français* 39–41 (1996/1997), pp. 577–635.

6   Rothwell NM 97 (1997) 423–36. L. Wright, *Sources of London English*, has assimilated the message: she gives Anglo-Norman as the etymological source of English, but sometimes the River Thames's waters reach the Continent. One example: *gorce* 'a type of fishing weir' is said to stem from AF *gortz* 'stream, flood' (pp. 63–4). References: AND **gort** and OED (1706!). But DEAF G 1024 has furnished since 1989 the information (3°) that the sense is attested since c.1045 in Normandy, then in Raschi's glosses (Troyes), in Paris, and in Anglo-Norman.

7   Cf., as an example of former statements on these principles (besides the practice in the OED – to give an example), E. Weekley, 'Etymologies, Chiefly Anglo-French', in *Transactions of the Philological Society* (1907–10), pp. 288–331 (to be discussed again), or H. Käsmann, *Studien zum kirchlichen Wortschatz des Mittelenglischen, 1100–1350. Ein Beitrag zum Problem der Sprachmischung* (Tübingen, 1961). Seemingly, works like these are forgotten quickly, and rediscovered from time to time, or not, so that knowledge does not grow evenly. This is ineffective and inefficient.

8   R. Sharpe, 'Modern Dictionaries of Medieval Latin', in *Bilan et perspectives des études médiévales en Europe. Actes du premier Congrès européen d'Etudes Médiévales, Spoleto, 27–29 mai 1993*, ed. J. Hamesse (Louvain-la-Neuve, 1995), pp. 289–304, esp. p. 300. The topos of the defective knowledge of medieval speakers or authors is dangerous. For the current example see note 13 below.

Sharpe gives 33 occurrences of the word, dating from 1202 to 1319, and showing a broad (Sharpe says 'dramatic') variety of spellings, grammatical termination and gender. He thinks that the 'variations show clearly that the word in the mind of the clerks is a French word, though it is not recorded in the principal dictionaries of Old French' [301]. He only found one single example in the *Anglo-Norman Dictionary*, i.e. *garoil* in Walter of Bibbesworth, with the definition 'trap'. Even if our DEAF is not a 'principal dictionary of Old French', it does contain the word (and has done since 1974). Furthermore, Godefroy, Tobler-Lommatzsch and the FEW give the word, together with other examples and another meaning, namely 'banner'.

Now, let us view the matter from the other side of the wattle. The article in DEAF G 334 gives only the information found already in older dictionaries, especially that in the FEW where the word is classed amongst the materials of unknown origin.[9] Its 'etymology' adds only a misleading inspiration: 'Etymologie inconnue, probablement ancien anglais ou ancien nordique'. No use has been made of the *Revised Medieval Latin Word-List*, yet it is quoted elsewhere in that fascicle of the DEAF.[10] The overall result is an article that will have to be entirely replaced.

The case is of metalexicographical interest. The article (10 lines) fails to use the materials offered by the sources cited in the article itself. *Bibbesworth*, ed. A. Owen, 261; 266 is indicated, but the *varia lectio* and the glosses have not even been read.[11] *Femina*, ed. Wright, 7,9 and 110,9 are cited in DEAF, but not read or understood: line 7,9 gives the 'riddle', the two homonyms to be explained, the explanation follows in line 7,20: that is where the erroneous identification of *garoile* as *baner* comes from (*Homme fiche soun baner en terre Pur le barbycan defendre*; the text should have given *garoyle*, just as in 7,9). The correction to the definition 'banner', proposed for *Bibbesworth* by Vising, *Studia Neophilologica*, 15,203, relies on BibbF (his true object of study), not on *Bibbesworth* itself which is the original text; this error is now fixed in the DEAF. If Vising, or the DEAF, had read and understood both Bibb and BibbF, they could have recognised the word and the text and they could have explained the text of BibbF as unsatisfactory. (Note the methodological error of Vising, maintained in DEAF: he uses a difficult passage in a secondary version to correct a much clearer passage in an original version.) The third occurrence of the word, culled by Gdf from the *Plainte de Henry de Lacy* (also in BibbO, glossary), is given in DEAF without quotation. Again, the line quoted in Gdf (*Car de verre est vostre garoil*) has not been understood (nor was it by Gdf who gives '?' instead of a definition). Why has the source not been consulted? If one cannot understand a quotation, one cannot confirm the semantic or etymological identifica-

---

9 FEW 23,136a reads as follows: Agn. *garoil* s. 'bannière' Bibb [note: Die definition 'piège, trappe' in Bibb ist falsch, StNph 15,203.], *garoyle* (c.1400, StNph 15,203).

10 For instance DEAF G 254,21.

11 The text of Bibbesworth, listing and explaining words, especially homonyms, runs as follows: *il i ad jaroil* [= a ducks quacking] *e garoile, La difference dire vous voile: Li ane jaroile en rivere si hom de falcoun la quere, Mes devant un vile en guere Afichom le garoil en tere Pur le barbecan defendre A l'assaut* (BibbR 263–70). The glossary of *Bibbesworth*, ed. A. Owen, defines 'piège, trappe', relying on the Middle English gloss *trappe* 'trap', whence AND 'trap'.

tion offered! The source has been known since 1843 (Wright, *Reliquiae antiquae*). We read in *Plainte de Henry de Lacy*, ed. Thiolier-Méjean, 48 (AN, end of thirteenth century): *Tost vus deveroient maubaillir Li maufee* (the Saracens) *a lur assaillir, Car de verre est vostre garoil* – your palisade is made of glass, i.e. your defence is useless.[12] This article in DEAF is a sound example of slip-shod lexicography: the books which could have been opened have not really been consulted, two versions of one text have not been compared (Bibb + BibbF), an identification has been effected without any evidence (PlainteLacy), the customary dictionaries have not all been used, no research has been carried out, and a speculative etymology has been supplied without any hint of proof. Finally, the qualification of the word as Anglo-Norman must be modified, see below.

The stereoscopic view from both sides of the wattle leads to fuller information. The medieval Latin forms, *garuilli, garoillio, jarellum, jarullios,* and so on, point to an Anglo-Norman *garoil* or **jaroil* and to a hypothetical French **jaroil*. The medieval Latin contexts drawn from Close Rolls, Liberate Rolls and royal accounts, are very clear regarding the meaning of the word – the *garoil* is a solid wattle or palisade typically surrounding fortifications, possibly the ditch, as a further protection or obstacle to aggressors. But contexts like *garoillum qui est circa castrum nostrum vento prostratus et fractus* (1225) or, *garillum quod est circa predictum castrum et quod nuper prostratum fuit per tempestatem venti* (1241), show that the *garoil* was not a permanent construction, but one used only to slow down the attack of an enemy.

We also see with satisfaction that the Middle English gloss in Bibbesworth, *the trappe*, is not really erroneous: the wattle hinders the enemy's movements beneath the wall and the overall situation in front of the fortress can be compared to a trap. Other manuscripts give the glosses *postgate* (261; 266) and *stekes* (266): they confirm entirely the meaning found for *garillum*.[13] The meaning given in the AND, 'trap', is in fact not the result of an analysis of the text, but the translation of the Middle English gloss *trappe*. Even if the other glosses, *postgate* and *stekes*, did not exist, the gloss *trappe* could not stand as evidence of the sense 'trap' for the word *garoil*. This is due to the general function of the gloss: a gloss is neither a translation nor a definition of a word, it is an approximation, an attempt to come near to the meaning of the word in a given context or, even, an approach to the onomasiological field surrounding the meaning aimed at and, very often, appropriate in this contextual situation alone. The other glosses are of the same quality: *stekes* gives the idea of two or more posts or perches, not of a palisade, the *postgate* is a gate, again not a palisade. The three glosses cover, to different degrees, only part of the possible

---

12 If the one line had been understood [N.B. with the meaning 'banner' given to the word], why should a banner be made of glass? The '?' in Gdf was much better.

13 The other OF name of the object was *paliz.* Its equivalent in Anglo-Latin was *palitium*, a word more common than *garillum*: see Latham (RMLWL), and Middle English *palis*, 1296–a1500, MED 7,573a; OED P 394c (English *palisade* dates from 1600). The MED contains no entry similar to *garoil/jaroil*.

meaning of *garoil*. As long as we have not gathered enough examples, we cannot be sure of the meaning. (Very often we even need the complete etymology.)[14]

Now, in order to complete our knowledge about the word, let us take another bold step, a step no one has dared to take in this century: let us open Du Cange. Under the heading **garrolium** (DC 4,38a) we find, culled from a document of 1202, *pro garrolio Vernonis reficiendo* (Vernon in Normandy)[15] and *pro veteri garullio reficiendo, & pro liciis*;[16] under the heading **jarolium** (DC 4,280b), is cited another document of 1202 (at Evreux): *Pro liciis circa fossatos faciendis, & pro jarolio villae parando*;[17] finally, there is an example under **legariol** (DC 5,58b): *ad firmandum castrum adducunt pallum et legariol* (l. *le gariol*), at Nonancourt near Evreux, Upper Normandy, in 1215. The last sample cited gives the French word without any latinisation and with the French article (whether the agglutination is real may be doubted).

The form *jaroil (or *garoil*) is now furnished with a precise definition, which is '(light) palisade' and we know its geographical distribution, which includes the Continent, so that we can try to find an etymology. The etymon should contain the base **gar-* and, probably, the ending *-ŭcŭlu*. This *garŭcŭlu compares to *genŭcŭlu*, the ancestor of Old French *genoil*, French *genou* 'knee' (see DEAF G 491). The family of Gaulish ***garra** 'part of the leg', grouped in FEW 4,66a, might give our word a home. This would presuppose a word-formation parallel to *genoil* and a semantic development to *'post'; cf. especially Vallée d'Yères (North-Eastern Normandy) *garille* (<*gar-īcŭlu) 'jambe' (68a), Aunis Saint. *éjarrer* 'ébrancher' (69b), Occ. *engarrar*, etc. 'entraver' (66a), etc., also French *jarret* 'part of leg rear of the knee' (66b). Cf. French *jambe* 'leg' and its multiple technical meanings, especially 'post'.[18] The ending *-ŭcŭlu* is rare and unproductive, so that the variants, ML *garillum* (1244), *jarillum* (1257), *jarellum* (1291, etc.), are useful for supposing another suffix at the origin or in the mind of the speaker or writer, especially *-īcŭlu*, a suffix forming designations of tools (cf. *garille* quoted), and conceivably with attraction from *genŭcŭlu/genoil*.[19] We finally obtain confirmation of what Sharpe, as an experienced lexicographer, already felt: the word really is French, it is Anglo-Norman, and it is originally continental.

Naturally, the case of *garoil/garillum* is not unique. We shall group some examples according to lexical, semantic and graphic criteria that give evidence of the frequency of similar interference.

[14] Rothwell, *Modern Language Review* 88 (1993), pp. 581–99, describes the 'role of the multilingual gloss' in a more positivistic manner – he sees the glosses as a rich source for lexicography, which is entirely true, but their good use needs good skill. Cf. Möhren, 'Edition et lexicographie', in M.-D. Gleßgen and F. Lebsanft, eds, *Alte und neue Philologie* (Tübingen, 1997), pp. 153–66, esp. p. 160.

[15] Nic. Brussel, *Nouvel examen de l'usage général des fiefs en France*, 2 vols (Paris, 1727), p. 2, app., *Compte gen. des rev. du roy pendant l'année 1202*, CCIX, a [DC *garriolo* incorrect].

[16] At Anetum [prob. Anet, south-east of Evreux], 1202, in Brussel (see previous note), CXLVII [DC 'CXLVIII' incorrect]. DC tries a comparison with Isidore's *vara*, but the initial *j-* is an obstacle.

[17] Brussel, *Nouv. ex.* 2, app. CXCVI, a [under the date of 1203].

[18] See FEW 2¹,114b–115b, for instance St-Pol (Pas-de-Calais) *gambillon* 'tronçon d'une grosse branche raccourcie à longueur de bûche', 115a, ε.

[19] Less probable is a comparison with the materials found under the etymon *CARRA, FEW 2¹, 409b.

(i) Lexical

1. Under the heading **explanare** the FEW 3,310b has only one example, *explaner* 'expliquer' drawn from Cotgrave (Cotgr) 1611, and there is no other etymon from the same family. The FEW ignores GdfC 9,585a where we find two samples of *explanation* from the fifteenth century.[20] The AND 288b gives *explanacioun* with one quotation from 1324. The rare family is reinforced by one sample in the continental translation of John of Salisbury's *Policraticus*, ed. Brucker (Prol. 52) (*explanacion*, Paris 1372) and by one Anglo-Latin *explanativus* (c.1375) in Latham. (Nothing important in DC). The picture is chronologically completed by LathamDict (DMLBS) which culled *explanare* from Aldhelm (end of seventh century), Bede (beginning of eighth century), Alcuin (end of eighth century), Andrieu de S. Victor etc. We note that the whole family has been borrowed both on the Continent and on the British Isles, but that it was much stronger in Britain. It is then possible to consider the French sample in Cotgr 1611 as possibly calqued on the English word. The situation remained the same as far as the modern versions of the two languages: non-existent in French, current in English. Without English and Anglo-Latin, the history of that family in French cannot be written.

2. The MED 4,325b dates **greywerk** 'a gray fur; prob. the fur of the back of the Russian gray squirrel in winter' from 1349. We find an earlier example as a ME gloss in Liber Horn (LHorn) f. 222v (dated 1311): *graiwerk* glosses Anglo-Norman *grisovere*, see DEAF G 1365.[21]

3. Anglo-Latin **grisetum** is given in DMLBS 1107b with an example dated 's978'. The history of French *gris* is not likely to allow such an early date. The DMLBS is not wrong, as the date is given as a historical, not as a linguistic, date. But the indication is dangerous. Cf. *Mélanges Höfler* 305–6 with n. 32.

4. It has been suggested that French **gisarme/guisarme** 'gisarme' originates from Western France, but the word is rare and late in Britain (Latin only from 1242, English c.1300), which argues against a regional origin. See DEAF G 1654, 24–35.[22]

5. English **ha**, in the sense of Shakespeare's much-repeated line *Ha? Let me see*, is not attested in Old English.[23] So, it is probable that Middle English *ha* is a borrowing from French, at least as a unit of literary usage. This is confirmed by the late appearance of the word in Anglo-Latin. See DEAF H 4,28.

---

20 The word is missing in Godefroy, *Lexique de l'ancien français*, and Wartburg had slips only from this derivative dictionary. It will be up to the future DMF to explain if fifteeenth-century texts borrowed the word directly from Latin (which is probable) or if their authors were inspired by insular sources.

21 See also Möhren in *Mélanges M. Höfler*, p. 307.

22 New etymon; to be corrected in OED*Sh*, etc.

23 Except in the *ha ha* of laughter. OED and OED*Sh* incorrectly blend *ha* and *ha ha* of laughter.

6. Anglo-Norman **halimot** appears rather late (1419, AND 349a; DEAF H 102,2), but Anglo-Latin and English date the word back to c.1120 and 1150–54 respectively. Thus, it does not seem unduly bold to advance the opinion that the Old French language borrowed the word with a figurative sense ('action de débattre une question, débat') as early as the thirteenth century (DEAF H 101).

7. Anglo-Norman **hallos** 'a transport vessel' pl. (AND 349a) has to be compared with medieval Latin *calupus*, attested in Gascony only (Latham 64b; DMLBS 246c). This fact renders invalid different etymologies[24] and clearly shows that the word is a borrowing of a specific sea-term in the *Life of St Edmund*. See DEAF H 105 (Dörr).

8. For English **to hamald** 'to prove (something withholden or claimed by another) to be one's own property' the OED H 48b has only two examples, dating from 1575 and 1609. These must be antedated by Anglo-Latin *hamhaldare*, fourteenth century according to DMLBS 1133a, and also by a citation in DC 4,157b (fourteenth century). The first date is probably 1321, given from RotParl[1]M by AND (see DEAF H 116).

9. English **henbane** occurs in Anglo-Norman texts, sometimes qualified as English, sometimes not. This is typical of the way words float between these three complementary idioms. See DEAF H 131 (Dörr).

10. Middle English **harras** is borrowed from French (English since 1303). The variant form *harrys* is dated c.1475 in MED 4,477b. An English gloss to the Anglo-Norman Bibbesworth (ed. Owen) 227, *haris*, antedates the -*is*- form to the first half of the fifteenth century (date of MS). (In modern English, *haras* is considered a more recent importation of French *harras*, and the pronunciation is modified accordingly.) Cf. DEAF H 179,15.

11. English **hasp** 'a contrivance for fastening a door or lid' is Old English, Middle English and Anglo-Latin. Anglo-Norman *haspe* fills a chronological gap within the series of examples, see DEAF.[25]

(ii) Semantic

1. The fragmentary transmission of Anglo-Norman or Anglo-Latin or English leads sometimes to unfounded hypotheses about the precise sense of a word. The confrontation of all known materials of the three languages, plus the conti-

---

[24] The word is found in five different articles of the *FEW*. No use has been made of the *Word-List* in that work.

[25] Cf. the eloquent example *depart/departure*, Rothwell NM 97,425 (cf. DMLBS 615a *departire*, 'to depart, retire' sixteenth/seventeenth century only). One might enlarge the scope of this to morphology, for example the formation of English words with French suffixes (ex: *lastage* Wright-Lond p. 129).

nental ones, can often help to get away from lexicographical guess-work. The operation in the field of semantics is even more delicate than that in the area of lexical units.[26] Cf. the opinion of Christmann: 'Hier, in der Lexikologie, liegt das Hauptinteresse dieser mittellateinischen Forschungen für den Sprachwissenschaftler. Er hat begonnen [!], sie zur Kenntnis zu nehmen, sie aber noch lange nicht ausgeschöpft.'[27] One of his examples is Middle High German *ritter* which must be analysed semantically against the background of Latin *miles* and French *chevalier*.[28] We all remember also the older and still current meanings of English *world*, and German *welt*, and their etymology, depending on the semantic influence of Latin *saeculum*.[29]

2. Anglo-Norman **daie** is defined as 'dairymaid' in the AND 140b. This is not erroneous, but we find the *daie*, woman or man, fulfilling also the task of a keeper of small farm animals and poultry not leaving the farm for pasturing. Anglo-Latin and Middle English confirm the functions of the *daie*. It is interesting to see that the functions of the continental *laitiere* have been very similar and that its sense has widened accordingly (see MöhrenLand 147; 315).

3. Anglo-Norman and French **galilee** (*galyleie, galerie*) has the meaning 'gallery'. The probable older meaning, 'porch (at the west end) of the church' (cf. English *galilee*) can be found with certainty only in medieval Latin. See DEAF G 1695.

4. French **guivre** 'snake' has developed the meaning 'beam' in Anglo-Norman, which is confirmed by Anglo-Latin and English. See DEAF G 1674,29; 1677,5.

5. The possible links between English *hall*, Latin *aula* and French *hale* (*haule, aule*, etc.) need further elucidation.[30]

6. Anglo-Norman **pelette**, in the sense of 'sheared skin (of sheep)', has not yet been recorded in the lexicography of French. The AND has an example, but did not recognise it.[31] There is another clear example in *Seneschaucie* (see Möhren, *Wort- und sachgeschichtliche Untersuchungen . . .*, 221). A mere

---

26 Cf. Möhren, 'Unité et diversité du champ sémasiologique – l'exemple de l'*Anglo-Norman Dictionary*', *MélRothwell*, pp. 127–46, esp. p. 133. This article aims to inspire theoretically-based semantic awareness on the part of lexicographers, philologists and linguists. The material is exemplary, not specific (cf. *MélRothwell*, p. 282a).

27 H. H. Christmann, 'Sprachwissenschaft im Dienst der Mediävistik – Sprachwissenschaft als Mediävistik', in J. O. Fichte et al., eds., *Zusammenhänge, Einflüsse, Wirkungen. Kongressakten zum ersten Symposium des Mediävistenverbandes in Tübingen, 1984* (Berlin/New York, 1986), pp. 1–26, esp. p. 11. N.B. the article is dedicated to the memory of Manfred Bambeck (see footnote 42 below).

28 J. Bumke, *Studien zum Ritterbegriff im 12. und 13. Jahrhundert*, and articles written on the subject. See Christmann's article. The same must be true for English *knight*.

29 Not mentioned in OED*Sh* 1978.

30 Not studied by Stephen Dörr in DEAF H 94; he does not believe in interference here.

31 See its second quotation. The definition '(little) skin' is not entirely satisfying.

glance into Anglo-Latin lexicography proves that the sense was in fact current (cf. ibid., 30–31).

(iii) Graphic

1. The medieval scribe and the educated speaker knew about the graphical code of each language. Sometimes we find an explicit reflex from this knowledge. In *Orthographia Gallica*, ed. Johnson, F35 we read the following phonetic explanation: *Et quant S est joynt [a la T], ele avera le soun de H, come 'est', 'plest' serront sonez 'eght', 'pleght'*. This means that the *s* is not pronounced, but is similar to an aspiration. This information is only accessible for the reader who knows the value of the Middle English graph *gh*. It is very amusing to read in the Yearbook of 1304 (Yearbooks Ed. I, 32,129) that the remission of a court-case is deferred because the object of the case is situated in *Ersam*, not in *Hersam*. The judge makes clear: *H n'est pas lettre*. That is to say, if a place-name is written by error without its English initial *h*, this cannot render invalid the plea. See DEAF H 2,20 with footnote 4.

2. The interjection *ha*, common enough, occurs in Middle French with two *a*: *haa* (from 1364 on). Similarly, Middle English *ha* becomes also *haa* (from c.1440 on, MED 4,425a), exactly as does Anglo-Latin (see DMLBS 1121a). This is proof (if it were necessary) that even as far as scribal habits are concerned, the British Isles were not isolated.

3. Anglo-Latin *harou* is said to stem from French *haro* (DMLBS 1136c). As it is certain that the word was known in the British Isles with the sense deriving from legal usage in Normandy, we must assume, rather, that the word corresponds to Norman *harou*. See DEAF H 169.

4. Anglo-Norman and English *hayward* is well documented. The reading *hayword* may be doubtful (MöhrenLand 189n86). But we now find it confirmed in the DMLBS 193b (sub [*]*berbicarius*) in a document dated 1284, so that we can conclude that the ending might be phonetic.

An important lesson to be retained is the fact that the scrutinizing of all available materials does not just shed light on oddities in a shady corner of Anglo-Norman or Scottish Latin, but that the history of French or of medieval Latin cannot be written without research which ranges as widely as possible. If we do not want to fall into pure exegesis of easily-attained, predigested bits, we must remove our blinkers. I must say that the British Isles are not the most obvious place for such a comment, as the Continent must envy their undertakings on first-hand material, such as the AND and the DMLBS.[32] On the other hand, the special condition of medieval Britain

---

32 Rothwell's comment is even more true on the Continent: 'Anglo-Norman is doubtless not only the field of study where pious repetition of the views of past scholars has been used as a convenient substitute for thought based on a reading of first-hand sources, but it provides an excellent illustration

needs special care. Nowhere else did there exist a vernacular language in the role of an official language with authoritative prestige comparable to that of Latin. That is why we have documents and treatises written in the vernacular much earlier and more commonly on the British Isles than on the Continent.[33] Depending on the communicative situation, a given English speaker of the fourteenth century would use English or French or Latin; when writing he would use Latin or French, but between his ears he had the three languages. They were clearly distinct, but borrowing from one language to another, and especially from the authoritative languages into English, was natural and frequent. The result is not necessarily a macaronic text (or speech), but, depending on the subject, blending might have been the most effective way of introducing the most convenient term without regard to its origin. We can assume that speakers or writers felt at ease when mixing these units.[34] Each language is potentially blended into the other (to very different degrees) by both its origin and by active use. The non-French elements did not have, for a French-speaking person, the character of foreignness they would have nowadays, just as non-English did not have such an effect to speakers of English. Speaking in terms of linguistic integration, the foreign elements were latently in the process of being integrated. So, philological expertise from all relevant languages is necessary for lexicographical research into any of the languages concerned. This is true especially for Latin: if Latin is the mother language of French, it is also at least the aunt language of English, as is Anglo-French, and medieval Latin is the godmother of all three of them.[35]

These inter-dependencies make clear that the Continent is not cut off at all. Just as Anglo-Latin has never been isolated from European medieval Latin, Anglo-Norman was an integral part of continental French, at least from its beginnings and throughout the thirteenth century. After that time the reciprocal nature of the contact diminished, but for the lexicographer things remain unchanged, as a fourteenth- or fifteenth-century Anglo-Norman word might well be evidence for a continental French word. Rothwell is right in pointing out again and again that Anglo-Norman is the first-hand source-language for Romance elements in English (especially regarding the *meaning* of borrowed words), and we must keep in mind that every

---

of the dangers arising from this practice', 'Playing "follow my leader" in AN Studies', *Journal of French Language Studies* 6 (1996), p. 177.

33   For a different view: D. A. Trotter, *Zeitschrift für romanische Philologie* 113 (1997), p. 139.

34   That is what Trotter likes to call Laura-Wright-Texts. See WrightLond and her article in MélRothwell, pp. 223–60. For words which are not at all, or only halfway, integrated, compare Platearius in Hunt, *Anglo-Norman Medicine*, p. 161, or Trotter, *Revue de Linguistique Romane*, 59,639 on *De quatuor-decim partibus beatitudinis*. See as an example **horhune** in DEAF ('Lettre d'Hippocrate', ed. C. de Tovar (Strasbourg thesis [1970]), 70 p. 294): the word with '.a.' is English, without it we consider it French (!?). The mixing of languages can be found equally on the Continent: DC has lots of bilingual quotations. Cf. in J. Monicat and J. Bussard, *Recueil des Actes de Philippe Auguste*, no. 1384, doc. 1215 *mille circulos de coldre et de charme ad duplarios in landis foreste nostre*. Or the trilingual mixing of Flemish, French and Latin in some documents from Flanders.

35   Cf. the *Dictionnaire de la littérature française. Le moyen âge* (DLF²) which included articles on French or Latin authors or texts without any discrimination. We also know that research on narrative motifs for instance cannot be carried out within one medieval language alone.

French word is potentially an Anglo-Norman word. Furthermore, the British Isles continued to be a living part of Europe as a cultural entity, where Latin played its role, but also French, especially for English. It is again Rothwell who has demonstrated convincingly that Chaucer thought French and Latin to be natural parts of English as a literary vehicle and that Chaucer integrated Anglo-Norman and continental French together with Latin into his poetic language.[36]

What Ekkehart IV of Saint Gall in the eleventh century called *Scotis semilatinis corruptius scripta*[37] and what was called in the fourteenth century *latyn corumpus* or *latyn corupt*,[38] or, if we turn to the vernacular, what was called 'Marlborough French' by Walter Map in 1180: *Merleburgam, ubi fons est quem si quis, ut aiunt, gustaverit, Gallice barbarizat, unde cum vitiose quis illa lingua loquitur, dicimus eum loqui gallicum Merleburgae*[39] (not to be confused with Etiemble's *Franglais*), have all probably been, in their own ways, vivid languages capable of integrating needed or convenient or pleasing elements. This integrative capacity – we might call it tolerance – leads regularly to borrowings of, for instance, Picardisms into Anglo-Norman, as in the case of the rare word *bibuef.* Such a word, certainly considered common French, might remain technical and literary, but it might become familiar too and, at any rate, it is an object of lexicographical research.[40]

One and a half centuries ago Delisle demonstrated that rich material can be culled from very old medieval Latin for the French vernacular, as did Bambeck four decades ago.[41] The repercussions of their work have been limited.[42] In Britain recent works have rediscovered with great success the same vein, just as Godefroy did a century ago when using Lacurne of the eighteenth century, who had already discovered Du Cange, who was another century older and who had used Bede, Aldhelm

---

36 'The Trilingual England of Geoffrey Chaucer', *Studies in the Age of Chaucer* 16 (1994), pp. 45–67. Of great interest is also the appendix 'Der aktive Latein-Wortschatz als integratives Element des althochdeutschen Satzes', in H. Backes, ed., *Die Hochzeit Merkurs und der Philologie. Studien zu Notkers Martian-Übersetzung* (Sigmaringen, 1982), pp. 162–91, of the type *du gibest uultum unde aspectum dien anderen sternon.*

37 Cited in W. Berschin, *Biographie und Epochenstil*, 3,407 n. 136.

38 *Fouke le Fitz Waryn* (ANTS), 43,15; 56,17, beginning of fourteenth century, cited by Rothwell, *Studies in the Age of Chaucer* 16 (1994), p. 53 n. 21.

39 Gautier Map, *De nugis curialium*, V 6, cited in *Privilège aux Bretons*, ed. Faral, p. 34 n. 4.

40 See Gilles Roques RLiR 59 (1995), p. 636 and in MélRothwell: 'Des interférences picardes dans l'*Anglo-Norman Dictionary*', pp. 191–8 (*bibuef*, a plant, in 'Roger of Salerno', ed. Hunt (*Anglo-Norman Medicine*), I 13 p. 139). See also T. de Jong, 'L'Anglo-Normand du XIIIe siècle', *Mélanges Dees* (1988), pp. 103–12, a localisation test of AN according to the materials and principles of DeesAtlas; the results are problematic but interesting (from 96 documents 89 could have their origin in Normandy and western France [Normandy alone 38], 3 in Paris, 4 in other regions).

41 L. Delisle, *Etudes sur la condition de la classe agricole* (1851); M. Bambeck, *Lateinisch–romanische Wortstudien* (1959); Bambeck, *Boden und Werkwelt* (1968); Bambeck, *Mélanges Gamillscheg* (Verba et vocabula) (1968). See DEAFBibl 1993; sources in part doubtful, often from later copies.

42 More recently, Pfister, in a short review-article on the Piedmont-project of Gasca Queirazza and his disciples, did the same for northern Italian: M. Pfister, 'L'importanza del Glossario latino medievale piemontese per la lessicografia italiana', *Miscellanea di studi romanzi offerta a G. Gasca Queirazza*, s.l. (Orso) s.d., 2,849–862. With reference to Baldinger, Hubschmid, Aebischer, but not to Bambeck. The ideal is double authorship like that of Paul Staniforth, involved in editorial work for both the AND and the DMLBS.

and Isidore. Seemingly, it is necessary regularly to reactivate knowledge of the past. This historical dimension is a variant of the diachronic perspective in linguistics – it is one of the volets of the triptych which symbolises linguistic research in Britain and elsewhere. The second volet symbolises the multilingual aspect: if Britain was multilingual in the past, research into the past (and of its present state) must be multilingual, or multilinguistic, as the philology of one language alone is not equipped to obtain durable results. The centre table of the triptych should not depict ugly creatures like carelessness, haste, superficiality and plagiarism, but a sumptuous Minerva, accompanied by the virtues and surrounded by the branches of science. Our own branch needs the constant multilinguistic approach, and we need to be each other's supporters: 'This is your devoted friend, sir, the manifold Linguist', as Shakespeare said in *All's well, that ends well* (IV. iii. 236).

Medieval Multilingualism and the Revision of the OED

EDMUND WEINER

1. The revision of the OED

THE SECOND EDITION of the *Oxford English Dictionary*,[1] published in 1989, represented an integration of the first edition and the four-volume Supplement, but not a thoroughgoing revision. A further OED project is now under way and is planned to culminate in 2010. This involves a revision of the Dictionary that will affect all its aspects: not only new words and senses, but definitions, etymology, pronunciation, and documentation. OED's documentation, founded on the use of excerpts from written texts dating from Old English to the present day, includes in its compass medieval multilingual texts. This paper looks at the use made of such texts in the existing OED (OED2), which is for present purposes virtually identical with the first edition (OED1), and at the role they will play in the Dictionary's third edition (OED3).

2. The revision of OED's documentation

Documentation in the third edition of the OED will be revised and expanded. The majority of the quotations included in the second edition will be carried over to the third edition, but most of them will be subject to one or more of the following procedures. (i) Quotations taken from inferior or later editions will be converted (unless the requisite reading is that of a later edition), wherever possible, so that either the first edition, or the best modern critical edition (depending on the circumstances) is cited. (ii) The content of quotations will be rechecked and corrected. (iii) The bibliographical details (publication date, author's name, work title, and so on) of the citation will be harmonised across all occurrences of the same source and will be corrected when inaccurate.

At the same time, new quotations will be added, in order to improve the documentation, wherever possible, as follows. (i) Earlier examples will be added in order to extend the coverage back to the earliest known example of a word or sense. (ii) Later examples will be added in order to bring the coverage down to the present day or to the last known occurrence. (iii) Gap-filling examples will be inserted in order

---

[1]   J. A. Simpson and E. S. C. Weiner, *The Oxford English Dictionary*, 2nd edn (Oxford, 1989).

to provide fuller, more even coverage, if the state of the evidence warrants it. (iv) Occasionally inferior examples will be suppressed (so as not to appear in the published version, although they will be retained in the dictionary database) and replaced with better ones.

The revision and expansion of OED's documentation is a very considerable part of the overall task, and it naturally has important knock-on effects on definition (shedding new light on word meaning), entry structure (altering the chronological order of senses), and, not least, etymology (modifying the possible explanations for the appearance of a word in English).

3. Documentation of Middle English and Early Modern English in OED3

Of the four main historical periods covered by the OED, Middle English and Early Modern English will occasion the most labour. Old English materials represent only a small proportion of the whole and OED reflects only that part of the total corpus which survived beyond 1150, so that the revision of Old English will make relatively small demands on project time. The coverage of later Modern English (perhaps with the exception of the eighteenth century), is in relatively good shape thanks to the OED Supplement and to the programme of reading sources and writing new entries which has continued since the completion of the Supplement, and, on the whole, later Modern English sources are the easiest to research and recheck.

The revision of the Middle English and Early Modern English documentation are both on an extensive scale, but the methodology for each is very different. For Early Modern English we have undertaken an extensive new reading programme in order to expand the corpus of linguistic material available to us. The observations of Jürgen Schäfer on documentation in the OED[2] have been taken to heart. This reading is carried out with direct reference to OED2, so that we file only quotations that in some way modify the OED's contents (for example by antedating, evidencing words or senses that are not included, or supplementing badly evidenced uses). Additionally, the Michigan Early Modern English Materials were presented to the OED project about three years ago; these are used in the same way as materials from the OED's own reading programme.

In contrast, no extensive reading programme has been undertaken for Middle English, though certain newly available texts are being read. The reason is of course that in this sphere the OED has to bow to the primacy of the MED, and to a more limited extent, the DOST. These projects between them have already assembled the overwhelming majority of the available lexical evidence. The main effort of the OED project is concentrated on a painstaking comparison between the coverage of each word in these two dictionaries and the corresponding entries in the OED. This comparison has a double outcome. (i) Every quotation in the OED which has an equivalent in either of these dictionaries is corrected to agree with the latter. Both the bibliographical citation and the quotation text are thereby converted to a reliable,

2   J. Schäfer, *Documentation in the OED* (Oxford, 1980).

consistent form. (ii) Earlier examples of each word and sense, and to a lesser extent later and gap-filling examples, are then identified and added. This activity naturally has to follow the bibliographical work, because it is the latter which provides the existing OED quotations with more accurate dates.

4. The use of non-literary texts

There is therefore in general a very marked contrast between our approach to Middle English documentation and our approach to Early Modern English documentation. However, one development on the Early Modern English front is enlightening for the consideration of the use of multilingual medieval documents in the third edition.

In the Early Modern English period we are expanding the use of non-literary evidence as compared with the second edition. The non-literary texts from which we draw evidence include wills, inventories, and accounts, both domestic and ecclesiastical. We have found that very often the history of a modern English word known at present from chiefly literary sources, or known from late regional glossaries, is greatly enhanced by evidence drawn from non-literary sources, especially in antedating the word or sense, often by a considerable span of years. There is no guarantee that literary authors in any age before the nineteenth century would conveniently mention all the items and occupations of everyday life. Many of the concerns of the kitchen, the workshop, and the farmyard need never feature in literature at all. If we are to find attestations of this kind of vocabulary, account books, wills, and similar documents are much more likely sources. As one would expect, if the records exist, a word is likely to be attested in what one might call 'ordinary everyday use' before it appears in the 'artificial' environment of literary writing.[3]

Before the first half of the sixteenth century, when English language wills and inventories become common, there are very few vernacular non-literary documents. We find that the part played by English-language non-literary texts in supplementing the evidence of literature in Early Modern English, is played, in the medieval period, by multilingual documents. For the most part these are Latin documents in which English words are embedded, though there are also some French documents of this type.

5. Multilingual texts in the first (and second) edition of the OED

Naturally multilingual texts were used by the editors of the first edition of the OED, who were well aware of their potential to supply the deficiencies of literary texts. It is difficult to obtain a clear idea of the number of texts used and their frequency in the first edition, even using a computerised version of the dictionary. It seems that a

---

[3]   For further discussion of this topic, see E. S. C. Weiner, 'Local History and Lexicography', *The Local Historian* 24 (1994), pp. 164–73, and E. S. C. Weiner, 'The Use of Non-Literary Texts for the Study of Dialect Lexis', in E. W. Schneider, ed., *Englishes Around the World: Studies in honour of Manfred Görlach* (Amsterdam/Philadelphia, 1997).

rather small number of texts were employed and that therefore the same documents, or collections of documents, are often cited. For example, the *Durham account rolls*[4] are quoted more than 700 times, *Testamenta Eboracensia*[5] more than 500 times, and the *Ripon Chapter Accounts*[6] more than 100 times.

It is worthwhile pausing to look briefly at some notable features of the data contained in these sources. Firstly, they often supply the earliest example or examples of a word or sense, irrespective of whether the latter is common or rare. This is especially true of occupation titles, e.g. for **gunmaker**, 'Joh'i Gonmaker'.[7] Secondly, they often provide gap-filling examples from the later Middle English period, even though literary sources are more abundant then than earlier; e.g. for **gutter** *n.* 3[1] a, second example, 'Pro emendacione et le pavyng j gutter juxta capellam',[8] or at **buckskin** *n.* 1, second example, 'Unam longam tunicam de bukskynnes'.[9] Thirdly, the multilingual aspect of the text is very often in fact a kind of informal gloss introduced by a word such as *vocatum*, e.g. at **balk** *n.*[1] 12 (first example) 'Unum instrumentum ferreum in camino aulae, vocatum balk'.[10] Fourthly, we find in this material a limited trilingualism: often the French definite article is used as a transition between the Latin context and the English word or phrase, e.g. at **goose-house** *n.* 1 (first example) 'Pro le flaggynge de le goyshous'[11] or at *bell-string*, s.v. **bell** *n.*[1] 12 (only example) 'Le bell-strynges sunt defectiva'.[12]

6. Multilingual texts in the third edition of the OED

In the last part of this article I shall consider the characteristic uses of multilingual texts in OED3. I have already explained the extensive use of MED and DOST in the revision and mentioned the limited but targeted data collection. I shall now look statistically at the results of this in a range of text that has been provisionally edited. Work on the third edition began with the letter M. Primary revision, in other words the incorporation of new quotations into the text and the accompanying redrafting of definitions, is now well advanced into the letter P. Text in approved, near-final form, however, is still relatively limited, being confined to the early part of M.

In this area I have made a computer search of the range of entries between MA and MILL, a total of 7658 OED3 entries. Of these, only 697 (9%) are entries for words recorded as far back as Middle English. Of these 697, 52 items are words or

---

4   C. Fowler, ed., *Extracts from the account rolls of the abbey of Durham from the original MSS* (Surtees Society 99 (1898), 100 (1899), 103 (1901)).

5   J. Raine, ed., *Testamenta Eboracensia; or wills registered at York* (Surtees Society 4 (1836), 30 (1855), 45 (1865), 53 (1869)).

6   J. T. Fowler, ed., *Acts of chapter of the collegiate church of SS Peter and Wilfrid, Ripon, A.D. 1452 – A.D. 1506* (Surtees Society 64, 1875).

7   1385–6 *Durham Account Rolls* 390.

8   1449–50 *Durham Account Rolls* 276 (the first example is from the same source).

9   1465 *Ripon Chapter Accounts* 159 (the first example is from *Testamenta Eboracensia*).

10 1432 *Testamenta Eboracensia* (1855) II. 23.

11 1474–5 *Durham Account Rolls* I. 95.

12 1484 *Ripon Chapter Accounts* 222.

senses which are illustrated by quotations from multilingual sources in OED3. Half of these entries occur with such quotations in OED2, and of these, half are augmented in OED3 with new quotations of the same sort while the other half remain the same. The other half of the 52 items are illustrated by quotations from medieval multilingual sources for the first time in OED3. In other words, in the sample OED3 doubles the number of entries which make use of such quotations, but such quotations are newly added in OED3 to 75% of entries which use them.

Turning our attention from the entries to the quotations in the range, there are in all 76 quotations from medieval multilingual sources. 34 (45%) are the same quotations as are already found in OED2. 32 (42%) are antedatings of OED2 entries. 8 others are important gap-filling examples, and 2 others illustrate new items: altogether, 42 (55%) of the examples are significant new additions to the text. As one might expect, little or nothing is added that has no important effect on the coverage of the OED, either in terms of dating chronology or in terms of vocabulary range. But it is interesting that OED3 more than doubles the number of quotations from medieval multilingual sources. It is important to remember that this achievement is based almost entirely on the labours of others. All but five of the new quotations come from MED and one from DOST. But four quotations come from sources acquired in the course of our own reading and research. For example, at **mereswine** n., 'dolphin', this 1311 quotation which was not available to the MED helps to fill the gap in OED2 between an Old English quotation and a circa 1325 quotation (now redated by MED ante 1400): 'Item unum mereswyn debet vnum denarium'.[13] We expect to continue to supplement the MED contribution with data like this, drawn from recently published works. Another good example, taken from a later range of text, is this ante 1336 example (antedating all other evidence) for sense 1 a of **nag** n.[1], 'a small riding-horse or pony': 'Item in i ferro anteriore pro le nagg et i remocione pro morel ii d'.[14]

7. Types of multilingual text used in OED3

Any careful user of MED will note that the range of multilingual texts used is much broader. In the interval since the compilation of OED1, a great range of such sources has become available, some in the form of collections, such as account rolls, others in studies containing excerpted material, such as occupational name studies. There are in the sample several occupational and surname studies, e.g. Fransson's *Middle English Surnames* (1935),[15] Otto's *Handwerkernamen* (1938),[16] and Thuresson's *Middle English Occupational Terms* (1950).[17] There are thematic studies such as

---

[13] L. Wright, *Sources of London English: Medieval Thames Vocabulary* (Oxford, 1996), p. 106.

[14] C. M. Woolgar, *Household Accounts of Medieval England* (Records of Social and Economic History, New Series XVII) (Oxford, 1992), p. 182.

[15] G. Fransson, *Middle English Surnames of Occupation 1100–1350* (Lund Studies in English 3) (Lund, 1935).

[16] G. Otto, *Die Handwerkernamen im Mittelenglischen* (Bottrop, 1938).

[17] B. Thuresson, *Middle English Occupational Terms* (Lund Studies in English 19) (Lund, 1950).

Löfvenberg's *Contributions to Middle English Lexicography and Etymology* (1946)[18] and Salzman's *Building in England* (1952).[19] And there are document collections that appeared after this part, if not the whole, of OED1 was published, such as Capes's *Charters and Records of Hereford Cathedral* (1908)[20] and Page's *Wellingborough Manorial Accounts* (1935).[21] OED3 will naturally reflect this wider range of sources. But it is also noticeable that sources already used by OED1, such as *Testamenta Eboracensia*, have yielded up new examples to the more complete excerpting carried out by the MED project.

8. Types of vocabulary

The other matter of interest is the kind of vocabulary illustrated by medieval multi-lingual texts. It comes as no surprise that the vast majority of the words are nouns, most of them with fairly concrete reference. In the sample, the following categories of noun occur, in the following numbers:

occupation (e.g. *marbler, matter*)   10
materials (e.g. *maple, marl*)   7
animals (e.g. *mackerel, mallard*)   5
foodstuffs (e.g. *mace, malvoisie*)   5
clothing terms, implements, measures, administrative terms   4
heraldic terms and plants   2

These are obviously the kinds of item one would expect to find in the documentary sources we are considering. Nevertheless, in the sample also occurred the verb *mail* 'wrap up (goods)', the verbal noun *maying* 'celebrating May Day', and the adjective *meruw* 'finely adjusted' (applied to scales).

9. Conclusion

Medieval multilingual texts will play an important part in enhancing the documentation of certain kinds of word and sense in OED3, particularly in providing the earliest example of many items. In its employment of such texts OED3 will depend in one way or another on the work of previous scholars – largely, but not entirely, that of the MED and DOST lexicographers. OED3's distinctive contribution will be made in its careful selection and marshalling of this data so as to expand and enhance our knowledge of the early development of many English words.

---

[18] M. T. Löfvenberg, *Contributions to Middle English Lexicography and Etymology* (Lund, 1946).
[19] L. F. Salzman, *Building in England* (Oxford, 1952; reprinted with corrections and an appendix of building contracts, 1967).
[20] W. W. Capes, *Charters and Records of Hereford Cathedral* (Hereford, 1908).
[21] F. M. Page, *Wellingborough Manorial Accounts, AD 1258–1323, from the account rolls of Crowland Abbey* (Kettering, 1935).

The Language and Vocabulary of the Fourteenth- and Early Fifteenth-Century Records of the Goldsmiths' Company*

LISA JEFFERSON

THE Worshipful Company of the Goldsmiths of London traces its history as an organised guild back to the twelfth century, although its full official legal existence as a corporate body dates only from 1327 when it received its first royal charter from Edward III.[1] This charter, in French, survives in four contemporary or almost contemporary copies, one of which is in the Company's first Court Minute Book.[2] This Minute Book, or 'Wardens' Accounts and Court Minute Book A + a' as the labelled title on its nineteenth-century binding proclaims, has a companion volume, now known as 'Minute Book A + b', which is housed in a parallel binding, both volumes being kept in the archives at Goldsmiths' Hall in the City of London. These two paper record books contain the year-by-year accounts, financial and historical, written up by the current clerk of the Company, mainly in French, from 1334 until 1446. They have been used, selectively and in modern English translated extracts, by historians of the Company but they have never been published, although I hope to rectify this soon, for the wealth of information they contain is of enormous interest, not the least of which is the linguistic record of precisely datable use of the French language in England during the fourteenth and early fifteenth centuries.

Minute Book A + a records its own purchase in 1358:

---

* I acknowledge with gratitude the permission given by The Worshipful Company of Goldsmiths to work in their archives and to publish extracts from their documents. I should like also to record my gratitude to the Librarian of the Goldsmiths' Company, Mr David Beasley, who has given me unstinting assistance and has helped me to puzzle out many a baffling entry in the Company's records; my thanks go also to Mr John Cherry, Deputy Keeper, Department of Medieval and Later Antiquities, The British Museum, whose expert knowledge of surviving medieval jewellery, gold- and silverware has been invaluable and who has generously spared time to answer many of my queries; to Dr David Howlett, who allowed me access to the files of the DMLBS; and to Professor W. Rothwell and Professor David Trotter who made most helpful comments on an earlier draft of this paper.

[1] T. F. Reddaway and L. E. M. Walker, *The Early History of the Goldsmiths' Company, 1327–1509* (London, 1975), pp. xix–xxvi (hereafter *Early History*). This is the standard and most up-to-date work on all aspects of the Company and its individual members during the early centuries of its existence, and it includes a good bibliography of both primary and secondary sources for the Company's history.

[2] PRO C66/166 m. 13; Corporation of London Records Office, Plea and Memoranda Roll A 1 b, m. 21; Corporation of London Records Office, Letter-Bk. G, f. civ; Goldsmiths' Company Minute Book A + a, p. 19.

Item, j graunt papere achaté par les avantditz iiij gardeyns pur registrer totes maneres remembrances qe sount ou serount faitez par la compaignie du dit orfeverie, dount les costages du dit papere amont – xiij s. iiij d.

It is clear that the records of years prior to 1358 have been copied up at this date into this new formal register,[3] which is then continued from year to year, in a variety of hands, those no doubt of the clerk or acting clerk of the Company, who at the end of each accounting year makes an official statement for the Wardens of the financial transactions made and disciplinary hearings held during the preceding year, together with any ordinances and statutes officially promulgated. In 1371 the first Minute Book records the purchase of another register:

Item, lez dites gardeyns acomptent avoir paié pur j novel papier achaté qe currera dez gardeyns en gardeyns et qe ceste graunt papier sera mys pur j lyggere, a gyser en une cofre ovesqez aultres choses: pris del novelle papier – ij s. x d.

This entry has an exact parallel, written in the same hand, on the first page of the second Minute Book:

Item, les dites Gardeyns acomptent avoir achaté ceste novelle papier qe currera des Gardeyns en gardeyns, et qe l'altre graunt papier sera gysant en une cofre ovesqe aultres choses pur un remembrauncer; pris de ceste novelle papier – ij s. x d.

The first book, which is indeed very large (90 folios measuring 398 x 275mm) and which cost 13s 4d, is thus termed interchangeably 'un lyggere' and 'un remembrauncer', both of which words are new to the AND, as is the usage of 'currera' – *qe currera des gardeyns en gardeyns* = 'which will pass (or be passed) from warden to warden'.

The contents of the two registers range very widely. Some of the early entries in the second book are duplicated in the first, the hand being the same in both, the wording at times identical but also at times showing interesting small differences. This second book is however far less complete than the first, its use by the wardens being apparently somewhat erratic after the initial flush of enthusiasm for it. It does however contain some highly significant entries not paralleled, for whatever reason, in the large ledger.

Apart from these two books, the Goldsmiths' Company possesses a number of copies of fourteenth- and fifteenth-century deeds and ordinances, some of them in French and therefore of use to the AND and others concerned with the medieval French language in England, these being entered in the *Register of Deeds*, two large fat volumes of parchment written up between 1417 and 1473 (with some later addi-

---

3 Lorna Walker (*Early History*, p. 54, n. 45) thought that this entry referred to another ledger, but this is contradicted by the evidence of the watermarks (the same one throughout the book) and that of the script: the same hand has written in the accounts of the years from 1334 until 1357, all in clearly parallel format, while another scribe has been set the task at this point of copying into this ledger various Latin documents relating to title to lands and properties owned by the Company and the copy, in French, of the 1327 royal charter.

tions), in modern bindings but with their original parchment guard-leaves preserved, and whose purchase is once again recorded in the first Minute Book:

> Fait a remembrer qe el temps de William Fytzhughe, Johan Hilles, Richard Wedyalle et Johan Walsche est ordeigné et escript et en le Tresorye mys un libre de velom contenant iiij^C foilles saunz lez custodyes, c'est assavoir iiij en primer comencement et iiij en le ffyn; le quelle libre fuist ordeigné al entent et profyt de tout la Cumpanye et pur ceo qe avant cez heures divercez evydencez ount esté embesylez et detraez, lez avantdytz gardeins ount lessé entrer toutz lez avantditz evydencez en l'avantdit libre pur le pluis record. Et lez avantditz evydencez chescun par soy mesmes come as ditz tenementz apparteignent en diverse kofyns et boxez mys, et issynt lez ditz boxez billez a dire qe de tielx tenementz specefyent, en chescun boxe quantz evydencez escriptz come en le libre est specefyé, auxi bien copiez come aultres chartres ensealez, les quelx copiez lez avantditz gardeins en defaut dez evydencez perduz et anientisez ount lez avantditz copiez hors de Guyldehall retraez et portez. Que le kalender qe ysy est mys . . .[4]

French is the language of a few early documents (*evydencez*) copied here, but Latin is the language of most, and the table of contents (the *kalender* referred to above) has been given in this language. English however is used for the very first headings: on the verso facing the first page of text is written in alternate red and blue ink:

> This book was bygon made and ordeynyd by William Fitz Hugh, John Hylles, Richard Wydyale, John Walsshe, beyng that tyme Wardeyns of ye crafte in ye yeer of our lord a. M^l CCCC xvij and in ye yeer of ye regne of Kyng Harry the fyvethe aftir ye conquest ye syxte yeer . . .

and above the text, in red ink, on the first folio is written:

> This prolog is wrytyn in englysshe to euery mannys undirstondyng in ye C iiijxx & ix leef of this book

and indeed a translation of the following Latin text of the prologue is found on f. 189 and in the same hand. This prologue explains the purpose of the book and is followed by the list of contents.

It would seem that Latin was considered the official language of record but that English was at this date (1417) considered the language that everyone would understand. However, no translations are provided for the Latin and French texts (apart from the Prologue), the account books continue at this date in good French, and though perhaps not everyone understood French, clearly many did.

To return to the contents of the early Minute Books: the large ledger starts its account of each year with a heading stating that 'Ces sount les nouns de gardeyns del orfaverie de Londoun en l'an du regne le roi Edward tiercz apres le conquest . . .', the regnal year being given, from 8 Edward III (1334–35) onwards, followed by

---

4   p. 120 (the writing breaks off at this point).

the list of the names of the four Wardens, who held office on a yearly basis, the Company's year running from each feastday of their patron, St Dunstan (19 May) until the next. Each year the Wardens were responsible for rendering the financial accounts, recording the monies received from fees paid on entry into and exit from apprenticeship terms, and on entry into the freedom and/or the livery of the Company, the sums charged at this early date varying greatly from individual to individual.[5] Monies were also received by will and testament, or by gift, or as contributions towards a specific expense. Fines levied – the amounts paid as fines, though sometimes low, sometimes remitted, and sometimes left unpaid, were often of quite hefty proportions, either in money or in kind – were another source of income, and the case brought against the miscreant, his misdemeanours and misconduct, produce for us now amusing reading matter and most useful information, and constitute a rich source of vocabulary for lexicographers. The sometimes very detailed record of events leading to the fine provide us with a great variety of technical and non-technical vocabulary concerned with the gold, silver and jewellery trade.

Monies disbursed by or on behalf of the Wardens and Company are also accounted for. They were responsible for a chapel at St Paul's Cathedral and each year record the cost of lighting this, as of providing candles and lamps elsewhere:

> Item, pur la lumere al hospital Seint Jake outre la quilette ové les standars de S. Pol qe amounte xxxv ll. summa vj s. (*A* + *a*, p. 5)

On St Dunstan's Day, the feastday of the guild's patron saint, the cathedral bell was tolled at noon, and this involved regular expense (including *beverage*, as it is frequently termed, to unnamed persons, presumably the bell-ringer(s)):

> Item, pur le sonere Noune et pur le beverage a Seynt Pol – v s. iij d. (*A* + *a*, p. 6)

> En primes pur soner le grant sonaile de Seint Poul – iij s. iiij d. Item, en payn, formage, et cervoise mesme temps – iij s. iiij d. (*A* + *a*, p. 61)

> Primes pur soner le graunt sonel de Seint Dunston al esglise de Seint Poul et pur la lumiere a l'esglise de Seint Johan Zakarie – xx s. (*A* + *b*, p. 1)

Other regular expenses were the provision of wax for candles for poor people:

> Item, en cire novelement fait encountre le jour de Seint Donston – xiij s. xj d.
> Item, en disches pur lé serges fait mesme an – iiij s. ij d. (*A* + *a*, p. 61)

support by alms-giving of the poor and needy members of the craft:

> Item, doné a deux poveres hommes a contre Noel – vj s. viij d. Item, a mesme deux hommes et une femme et un altre homme del amoigne en mesme l'an – Cvj s. viij d. (*A* + *a*, p. 29)

burial and funeral expenses of members:

---

5   See *Early History*, pp. 78–9, 107–8, 121–3, 125–6, 133–4 for fees etc. charged.

Item, pur l'enterement William de Hinge – xvij d. (*A* + *a*, p. 3) – Item, en sepulture de iij povres – iiij s. viij d. (*A* + *a*, p. 6)

expenses connected with bequests to the Company:

Item, lez ditz gardeinz ount paiez et deliverez a la compeignie del devys du testament William de Burtoun al almoigne de Seint Dunston xiij s. iiij d. Et xxvj s. viij d. queux il remaneit en dette de la compeignie, dont lez dit gardeinz ount fait une acquitance as executours le dit William. (*A* + *a*, p. 43)

expenses incurred at the annual dinner held on St Dunstan's Day:

Adeprimes les costages de la feste de Seint Dunston a le diner des dites gardeyns outre le quilette amont a x li. x s. (*A* + *a*, p. 22) – Item, les dites gardeyns despenderunt le jour de Seint Dunston en les chaumps en vyn, blaunderelles, menestralles et autres choses – xxx s. (*A* + *a*, p. 32)

and at other meetings and assemblies:

Fait a remembrer en le temps de lez gardayns avantditz c'est a dire Robert Lucas, Johan Coraunt, Harri Bamme, Harri Malmayns, al comencement de lour office par assent de bons gentz de le compaignie et comunes, ils fount une feste a quele feste furont seignours et dames, adeprimes ma treshonurable Madame Izabelle file Roy d'Engleterre, et sa file Countasse de Oxinfford et le seignur de Latemer et le principal mestre de Seynt Johan de Clerkenwell et le Maire de Loundres ovesqes alutres [*sic*] bons gentz de la cité. Par quoy lez ditz gardayns furount a grauntz costagez, par quoy lez ditz gardayns prieunt qe ils purrount estre alowé de sez grantz costagez ové alutrement [*sic*] qe chescun dez gardayns qe vient apres qe ils fount une feste desus une payne fait entre lez bons gentz et comunes de dit mester. (*A* + *a*, p. 55)

expenses run up whilst taking part in civic ceremonies:

Item, a les mynstrales pur chivacher ové le vicecompte – vj s. (*A* + *b*, p. 30)

Item, paié a menstrales pur chivacher vers le roy et vers le meire – iij li. xiij s. iiij d. Item pur baneres a lour trompes – xxvj s. viij d. dount resceu de ceo qe fuist quilez de gros – xxvj s. vj d. Item, pur drap achaté a viij menstreles – xxviij s. iiij d. (*A* + *a*, p. 67)

legal expenses of various kinds:

Item, fait a remembrer qe lez avantditz gardeyns acomptent en despences et diverses coustages vers la lei, de pursure pur iij fauces lyens des hanaps des maszer, queux lienz estoyent de latoun et endorrez, pur queux hanaps les dites gentz avoient lour juggement del pillori, q'amounte en tout – vij s. j d. (*A* + *b*, p. 4)

Fait a remembrer qe les ditz gardeinz paieront as gentz de ley et a lour conseil al Guyhalle et as gentz de lour conseil de ley cristyene en tut pur le suite encontre Thomas Berche, tutez choses acomptez – xliij s. iiij d. (*A* + *a*, p. 38)

and so on.

Two of the civic ceremonies whose costs are accounted for in these Minute Books were very grand affairs and of great historical importance.[6] The first was organised for the coronation of Richard II in 1377 and was the first English civic pageant for which any detailed description survives; the second was for the reception of Anne of Bohemia, Richard II's first wife in 1382. The Goldsmiths took part in these pageants and at both their chief set piece was a *somercastell*, a word listed in the OED and MED only as a siege engine, but here clearly being used in peacetime and ceremonially. The word has of course nothing to do with the season of the year when it was used, but derives from the French *somer* – 'a packhorse' or 'a horse load', since it was a castle or more probably a tower that could be carried on horseback to its temporary destination. Other new vocabulary surfaces in these sets of accounts: the mysterious *seluerskynnes*, which were most probably silvered-over hides used to cover the framework of the somercastell,[7] and *seluerwir*, silver wire that would look decorative as well as serving a useful purpose. *Orsandy* = 'arsedine'[8] was used for something we know not what in 1377 (perhaps to decorate the somercastell with gold-coloured patterns), and in 1382 leaves were painted with diaper patterns and used apparently as confetti: 'Item, pur foyll' a diaprer a getter sur le royne – v s.' (*A + a*, p. 57).

More everyday occurrences provide equal interest. The ledger contains also the full texts of various sets of statutes and ordinances dealing with rules governing the work of gold- and silversmiths, empowering the Company to take action against those who infringed these rules, while also regulating the running of the Company and defining its legal powers. These early ordinances are all in French, and provide us with a rich source of vocabulary and language usage referring to the everyday working lives of the goldsmiths, e.g.

> Et auxint plousours qe se fount del dit mestier des orfeveres tignent lour shopes en veneles oscures et rues foreines et achatent vessells d'or et d'argent en musset et ne mye en querant si le vessel soit emblé ou de loial purchaz et meintenant le mettent al fieu et fount translater en plate et le vendent as marchauntz passajours pur le porter hors de ceste terre et ensement fount fauces overaignes d'or et d'argent come de coronaux, fermeux, aneux et altres jeux es queux ils mettent veirres de diverses colours contrefaitz a perrie et mettent plus de lai en l'argent qe faire ne deussent, les queux ils vendent as mercers et as autres qi de ceo ne ount conissance. (*A + a*, p. 19)

> Et si nul de la confrarie meurt, toutz viendront a l'enterement s'ils n'eiont resonable encheson, sur peine de ij deniers a doner pur l'alme. Et si nul de la confrarie moert hors de la ville, qe l'em fra pur lui si com il fust mort en la ville. Et ceux qe murront qe sont de la confrarie regardent a la confrarie a lour voluntez [*i.e. in their wills*] pur lour almes. Et qe nul overe pir oor de l'asay ne pir argent de la moneie.

---

6   For a full account, see Richard H. Osberg, 'The Goldsmiths' "Chastell" of 1377', *Theatre Survey* 27 (1986), pp. 1–15.
7   See Appendix, below.
8   See Appendix, below.

Et qe nul n'eit forsqe une manere de pois, et ceo soit encelez. Et qe nul ne see faux piere en or ne dreit piere en quivere n'en latun, c'est assaver en anel ne en firmail ne en ceinture, ne deorrer nul de ceo trois. (*A* + *a*, p. 41)

French is the language used throughout except in a very few cases and until well past the turn of the fifteenth century. To deal first with exceptions to the use of French: the copies on pp. 14–18 of legal documents relating to land and property holdings are in Latin – as one would expect. The ledger occasionally shows an anno-tated marginal remark in Latin, the date at which this might have been added being difficult to determine but being if not contemporary then nearly so; these occur for instance above the copy of the first royal charter on p. 19: 'Anno primo E. tercij / Prima Carta Aur' Auctoritate parliamenti' and the charter relating to Bordeaux and the duchy of Guyenne on p. 20: 'Carta Civitatis Burdegalie in ducatu Acquitanie', as also to the ordinance picked out for mention on p. 32: 'Prima ordinacio de non venantibus' and the precedent set by a fine imposed in 42 Edward III and recorded on p. 36: 'Pena pro vendicione operis aurifabr'. . .'. This penalty was imposed on one John Chapler, who was in the habit of taking silverware to sell on Cornhill, contrary to the customs and ordinances of the guild; when challenged, John Chapler 'disoit q'il voleit feare maugré lour et parla malveis paroles et maliciouses a eaux et fust desobeisant et rebel as ditez gardeinz', for which he was led off to cool his heels in Newgate Prison; two friends of his then undertook to get him out by vouching for his future good behaviour and tied him down with a legal deed of obligation, the words of which are recorded here: 'et les paroles del obligacioun ensuont: Noverint universi presentes me Johannem Chapler aurifabrem . . .'. The legal document is in Latin and is being copied here verbatim, whereas the case is otherwise recorded in French, with the revealing little slip at the beginning of giving the name as 'Johannis Chapler' rather than Johan as it occurs thereafter, the Latin form occasioned very probably by the presence in front of the scribe of the Latin legal document.

For whatever reason, the end of Edward III's reign and the start of that of Richard II seems to have led to some upset in the recording of the Company's affairs: we find on p. 53 Latin being used for the brief headings over a list of names and on p. 54 English is used to record the receipt of two fines levied on aliens. French is then however reverted to and is used throughout the reigns of Richard II and Henry IV (apart again from the copying of a Latin document on p. 98: 'La copie del brief purchasez par Roger Osbourne: Henricus dei gratia Rex Anglie et Francie et Dominus Hibernie vic' London' salutem. Precipimus vobis quod William Chipstede . . .') until the last years of the latter's reign, when a new scribe took over (p. 100), began his work writing in Latin, perhaps from force of habit acquired at his previous job, and then quite naturally and fluently went into French as he realised this was the way things were done here at the Goldsmiths'. A few pages later however (p. 104) the French again breaks down and Latin is used to record matters previously dealt with in French, although this is again a temporary lapse and French is reverted to. The move away from French becomes very evident once one gets to the records from Henry V's reign. This king's promotion of the cause of the English language is well documented,[9] but before English is introduced we find a long series of pages where French and Latin alternate. The hands are not different, the same scribes are equally able to write in Latin and French and it remains a mystery why and how they chose to record the case against one errant goldsmith in Latin and that against another in French. From the eighth year of Henry V's reign (1420–1), English begins to be used as a language of record, but not exclusively by any manner of means. The ledger indeed for a few years shows a bewildering mixture of languages, English being used for some entries, Latin for others, and French still holding its own though to an ever-decreasing extent. When used, the French is however still fully competent and fluent, e.g.

> Fait a remembrer qe le ij^de jour de Novembre l'an du regne le Roy Henry vj viij^e qe pur taunt qe William Reygate revyla et disoit maliciouses et faulx paroles de Johan Patteslee,[10] un des audermans de Loundres qe adevant estoit gardein de la mistier des orfevres, come le le dit William conust luy mesmes, agardez feust par les gardeins qe le dit William paiera xx s. al almoigne de Seint Dunstan dount il paiera vj s. viij d. et les autres xiij s. iiij d. feurent pardonez. – vj s. viij d. (*A* + *a*, p. 149)

After French disappears from the recorded details entered in the book each year, it is retained for a short while in the standard formula beginning each year's entry ('Ceux sount lez nouns dez gardeins eslutz al ffeste de Seint Dunston l'an du regne le Roi Henry . . .'), until in 13 Henry VI (1435) the inevitable happens: 'Theise ben the namys off the Wardeynys of the craft of goldsmithis chosyn in the feste of Seynt Dunston in the yere of Kyng Henry the vj^to after the conquest xiij thanne beinge' (*A* + *a*, p. 161).

The situation is in every way similar in Minute Book A + b, the smaller record book intended for the wardens themselves to keep. The language of record is French, the fluency and competency of this being with one exception of the same standard as that in the large ledger, unsurprisingly, since the same scribe was keeping both registers. The exception occurs on pp. 17–20, dealing with the last years of Edward III's reign, which are written in a different and rather poor hand, one that does not occur in the large ledger. The obvious inference is that this is the hand of one of the Wardens who has chosen to write up the records himself. His French is still fluent, but the spelling bears many more marks of its English home-ground than is usual in the big ledger. French is used throughout the records kept during the reign of Richard II and for the first years of Henry IV, until in the fourth year of the latter's reign (1402–3) a most interesting case appears. A series of fines for various misdemeanours are being recorded and in the midst of these, all recorded in French, one case, that of Walter Prata, is written up entirely in English. The case is a long one, the offender clearly an habitual criminal who disrupted and disturbed the whole craft and Company by his stealing, lying, cheating, embezzling, burgling

---

[9]   See e.g. John H. Fisher, 'A Language Policy for Lancastrian England', *PMLA* (October 1992), pp. 1168–80, which contains a good bibliography of previous scholarship on the subject.

[10] Or Paddesley: see *Early History*, pp. 300–1 for biographical notes on this man.

and by his ultimate refusal to make amends in any way.[11] Whether the record of the case against him breaks into English deliberately – to ensure that there be none who cannot fully understand the charges and the full authority of his expulsion – or whether it was inadvertent – the case having been heard in English, the clerk on hand to record the proceedings, and then copying up his notes verbatim forgetting in the heat of the moment to translate – we cannot know the reasons now. That it may have been in order to ensure full comprehension of all is perhaps borne out by an entry four years later (1406–7) in the large ledger of a similarly convoluted and serious set of charges, this time involving one William Chipstede. The record of this is in French, but in three places an interlinear gloss in English has been added to explicate certain words: *puys* is glossed as 'aftward', *tuez* as 'slayn', and *enoutre* as 'more ouere'. These words are apparently written by the same hand as that of the main text, were demonstrably written in after the main text, and one imagines perhaps that the clerk was reading it through to someone who hesitated at those points, the clerk translating for him and writing the words in as he did so. (It may be noted that this same case gave rise to two other documents copied up into the ledger here: a legal brief which is in Latin, and a letter of support of Chipstede's cause from the Queen herself – this latter being in French.)[12]

The evidence of the archival records of the Goldsmiths' Company shows clearly that for written records throughout the fourteenth century and until well into the fifteenth a completely trilingual situation existed.[13] Legal documents such as deeds to property, official writs, wills and bequests, were in Latin. The oath to be sworn at the Guildhall of those admitted to the freedom of the City is given in French (A + b, p. 45 (4 Henry IV = 1402–3)); however, the only slightly later texts given (in Book A + b) of the oaths to be sworn on entry into office of the Wardens are in English (A + b, p. 74), as are those to be sworn by 'Dutchmen' given permission to work and trade in London (A + b, pp. 64, 66). The record of the permission given is however in French:

> Hanes Cokeban est jurré [et] voil paier ij nobles pur estre suffry tank al feste des Paskes et s'il demure en outre graunte de faire fyn ové les gardeyns. . . . Wynant van Coloigne est jurrez et ad graunté de paier pur estre suffriz xl s., c'est assavoir al feste de Noell et le Purificacion de Nostre Dame et overa par terme de les ans qe est obligez. (*A + b*, p. 67)

The ordinances for goldsmiths and ancillary workers (vessellers, enamellers and

---

11 Among his crimes one can pick out as examples: 'Also he tak a Wey his maystres sal armonyak & salt pete for to make a Watir of & profrede to a man x s. for to lerne to make it. Also he countrefeted the keye of his maystres countour chambr & of his cheste . . .'.

12 Henry IV's second wife was Joane, daughter of Charles II of Navarre and widow of John de Montfort, Duke of Brittany; her letters were addressed to the Mayor of London and the Wardens of the Goldsmiths' Company, and it was clearly expected that they would understand fully the French.

13 See further on this: W. Rothwell, 'The Trilingual England of Geffrey Chaucer', *Studies in the Age of Chaucer* 16 (1994), pp. 45–67. See also Linda Ehrsam Voigts, 'What's the Word? Bilingualism in Late Medieval England', *Speculum* 71 (1996), pp. 813–26: this article deals with Latin and English in scientific and medical writings.

engravers of seals, burnishers), written up in Minute Book A + a at various points during the fourteenth and early fifteenth centuries, are all in French. The ordinances for spangle-makers, dating from 5 Henry IV (1403–4), copied into Book A + b (p. 52), are however in English, as are the later ones (1435) given for the finers (those who refined the metals) (A + b, pp. 81–3).

French was fully and fluently understood and used as a language of record, and the ease with which objects of goldsmithry are referred to and described in French makes one believe that this language was also frequently used orally, in business deals of all kinds. There was a vast amount of commerce between England and the Continent, foreign goldsmiths coming over in particular from the Low Countries, Burgundian lands where French was current. In addition, we know from other records that the goldsmiths' dealings with the court and with the aristocracy of the land were perhaps conducted in French, and were certainly recorded in that language. The Public Record Office in London contains a number of medieval inventories of jewellery and plate, almost all of which are in French: for instance, Nicholas Twyford, four times Prime Warden of the Goldsmiths, was called in to make a valuation of all the table plate, ecclesiastical vessels and personal jewellery belonging to Richard II at the beginning of his reign and presumably inherited from his grandfather Edward III.[14] John of Gaunt's Register records his large holdings of precious plate and jewels.[15] John of Bedford's clerks and household officers drew up inventories of his quite splendid holdings of valuable goods (many acquired from French royal and other collections during his regency of France), the language of some of these being in French, some English, and with some small use of Latin also.[16]

However, one field of vocabulary is heavily anglicised – that of the building trade. Whereas a goldsmith from Paris would, one imagines, have had little difficulty in communicating with his opposite numbers in London, the same is clearly not true for plumbers, carpenters, plasterers and tilers. The first recorded entry concerning the Goldsmiths' building expenses (that of their first communal Hall) is very brief and poses few problems for it goes into no details:

pur un sale et quezine et pantri et botylrie et ij chaumbris ové dowble gette – C xxxvj li. iij d.

But when extensions were made to this later and a full account was rendered and recorded, the vocabulary used often becomes distinctly anglicised, e.g.

Item, al tyler xij s. Item pur iiij^{Ml} tieles, pris xxvj s. viij d. Item, pur rooftiel – ij s.

14 PRO E101/400/6.
15 Ed. S. Armitage-Smith, *John of Gaunt's Register (1371–75)*, Camden Society, 3rd ser. 20 and 21 (1911); ed. E. C. Lodge and R. Somerville, *John of Gaunt's Register (1379–83)*, Camden Society, 3rd ser. 56 and 57 (1937).
16 See Jenny Stratford, *The Bedford Inventories: The Worldly Goods of John, Duke of Bedford, Regent of France (1389–1435)*, Reports of the Research Committee of the Society of Antiquaries of London, no. XLIX (London, 1993).

vij d. Item, pur tylpyns vij d. ob. Item, pur lathes al celour – x s. x d. Item pur lathenaylle a tut l'overaygne – xx s. v d. ob.

Some of the vocabulary used is purely French: *baillé . . . en erres, par le jour, a cause de, voider, grees* (steps, stairs), *les mures del parlour, pur amender les autres defautes*, etc.; some is anglicised French: *un masoun, un carpenter, pur un autre servant, soun vadlet*, etc.; but much is purely English or gallicised English: *lattenaylle, un daubere, iiij hokes pur le seler, rooftiel, tylpyns*, etc. These are clearly local materials and local workmen, whose language is English. The clerk of the Goldsmiths' Company has an excellent command of the French language, but is unable to translate the names of such objects as roof-tiles and tile-pins into that language, although he has no difficulty with the language of accountancy: *baillé en erres, pur le masoun pur soun travaill*, etc.

The vocabulary of goldsmithry is in contrast almost entirely French, with a few exceptions: 'Item petites bedes de coper en un pice de drap linge', and the so-far-unexplained 'ryng' which would appear to be a different sort of ring to an *anel*:

Item, deliveré en anelx d'or faux et stoppés de coper: En primes un anelle fait al manere d'un signet stoppé de coper. Item iij rynges dj round coveré d'or et stoppé de latoun. Item j anelle d'or bon, pois v s., ové un verre. Item un autre anelle coveré d'or stoppé de plumb ové un verre. (*A + a*, p. 86)

The above passage dates from 22–23 Richard II (1398–9) and apart from the 'ryng' we see also the English form 'coper' and the acephalous and English form 'stoppé'. One can find a few examples of these intrusions earlier (e.g. *et autres yngotys peces – A + a*, p. 67; *Item, ij bokclaspes de coper endorrez – A + a*, p. 79), and increasingly from here on we find English words or English forms introduced into the French: *bolkuppys . . . pleynkuppys* (*A + a*, p. 112); *foundue en trois wegges* (Reg. Deeds, f. 379r – 30 May 8 Henry IV in a mid-fifteenth-century copy); *un barre al maner d'un squirell'* (*A + a*, p. 97).

From 1362 the official spoken language of the courts of law in England was supposedly English (although some French may still have been used), but legal documents were very generally issued in Latin, and Latin provided the names for various types of court procedures as of such documents. The references to legal costs in the Goldsmiths' records thus often show language contamination from these Latin sources. One expects of course a straight citation: 'Et le dite Roger Osbourne encountre la ffraunchise du dite cité et encountre soun serement fait al dite mestier pursua al chaunceler d'Engleterre pur avoir le dite William Chipstede devant le dite Chaunceler par brief appellé *corpus cum causa*' (p. 98); but one finds also such bastard mixes as *lettre obligatorie*:

Et de ceo ledit Giffrey est obligé a les ditz gardeyns en viij li. par une lettre obligatorie.

Fait a remembrer qe Estephene Clerc est obligé a lesditz gardeyns en x marcz d'esterlingz par une lettre obligatorie. (p. 50)

The vocabulary culled from the Goldsmiths' archives and listed here below in the Appendix to this article for specific comment represents only a fraction of what can be gained from these records. AND2 will include as short quotations many further words and phrases gleaned from this source that will provide sometimes better examples, or later ones, of a word previously attested, sometimes new spellings, or newly attested collocations, and also further attestations of specific meanings of words and phrases with variable usage. Historians of the Goldsmiths' Company have already used this archive,[17] but have seemingly in some cases misunderstood the language,[18] or perhaps not mentioned certain interesting misdemeanour cases since the details appeared obscure.[19] Linguists and lexicographers can be of use to historians, but conversely the former can often only attain their knowledge from experts in a field, in this case that of medieval jewellery and gold- and silverware.[20] By no means all the words I have picked out to comment upon relate to gold- and silversmithing. The great value to linguists and lexicographers of the Goldsmiths' Company fourteenth-century records lies only partly in their technical vocabulary, for one finds here also a wealth of examples of everyday vocabulary, legal terms, words relating to other crafts e.g. the building trade, etc. I hope in due course to be able to publish the full text of the early Goldsmiths' Minute Books and thus make this material available to all.

17   Prior to the work of Reddaway and Walker one should mention W. S. Prideaux, *Memorials of the Goldsmiths' Company . . .*, 2 vols, vol. I (London, printed for private circulation, 1896); W. Herbert, *The History of the Twelve Great Livery Companies of London*, 2 vols (London, 1834), vol. II.

18   E.g. *Early History*, p. 48 where *alkenamie* has been interpreted as 'alchemy' rather than the metallic substance (see below); Prideaux, *passim*, instead of giving an English translation as usual, quotes in French for a number of dubious points e.g. see pp. 10–11; on p. 11 he mistakenly translates *lyens* as 'handles' (see Appendix).

19   Prideaux is admittedly only claiming to summarise the most important events of each year, but many notable cases are omitted from his summaries of the fourteenth-century records.

20   Later works of reference than those dealing with medieval times can also often provide the information one needs, since craft practices endure for centuries. Cited below and among the reference books I have used, most of which have good bibliographies: R. W. Lightbown, *Mediaeval European Jewellery* (London, 1992); R. W. Lightbown, *Secular Goldsmiths' Work in Medieval France: A History*, Reports of the Research Committee of the Society of Antiquaries of London, no. XXXVI (London, 1978); R. W. Lightbown, *French Silver* (London, 1978); P. Glanville, *Silver in England* (London, 1987); C. Oman, *English Silversmiths' Work Civil and Domestic* (London, 1965); C. Oman, *English Domestic Silver* (London, 1934; 7th edn 1968); C. Oman, *Victoria and Albert Museum Catalogue of Rings 1930* (Ipswich, 1993); C. Oman, *British Rings 800–1914* (London, 1974); J. Alexander and P. Binski, eds, *Age of Chivalry: Art in Plantagenet England 1200–1400* (London, 1987); S. Brault-Lerch, *Les Orfèvres de Franche-Comté et de la Principauté de Montbéliard du moyen âge au XIXe siècle* (*Dictionnaire des poinçons de l'orfèvrerie provinciale française*, 1) (Geneva, 1976) – and all the other volumes in this series; L. Douet-D'Arcq, *Comptes de l'argenterie des rois de France au XIVe siècle* (Paris, 1851), pp. 345–408: 'Table des mots techniques'; L. Douet D'Arcq, *Nouveau recueil de comptes de l'argenterie des rois de France* (Paris, 1874); C. J. Jackson, *An Illustrated History of English Plate*, 2 vols (London, 1911).

Appendix[21]

acord/acordance – faitz d'une acord/acordance – 'standardised, of one standard officially agreed weight': Fait a remembrer qe en le temps dez gardeins suditez furent totz les poys dez orfeveres par tote la cité de Loundres assises (*sized*) et faitz d'une acord. *A + a*, p. 24. (1361) . . . qe les poys soient faitz de une acordance; et qe nul ne poise mes qe des poys merchez. *A + a*, p. 42. (1370)

The words **acord** and **acordance** are certainly found listed in all the dictionaries of medieval French, but the meanings given always refer to agreement, harmony and concord, or alliances, not to actual physical concordance between two or more objects, in this case weights.

akere, acre = 'an acorn-knop': Item, pur un doszeyne de quilheres, c'est assavoir ové pomelles et akeres . . . *A + a*, p. 33. (1367) . . . qe come le dit Johan, en temps qe T.P., T.E., R.R., et W.M. furent Wardeyns, fist esquels de faux metalle et les acres endorrez . . . *Reg. Deeds*, f. 376.

This is an entirely English word (ME **aker, akir, akorn**, etc. derived from OE **aecern**), an acorn, and used by extension for any decorative representation of these attractively-shaped fruits. As finals for spoons they were popular, and indeed the rounded form made its use as a knop on e.g. lids and covers equally frequent. The specialist books on medieval silverware and china show many examples of this,[22] but lexicographers are in general behind in their coverage of this material. The MED gives a 1420 quotation of 'A dosyn off siluer sponys with acharnus ouerguld' and a 1450 quotation of 'a couered pece with a gilted knop of acorns leves'. The OED lists acorn knop only as 'a knop or protuberance on the stem of a drinking glass, tooled in the form of an acorn' with a 1960 quotation.[23] It is interesting therefore to note that the example from the Goldsmiths' records of 1367 is the earliest recorded use of the word **akere** in this sense, and that the word, though English, comes in an entirely French passage.

alkenamie = 'alchemy, a metallic composition, a yellowish alloy, imitating gold': Item, pur ceo qe Aleyn Palmer, Simond atte Wode, Hanes Bugelyn, et Thomas Richardson, pedder, et j frere carme furrount arestez pur xxij esquilers lesqueux furent trovez en le mayn le avant dit Simond et j cuppe qe fuist trové en le mayn Johan van Berwe, Duchman, qe furront de Alkenamye et faux argent, et j staylet (?*little stele*?) pece trové en le mayn du dit Simond et autres yngotys peces trovez ové le dite Aleyn Palmer pur queux ils furrount emprisonez en temps Nicholas Extoun, meire, et les

---

[21] For the dictionaries cited here, see the list of abbreviations at the beginning of this volume.

[22] See e.g. Oman, *English Domestic Silver*, p. 38 and plate V; Lightbown, *French Silver*, no. 10; *Age of Chivalry*, nos. 209, 210 pp. 280–1 and no. 541 p. 435.

[23] The situation is similar for the Latin **glans** and French **gland**, for which only FEW lists a sense of 'petit morceau de métal, de bois, petite houppe d'étoffe, de forme ovoïde, et destiné à l'ornementation' with a dating of 'seit 1379'.

chosez avant nomez lessez en le chaumbre del Gildehalle, as costages des ditz gardeyns – xxvj s. viij d. *A* + *a*, p. 67. (1386–88)

Alchemy, the notorious search for a method of transmuting base metals into gold, is less well-known as a word denoting the results of such labours (dishonestly presented as successful). Dictionaries do however list it, the earliest attestation being it seems from a Latin document of 1287 listed in DMLBS 1.59a sub **alchimia** ('. . . et misit alkemiam et falsum metallum . . .').[24] The MED's earliest citation is (a1393), while that of the OED is 1440. G lists this meaning only in the Complément, and with no quotation earlier than the sixteenth century (1536 and 1570). FEW (1.70a)[25] also gives the sixteenth century for the word in the sense of 'métal de composition alchimique', although DHLF gives 1447 for **arquemie**: 'un alliage de composition alchimique' (1.43a). The passage from the Goldsmiths' records takes the earliest attestation in French of the word in this sense back to 1387, still a century after its first recorded use in Latin.

ameillour = 'enameller' . . . ordeiné est et assentu qe toutz ameillours et taillours des seals (*seal-cutters/seal gravers*) rendront a chescun son pois d'or et d'argent solom lour pouwer . . . *A* + *a*, p. 40. (1370)

Enamel, enamel work and enamelling and the words for them in various medieval languages are easy to find in dictionaries, but the men (or women) who did the work are more difficult to trace.[26] The DMLBS has nothing. G Comp. 532c lists **esmailleur** but with no date. The MED however correctly lists **amelour** as coming from AF, but its only citations are as men's surnames, the earliest being 1311.

anelet, anelette = 'annulet (a small ring or circle used decoratively)' Item, pur ceo qe Richard Litlee fuist trové en defaute de vj boses appellé anelettes pur un jakke, queux pois' j li. le quel li. ne vaut forsque xx s. pur quel fauxté il se mist en grace de ses gardeyns. *A* + *b*, p. 46. (1403)

G, DMLBS and MED give only the meanings of a real ring (whether as a finger-ring, or a ringlet of hair, or a metal ring serving some useful purpose), but the OED and FEW (24.556b) both also cite the heraldic meaning of the decorative small circle worn as a charge on a coat of arms, the OED from 1572, FEW only with a 1681 reference. This usage as a decorative representation of the object is similar to the heraldic usage. Other earlier heraldic examples can also be found than those in the OED and FEW referred to above, e.g. 'Grimaldi's Roll', 88: 'a sys anelettes'.[27]

apporter = 'to behave': Nespurqaunt pur ceo qe nous sumes enformés a present coment le dite William luy ad apporté nyent graciousement devers vous ne les

---

24 Gaol Delivery Rolls (1271–1476), PRO (Just. Itin. 3), 36/1 r. 24d.

25 The word does not appear to be listed in FEW 24.

26 This is only true of dictionaries, for specialist works on the subject have traced many individuals: see e.g. Lightbown, *Secular Goldsmiths' Work*, p. 83; V. Gay, *Glossaire archéologique du moyen âge et de la Renaissance*, 2 vols (Paris, 1887–1928), sub **esmailleur**).

27 Cited in G. J. Brault, *Early Blazon* . . . (2nd edn, Woodbridge, 1997), p. 106, where other examples may also be found cited.

mestres de soun art des orfevers dount il nous displest a cause de soun orgelouseté et necligence celle partie . . . *A + a*, p. 98. (1406/7)

The passage is a quotation from a letter from the Queen explaining her earlier support of the miscreant William Chipstede, a relative of her private chaplain, and that follows the above-quoted acknowledgement of William's error by a request for clemency. William's ungracious behaviour included plotting to kill the wardens of the company, maligning them publicly, and renouncing the trade of goldsmith ('le dite William Chipstede ad renunciez la mestier d'orfeverie et dist eovertement q'il ne voille estre al governayle de sez gardeyns ne unqes claymer d'estre orfevere pur M^l li.'). The noun *aport, port* in the sense of 'behaviour' is well attested, but this appears to be the first attestation of the verb *apporter* in the sense of 'to behave, conduct oneself' since no French or Latin dictionary lists such a meaning. The extension from *aport* = 'behaviour' to *apporter* = 'to behave' is in no way surprising, but the strong presence of the verb in the sense of 'to bring' might have 'blocked' frequent use in this other sense.

argent . . . argent blank = 'ungilded silver'; (also as just **blanc, blank**): Fait a remembrer qe mesme an fuist ordeigné qe nuly du dite mestier n'achate de nulle estraunger le livre d'argent blank debrosez (*broken up bits of ungilded silver plate*) pluys chere qe le livre a xxvij s. . . . *A + a*, p. 77. (1393–5) – Item, pur ceo qe Thomas Wylwes fist un bond blank a un estraunger et mesme estraunger fist endorrer mesme bond et reporta au dite Thomas pur mettre sur le hanap . . . *A + b*, p. 43. (1402–3)

No dictionary of medieval French lists this use of *blanc/blank* in the sense of 'ungilded (silver)'. They do however list it under the meanings of a coin: G Comp.328a: 'petite pièce de monnaie qui valait cinq deniers', which appears in English as *blaunk* (MED 1.958b) and in Latin as *blancus* (Du Cange 1.698c; DMLBS 1.202c). The DMLBS also lists for **blancus** the sense of 'blanched = tested by assay', a meaning not listed in the OED, which does however give both 'to make metals white . . .' and 'to remove the dark crust from an alloy after annealing' II.258b. FEW (25.192a) lists *argent blanc* as 'argent mat, non poli' with datings from 1360–1595 (since it is otherwise the *éclat* and gleam of both silver and whiteness that lend themselves to metonymic uses, one is surprised by this usage). The meaning of 'ungilded (silver)' was evidently in common use. Apart from the examples cited here, one may for instance note its use in various fourteenth-century documents[28] (although in some cases it could be debatable as to whether it meant 'unpolished' or 'ungilded', the Goldsmiths' examples seem clear as do the Bedford examples cited below). It is also found frequently in the mid-fifteenth-century inventories of John of Bedford's worldly goods,[29] e.g. 'Item, une grosse pomme

---

[28] e.g. Item, deux bacyns veill' d'argent blancs – pris vij li. . . . . Item, un sonet d'argent tout blanc, poisant vj s. viij d. – pris viij s. iiij d. . . . . Item, deux eawers d'argent blancs . . . Item, un chaufour d'argent blanc gravé en le tenelle ové les armes quarterés, poisant iiij li. iiij d. – pris Cij s. (PRO E101/400/6).

[29] Edited by Stratford, *Bedford Inventories.*

d'argent, moitié doré moitié blanche, au mettre de feu dedens pour chaufer les mains de prestre quant il fait froit' . . . (*Bedford Inventories* B131). – 'Premierement, ung ymaige de Nostre Seigneur . . . . . . tenant en sa main senestre ung pomme ronde, a ung croix par dessus, a une piece se terant sur blanc en la poietrine appellé doublet' . . . (*Bedford Inventories* B105).

argent fin . . . grauntasmes pur nous et noz heirs qe nul marchant privé n'estrangé ne porte en nostre dite roialme nulle manere de monoie forgé mesqe plate d'argent fyn . . . *A + a*, p. 20. (1358)

The FEW (25.192a) lists *argent fin* as appearing from the twelfth to the fifteenth centuries in Old Provençal in the meaning 'argent pur' and in modern Occitan as 'argent de coupelle' i.e. cupellated or refined silver. G and TL have no cited instances, nor has the DMLBS, but Du Cange (1.389a–b) has a long section on *Argentum Regis, Argentum Finum, Gallice Argent le Roy, Argent fin* which details the difference (*une maille*) between the two and the reasons for the two appellations: 'car anciennement quant l'Emperiere faisoit monnoie, l'en disoit en ses monnoies d'Argent Fin, et ainsi faisoit l'en ès monnoies des Rois, Ducs, Princes, et Comtes, qui tenoient de luy. Et afin que il ne semblast que le Roy de France fut homme de l'Emperiere, et que il venist de lui, il fu ordené par le Conseil des Pers de France, que l'en dirait, Argent le Roy, qui est à une maille prés d'Argent Fin' (*Registrum Camerae Computorum Parisiensis*, f. 205). The fourteenth-century goldsmiths of London had no such political-linguistic problems, however, and would seem to be using the phrase in opposition to 'monoie forgé' to mean 'cupellated, refined silver'.

assai = 'assay' Et qe nul overe pir oor de l'asay ne pir argent de la moneie. *A + a*, p. 41. (1371) . . . fust ordeiné et assentu qe chescun an deivont aler as divers feires les gardeinz qe seront pur l'an pur assay feare des choses touchant le mester d'orfeverie, et ferront lour assay des toutz choses touchant lour mester trovez en les meinz des merceres, haburdassheres come des orfeveres, et si bien en feires pardehors villes come en villes. *A + a*, p. 48. (1372) – . . . les ditz gardeins et touz autres qi ount esté gardeyns de la dite mistier en la dite citee de temps dount memorie ne court ount ewez et usez d'avoir la serche, surviu, assaie et governaunce de tout manere oor et argent overez, si bien deinz mesme la citee comme aillours deinz vostre roialme d'Engleterre . . . *Reg. Deeds*, f. 377r.

The Modern English word *assay* derives from AF *essai* (ultimately from the Latin *exagium*), and although the OED gives the etymology as from OF, the MED's listing as from both AF and CF seems better informed, at least as far as one can see from the present lexicographical situation. In the non-specific sense of 'a test, trial', the word certainly occurs in a number of contexts in continental French of the Middle Ages (TL 3.1283–5), but in the technical sense of the testing of a metal to determine the quantity of ore or alloy G and TL both list only one instance from Chrétien's *Cligès* (l. 4246: Por ce toche an l'or a l'essai / Qu'on vieut savoir se il est fins). No later examples are given,[30] but we can now supply the above quotations. In England

[30] See however the Larousse, *Grand dictionnaire universel du XIX*^{e} *siècle* (Slatkine reprint, 1982),

the word took on an even more specific meaning, that of the London standard of quality of the metal gold, a meaning cited by the MED from 1457 (1.435b), although the OED gives only the more generic usage as 'approved quality, proof, temper of metal etc.' or 'standard of fineness in the precious metals', its earliest quotation being of 1430. The examples below all predate this.

Et qe nul overe pir oor de l'asay, ne pir argent de la moneie. *A + a*, p. 41. (1370) – . . . et qe l'en overast or del assay ou meillour et nul peiour . . . *A + a*, p. 40. (1370) . . . qe or fust trové en meyn d'orfevere ou marchant qe ne vausist le assay, en fermaux ou en aneaux ou en autres choses, q'ils fussont debrusez . . . *A + a*, p. 40. (1370)

As a verb, *assaier/essaier* is not listed in G or TL with the technical meaning, although one suspects that it nevertheless existed. The goldsmiths of London certainly employed it:

Et qe nul manere de vessel d'argent ne soit porté hors des mains des ov[ere]res tauntqe ele soit assaié par les gardeins del mester et qe ele [soit] signee de une teste de leopart. *A + a*, p. 41. (1370) – Et qe les gardeins del mester aillont de shope en shope entre les overers assaiaunt qe le or soit tiel comme la touche avandit. *A + a*, p. 41.[31] (1370)

asseer . . . asseer les pois = 'to size, regulate weights and measures in relation to a fixed standard' Fait a remembrer qe en le temps dez gardeins suditez furent totz les poys dez orfeveres par tote la cité de Loundres assises ('sized') et faitz d'une acord. *A + a*, p. 24. (1361) – Item, pur ceo qe Henri atte Felde, goldbetere, fuist trové en defaute d'iceo qe ses moldes ne furent fait de mesure ne assise qu'ils duissent estre, il fuist amerciez en xl s. . . . *A + b*, p. 51. (cf. assise = 'the assize (a prescribed standard of quality') . . . d'or overaunt meyns qe l'assise ent ordeyné . . . *A + a*, p. 112. (1412/13)

The noun *assise* or its equivalents in Latin and English is in the above sense well-attested in England, the word coming from the legal sitting that determined the standard and hence being applied to the standard itself. The verb however is difficult to find in dictionaries (the DMLBS example sub **assidere** (1.141c) 'to fix (a standard)' is not the same as actually to do the setting to this standard). It certainly passed from French into English as 'to size', the OED (15.579c) giving a 1400–50 quotation as its first example. Whether or not it was used in CF must remain in doubt until lexicographers have fully combed the available resources. A related word *sezaille* is found in G but not under its own headword: sub **tailleor** is listed *tailleresse*: 'ouvrière chargée de tailler les flans des monnaies, de leur donner le poids fixé' and the example cited, dated 1383, reads: 'Lesquelz flaons cellui ouvrier avoit tirez de la sezaille que la tailleresse avoit faite'.

VII.936–44 for excellent sections on the various methods of 'essai des monnaies et des matières d'or et d'argent'.

31   See Glanville, *Silver in England*, pp. 145–65: 'Touch, Assay and Hallmarking'; *Early History*, pp. 317–21.

almoigne: The alms donated by the goldsmiths were collected first from various sources into a Common Box and were known after their patron saint as the *almoigne de Seint Dunston*, the phrase referring to the funds rather than to the object they were kept in: . . . 'un certein somme de monee . . . al almoigne de Seinte Dunston en eide de sustenance des poveres de mesme le mester et en eide d'allowance des chapleins a chanter pur les almes de la confraternité des orpheveres' . . . *A + a*, p. 36. (1368) The phrase, in a number of variant spellings, is found on almost every page of the Goldsmiths' minute books, and each year the amount 'Doné al encrés del almoigne Seynt Dunston' by the outgoing and incoming wardens is recorded, as are the fines levied for misdemeanours, each of which resulted in a payment 'a l'amoyne de Sent Dounstoun' / 'al almoigne de Seinte Dunstoun'. There is no instance of the goldsmiths taking this usage further and applying it to the fines themselves, but in the Merchant Taylors' accounts an amount is listed each year as received 'de Almoigne: Item de veill' almoigne . . . Item de nouell' almoigne', these being, it must be assumed from all the evidence, the sums paid into the alms-box or common funds as a result of a fine or penalty. This extension of meaning of the word has not previously been listed in dictionaries, but was nevertheless understood by historians such as Clode.[32]

batelment: Item, purceo qe Johan Andrew fuist trové en defaute en le façoun de un batelment paia – ij s. *A + b*, p. 29. (1382–84)
Nothing is recorded in dictionaries of medieval French that would elucidate John Andrew's defective work, but all three of the languages of medieval England produce written evidence that an indented or crenelated rim or brim to a vessel e.g. a cup was known as a *batelment, batilment* or *batillamentum*.[33] The OED, MED and DMLBS all concur in deriving the word in its military-architectural sense from OF *batillement*, but on present evidence it would seem that the extension to an ornamental battlement on e.g. drinking cups was an insular development. The present citation from the Goldsmiths' predates by a few years the earliest citation in the DMLBS of 1390 (1.187c), and by a good half-century the English quotations of both the MED and OED (1.1010b) which date only from 1444.

bede: . . . j peir bedes de latoun endorré . . . Item petites bedes de coper en un pice de drap linge. *A + a*, p. 79. (1394–6) – Item pur ceo qe plusours disloialx artificers ymaginantz a desceyver le comune people fait de jour en autre firmeux, anelx, bedes . . . de cupre et de latoun, et les susorrount et susargentount semblables a or et argent et les vendent . . . *A + b*, p. 61. (1403/4)
The only points of note on this word are the dates (earlier than those in the MED and OED) and that its entirely English (and ultimately Germanic) nature obscured its

---

32   C. M. Clode, *Memorials of the Guild of Merchant Taylors of the Fraternity of St John the Baptist in the City of London and of its associated charities and institutions* (London, printed for private circulation, 1874); *The Early History of the Guild of Merchant Taylors' of the Fraternity of St John the Baptist, London, with notices of the lives of some of its eminent members*, 2 vols (London, printed for private circulation, 1888).

33   A good illustration though of a later date is plate 43 of Oman, *English Silversmiths' Work*.

meaning to Godefroy when he met it in a copy of a statute of Henry IV of England, the same as the last citation given above. G simply lists the word **bede** with a question-mark for its meaning (1.608b), and then gives three citations; for the second of these,[34] a glance at an English dictionary would have told him that it meant either a rosary or a bead of a rosary.[35] Du Cange also failed to appreciate the Englishness of the word in its Latin form, and for some reason listed **beda** (1.635b) with the sense of *armilla* (= 'bracelet'), although his sole quotation is from an English source of 1386 and clearly refers to rosaries (*duo paria de bedis de auro*).

belfray, belfrey, berfray = 'belfry' Primes, pur soner none en le belfray de Seint Poul de diverses costages – vij s. iij d. *A + a*, p. 49. (1373) – Primes, pur sonere noun le veile de Seint Dunstan en la Belfray de Seint Poule pur divers costages – vj s. viij d. *A + a*, p. 50. (1374) – En primes pur le sonour del grant sonel de Seint Poul et pur autres custages del berfray – viij s. ij d. *A + a*, p. 59. (1382) – En primes pur soner le graunt sonaille en le belfrey a Poules – iij s. iiij d. *A + a*, p. 79. (1394–6) – En primes pur soner le graunt sonail de Seint Poul et en autres costages en le belfray – vij s. vij d. *A + b*, p. 29. (1382–4)

The etymology of this word (< Germanic **bercvrit** < Frankish ***bergfripu** > AF *berfroi* = a movable wooden siege tower, a watchtower) is dealt with fully in the OED, which however states that the change from r to l while common in Latin forms of the word is exceptional in French and in English 'did not appear bef. 15th c., being probably at first a literary imitation of med. Lat.' FEW (1.332a) and the DHLF (1.203a) give the fifteenth century also as a date before which the word was not used in the sense of a bell-tower. The examples culled from the Goldsmiths' records show both the form of the word with *l* and with the meaning of a church bell-tower to have been current in the fourteenth century.

bende, bond(e) = 'an ornamental band (of metal, to be affixed to an item of silver-ware, a cup, etc.')[36] Item, Goffrey Wapol ad fayt treys bendis de argent . . . (c.1373) *A + b*, p. 19. Thomas Wylwes fist un bond blank a un estraunger et mesme estraunger fist endorrer mesme bond et reporta au dite Thomas pur mettre sur le hanap et mesme Thomas mist mesme bond sur le hanap . . . *A + b*, p. 43. – . . . Johan Turnour fitz a Simond Turnour fuist trové faux en bondes de cuppes qe furent faux et desceyvables . . . *A + b*, p. 49. (1403/4)

cupbonde – Purceo qe Johan Chervelle le xj[me] jour de Maij ffuist trové en default devaunt lez gardeins del overaigndе [*sic*] d'un Cupbonde ennorez . . . *A + a*, p. 101. (1407/8)

Of particular note here is perhaps that in 1403–4 a scribe will write 'bondes de cuppes' whereas just a few years later this appears as 'cupbonde'. Many further examples can be found from this period showing how English syntactical construc-tions were invading written French documents. One should note also the alternative

---

34 The other two belong together apparently as a separate lemma, both concerning doves in Lille.
35 See also Lightbown, *Mediaeval European Jewellery*, pp. 342–54 'Paternoster Beads'.
36 See e.g. plates 1–8 of Oman, *English Silversmiths' Work*.

word *lien* which is purely French, and which is also used for these ornamental bands on cups (see below).

biller = 'to label' ... Et lez avantditz evydencez chescun par soy mesmes come as ditz tenementz apparteignent en diverse kofyns et boxez mys, et issynt lez ditz boxez billez a dire qe de tielx tenementz specefyent, en chescun boxe quantz evydencez escriptz come en le libre est specefyé, . . . *A + a*, p. 120. (1418)

This sense of *biller* is not listed in any dictionary of French, nor does it appear in the MED's entry **billen** and would thus not appear to have existed in English with this meaning. However, the DMLBS lists **billare** = to label, its earliest quotation being 1300 followed by several others of the fourteenth century. The Goldsmiths' use of the word in French well into the fifteenth century gives room for speculation that it may one day turn up in English.

bombard = 'a 'bombard' = the bass shawm, a member of the bassoon family of wind instruments' . . . trumpes, clarions et pipes . . . Item, un bombard poisant iiij marcs (demj) j ounce et v d. de mesme pois ové le portour. *A + a*, p. 74. (1391/2)

This reference to the musical instrument whose name was taken from a piece of siege ordnance (presumably in reference to the noise it produced) is contemporaneous with the earliest quotations of its use in ME given in the MED and OED (1393). The DMLBS has no record of it, Du Cange's earliest citation of its use in French (1.719a) is from 1432, and G's quotations are also of a late date (Comp. 8.338b).

burcel, bursel, bussell = 'a bossell = the 'print' or ornamental medallion fixed in the bottom of a mazer or drinking bowl; this was sometimes raised up slightly'.[37]

Item pur ceo qe plusours disloialx artificers ymaginantz a desceyver le comune people fait de jour en autre firmeux, anelx, bedes, chaundelures, gipserrynges, chalices, hiltes et pomelx d'espeyes, pouderboxes, liens et burcelx pur hanapes, de cupre et de latoun, et les susorrount et susargentount semblables a or et argent et les vendent . . . *A + b*, p. 61.[38] (1403–4)

The OED's earliest example of this word (said to be a diminutive of boss) is dated 1495, and the MED lists two of 1439 and 1456 (but believes the word to derive from Latin BORCELLUM). The DMLBS derives the word **bursellum** from OF *borsel* and provides a good illustrative quotation of 1458. *Borsel* however only appears in G 1.689c with the meaning of a bump on the head, or swelling, as it does in TL (1.1079). The etymology of the word in this sense should perhaps be looked at again. These quotations from the Goldsmiths' records are certainly earlier than previously found attestations, but what is most surprising about this is that the OED elsewhere quotes from the same Statute of Henry IV that contains this word (sub

---

[37] Illustrations appear e.g. in plates 3, 4, 7 of Oman, *English Silversmiths' Work*; Glanville, *Silver in England*, fig. 3. In France it was known as a 'boulon': see Lightbown, *Secular Goldsmiths' Work*, p. 21.

[38] The word is spelt 'bursels' a few lines later, and is spelt 'bussells' in the somewhat later copy of this statute of 5 Henry IV in *Reg. Deeds*, f. 375v.

gipser 6.523c); had the editors noticed this they might have altered their remark that the word was 'perhaps already in OF' and have suggested an AF origin for it.

carole = 'a ring or circle of precious stones in a piece of jewellery' . . . et aneaux a bases caroles s'ils le voilont faire a double chaston . . . *A* + *a*, p. 42. (1370)
The word *carole*, originally meaning a dance and then applied to various rounded formations (as well as for other extended uses), must clearly here refer to a ring of small jewels or precious stones set decoratively around one large gemstone on a ring.[39] The DMLBS lists this meaning (**carola** 2.285c) with quotations from 1295 and 1331, as does Du Cange (2.193a) with quotations from continental sources. G, TL, FEW, DHLF along with the MED and OED seem not however to have picked up any examples of the word in such a context in either French or English. The Goldsmiths' use of it in 1370 proves that it existed at least in Anglo-French.

chape = 'chape (a pointed metal mount at the end of a scabbard or belt)': Et les ditz gardeins d'orfevers par vous, treshonourez seignurs, soyent comaundez d'apporter ou faire apporter en vostre honourable presence sibien les avaunditz chaundelers come un hylt et un chape de coper endorrez pur une espeye . . . *Reg. Deeds*, f. 375r. Although the word *chape / chapa* is given in the DMLBS and MED as from OF, the OED gives a derivation from late Latin CAPA, CAPPA = hood, cap cape, and suggests that the English use of it to refer to an ornamental metal plate may have been influenced by the Spanish and Portuguese use of *chapa* = 'plate, thin piece of metal with which anything may be plated'. In England certainly, as the quotations from the MED and OED make plain, the word often referred to a metal plate or mounting of a sheath or scabbard, particularly the part that covers the point, and would also seem to have been used of the whole sheath or scabbard. G, TL, DHLF and FEW list no occurrences of the word in this sense and nothing in anything approaching this sense until the nineteenth century (FEW 2.1.275b). Although OF may be the origin of the form of the word *chape* meaning cape or mantle, it seems from the evidence that the meaning of 'chape' (the word persists in English) cannot be attributed to continental OF but rather is specific to England.[40]

chastun, chaston, caston = 'bezel' ('the groove and projecting flange or lip by which . . . the stone of a jewel is retained in its setting' (OED)
Qe nul ne face anel s'il ne soit a double caston (with a double bezil) . . . *A* + *a*, p. 41. (1370) – . . . et la ou y ad double chaston qe le chaston desouth soit parté a treis parties qe un puisse veere parmy et le chaston paramont [soit] a baas filet (with a low fillet), et les nouches en mesme le manere; et aneaux a bases caroles s'ils le voilont faire a double chaston en la fourme avandit. *A* + *a*, p. 42. (1370)
G does not list this word but TL includes it with the meaning 'Ringkasten' (2.309–10); the DMLBS (**casto** 2.295b) and AND1 give its meaning as 'setting (of a gem)' but jewellers distinguish between the setting and the bezel and the OED defi-

---

[39] See e.g. Oman, *British Rings*, plates 6, 7, 8, 19.
[40] Illustrations can be found in e.g. *Age of Chivalry*, no. 176 p. 263 and no. 730 p. 526.

nition is accurate.[41] One may also note that the modern English word *bezel* is said to come from OF *besel/biseau* but this word is not listed in G or TL, and the DHLF which says the word is 'd'abord attesté en orfèvrerie à propos d'un chaton taillé en biais servant à enchâsser l'émail d'un bijou' gives no date or source for this usage.[42]

colers appellez S, 'S' = 'collars of SS' (livery collars formed of chains of linked letters 'S' – the livery of the house of Lancaster, granted by Henrys IV, V, and VI): Purceo qe Johan Cottoun ffuist trové en defaut del overaigne dez colers appellez 'S', des queux S quatre sount en garde come appiert par un bille le xxme jour d'apprille, il ad payé a celle temps – iij s. iiij d. *A + a*, p. 101. (1406–8).
The quotation dates from 1406–8 and is thus contemporaneous with the OED's and MED's earliest citation of 1407 and much earlier than the DMLBS's 1440 date (2.378a).[43] It is not perhaps surprising that continental dictionaries, while they list the meaning of *collier* (in whatever form) as a chain worn about the neck as an ornament or badge of office, have not picked up the 'colers appellez S' which might certainly turn up in French documents.

coronal = 'coronal' . . . et ensement fount fauces overaignes d'or et d'argent come de coronaux, fermeux, aneux et altres jueux . . . *A + a*, p. 19. (1327, copied in 1358)
The word 'coronal' in the sense of a circlet for the head, usually made of gold and with inlaid gems,[44] occurs only in AF and has never been attested in CF. It appears also in insular Medieval Latin and ME, and is recorded in the DMLBS from 1332, in the MED from a1393, and in the OED from c1330. The OED gives its etymology as 'app. repr. an AngloFr. *coronal . . .', and it is thus good to be able to supply with the above quotation a missing link. However, although the word does not appear in this sense in G, TL or Du Cange, the FEW has picked it up (2.ii.1209a) with a vague '14.jh.' date.

corps = 'corse' ('a ribbon or band of silk (or other material) serving as a ground for ornamentation with metalwork or embroidery, and used as a girdle, garter, etc.' OED).[45] Item, Gerard van Sweck, pur ceo q'il fust trové en defaut de j seinture q'il avoit fait al Ducz de Lancastre d'or, et puis fust mandé a lui pur remuer et enclower sur j novel corps et les clowes furent soudez d'esteym . . . *A + a*, p. 39. (1369)
Once again we appear to have a word which has come into English from OF in its original, basic sense (*cors* = body), but which has then been used in Britain in a context not so far attested for continental French. Clearly such a word as *cors* (or

---

41 On medieval bezelled rings see Oman, *British Rings*, pp. 15–22; Oman comments on the oddity of the ruling given in the first quotation above (p. 14, n. 3) but has no explanation; see also Oman, *Victoria and Albert Museum Catalogue of Rings*.
42 Professor Rothwell has pointed to the mysterious 'bisseaus' that occur in Bibbesworth 1056, glossed in ME as 'paringes' and which would seem to mean perhaps crusts of bread.
43 The earliest surviving representations of one dates from c.1370–80: see Lightbown, *Mediaeval European Jewellery*, pp. 245–50 'Livery Collars'.
44 See Lightbown, *Mediaeval European Jewellery*, pp. 121–31 and plates 13, 15.
45 See Lightbown, *Mediaeval European Jewellery*, pp. 306–41 'Girdles and Belts'; *Age of Chivalry*, no. 609 p. 473.

corpus in its Latin form) is inevitably going to be applied in a number of extended uses, and many such are indeed listed in G, TL, Du Cange and most comprehensively in FEW (**corpus** 2.ii.1212–19). Interestingly, the DMLBS has no examples of this usage. The MED (2.i.625b) lists it, its first quotation being of 1382, whereas the OED's earliest text is of 1440.

coster = 'coster = a hanging for the sides of a bed, the walls of a room etc.' Item, des exec' de Alice Chichestre en moneye – x li. et j sale (*the hangings for a room*) ové iiij costers, iiij banqers et xxiiij quissyns (*cushions*) de plume. (*feathers*) *A* + *a*, p. 59. (1382/3)
In OF the form of this word was *costier* or *costiere* and it is attested in G as the masculine form from 1316 Artois and in TL as the feminine form from one twelfth- and one thirteenth-century text.[46] The DMLBS gives the derivation of the Latin word **costera** (which has several meanings) as from AN *costere*, OF *costiere*, its earliest citation in this sense being of 1371. The MED on the other hand gives the derivation of ME *coster* as from AL *costera*, its earliest quotation given being in Latin and of 1345–9, the next being in French, the word in the form *costres*, and the date 1376, and the first English citation here dates from 1395. The OED's etymology is from AF *coster* = OF *costier*, and its first quotation is a mixed language one of 1385 where the word *costers* is placed in the midst of a Latin sentence (*Duo costers panni magni de velvetto*) and could thus be accounted as either a French or an English interjection.

custodye = 'guard-leaf': Fait a remembrer qe el temps de William Fytzhughe, Johan Hilles, Richard Wedyalle et Johan Walsche est ordeigné et escript et en le Tresorye mys un libre de velom contenant iiijC foill' saunz lez custodyes, c'est assavoir iiij en primer comencement et iiij en le ffyn;[47] le quelle libre . . . *A* + *a*, p. 120. (1418/19)
This sense had been given to the Latin word *custodia* in England since at least 1245, the earliest citation given in the DMLBS (2.544c; cf. also 2.546c sub **custos**). The MED and OED do not record it in English (although the OED gives for *custody* a meaning of 'a case for keeping a thing in' with a citation from Caxton's 1483 Golden Legend 240/3: 'His bookes whiche had not a custodye (nullum habentes conservatorium) fyl in the water'. G and FEW record this latter meaning but not that of guard-leaves to a book, but Du Cange (2.724c) has recorded several uses of the word in a 1295 document from St Paul's in London. On present evidence it therefore looks as if the word existed in this sense in both its Latin and French forms in medieval England but did not pass into the English language, and that it was not used on the continent.

customer = 'customer' Item, pur ceo qe Philip Castille vendust a un Thomas, servant de Henri Grene, orfevere, un anelle d'or pur iiij s. et i d. et vendust mesme anelle a un des customers du dite Henri, au quel customer le dite Phelip covertement

---

46 *Partonopeus de Blois*, ed. Crapelet (Paris, 1834), l. 10305; *Der Roman von Escanor von Gerard von Amiens*, ed. H. Michelant (Tübingen, 1886), l. 16039.
47 These guardleaves all survive and are bound into what is now known as the *Register of Deeds*.

dist qe le anelle ne custa pluys qe iiij s. et j d. en disclaundre du dite Thomas et perde de soun customer. *A* + *a*, p. 93. (1402/3) – Item, pur ceo qe Thomas Oxenforde ad disclaundré Huchon (= Hugh) Wetherby en disaunt qe ne savoit eoverer ne faire un cuppe, par quel perdust soun customer, pur quel il fuist juggez de paier vj s. viij d. *A* + *b*, p. 45.

These examples of the use of the word 'customer' in a French text and in its modern English sense predate by a few years the MED's earliest citation of 1409 (the OED only lists it from c.1480). The French 'coustumier' and Latin 'custumarius' have very different meanings, including that of a customary tenant, a meaning which also existed in AF and ME. The meaning of a buyer or purchaser is specific to England.

custumable = 'in the habit of (doing something)': Item, pur ceo qe ascunz de mesme le mester sont custumables d'aler al Guyhalle et d'enfrancher apprentiz . . . sanz assent des gardeinz . . . *A* + *a*, p. 42. (1370)

This word is not recorded in continental OF with this meaning and once again it seems that it is a purely insular extension of sense, found in both AF and ME (the earliest citation in both the MED and OED is from c.1303), so that although the form of the word may be correctly said to come from OF (OED 4.168b), its use in this sense does not.

desk = 'a sloping board, a reckoning-board' J. G . . . fist esquels de faux metalle et les acres endorrez et puis . . . ad mys campernolle d'esteigne en une ceynture d'argent . . . et ore ad fait une ceynture ové barres d'esteigne et penduz en soun desk overtement pur vendre, a graunt disceite del peple du roialme . . . *Reg. Deeds*, f. 376. (1395/6)

The word ultimately derives from L. DISCUS but is found in its French derivative form only in England and not in France (see OED 4.524b on the etymology). It is recorded in the OED and MED in many senses, the most usual being that of a writing or reading desk. The DMLBS also lists a wide range of meanings for **discus** (2.684a–c), one of which (4e) is a reckoning-board for which it supplies a 1483 quotation from the *Catholicon Anglicum*. If this is the meaning here, which seems possible, then it represents an earlier use of the word in that sense. It may alternatively refer simply to a sloping board used as a sales counter.

filet = 'fillet': . . . la ou y ad double chaston (*double bezil*) qe le chaston desouth soit parté a treis parties qe un puisse veere parmy et le chaston paramont [soit] a baas filet (with a low fillet), et les nouches en mesme le manere. *A* + *a*, p. 42. (1370)

The word *filet* is a diminutive of 'fil' = a thread, 'ce qu'on a filé' and has been used in both French and English to denote a wide number of objects with a long thin shape. This particular usage however, that of an ornamental edging around something, has only previously been picked up by the MED in a passage dated a1425 (a1382) and referring to rings.

fieu = 'fire assay, cupellation' (used to test the quality of gold and silver): Ore novelement les marchantz susditz auxibien privés come estraungés amesnent de estraunges terres en ceste terre esterling contrefait, dount la livere ne vaut forsqe sesze sols del droit esterling et de cele monoye ne poet homme avoir conissance s'il ne soit par fieu. *A + a*, p. 19. (1327 copied in 1358) . . . **mettre al fieu** – *to melt down (silver)* . . . et achatent vessells d'or et d'argent en musset et ne mye en querant si le vessel soit emblé ou de loial purchaz et meintenant le mettent al fieu et fount translater en plate et le vendent as marchauntz passajours pur le porter hors de ceste terre . . . *A + a*, p. 19. (1327 copied in 1358)

The FEW only lists this sense of the word ('bas fourneau où s'opère la réduction du métal' as from 1872 (3.656b)) and yet it clearly must have been in use centuries before, although one cannot find it in any other dictionary.

gipserring, gipsering = 'a ring or circlet of metal used to attach a gipser to a girdle' Item pur ceo qe plusours disloialx artificers ymaginantz a desceyver le comune people fait de jour en autre firmeux, anelx, bedes, chaundelures, gipserrynges,[48] chalices, hiltes et pomelx d'espeyes, pouderboxes, liens et burcelx pur hanapes, de cupre et de latoun, et les susorrount et susargentount semblables a or et argent et les vendent . . . *A + b*, p. 61. (1403/4)

Gipsers were ornamental pouches attached to a girdle or sash by means of a ring. The MED (4.128b) derives the word from OF *gibeciere, gipsiere* '= a game-bag', and cites the word first from a translation and then in English from Chaucer c.1387–95. G lists it in his Comp. 698a with examples from the *Clef d'Amors* and then from documents of 1389 onwards. Surprisingly, the word has not been found in Latin form in England (the DMLBS lists **gibbus**, but not this possible derivative). Du Cange has however picked it up in several examples from the Continent (3.517c), and although FEW rejects the derivation from GIBBUS (4.133b), the OED rejects the alternative derivation from *gibier* (6.523c), the DHLF, quoting both theories, seems to accept the GIBBUS hypothesis (1.887b), but the DEAF opts for the derivation from *gibiez* (G699–700). Whatever may be the case as to the correct etymology, the word *gipser* is clearly of OF origin, but the addition of the purely English *ring* to form the compound *gipser(r)ing* has produced another of the many words of mixed origin. The OED quotes another version of our example above, but prefacing it with an 'attrib.', and not choosing to consider the word as an independent compound although it prints the example thus.

hendrer = 'to hinder, impede': . . . qe si lez termes qe sount a dit Walter relessez par le dit Johan Colney ne soit fait par fraude ne collusion parcount la Companye d'Orfeverie ne nulle d'eux ne soient empechez ne defamez ne par le dit Walter ne sez termes hendrez . . . *A + a*, p. 108. (1411/12)

This must be the ME verb *hindren* given a French form. It is recorded in the MED with the senses of 'to cause harm or injury', 'to bring sb. or sth. into ill-repute' and 'to hold back, impede, obstruct' and any of these might have been the intended sense here. No French dictionary has previously picked up this word which may have been somewhat idiosyncratic.

---

[48] 'gipserynges' in the same Statute copied out in the Goldsmiths' *Register of Deeds*, f. 375v.

judas = 'a "Judas"; a kind of wooden candle-holder': Item, pur lumere de Seint Dunstoun pur ix Judas, le fesour vij s. Item pur peynture de mesme les Judas iij s. Item pur ix disshes pur les tapres – iij s. ix d. Item in cire – xviij s. viij d. *A* + *a*, p. 59. (1382/3)

The OED supplies a full description of a 'Judas' in a quotation from 1877: 'The paschal candlestick in churches, which was usually of brass, had seven branches, from the seventh or middle one of which a tall thick piece of wood, painted like a candle, and called the Judas of the Paschal, rose nearly to the roof, and on the top of this was placed at Eastertide the paschal candle of wax.' The OED's earliest citation is from 1402–3 and is in Latin, its earliest English quotation being from 1453. The MED lists it (5.417a) from 1405 and says it is also a kind of small candle. The DMLBS however can provide a citation from 1310 (1507a). No French dictionary lists it and one must presume it to have been purely insular in use. In the passage from the Goldsmiths' records it would seem that the reference must be to a type of candle-holder, rather than a candle.

latrocinie = 'theft, larceny' Item pur ceo qe Johan Scherston ad eovertement disclaundrez William Hert de latrocinie . . . *A* + *b*, p. 40. (1402/3)

The Latin LATROCINIUM gave the French *larcin* and the English *larceny*, and in English the learned form *latrociny/latrosinie* is recorded from c.1430 to 1657 (OED 8.692a; MED 6.696b). No French dictionary records the word, although G lists (4.737a–b) **latrocinal, latrocination, latrocineusement**.

lemayle = 'metal filings, limail, lemel' . . . **lemayle d'argent** – 'silver filings': Item, l'autre ffausçune ffust de le poys de un mark de sablount qe ffust mellé ové lemayle d'argent et vendu pur argent a Thomas de Brandam. *A* + *a*, p. 32. (1365)

In modern English the word is more usually *lemel* and refers generally to waste, filings of no possible use. In the Middle Ages, and indeed until much later, such filings of precious metals could be collected up by the workman for re-use – but clearly re-use as practised by John of Bruges was illegal! G (4.786a) lists the word **limaille** used first in a Latin text of 1340–1 and then for 1379–80 onwards. The MED gives *limaille* as derived from OF and its first quotation of 1357–8 is from a mixed-language document. The vowel change from *limail* to *lemel* is already evident in the Goldsmiths' records of 1365.

leopard, la teste de leopard = 'leopard's head mark': – Et qe un [ou] deux de chescune citee ou ville avandites veignent a Loundres pur le dit mestier de quere lour certeine touche d'or et ensement le pounceoun ové la teste de leopard pur mercher lour overaignes come auncienement feust ordeiné. *A* + *a*, p. 19. (1327 in copy of 1358) – . . . et qe un ou deux du dit mestier de chescun cité ou ville avantdites veignent a nostre chastel de Burdeux a nostre Conestable illocqes, pur le dit mestier, de quere lour certein touche d'or et ensement le punchoun ové la teste de leopard pur mercher lour overages. *A* + *a*, p. 21. (1358)

Dictionaries of French and Latin do not record this usage, although they do record the heraldic significance of the leopard in the royal arms of England, and the gold coin, known as a leopard, struck by Edward III in c.1344.[49] The leopard's head appears only in the MED (6.837b) as an assay mark for silver, its earliest citation being of 1423. The OED has a very odd entry (8.832c): 'The leopard's (i.e. lion's) head seems to have been used as an assay-mark for silver' with just one quotation of 1423. This mark was however in use from 1300,[50] and as these quotations from the Goldsmiths' records make clear, in well-established use in both England and Gascony from at least the beginning of Edward III's reign.[51] The valuation of Edward III's jewellery and plate made at the beginning of his successor's reign (PRO E101/400/6) lists objects with leopards' heads: 'Item, un peir bacins d'argent ové les swages enorrez et esm' dedeins en les fountes de testes de leopardz, poisant Cxj s. iij d. – pris vij li.', and also a number of objects with just a leopard mark, which may have been rather a mark of royal ownership than an assay mark ('Item, xxiij saucers d'argent blancs merchez par dehors en les bordours d'un leopard . . . pris xx li. Item, xvj esquelles d'argent d'une sort merchez en les bordours par dehors d'un leopard et flourdeliz – pris xxviij li. xiij s. iiij d. Item xij chargeours d'argent d'une sort mercheez en les bordours par dehors d'un leopard – pris xxx li.')

lien = 'a band, bound to a cup or other object': Item, fait a remembrer qe lez avant-ditz gardeyns acomptent en despences et diverses coustages vers la lei, de pursure pur iij fauces lyens des hanaps des maszer, queux lienz estoyent de latoun et endorrez . . . *A* + *b*, p. 4. . . . Johan Wadyngton pur ij marc ad iij lienz d'argent pur mazers, quel est en le cheste. *A* + *b*, p. 5. . . . Item pur ceo qe plusours disloialx artificers ymaginantz a desceyver le comune people fait de jour en autre firmeux, anelx, bedes, chaundelures, gipserrynges, chalices, hiltes et pomelx d'espeyes, pouderboxes, liens et burcelx pur hanapes, de cupre et de latoun, et les susorrount et susargentount semblables a or et argent . . . *A* + *b*, p. 61. . . . lienes et bussells pur hanapes . . . lienx et busselx pur hanapes . . . *Reg. Deeds*, f. 375v.

The French word **lien** is listed in G (Comp. 80c) as a 'chose flexible, d'une certaine longueur, dont on entoure les parties d'un objet, ou plusieurs objets pour les joindre ensemble' which covers the meaning of the word in the above passages; these must refer to silver (or supposedly silver) bands around the rim of a mazer etc. or else strips linking the base and the rim.[52] FEW (**ligamen** 5.317–19) lists a large number of specific uses of the word *lien* but none that refer to bands on cups, although the word must surely have been used in continental French. The DMLBS however gives the etymology of *lien* (1606b) and *lienum* (1606c) as from AN and ME with AF *liien* listed after these other two languages; the meanings picked up for these two words do not however include the specific one found here, which does though appear sub **ligamen** (1607a) with a date of 1286 for its first attestation. One notes in

---

[49] See *Age of Chivalry*, no. 616 p. 477 and no. 661 p. 491.

[50] See Glanville, *Silver in England*, p. 145.

[51] See *Age of Chivalry*, pp. 165–7 and fig. 116.

[52] I am indebted for this information to John Cherry. See e.g. R. W. Lightbown, *Secular Goldsmiths' Work in Medieval France*, plate LXXII; Lightbown, *French Silver*, no. 1; Glanville, *Silver in England*, fig. 2.

the Goldsmiths' records the parallel use of the English word 'bond' and 'cupbonde' (see above).

limit: . . . les ditz gardeinz examineront les parties et si trové soit qe la dette soit duwe, les ditz gardeinz front redresser qe la dite dette soit meintenant paié ou autrement lymit dit j certein jour del paiement et si la dette ne soit mye paié al jour assis adonqes eiont les ditz gardeinz pouwer de prendre destresse des ditz orfeveres qe sont dettours . . . *A + a*, p. 40. (1370)

The word *limit(e)* is of course well-recorded in all dictionaries, but this precise use as a fixed date set does not appear, except under the verb **limiten** in the MED (6.1058b) which is there listed with the sense of to fix a date.

lokette = 'a locket (a metal mount)' Item, pur ceo qe Johan Welforde fuist trové en defaute le xxje jour de Juni, de ij lokettes et un harnois d'un corn d'argent (*a drinking-horn*) qe le livre fuist peiour de vij d., fuist condempnez en ij s. *A + b*, p. 39. (1402–3)

Locquet, loquette appears in continental French (although the word is cognate with *lock* and of Germanic origin) with the meanings of 'lock', 'latch' or 'bolt' (G 5.31a, 31c) and these meanings are listed for the English word 'locket' and ME 'loket', but in English another meaning exists, that of 'a metal plate or band on a scabbard', or, as in its present context, on other objects. Metal plates or bands were affixed to a drinking-horn and formed part of their 'harness' or ornamental fittings.[53] The DMLBS gives for **lokettus** the meaning of a metal plate or bar as attested from 1290, and refers with a 'cf.' to an etymology perhaps from OF *loquet* or ME *loket*.

lomb = 'loam, clay, esp. that used for daubing walls' Item pur C charrettés de lomb et sond – xxvj s. viij d. *A + a*, p. 60. (1382/3)

The word is clearly an English one and is not listed in dictionaries of either French or Latin. The MED lists the form *lomb(e* but labels it erroneous (sub **lom** 6.1176b). This form was certainly widely current and appears not only as here in the Goldsmiths' records but also in those of the Merchant Taylors: Item pur ij lodis lombe et pur dawberis iij s. vj d. *Mch Tayl Accts* 1.Hen.IV. – pur un lode de lombe al furneis – iiij d. *Mch Tayl Accts* 9.Hen.IV.

lowerie = 'rent, hire': Les amerciament mesme l'an de Johan de Kelleseye et Johan fiz Roger pur le lowerie d'une shope – vj [s.] viij d. *A + a*, p. 5. (1340 copied in 1358)

G (5.15a) lists the word **loerie/louerie** in the sense of 'loyer, location' but his earliest citation is of 1408–9. The word seems to have remained entirely French and did not apparently pass into English in any form.

lyggere = 'a ledger, record book': Item, lez dites gardeyns acomptent avoir paié pur j novel papier achaté, qe currera dez gardeyns en gardeyns; et qe ceste graunt papier sera mys pur j lyggere, a gyser en une cofre ovesqez aultres choses: pris del novelle

---

[53] See e.g. Oman, *English Silversmiths' Work*, plate 5; *Age of Chivalry*, nos. 544, 545 pp. 437–8.

papier – ij s. x d. *A + a*, p. 45. (1371) Item, les dites Gardeyns acomptent avoir achaté ceste novelle papier qe currera des Gardeyns en gardeyns, et qe l'altre graunt papier sera gysant en une cofre ovesqe aultres choses pur un remembrauncer; pris de ceste novelle papier – ij s. x d. *A + b*, p. 1. (1371)
These parallel entries in the Wardens' Accounts Books were both written in 1371 at the time of the purchase of a new record book; what is being referred to as 'ceste novelle papier' here is now Wardens' Account Book 1B, and 'ceste graunt papier' is Wardens' Account Book 1A, which is indeed on much larger paper than the other. The word 'lyggere' is purely English and is recorded in the MED (**ligger** 6.1004a) and OED as a large and not easily portable breviary, but the above quotation shows that its more general sense of a book that lies permanently in some place, or that of a record-book was current by 1371, almost two centuries before the OED's first citations of 1538 and 1550 (8.789a).

malousement, malowsement = 'maliciously': Fait a remembrer pur ceo qe William Letherpole dispetousement revyla et disclaundra sez gardeins et eux disclaundra de robbery, et auxi revyla un Roger Barneston malousement a son schoppe en Chepe . . . *A + a*, p. 111. (1412/13) – . . . l'avantdit Robert batust l'avantdit Maykyn malowsement cy come devant lez avantditz gardeins de record fust trové. *A + a*, p. 119. (1418/19)
G lists **malous** = 'mauvais' (5.126a) but no adverb derived from this form. The MED lists what it calls an erroneous form: 'maliously', sub **maliciousli** (7.99b), but since the quotation from Lydgate in which the word occurs is in verse the error must be doubtful and the above two instances of the word in the early fifteenth-century records of the Goldsmiths show it to have existed in both French and English forms.

melter = 'to melt, smelt' Item, pur ceo qe Robert Howes fuist trové en defaute pur ceo qe monstra a –[54] estraungers les privités del mestier en melter d'argent . . . *A + b*, p. 40. (1402/3)
The ME verb *melten* has clearly here been given a French form. This type of formation is commonly found in the early fifteenth century in official records kept in French by English scribes. Cf. Item pur iiij laborers par xliiij jours a deboter lez velx maisons, ripper tiles, digger vowtes pur privés et autres fundementz, et de voider le terre a v d. ob. – iiij li. viij d. *Mch Tayl Accts* 3.Hen.V.

multeplier . . . multeplicacion: Item, ordeigné est et establez qe nully desore enavant use de multeplier or ou argent ne use le art de multeplicacion et si nully le face et d'iceo soit atteynt, q'il encourge le peyne de ffelonye en ceo caas. *A + b*, p. 61. (1403/4)
The felony involved here may be one of two things: first, that of splitting a piece of gold or silver or of gold- or silver-foil into two in order to make it go further.[55] Since gold and silver objects were sold by weight, it would seem that the likely moment

---

[54] 'un' has been crossed out and an indecipherable number written over.
[55] John Cherry sides with this interpretation.

when a goldsmith might be tempted to 'multiply' might be if he had been given a set amount of metal or metal foil to carry out some specific piece of work and was either hoping it would not be weighed once made, or was intending to make up the weight by some other felonious means. The word was certainly used in the fifteenth century in England to refer to the counterfeiting of money and AND1 has such a quotation, listed only however with the given meaning of 'multiplying, increase' from the *Rotuli Parliamentorum*, iii 540.[56] RMLWL also gives sub **multiplex** the *multiplicator cunagii* of 1437 with the meaning of 'coiner, counterfeiter'. In continental French no such usage has been recorded before 1646 (*multiplier les armes du roi = faire de la fausse monnaie*: FEW 6.ii.204b) and 1718 (*multiplication des espèces = fausse monnaie* FEW 6.ii.205a). The other possible meaning is that of alchemy, and this meaning is recorded in English and in insular Latin, and seems perhaps the more likely explanation of the prohibition ordained. Du Cange cites from a 1456 charter of Henry VI of England the word *multiplicatores* and gives a full passage from it: 'Quia timor poenalis ab investigatione et practica tantorum secretorum multos viros ingeniosos, naturalibus scientiis doctissimos . . . ab multis diebus hucusque abduxit . . . ne ipsi in poenam incidant cujusdam statuti tempore regni Henrici avi nostri contra Multiplicatores editi et provisi . . .' (4.569c–570a), while RMLWL gives a 1456 date for **multiplicatio** = alchemical transmutation and a 1418 date for **multiplico (metalla)** – to transmute in an alchemical sense. The OED records this sense of the words from 1386 (Chaucer) and 1390 (Gower) and has also a 1543 translation of the above prohibition of the reign of Henry IV which is being alluded to in Du Cange's passage (10.89a). The MED also cites this same passage but from the *Statutes of the Realm*, 2.144.[57] There seems to be no record of this usage from the continent and one must presume it to have been purely insular.

note = 'a "nut", a nut cup, a coconut cup': Johan de Tourstrete avoit mys en une pee d'argent de une hanap qe l'en appelle une Note certein plum en deceite . . . *A + a*, p. 48. (1372) – Purceo qe Johan Chervelle fuist trové en defaut del overaigne del garnyschour d'un Note le xme jour d'aprille et issint trové par dieux foitz, dount ad payé al almoigne de Seint Dunstoun – iij s. iiij d. *A + a*, p. 101. (1407/8)
The coconut cup, a kind of goblet made from a coconut or other large nut, whose shell, cut open at one end, is mounted in metal, was a popular object in the Middle

---

56 *Rotuli Parliamentorum*, vols i–iii, Record Commission, London, 1767–77.
57 It has also tracked an allusion to one actual method used:

> Arestotle he was arste in Alexander tyme,
> And was a fyne philozophire and a fynour noble,
> He gerte Alexander to graythe and gete golde when hym liste,
> And multiplye metalles with mercurye watirs,
> And with his ewe ardaunt and arsneke pouders,
> With salpetir and sal-jeme and siche many othire,
> And menge his metalles and make fyne siluere
> And was a blaunchere of the best thurgh blaste of his fyre.

'The Parlement of the Thre Ages', ed. I. Gollancz, *Select Early English Poems I* (London, 1913), ll. 586–93.

Ages and a number of specimens survive.[58] In Latin they were called either *nux* (Du Cange 4.664c with a 1420 quotation) or *poculum nuceum*, although RMLWL has no quotation before c.1508 for this. The DMLBS files however contain several thirteenth- and fourteenth-century citations e.g. 'de uno cipho de nuce', 'j nux nigra pro cipho', the word *nux* standing alone for a cup made of it in documents from 1315 and 1334. In French they were known as *nois(e)*, GComp. 206a giving only a 1507 citation for nois, whereas *noise* is cited 5.517a from the Year Books of the reign of Edward I. The English appellation 'nut' or 'note' is recorded from 1337 in the OED but the text cited is in fact an 1868 translation and the original needs to be traced. The AND1 has unknowingly found the same quotation as G from the Year Books but has only listed it under **herneschcer** ('une noyse herneysé d'argent' 354b). Under **noise, noice** it could now be joined by 'Item, un noice garni d'argent enorré, poisant xviij s. vj d. – pris xxvj s. viij d. . . . Item, un poet d'un potelle d'un noice noire garni d'argent enorrez – pris lx s. PRO E101/400/6 (1378–9). Since the French words for the object existed and were used in England in 1378/9, it is interesting to note the Goldsmiths's use of the English word in 1372.

or – oor ars . . . Qe nul ne vend oor ars s'il ne soit dreit fyn. *A + a*, p. 42. (1370)
One presumes this must mean gold that has been refined by cupellation, but I cannot find any other examples of this in any dictionary. The same is true of the following expressions relating to gold:

feble or = 'gold below the official touch standard, below the official standard of purity': Item, Water de Algate et de Thomas Bamme pur j fermail oeveré de feble or – iij s. iiij d. *A + a*, p. 2. (1336 copied in 1358)
or tochant le allay de .v. = 'gold of the assay of the fifth = 19.2 carats (the Touch of Paris)':[59] . . . Item, pur ceo qe le xije jour de Juin l'an du regne le Roy Henri quarte puisse le conqueste tierce, Johan Pecche fuist trové en defaulte en eoveraigne d'argent et d'iceo fuist atteynt, adjugé est et ordei[g]né qe si mesme Johan disoremés soit trové en defaute et ne eovere argent bon et loialle come l'esterlyng et l'or tochant le allay de .v. qe paiera al almoigne de Seint Donston C s. *A + a*, p. 90. (1401/2)
or . . . or entier: Item pur ceo qe plusours disloialx artificers ymaginantz a desceyver le comune people fait de jour en autre firmeux, anelx, bedes . . . de cupre et de latoun, et les susorrount et susargentount semblables a or et argent et les vendent et mettent a gage . . . pur or entier et argent entier . . . *A + b*, p. 61.
or . . . or overaunt = 'wrought gold, or gold ready to be wrought/worked': . . . si l'avantdit Henri soit trové desoreenavant faulx ou defectyf en argent ou or overaunt . . . *A + a*, p. 112. (1413/14) . . . **or overaunt meins qe l'assise** = 'gold of a lower quality than the law decrees' . . . et issint fuist trové ové aultre piers faulx countre-

---

58 See e.g. Oman, *English Silversmiths' Work*, plates 25, 41; Oman, *English Domestic Silver*, plate 38; Glanville, fig. 4; Lightbown, *Secular Goldsmiths' Work*, plates XXVIII, XXIX and pp. 26, 53–61.
59 This standard was revised in 1478: see Reddaway and Walker, p. 233 note 1 and pp. 317–21; see also W. Badcock, *A New Touchstone for Gold and Silver Wares* (London, 1677; reprinted Shannon, Ireland, 1970).

faitz et ové d'or overaunt meyns qe l'assise ent ordeyné *A* + *a*, p. 112. (1412/13) – Fait a remembrer qe le iije jour d'aprille l'an du Roy Henri quint puis le conquest primer, William Gootlee fuist trové faulx come de son argent overant et issint ad sovent esté trové . . . *A* + *a*, p. 112. (1413/14)

G (5.675b) lists **ouvrant** in the sense of 'ouvrable' with a quotation from 1382–3 referring to 'jours ouvrans'; the present example represents a much more concrete sense of the word.

orsandy = 'arsedine = a gold-coloured alloy of copper and zinc rolled into very thin leaf, and used to ornament objects.': Item pur foyl et orsandy – xxj s. *A* + *b*, p. 21. (1377–8)

The one example in the Goldsmiths' records comes in the wardens' accounts set out for the year ending on St Dunstan's Day 1 Richard II (1378); the item is listed among the expenses associated with the Company's participation in the pageantry accompanying the coronation of Richard II on 17 July 1377.[60] The OED seems to be the only dictionary to list this word, which it does under **arsedine** and **orsidue**, giving then a range of alternate spellings; its earliest example is a quotation of 1472–8. The OED says that the etymology is unknown, and may have nothing to do with **or**. One wonders if it might be at all related to 'arsenic' (see above, sub **multiplier**).

pensez qe . . . = 'Memorandum, Memo': Pensez qe Richard Burnham ad vendu son apprentys pur C. s. sans congé ou gree faire a les gardeins. *A* + *a*, p. 50. (1373) – Faite a remembrer qe . . . Fait a remembrer qe . . . Pensez qe Geffray Walpole vint devant les bones gentz de dit mester . . . *A* + *a*, p. 51. (1374)

G and TL do not record this usage.

pile = 'a pile of weights: a technical term referring to the stacking pile of weights of a different weight each that fitted one with or upon the other and built up into a solid cone, a pyramid or other shape': Item, Johan Frere purceo qe fuist trové en defaute de sez poises c'est assavoir de ij piles l'un fuist trop poisaunt l'autre trop leggier encountre l'ordeignance ent fait . . . *A* + *a*, p. 93. (1402/3) – Item, pur ceo qe Johan Frere fuist trové en defaute de ij piles du pois poisant viij marcz, dount l'un fuist trop legier et l'autre trop poisans par ij unces . . . *A* + *b*, p. 39. (1402/3) – Fayt a remembrer qe William Fytzhughe, Johan Hilles, Richard Wedyalle et Johan Walsche, lez gardeins avantescriptz pur l'an esteantz, ount ordeignez et faitz et en lour Tresorye mys en garde un Pyle de xvj marcz de troye pur estre un standard pur governer toutes lez poysez au dit mistier appurtenantz en temps avenir. *A* + *a*, p. 119. (1418/19)

The word *pile* in this sense is recorded by G (6.158a) from 1361 and *pila* is recorded by Du Cange (5.253b) from 1332. It is therefore undoubtedly a continental French term. RMLWL has it only from 1491, but the DMLBS files contain a citation from

---

[60] For a very interesting account of this which uses the Goldsmiths' records for this year, see Osberg, 'The Goldsmiths' "Chastell" of 1377'.

1449.[61] The MED (which unfortunately glosses the word only as 'some sort of weighing device') has picked up a 1423 usage (9.921b). The OED's earliest citation of it is 1440, but doubt is expressed by the editors whether that is certainly the sense of the word in any of their quotations earlier than 1611. The above citations from the Goldsmiths' records therefore help to establish the word and predate by a few years all previous attestations in whichever of the three languages of medieval England.

pise: . . . qe les poys soient faitz de une acordance; et qe nul ne poise mes qe des poys merchez. Qe nul ne tigne pise. *A + a*, p. 42. (1370)
The DMLBS files contain a number of fourteenth-century citations of the word *pisa* used for 'a way' (= a unit of weight). In the Goldsmiths' records the word must mean not a measurement of weight but the instrument with which this was done, and why it should not be done with one particular variety is not explained. G quotes from the sixteenth century *Mémoire pour les habitants de Douai contre le seigneur de Mortagne* (Arch. mun. Mortagne): 'Et convient notter que il y a difference entre une pise et une poise, parce que une pise ne contient que cent .xx. livres, et la poise comme dict est cent .lxv. livres d'Anvers ou Vallenchiennes, ou cent .iiiixx. livres de Tournay, Douay, Lille et aultres villes ou est samblable poix.' G also quotes an eighteenth century text: Pièce du 18 déc. 1717, *Bulletin du comité flamand de France*, V, 134: 'Savoir que quatorze woghes et demie de fromage au poids de l'abbaye de Bourbourg composent onze pises et demie et onze pierres au poids de la ville; que la pise ou poise contient cent quatre vingt livres et la pierre quatre livres . . .'. Whether or not these quotations illuminate the precise prohibition in the Goldsmiths' ordinances of 1370 remains doubtful.

porteresse = 'hawker, itinerant female merchant, saleswoman': Et qe nul ne baille rienz qe appent a orphevere ne a porteresse ne a portour, s'il ne vend sanz rien returner *A + a*, p. 41. (1370) – Item, pur ceo qe est defenduz par la ordinance qe nul ne baillereit rienz a vendre a nulle porteresse, trové fust qe Thomas Horntoft bailla a sa femme diverses aneux, ffermailles et altres choses del mestier, de quelle chose le dit Thomas estoit atteynt et se confessa, de paier al almoigne de Seint Dunston – x s. et les paia. *A + a*, p. 44. (1370)
TL lists **porteresse** only in the sense of 'Trägerin' (7.1602) as does G (6.317a) although the latter gives an undated quotation where the sense seems clearly to be that of a hawker ('Print et embla une petite sainture . . . qu'il vendi v sols par. a une porteresse de frepperie' *Reg. du Chât.*, II, 501). In England the meaning of a female doorkeeper is recorded by the MED and OED, but no instances are given of the above meaning.

pounceoun (also *pounchon, punchoun, punçon*) = 'punch, puncheon, die' Et qe un [ou] deux de chescune citee ou ville avandites veignent a Loundres pur le dit mestier de quere lour certeine touche d'or et ensement le pounceoun ové la teste de leopard pur mercher lour overaignes come auncienement feust ordeiné. *A + a*, p. 19. (1327

---

61 'unam pilam eneam . . . pro auro et argento ponderand" KR Acc. 294/6 (= PRO E101/294/6).

document copied in Goldsmiths' minute book in 1358; the word appears several more times later)

G records the *poinçon* from the thirteenth century, but, for the sense of an 'outil servant à imprimer sur les ouvrages d'or et d'argent une marque indiquant qu'ils sont à un certain titre', his earliest citation is from 1569 (Comp. 366b). The OED has recorded such a *punschion* in England in 1504 (12.837a, sub **puncheon**). RMLWL however (383a) records a **punchona** from 1358, the date when the Goldsmiths' copied this much earlier ordinance from the first year of Edward III's reign, and the DMLBS files reveal that the word is found in a Latin version of exactly the same ordinance regulating goldsmiths' work and picked up previously by Du Cange (569a). The DMLBS files record it also from the English-held regions of south-west France where the same rules were enforced (*Archives historiques de la Gironde*, XVI, p. 138).[62]

quilet, quilette, quiliere = 'monies collected' Doné al entree cest an ix? hors pris la quilette des aprentiz – xvj mars. *A* + *a*, p. 1. (1335 copied in 1358) – Doné al encresse mesme l'an hors pris la quilete de apprentiz et de mercimentz – xx marcz. *A* + *a*, p. 2. (1335 copied in 1358) – Doné al encress horpris lé quylettes des apprentiz et d'amerciamentz mesme cel an – viiij li. x s. *A* + *a*, p. 3. (1337 copied in 1358) – Item, en despens de lumere outre la quilette – v s. x d. *A* + *a*, p. 3. (1338 copied in 1358) . . . Item, pur la lumere al hospital Seynt Jake outre la quilette qe amounte xxxij lb. summa vji s. *A* + *a*, p. 4. (1339 copied in 1358) . . . Item, en lumere a Seint Pol prieu puis qi le quiliere . . . *A* + *a*, p. 6. (1342 copied in 1358) – Item, pur sonail de Seint Paul et pur costages del lumere al glyse Seint Jehan Zakerie outre la quilet – xv s. vj d. *A* + *a*, p. 29. (1363)

The MED records **quilet** in the sense of a collection, deriving it from OF *coilloite*. In G (2.391b) the *cueillete* is given with a meaning of 'levée d'argent' and *quilloitte, quilote* are listed also. One cannot be certain how the Goldsmiths might have pronounced the word in 1335 but its form suggests that it was already nearer to the ME pronunciation, and that the MED should perhaps consider AF as the intermediary and immediate source between OF and ME.

remembrauncer = 'a record book, an official record': . . . l'altre graunt papier sera gysant en une cofre ovesqe aultres choses pur un remembrauncer *A* + *b*, p. 1. (see **lyggere** above for fuller quotation).

With the meaning of a record book kept as an official record, which in this passage it seems clearly to have, one can find no citation for this word in any dictionary in either its French, Latin or English form, except in AND1 which quotes the meaning 'official record'. (G has **remembrance** with the meaning of 'écrit-mémoire' (6.778b-c) and FEW lists *remembransa* with this sense in Provençal from c.1200 (10.238a). The *-er* ending here would appear however to be an English addition to a

---

[62] On *poinçons* used in France see the series of volumes in *Dictionnaire des poinçons de l'orfèvrerie provinciale française* (Geneva, 1976–); these volumes contain a wealth of information about goldsmiths, their work and their working conditions etc.

French word. The OED's citations of the word with this meaning are no earlier than 1671.

sale = 'the hangings for a room': Item, des exec' de Alice Chichestre en moneye – x li. et j sale ové iiij costers, iiij banqers et xxiiij quissyns (*cushions*) de plume. (*feathers*) *A* + *a*, p. 59. (1382/3)

Dictionaries of medieval French and medieval Latin do not record this sense of the word, but the MED has picked it up in 1414. The above citation from the Goldsmiths' records is not the earliest attestation, for I have also found it used in a document of 1368–9:

> Nous vous mandons qe a Richard Mareschall, Gardein de noz litz et sales deinz nostre Chastel de Windesore facez liverer une sale embroidré de diverses oeverages d'or et de soy contenante un dorser ové quatre cousters d'une suite pur demorer pur l'estore de nostre sale deinz nostre chastel susdite . . . PRO E101/395/2/130. (1368–70)

selverskynne = '?' (probably leather with a silver covering) Item, pur selverskynnes – iij s. iiij d. . . . Item pur selverskynnes viij s. x d. ob. *A* + *a*, p. 57. For the full passage in which this occurs see below: **somercastell**.

The word is clearly ME but is not listed in the MED. It has been discussed by Osberg (see sub **somercastell**), who suggests that the 'seluerskynnes', although he can find no other instance of such a usage, could be = seluer = a form of 'celure' which as he says the MED gives as 'panelling or some other ornamental covering for walls or ceilings' and that these were leather hangings; alternatively he suggests silvered hides, a suggestion I find more plausible.[63]

selverwir = 'silver wire, silver thread' Feat a remembrer qe le vendirdy aprés le feste del Epiphanie cest an les meir et aldermans et comunes furent arrayés pur chevacher encontre la Reyne soer al Emperour et par cause qe touz les miesters de la cité avoyent en charge q'ils ne duissent avoyr autre vesture qe rouge et blank, les orfevers furent arrayez de mesme les colours, et pur ceo qe touz autres miesters avoynt divers conisances, les ditz orfevers furent en le rouge partie barrés de selverwir et poudrés de treys foylles d'argent (1381) *A* + *a*, p. 57.

This is again an ME word not listed in the MED.

somercastell = 'a summer-castle': – Et feat a remembrer qe desuis Chepe feut un somercastell bien arrayés, pendant en quel furent treys virgyns pur getter foylle, quel castel costa: / En primes pur vj verges de rouge pris le verge xviij d. / J verge et j quart rouge pris le verge – xxx d. / iij verges blank pris le verge xxviij d. / Johan Caroun pur carpentrie – xliij d. / Item pur j corde vj s. viij d. / Item pur selverskynnes viij s. x d. ob. / Summa xxxv s. ix d. ob. / dount ressu pur le drap et le corde – x s. *A* + *a*, p. 57.

---

[63] Osberg adds that siege-towers were often fronted with leather to protect the attackers from defensive shot, and that silvered hides might provide 'the illusion of "lamynes of yron", the thin sheets of protection advocated by Vegetius' (p. 6).

This 'castle' was erected as part of the civic pageant organised in the City of London to celebrate the coronation of Richard II. It has been discussed at length in a most interesting article by Richard H. Osberg.[64] As he points out, dictionaries such as the OED and MED give this word in its sense of a movable tower used in sieges, but here it is clearly peace-time and the edifice is being used for pageantry and ceremonial procession. *Somercastell* should therefore be glossed with the additional meaning of a decorative model castle or tower, constructed on the model of the siege-engine of that name, made of wood and with cloth and leather hangings, used as a decorative stand in pageants and processions.

trover = 'to find funds for alms for, to provide for, to support financially': Item, estre ceo troverent deux poveres hommes del mister par un an – iiij li. xv s. ij d. *A + a*, p. 30. (1365) – Les bones gentz concilerent ensemble et ly mist en lour grace en ceste fourme: q'il paieroit un pipe de vyn et q'il troveroit un povere homme de mesme le mister xij d. la semaigne continuant un an entier. *A + a*, p. 24. (1360) **trové . . . les povres trovés** – *the poor of the craft who are being supported by alms given by the company from its funds* Item, paié a les povres trovés del almoigne countre Noel – vj s. viij d. *A + a*, p. 12. (1355, copied in 1358)

The sense of the word in the above passages, 'to provide for' is one that is not recorded in CF except in a specific sense of finding some particular thing for someone else (TL 10.696), but it is, interestingly, found for each of the verbs meaning 'to find' in all three of the languages of medieval England, different as these are. RMLWL records **invenio** in this sense from c.1353 and **inventio** meaning 'provision' from the thirteenth century and with the meaning of 'maintenance, keep' from 1407. The OED has citations from c.1200 onwards for the verb *find* with the meaning 'to procure sth for the use of sb', 'to supply, provide, furnish', and the sense is found also in the phrase *all found* = with all customary articles of food etc. provided. AND1 has already noted this meaning (828a) but the above quotations add in particular the p.p. used as an adj.

veer, verre, veirre – piere de veer = 'an imitation gemstone made of glass': – Les amerciamentz qe ne sont paiez: . . . Thomas de Algate pur verre mys en or demj marc. *A + a*, p. 1. (1335 copied in 1358) – . . . et ensement fount fauces overaignes d'or et d'argent come de coronaux, fermeux, aneux et altres jeux es queux ils mettent veirres de diverses colours contrefaitz a perrie . . . *A + a*, p. 19. (1327 copied in 1358) – Fait a remembrer qe Godekyn, orfevere, myst en j anel d'or j piere de veer, en grant damage et esclandre del mester d'orfeverie . . . *A + a*, p. 47. (1372) – Item, deliveré en anelx d'or faux et stoppés de coper: . . . Item j anelle d'or bon pois v s. ové un verre. Item un autre anelle coveré d'or stoppé de plumb ové un verre. *A + a*, p. 86. (1399)

It was forbidden to set glass stones in gold or silver, and conversely it was forbidden to set real gemstones in a base metal. Understandably, it was the former prohibition that unscrupulous goldsmiths were tempted to infringe and when caught doing so

---

64 'The Goldsmiths' "Chastell" of 1377'.

found the details recorded for posterity along with the fines or other penalties imposed. Dictionaries of French have not previously however picked up on this usage. G (Comp. 848b) lists **verre** with the meaning of 'objet en verre' but not specifically as an imitation gemstone. TL does not give this meaning but cites one passage that would seem nevertheless to mean this: 'Tant com jesme (gemma) sormonte voire'[65] (11.669 sub **voirre**). FEW and the DHLF have nothing.

vesseler = 'vesseller': Fait a remembrer qe une ordinance fust ordiné entre les vesselers qe null de eux vende null vessel a null estranger meins le lb de ij s. south peine de xl s. appaier al almoigne de Seint Dunstoun, et un William Yrissh qe l'en appelle William fitz Hughe fust trové qe il vendy a Cornhull une dozeine d'esquelys le lb meyns de xviij d. *A + a*, p. 49. (1373)
The OED gives the first meaning of *vessel* as 'vessels or utensils for the table or for use in the household, esp. those made of gold or silver; = plate', but it does not list the men who dealt in such goods. Latin dictionaries have not picked it up either, and G for **vaiseleur** lists only the meaning of 'tonnelier'. FEW however records *veisselier* as 'fabricant de vaisselle' in Lyon in 1295[66] and once later in 1489.

wast = 'the consumption of a certain amount of a candle': Item, pur le wast de ij torches xxij d. *A + a*, p. 59. (1382/3) – Item en costages de cire pur les vij serges du pois iijxx li. et xv et pur le wast de les torches et le façoun – xxxviij s. j d. ob. *A + b*, p. 29. (1383/4)
Neither the dictionaries of French or Latin list this, but the OED (19.957c) records an obsolete meaning for *waste* = 'the consumption of candles etc. at a funeral or obit' and provides citations from 1477–9 until 1556–7. The present instances are thus nearly a century earlier than the first in the OED, and one may note also that the word is found used in the early fifteenth century in the records of the Merchant Taylors' Company, sometimes appearing as gast: Item pur lowaunce et gast de ij torches al enterement Henri Mason – ij s. *Mch Tayl Accts* 6.Hen.IV. Item, paié pur le wast des xij torches vers le Roy et pur pain et servoise a lez torcheberers en tout – xxviij s. ij d. *Mch Tayl Accts* 1.Hen.VI. – Item pur ij torches et le wast pur l'enterment de Sparke – ij s. viij d. *Mch Tayl Accts* 3.Hen.VI.

---

[65] *Fabliaux et Contes*, ed. Barbazan and Méon (Paris, 1808), IV 328, 65.
[66] The DHLF cites what must be the same Lyon text with the spelling **vaisselier**.

Aspects of Lexical and Morphosyntactical Mixing in the Languages of Medieval England

WILLIAM ROTHWELL

THE PURPOSE OF the present paper is to provide examples from just one text of the different ways in which the three languages of medieval England – Latin, French and English – were intertwined in the later Middle Ages.[1] The two substantial volumes of the *York Memorandum Book*[2] provide some five hundred pages of records detailing the administrative and commercial life of the second city in England over the years between 1376 and 1493, setting down in full charters, ordinances of the various trade associations, legal cases involving citizens and so on. Similar records existing for other cities such as Durham and Leicester[3] could be used to supplement the present findings in any subsequent fuller study. The evidence gathered from the *Memorandum Book* will be treated as giving an indication of the position of Latin, French and English in the sphere of written record only, without any inference regarding spoken language.

Before turning to the *York Memorandum Book*, however, just one quotation from Chaucer will be examined in order to show that the evidence from an administrative text drafted by unknown clerks of unproven linguistic competence is not totally at odds with that provided by one of the greatest practitioners of English who was in daily contact with all three languages regularly used in medieval England.[4]

> Thow blamest Crist and seist ful bitterly
> He mysdeparteth richesse temporal;
> . . .
> O riche marchauntz . . .
> Youre bagges been nat fild with ambes as,
> But with sys cynk, that renneth for youre chaunce[5]

---

[1] Despite the assertion that 'it can in no way be considered reasonable to suppose that any of the conditions for pidginisation, creolisation, or *language mixture* existed between English and French in the Middle Ages'; S. G. Thomason and T. Kaufman, *Language Contact, Creolization and Genetic Linguistics* (Berkeley, 1988), p. 309. My emphasis.

[2] Ed. Maud Sellers, Surtees Society, vols 120 (1911) and 125 (1914).

[3] *Durham Account Rolls*, ed. Canon Fowler, Surtees Society vols 99 (1898), 100 (1898), 103 (1901); *Records of the Borough of Leicester*, ed. Mary Bateson, 2 vols (London, 1899 and 1901).

[4] See W. Rothwell, 'The Trilingual England of Geoffrey Chaucer', *Studies in the Age of Chaucer* 16 (1994), pp. 45–67.

[5] 'Introduction to the Man of Law's Tale', in *The Riverside Chaucer*, ed. Larry D. Benson (Oxford, 1987), p. 88, vv. 106–7 and 122–5.

Although the presence of French words is very clear and has long been recognised, some very odd ideas as to their provenance still persist. In a recent book, *The Empire of Words: The Reign of the* OED,[6] John Willinsky quotes without demur a passage from Owen Barfield written seventy years ago on the role of English and French in the late fourteenth century. Barfield writes of the modern poet envying 'Chaucer with this enormous store of fresh, unspoiled English words ready to his hand and unlimited treasury across the Channel from which he could pick a brand-new one whenever he wanted it'.[7] Apparently convinced by this fanciful and utopian picture of Chaucer's working practices, Willinsky simply puts the second edition of the OED through his computer and declares roundly that: 'Chaucer coins more new words in English than any other author' (p. 196). However, he does not understand the reality of the linguistic situation in late medieval England, so that, whilst the computer might be able to pick out for him all the dictionary entries in which Chaucer's name appears before the earliest attestation of a word, this facile exercise cannot tell him whether such words were already current in England in either French or Latin documents, or whether they even existed in continental French for Chaucer to borrow. For the computer to provide any meaningful assessment of the growth of English in the Middle Ages, it would have to analyse the entire contents of the *Middle English Dictionary*, the *Dictionary of Medieval Latin from British Sources* and the *Anglo-Norman Dictionary* as they all advance over a long time-scale, steadily recording the true state of written language in medieval England. It would then have to do the same with the vast dictionaries of continental medieval French in order to see whether developments in England were paralleled by similar growth in France itself. Both Barfield and Willinsky have their gaze firmly focused on the narrow literary sphere of Middle English, apparently in blissful ignorance of the fact that both French and Latin had been developing in an English society on English soil for hundreds of years, independently of either Rome or Paris, not only in the general field of imaginative literature, but also in a wide spectrum of administrative and technical texts.

In the snippet quoted above from *The Canterbury Tales* there is indeed no lack of French words that catch the eye immediately, but they had not been brought over by Chaucer from mainland France, culled from an 'unlimited treasury across the Channel from which he could pick a brand-new one whenever he wanted it,' a sort of private thesaurus accumulated perhaps as a result of his French family connections, his considerable time spent in France on government business, or his unquestioned record as a translator. *Blamer, riche, richesse, temporel* and *marchant*, completely anglicised by Chaucer's time, can all be traced back in the *Anglo-Norman Dictionary* to the early days of French in England and were used for generations before Chaucer was born, forming part of the everyday lexis of Anglo-French over a long period as it co-existed with Middle English. The dicing terms 'ambes as' and 'chaunce', however, not having been assimilated into modern English, might

---

6   (Princeton, New Jersey, 1994), p. 104.
7   *History in English Words* (London, 1926), p. 53.

possibly be assumed to be medieval 'borrowings' taken directly from continental French into Middle English. Not so: *ambes as* ('double one', hence an unlucky, losing throw of the dice) is used in a figurative sense in Anglo-French as early as c.1230, without the writer feeling any obligation to explain its meaning to his readers,[8] so that it must have arrived in England as a concrete dicing term well before 1230, whilst *chance* in Chaucer's sense of 'good fortune' is found even earlier, around the end of the twelfth century, again without explanation, its meaning evidently being taken for granted.[9] The numbers 'sys', and 'cynk' are so frequently found in both Anglo-French and Middle English that they too must be regarded as part of the dicing terminology, which, although ultimately of French origin, had obviously been part of the culture of medieval England for many decades before Chaucer.

In addition to showing the use of French and English terms in the same sentence, however, the few verses from the *Canterbury Tales* quoted above also reveal the practice of merging elements of the two languages to make up hybrid words. Christ faces the accusation that he 'mysdeparteth' earthly wealth. This compound verb shows just how difficult it can be to separate the two languages. The original French *partir* soon acquired a prefix *de(s)-* on both sides of the Channel: in fact, the earliest attestation of *departir* given in the Tobler-Lommatzsch *Altfranzösisches Wörterbuch* is taken from the Anglo-Norman *Comput* of 1113–19.[10] The verb was widely used in both Anglo-French and Middle English for generations before a second prefix 'mys-' was attached to it. Whether this prefix should be interpreted at face value as a purely Germanic element (English 'misjudge', 'misunderstand', 'misplace' etc., German *missachten, missbrauchen, misslingen*, etc.) is perhaps a moot point in view of the French *mésaventure, mésalliance, mépris*, etc. The essence of the matter, however, is that Chaucer's hybrid verb and his 'borrowed' words must have been readily understood and accepted by people fully accustomed to the kinds of linguistic mixing that will be shown to be prevalent also in documentary records.

Generally speaking, in the fourteenth century the base text of a document to be preserved for posterity would be either in Latin, often with French or English terms inserted, or in French, with the possible insertion of English terms. The 'foreign' elements in the communication would be treated in one of two ways: either they would be set down in something resembling their true form in their language of origin, or they would be adapted to conform to the morphological patterns of the base language – Latin or French. This means that the following simple types of mixing may be found: English words inserted without modification into a Latin text

---

8   Mes tost li sunt les dez turné Sur ambes as (var. amesas) e reversé Kar les dous oilz li sunt crevé Ainz ke li meis seit passé *St Modwenna*, eds A. T. Baker and A. Bell, ANTS VII (Oxford, 1947), vv. 8645-8. The sense is that the man's luck has run out and he is blinded within the month. Curiously enough, neither *ambes* nor *as* figures in the glossary to the text, the editors presumably crediting their readers with the same grasp of medieval dicing as was clearly current in the thirteenth century.
9   Ki ad femme de bone part, Ceo est cheance cum de hasart, *Le Petit Plet*, ed. Brian S. Merrilees, ANTS XX (Oxford, 1970), vv. 1533-4.
10 E nus les (*sc.* years) departum par quatre . . . *Philippe de Thaon: Comput*, ed. Ian Short, ANTS Plain Texts Series 2 (London, 1984), v. 2143.

(i); English words similarly introduced into a French text (ii); French words used without modification in a Latin text (iii); French words similarly used in an English text (iv). But there is more to the mixing process than that. On a somewhat deeper level we find English words dressed up as Latin in a Latin text (v), English words dressed up as French in a French text (vi), or French words dressed up as Latin in a Latin text (vii). Going still deeper into this process, it may be seen how French words are used in a specifically Anglo-French sense in a French text (viii). This mixing of the languages is by far the one most frequently found in the *York Memorandum Book*. Again, French words may be found in a Latin text dressed up as Latin, but with an English meaning (ix). On occasion, a single word may be made up of parts taken from different languages, as was seen in the extract from Chaucer, or a new word may be created by attaching a suffix to an existing word, either from the same language or from one language to another (x). Outside the area of word-formation there is also the question of grammatical endings to be considered (xi). These are often indicated by abbreviations in texts of this type, but, since the editor of the York documents does not set down the abbreviations used by the scribes or her policy for expanding them, it is impossible to be sure that any conclusions drawn from the printed text in this regard are accurate.[11] Some representative examples of each of these types of language mixing as found in the *York Memorandum Book* will be set out in the body of this paper, with further, but by no means exhaustive, examples to be found in the Appendix.

(i) English words unmodified in a Latin text:

j *brandreth* et j *spytt* . . ., unam ollam et unam pelvem . . ., j *waterkan* . . . i 78
quod nullus ammodo vendat gallum silvestrum, perdricem . . . carius quam pro duobus denariis, unum *tele* j d. ob., xij *feldfares* iiij d., xij alaudas . . . i 46

In many cases such insertions are self-explanatory, but not all are so straightforward.

unum *hopir* cum scala et unum *strikill* . . . i 10 (*hoper* i 13)

The 'hopper' presents no difficulties, being unquestionably English in origin. Similarly, according to both the OED and MED, *strikill*, a straight piece of wood for removing excess grain from a measure, comes from Old English. Neither mentions French, but the OED notes that the original sense ('pulley, small wheel') does not match the Middle English sense as here. Recently published Anglo-French glossarial texts, however, show that the Middle English sense of 'strikill' comes from French. They provide no fewer than seven attestations of varying French forms of *estric(h)e* used to render the Latin *(h)ostorium*, from the thirteenth century onwards, long before the quotation given in AND1. In one of these glossaries, however, two

---

11 Hans Goebl touches on this question with regard to continental records in his book *Die normandische Urkundensprache*, Österreichische Akademie der Wissenschaften 269 (Vienna, 1970), p. 125.

scribes differ in their translation of *ostorium*, the one putting *estric*, but the other using *roel* ('wheel'),[12] which ties in with the Old English sense of 'stricel' as given in the OED, but does not fit the Latin *hostorium* at all. How the scribe came to give this gloss is not clear, but the link between 'wheel' and 'strickle' must evidently have survived somewhere in England, despite not being attested so far for Middle English. The MED records just the modern sense, deriving the term from Old English, with the quotation from our present text being given as the earliest attestation for Middle English. Not being versed in Anglo-French, the compilers of neither dictionary would be minded to consider the possibility of a French origin for the word, given that in mainland France it is now confined to dialectal use in the agricultural area of Hainaut (Godefroy 3.353c). Anglo-Latin, however, confirms the Anglo-French origin of the word in England, having various forms of *(e)strica* from the late twelfth century, thus showing that even writers ostensibly using Latin are preferring a form calqued on Anglo-French to the 'correct' Latin *hostorium*. So, whilst the morphological shell of 'strickle' is inherited from Old English, the vital semantic content comes from French. Perversely, Godefroy's first quotation for *estrique* is no earlier than 1429 (3.653b), although the verb *estriquier* is attested from 1282 (3.653c), which raises once again the question of the inadequate representation of non-literary texts in the current dictionaries of medieval French.

ij *alterclathes*, ij towalia, . . ., j manipulus, j frontale de *whitebustion* . . ., unum vestimentum de *fustyan* . . . i 236

The two types of cloth here, 'bustion' and 'fustian', show that any neat and tidy separation of languages at this period and in this kind of document can often be illusory. The editor's printed form 'whitebustion' appears to show an English form, but when separated into 'white' and 'bustion', it becomes English and French. Godefroy lists three forms – *buttenne, bustane* and *buttanne* (1.763b), covered by just one quotation from Valenciennes in 1434, but the DMLBS has *bustianus* from the end of the fourteenth century, so it would appear that trade had made the word common to both sides of the Channel around that time, and so, probably, common to all three languages of record in later medieval England. *Fustian* is no simpler: it would seem to be recorded in both French and English at about the same time, the early thirteenth century. Godefroy's first attestation is taken from *Ogier le Danois* in the first half of the thirteenth century (9.676b), whilst the OED dates the term as appearing about 1200 (MED a.1225), but the DMLBS has it in a quotation from before 1130. If a term for a trade commodity is found in an Anglo-Latin record of the twelfth century, it is highly unlikely that it would not be current in Egland in the two vernaculars, Anglo-French and English, at the same time, as well as being similarly

---

12 Tony Hunt, *Teaching and Learning Latin in Thirteenth-Century England*, 3 vols (Cambridge, 1991), i 137, ii 40, 62, 88, 93, 164; also in Tony Hunt, 'Les Gloses en langue vulgaire dans les manuscrits du *De Nominibus Utensilium* d'Alexandre Nequam', *Revue de Linguistique Romane* 43 (1979), with the significant gloss: ostorium: estric, roel (248.71).

used across the Channel, whether or not its vernacular forms were recorded on parchment. Trade is no respecter of political or linguistic boundaries.

(ii) English words unmodified in a French text:

fymes en *bolles* ou en *scutelles* (also *skutelles*) i 164

The *scutelles* here would be large open baskets in which the rubbish would be carried for dumping in the Ouse.

que les bouchers de la dite citee facent une pounte sur la dite petit *stathe* i 15

A 'staith' is a landing-stage.

(wood) sanz (*ed.* sauz)[13] ascun *sappe* i 149
que nully . . . ne face porter a ascune *hukester* ascun payne a lour measons ibid. i 168
diverses choses et darrez . . . ount esté overez nounduement et *utterez* par la manere de *haukyng* i 151
que null pestour vend aucun roundell ne escu ne *chunx* de payn demayne i 169

The *roundell*, as its name implies, was a round loaf, the *escu* a triangular one, so it is difficult to avoid the conclusion that in *chunx* we have here a plural form of the modern English 'chunk', previously not attested before 1691.

(iii) French words unmodified in a Latin text:

quod linea trahatur directe a quodam lapide jacente subtus *le panne* ii 109
quod J.L. amoveat quemdam caminum, in quantum occupat super *le pan* predicti domini H. ii 112

The *pan(ne)* is a main beam that supports the rafters in a timber-framed house. The point at issue here is the extent to which a house may be allowed to protrude towards another building or a path.

Et quoad balingeram, quia malus ejusdem cum les *herynges* sunt fracte ad disruptionem i 33

In the context of a shattered mast on a vessel, the unexpected form *herynges* is to be understood not as the English 'herrings' but as a corruption of the Anglo-French *herneis*, commonly found as meaning 'equipment', 'tackle', not just 'harness (for a horse)'. Chaucer uses the word on several occasions in this sense – another of his French words that are not 'borrowed' from France.

---

13 This kind of elementary error on the part of the editor undermines confidence in her transcriptions of more difficult words.

(iv) French words unmodified in an English text:

> . . . will not obbey his *serchiours* i 133 (*seirch(e)ours* i 135)

The *serchours* were official inspectors responsible for ensuring the quality of workmanship amongst members of the various gilds.

> lettres . . . of his gude *conversacion* i 81

Conversacion here is to be understood in the medieval sense of 'behaviour, 'conduct', in use in both continental and insular French as well as English for many decades before this time.

> and if the market keper *encheson* (*ed. eucheson*) hym therfore and why he byes so mykill fyshhe . . . i 222

To *encheson* here means 'to interrogate', 'accuse' (cf. si dictus J. . . . *occasionetur* racione alicujus vendicionis . . . ii 14)

> . . . cukes and *regratours* i 224
> aswel be (= 'by') *denicens* as *forauntes* i 135 (*forraunt* ibid.)

The *regratours* here look French, but the term was used in English a century before this mention in the *York Memorandum Book* (cf. OED and MED). On the other hand, 'denicens' may perhaps be regarded as still being French, since this is the earliest example of it quoted by the dictionaries of English, and *forauntes* still has a 'French' look about it, on account of its ending, and is not found before the latter part of the fourteenth century. It is not attested with this form in France itself, another example of the difficulty of labelling words at this time as belonging unequivocally to one language or the other.

> no man that is *customer* to any of the sayd craft . . . ii 177 (also another 3 examples)

'Customer' obviously belongs to a 'word family' well-established on both sides of the Channel, but it never carried this meaning in continental French.

These few examples have been introduced merely as token representatives of a widespread and complex phenomenon. So integrated were Anglo-French and English that in hundreds of cases all over late fourteenth-century records it is virtually impossible to decide whether an originally French word is to be considered as still being French or having been already merged into English. However, whilst English words that are set in a French context usually belong to the category of concrete objects – tools, building materials, household items, etc., the French words found in an English context are in the main abstract.

(v) English words dressed up as Latin in a Latin text:

de tribus *shoppis* juxta hostium capelle i 5
vendere super *stallas* sua carnes bovinas i 5
quod nemo ponat ne jaciat bona seu mercandizas supra *stathas* i 42
in eadem civitate et *suburbio* ejusdem i 125
preter *wapentachium* de A. i 123
W.E. . . . marcandisas predictas . . . *skippavit* et frettavit . . . ii 56
fossatum cum *gutta* inter les Holmes et causeiam apud le Neutour ii 33

These examples reveal the vernacular lying beneath the veneer of Latin dictated by convention. The last two quotations also show that both vernaculars could be used thinly disguised in the same sentence. Whilst *skippavit* may be regarded as English, from Scandinavian, *frettavit* comes from the Anglo-French *fretter*, 'to charter (a vessel)'; *causeiam*, the modern French *chaussée*, is set alongside *gutta*, found elsewhere in the *Memorandum Book* in its Middle English form 'goote', 'a watercourse' (i 23), whilst 'Neutour' is an amalgam of the English 'new' and the French *tour*.

(vi) English words dressed up as French in a French text:

Et si ensy soit que aucun vouldra *compleiner* d'aucun furrur . . . i 61

This shows not only the anglicised move from the standard medieval French *complaindre* to the simpler first conjugation form in *-er*, but also in *compleiner de* the modern English meaning 'to complain about', 'make a complaint against'.

il n'artera ne *compellera* nulle persone . . . lesser d'avoir son or ou argent cunez en la dite toure de Londres ii 105
. . . pur ycelle (*sc.* piece of work) amender et *correcter* i 166
nous requerant diligentment noz lettres *compulsories* a lui graunter i 57

Although made to look like French, none of these words is actually found in French of the mainland.

toutes fellonies ou deroberies ou *burgaries* ii 261

Burgarie ('burglary') is not to be found in the dictionaries of medieval French, although it appears to be a perfectly plausible French term. Godefroy has *burger* meaning 'saccager, piller' (1.759b) and Tobler-Lommatzsch has *burgeor* 'Einbrecher, Plünderer' and also *burgessor* 'Räuber, Plünderer' (1.1205), but neither has *burgarie/burgerie*.

comune passage . . . ové totes maneres de *cariages*, charetz, chivaux . . . chargez de marchandisez i 38
lour *cariages* susditz descharger de lour chargez i 38

Although 'cariage' has a French look about it, it is not found in mainland France. In

England, however, it is recorded as early as Magna Carta[14] in the sense of 'transport (of goods)', and also in the *York Memorandum Book* – in Latinate disguise, admittedly – as 'right of passage with a cart: 'cum commune *passagium* et *cariagium* cum hominibus, equis et carectis . . .' (i 27).

> . . . d'*adder* et de menuser i 229

This a good example of the juxtaposing of English and French elements.

> overer torches . . . et prykettis et *perchours* et mortars et tapors i 56

This apparently straightforward list of forms of candle is, in fact, a complicated mixture in which the labels 'French' and 'English' can be used only with caution. The French *torche* had been long enough in England to have become acclimatised, so to speak, as had the *mortar* – originally a bowl containing oil and a wick; the Middle English 'percher' ('a candle on the end of a pole') is based on the originally French *perche* 'rod, pole' and has in the present context a French ending -*our*, but is not attested in the dictionaries of medieval French; *prykettis* (ME 'pricket') is a diminutive of the English 'prick' (i.e. 'spike'), but its Romance diminutive ending -*ette* gives it a deceptively French look; only 'tapors' is unambiguously English. All, however, could pass for French when put in a French context, as here.

On occasion, the Englishness of a form is not immediately obvious:

> que nul straunger . . . ne *seura* ('shall sew') en nulle lieu fors solement en la shop i 99

The context being regulations for tailors, *seura* must be the English verb 'to sew' fitted with a French third person singular ending -*ra* to give it a French appearance.

> que nulle meistre . . . *tewe* nulle manere de werk ne furrour i 60

The verb here is the modern English 'to taw', now used only of working leather, but having in Middle English a wider sense of 'to prepare', 'dress' a raw material.

(vii) French words dressed up as Latin in a Latin text:

> pro *bargea* dicte civitatis . . . i 30

The 'barge' was common to all three languages from a very early date, being first attested in the Anglo-Norman *Chanson de Roland*.

> et in magnam *cretenam* aque . . . cecidit de equo predicto i 45

This is the well-attested *cretine* 'flood'.

---

[14] [N]us viscontes . . . ne pregne les chevals ne les charettes d'aucun franc home pur faire *cariage*, 'A Vernacular French Text of Magna Carta', ed. J. C. Holt, *English Historical Review* 89 (1974), 360.30.

flotas meremii ad obstruendum archeas pontis i 33
admirallus flote navium i 225
infra *admirallitatem* predictam i 225 (cf. *admiralté* i 228)

The *admirallitas* was the area under the jurisdiction of the *admiral*.

vendere per *retalliam* i 57
(cf. . . . and after that *retailes* the same fysshe at thayr houses i 223)
. . . est verus *ligeus* domino nostro regi i 116
fossatum cum gutta inter les Holmes et *causeiam* ii 33
omnes pile, pali et *kidelli* in aqua de Ouse . . . i 45
pilos, palos et *kidellos* i 217/ pilorum, palorum et *kidellorum* ibid.

Anglo-French forms of all these terms have been attested, so the path of transmission is likely to have been through insular French, but *flotas/flote* with their two meanings coming down from Nordic/Anglo-Saxon as well as from continental French show once again that the linguistic state of medieval England was by no means simple. The *kidelli* quotations provide a good example of the unreliability of the datings given in current dictionaries. Although attested in Anglo-Latin as early as 1196 (RMLWL) and in Anglo-French as *kidel* in *Magna Carta* (para. 33) in 1215, Godefroy's earliest evidence of it in the form *guidel* comes from 1289.[15] Common sense would suggest that the object and the word for it were both in general use on both sides of the Channel from the twelfth century, if not before.

quod nullus shoppam levet nec occupet *cum* magister i 192

This decree is, of course, a straight translation from the Anglo-French, but the use of the apparently Latin *cum* in the French sense of *com(e)* meaning 'as', not the Latin 'with', shows how deeply entwined were the two languages.

(viii) Anglo-French words or continental French words used in an Anglo-French sense found in a French text:

le pleintif doit recoverer fors tantsoulement le *clere* dette ii 148
le pleintif recovera riens mes ceo q'est trové due *clerement* par enquest, cestassaver, le seingle *deuté* . . . ii 149.

Cler is also found dressed as Latin, *de claro* (i 5), and would appear to be confined to England in its present sense of 'clear of all demands', 'when all deductions have been made'. *Deuté* looks French, but is a purely Anglo-French term.

que nul . . . voise en haukyng ovesqez cardes novelx ne *eisnez* pur vendre i 79

The Middle English translation of this document given on p. 81 has 'alde' for *eisnez*,

---

[15] *guidel* 4.381b and 9.736b–c.

confirming that the word is being used in a purely English sense not attested for continental French.

> q'il purra trover sufficeantz plegges a *mayneparner* pur lui et pur ses faitz i 79
> ... le dit J. se trove plegges et *emnpernours* (*l. menpernours*) i 18

These two words belong to the peculiarly Anglo-French and then English legal 'word family' created around 'mainprize' – *meynpernaunce, mainpernour, meinpernable, meinprendre, meinprise.*

> que totes les tenementz ... serront ... en la registre ... *entree* et enroullez i 13
> pur *entré* del noun de attourné j. d. i 138 (also *entree* ibid.)

This sense of *entrer* and *entree* is not attested for continental French.

> pur chescun *record* issaunt des roulles, ... soit il *large* soit il meyns, vj. d. i 138

Both *record* and *large* are used here in a specifically English sense.

> que chescun ... qi a son primer *leve* (*l. levé?*) de shoppe et *occupacion* ... paye xl.
> d. i 149–50
> s'il soit assez sachant ... pur *occupier* come meistre i 111 (also i 149)
> (cf. qui incipiet *occupare* ut magister i 30; in prima *occupacione* sua ut magister
> ibid.; si quis ... shoppam *levaverit* ... quod solvat in prima *levacione* ... xiij s. i
> 156)

Lever in the sense of 'to set up, establish (a business, etc.)' is not found in continental French, but is attested in Anglo-French long before the *York Memorandum Book* (AND). Although *occuper* and *occupacion* are found in continental French, neither is recorded in the extended sense of 'to trade', 'to be in business' and 'trading', 'business'.

> *tastours* de cervoise i 164

In Anglo-French *taster* had developed semantically into 'to taste' by the early thirteenth century (*Saint Modwenna* 1706), and the present form *tastours* is simply a natural substantival formation based on this Anglo-French sense.

> si ascun servaunt du dit artifice soit trové ové *disloialté* a le valu de vj. d. ou oultre
> ... i 60

Continental French never attached a concrete meaning to the abstract concept of 'disloyalty'; the sense here is 'unworthy product', 'shoddy goods'.

> les ditz orfeverers apportent lours *touchez* et marche issint que lour darrés
> purroient estre *touché* ovesqez le *pounce* come l'astatut purport i 75
> si ascun meistre vende ... ascun choise d'ore ... avaunt q'il soit *touché* ovesqez le
> *commune touch* de la dite cité et le *pounce* de luy ... i 75

Although *touch* and *toucher* are well attested French words and are found in the specialised sense of authenticating precious metals, *pounce* meaning a 'punch', an instrument for impressing a seal, is not recorded for mainland France. It would appear to be an English shortening along the lines of 'luncheon/lunch'.

> si . . . aucun servant . . . par fraude et male ingein *proloigne* aucuns biens a le valu de . . . i 212
> (cf. that nan sadeller . . . *perloune* . . . na servant . . . i 183; in *perlunyng* of his gude i 182)

Continental Old French used *porloigner* not only in the senses of 'to put off' and 'to prolong', but also 'to keep from', 'deny access to'. Only in Anglo-French, however, was the meaning further developed to include the idea of unlawful removal or stealing.

> si ensy soit que . . . le *factour* de le *garment* soyt porté devant lez sercheours . . . i 98

Facteur, the learned form of the popular *faiteur*, is known to Godefroy (9.591b) only in the commercial sense of an agent, one who buys and sells for another. Tobler-Lommatzsch (3.1552) refers the reader to the entry *faitor* (3.1604), but its sole quotation containing *facteur* is glossed as 'Täter (eines Verbrechens)'. In the *York Memorandum Book* the term is used in the sense of one who makes or manufactures. The Anglo-French *garnement* has already been reduced here to the Middle English 'garment'.

> Et si nul servant au bouchers porte fumes (*l*. fumés?) et isseuz des bestez del bocherie al eawe de Ouse *descoverez* et sauncz drape desuys . . . i 18

This shows the specifically Anglo-Norman use of the negative prefix *de(s)-*, not, as in continental Old French, to negate an already existing state, but to indicate simple negativity. The offal is being transported without a cover over it, not with its cover removed. (See 'scutelles' above.)

> qe les *enditez* . . . soient *lessez en baile* pur resonable *fyne* doner i 137

None of these terms is found with this kind of legal sense in continental French. They serve as a reminder of the debt owed by the modern English legal register to Anglo-French.

Similarly, *place* in standard French has never had either the general sense occupied by *lieu* nor the legal sense of *cour*, both of which are found in the *Memorandum Book*, as elsewhere in Anglo-French:

> les carier a Everwyk ou altres *places* i 38
> par briefe al Eschekre ou en autre *place* de roy ii 255
> que . . . chescun mestre et servant ferrount lour overaigne del longure solonc l'assise des certeinz *ensamples* quels lours serront baillez . . . i 87

To judge from Godefroy (3.567a) and Tobler-Lommatzsch (3.1298–1300) continental French never used *essample* in the modern English sense of 'sample (of goods)', the glosses *échantillon* and *Muster* being absent from their pages. In England, however, this sense is already found in the *Liber Albus* (AND), long before the *York Memorandum Book*.

les ditz viscountz poent par usage tenir qeconqes prisoners . . . a lour *countours* come en les communes gaoles ii 151

This sense of *countour* which has given the historical 'compter', a 'sheriff's prison for debtors' is peculiar to Britain.

si ascun homme du dite artifice soit *conventu* (i.e. 'convicted') ou trové feisaunt disloialté i 94

Although this sense is recorded in Godefroy's *Complément* (9.189a), his two examples are much later than those available in Anglo-French.[16]

que nul mestre taillour ne covere (= 'conceal') nulles *cotoures* ne servantz en chaumbres en peine (*l.* privé)[17] nen appert i 98
que nul mestre taillour allowe (= 'hire') nul servant pur *coturer* ou *cuser* i 98

The form *cotoures* in the first quotation should perhaps be read as *cotourers*,[18] the noun made from the verb *coturer*, representing the standard OF *cousturer* (G.2.341b), but here in the sense of 'to seam' rather than the normally accepted 'to sew', with *cuser* being an anglicised form of *custre* 'to sew'.

. . . sur peyn de xl.d. appaierez taunt de foith com il serra trové *defautive* i 99

Although *defautive* looks thoroughly French, it is not listed in the French dictionaries.

le overaigne . . . ad estee *nounduement* et *nounable* overee i 61

The adverbs *nounduement* ('wrongfully, 'illegally') and *nounable[ment]* ('incompetently') are formed on the basis of the French *non/n(o)un* being treated as the equivalent of the English negative prefix 'un-', but are not so far recorded for continental French.

q'il soit fraunk homme nee, et de ses membres *dismaheymee* ou *dismembrez* i 61

The two adjectival past participles in this quotation are strange negatives used to express a positive state: the man chosen for the vacant post must be, literally, 'un-

---

16 Cf. *convencu* de felonie, *Magna Carta*, p. 360, para. 32.
17 The emendation here involves only the substitution of 'r' for 'e', letters that are easily confused in a manuscript. The standard locution *en privé* ought to be familiar to anyone dealing with these documents.
18 Cf. grande cope dez *cousterers* ou taillandres, *Manieres de Langage*, ed. A. M. Kristol, ANTS 53 (London, 1995), p. 6.9; *cousturers*, ibid., p. 34.19.

damaged/not maimed' and 'having lost no limbs'. The first of these forms is not found in continental French at all, the second is being used here in the opposite sense to that usually found in mainland France.

(ix) French words dressed up as Latin, used in an Anglo-French sense in a Latin text:

> predicta bargea fuit dimissa apud Southampton *male araita* i 30
> bargeam et balingeram *arraiatam* . . . i 32

The Anglo-French *arraier* carries this sense of making a vessel ready for sea, but it does not appear to be in the semantic range of continental French.

> W. de T. capellanus admissus est et presentatus ad *cantariam*, pro Missa matutinali en capella i 24
> J.C. capellanus resignavit *cantariam* suam ibid.

Cantariam 'chantry' appears to be a perfectly normal Latin term, but, although abundantly attested for Anglo-Latin (see DMLBS), Anglo-French (see AND) and Middle English, it is apparently unknown in the sense of 'chantry' in mainland France, being listed by Godefroy (2.58b) in this sense only in an Anglo-French quotation and known to Tobler-Lommatzsch only in the meanings of 'Singen' and 'Kirchengesang' (2.232).

> Que quidem *bunde* situate sunt . . . i 21

The well-attested Anglo-Latin *bunda* 'boundary(-stone)', like *cantaria*, is an Anglo-French word and is first attested in the *Voyage of St Brendan*.[19] It is here latinised to meet the linguistic conventions of the documents in hand.

> pro una *placea* terre in Hundegat i 9
> quod illa *placea* est alta via de Seintmarigate i 27

The Anglo-French *place* had been diverging semantically from its counterpart on the continent since the later twelfth century[20] and this is simply a Latinisation of an Anglo-French sense.

Since Latin was the first language of the law, it is only to be expected that a whole range of legal terms in Latin form would find their way into the *York Memorandum Book*. In the examples below the English scribes are clearly thinking their law in Anglo-French and simply tagging Latin flexional endings on to Anglo-French terms: the lexis is Anglo-French, the syntax Latin.

> mandare *warantum* pro nautis arestandis i 33
> ille qui . . . debite *convincatur* incurrat penes . . . i 217 (cf. *conventu* i 94)

---

[19] *The Anglo-Norman Voyage of St Brendan*, eds I. Short and B. Merrilees (Manchester, 1979), v. 1514.
[20] See AND.

mandare *warantum* pro nautis arestandis i 33
J.M. *attachiatus* est per corpus suum i 31
viginti solidis solutis in *hanaperio* nostro . . . ii 50
pro triacione in *scaccario* domini regis ii 73
. . . ac *lotto et scotto* ii 50
quod predictus D. *remisit* et *quietumclamavit* . . . pro hac *remissione, quietacla-mancia* . . . i 117
ballivi . . . ceperunt et *seisierunt* predictum equum i 23

(x) words made up of parts taken from different languages and fused to make a single hybrid word:

que drap entier . . . ne sera pas coloré *gaudegrene* ne sangwine de drap blanc i 114

The editor refers to the presence of *gaudegrene* in an unspecified edition of Chaucer and also in the *Promptorium parvulorum*. Willinsky's computer did not pick up this word, because it does not figure in the OED, but it would appear to be a compound of the (Anglo)-French *gaude* (i.e. 'woad') and the English 'green', i.e. 'blue-green'.[21]

nulles . . . qui vocatur *taskeman* . . . i 199
opus vocatum *taskewerk*; pro chippyng . . ., pro . . . i 199

The Middle English suffix 'man' is attached to the French *tasche* in the sense of 'a specified piece of work' to produce the meaning 'piece-worker', 'workman who is not regularly employed, but brought in to carry out a specified job of work'. *Taskewerk* is similarly formed to mean 'piecework'.

Et la *takilment* deinz la dite nief esteant . . . i 228

The Middle English root 'takil' is augmented by the Romance suffix *-ment*, but without any change of meaning.

pro xij paribus de *lynedboteux* i 194

An English past participle used as an adjective is here joined with a plural French noun to produce the hybrid 'lined boots'. The word-order is English, not French.

que nulle mestre ne ferra carier . . . forsque . . . un *summage* et di. (*sc.* of arrows) i 53
de quolibet *summagio* (*sc.* of fish) veniente ad eundem pontem viginti solidis solutis i 117
noluerunt portare *summagia* sive pondera ii 41

Long before the compilation of the *Memorandum Book* the Latin *summa* was being

---

21 I am informed by Professor J. D. Burnley that one of the Chaucer manuscripts does indeed contain this, but as separate words, not a compound.

used in both continental and insular French as *somme/summe*, meaning 'load'. Anglo-Latin had added the suffix *-agium*, to make *summagium* with the same meaning. It would appear that Anglo-French was now copying Anglo-Latin with its *summage*.

> que nulle *perfournesynges* soit mys en novel pelour . . . mes que soit halebrod i 60

This example is perhaps a little more complicated, in that the ending of 'perfournes' shows that the original French verb *parfournir* had already been anglicised into 'perfournish' (cf. *brandir*/brandish, *polir*/polish, *ravir*/ravish, etc.) before acquiring the English suffix *-ing* to make a noun denoting either an action ('giving', 'making', etc.) or the product of an action ('building', 'painting', etc.). Often such words can carry both senses in English.

> in *perlunyng* of his gude i 182

This is another example of the same phenomenon. The French verb *purloigner* 'to distance, take away' is used in Anglo-French to mean 'steal', 'embezzle' much as in modern English and here is given an English suffix of action '-ing', making it into a noun – 'in the purloining of his goods'.

> pro la *vaumpedyng* xij parium ocrearum lowsed aretro . . . i 194

This case shows the same mechanism in rather more complicated form. The root of *vaumpedyng* is the French noun *avantpié*. The full form of the word is found late in the thirteenth century in one of the two Anglo-French versions of the *Ancrene Riwle*: *chauces sanz avantpiez*,[22] but it had already lost its prefix in the Middle English version, becoming *vampé* by the middle of the century. Aphetic forms are found in both English and Anglo-French around this time, as is abundantly shown by glossary entries in *Teaching and Learning Latin . . .*: Hoc antepedale: *vampé* i 416, inpedias: *empenes, enpeyns, wanpeys, vampés, les pinnes* ii 129, inpedias: *gallice vampés* ii 149, tenea (impedia): *gallice vampie* (*l.* vampié?) ii 170. Treated as English,[23] this form is then fitted with the English suffix '-ing' giving the sense 'fitting of a vamp (to a shoe)'. This is a clear demonstration of the mixing of the two languages at a much deeper level than that of simple 'borrowing'.

(xi) Use of grammatical endings to make French nouns into Latin:

> adjudicaverunt ipsum T. *prisone* i 173
> commissus est *gaole* ibid.
> W.M. magister *craiere* vocate Marie de Y. ii 73
> pro xij paribus *de galages*: pro . . . xij parium *de lez galages*: pro . . . factura xij parium *galages*: pro sutura xij parium *galage* i 194

---

22 *The French Text of the Ancrene Riwle*, ed. J. A. Herbert, Early English Texts Society, Original Series, 219 (1944), p. 309.5.
23 Cf. 1 pare botarum et wampas de dubelsols, 4s. (1378–9), *Durham Account Rolls*, vol. 3, p. 587.

Whilst it may be argued that the final *e* of *prisone*, *gaole* and *craiere* could be interpreted as representing the classical Latin *ae* indicating a genitive or dative case, this cannot hold good for the four different treatments of *galages* 'clogs'. In the first two cases the presence of the preposition *de* indicates a straightforward French plural noun; in the third case it must still be French, although the preposition is missing; in the fourth case, however, the final *e* can hardly indicate a genitive plural. Any definitive evaluation of this point, however, can only be made after scrutiny of the manuscript in order to identify the precise nature of any abbreviation used.

On occasion a number of these different procedures can be found together in one single sentence:

pro xij paribus de galages, *shapyng* et *factura* earundem in mundum *hematis* i 194.

'Shapyng' is straightforward English, *factura* is straightforward Latin, whilst 'hematis' is the English verb 'to hem' fitted with a Latin ablative plural ending as called for by the preposition *pro*.

The extent to which the three languages of medieval England were merged in the compilation of records may be encapsulated in just two cases in the *York Memorandum Book* where all three are used in the same context. The first case concerns the verb *coillir*. The French *acoillir* is used aphetically in Anglo-French from the middle of the thirteenth century as *coillir* or *coiller*, meaning 'to invite'.[24] In the *York Memorandum Book* it means 'to offer employment to':

que nul mestre du dit artifice *cocera* (*l. colera*) ne procurera autrein servant . . . i 72
. . . *coille* oue procure . . . ascun servaunt . . . i 82
. . . *coille* or procure . . . any servant . . .' i 81
quod nullus dicti artificii *coliet* apprenticium alterius . . . i 85

The second example is the noun that has become the English 'pageant'. The *York Memorandum Book* contains many references to the Mystery Plays, the earliest being in Latin and coming from 1376:

De uno tenemento, in quo tres *pagine* Corporis Christi ponuntur i 10[25]

Other examples in Latin follow, but there is also one in Anglo-French, unfortunately undated:

. . .xl. d. a la *pagyne* des ditz pestours i 29

In the first half of the fifteenth century English forms appear and are used both as noun and adjective:

---

24 Mes si vous quillez (ME biddest) genz a festes . . . *Walter de Bibbesworth, Le Tretiz*, ed. W. Rothwell, ANTS Plain Texts Series 6 (London, 1990), v. 362.
25 Further examples: i 101, ii 32, 63, 172, 176, 179, 181, 281, 297, 298.

(1443–4) it is ordaned that the *pageant* of both the saide craftes . . . ii 181
(1409) it is ordand that the *padghand* maistres of the said crafte sall . . . ii 176
(1428?) thay asked of tham *pagand* sylver ii 179

The evidence from the *York Memorandum Book* shows that a wide range of differing combinations of Latin, French and English may be identified in the drafting of administrative documents around the turn of the fourteenth century, confirming Laura Wright's original claim that the use of mixed language for this type of document was recognised policy, not merely the haphazard product of scribal ignorance. Similar studies carried out on other compilations of municipal records dating from around this time would add support to this conclusion. Yet the suspicion that automatically springs to mind to account for the inclusion of English or French in a Latin text or English in a French text, namely that the scribes simply did not know the necessary terminology in Latin or French, could fit perfectly well into this scheme of things without invalidating the importance of the documents or dismissing as unintelligent whole generations of scribes who drafted them. This is undoubtedly the explanation for the English technical terms relating to the making of long-bows – 'pro chippyng . . .,' 'pro thwtyng . . .', 'pro dressyng . . .' (an originally French term given a specialised trade meaning in English), 'pro hornyng . . .' (i 199) and would apply also to terminology for weights and measures peculiar to England, and to English terms for areas of land or administrative areas like the 'wapentake', which turns up as *cum wapentachio* (i 124). The concept of 'technical vocabulary' would, however, have to be interpreted very generously to take in terms such as 'coverlet' alongside *lectum*, or 'spytt' in the same list as *unam ollam* (ii 78).

Before condemning the scribes of late medieval England for their ignorance, account must be taken of the situation in which they found themselves. On the one hand the recording of administrative documents steadily increasing in number and diversity called for an ever wider lexis, whilst on the other hand the conventions of the time demanded that such documents be couched in Latin or French. No one has ever remotely approached complete mastery of the lexis of his own language, let alone that of any other language, either in medieval or modern times. The vocabulary associated with machinery or skilled trades is no less foreign to translators today than it was to the medieval scribes, but the modern translator now usually works from the foreign language into his native tongue and has sophisticated lexicographical assistance that was not yet to hand in the early fifteenth century: Palsgrave's epoch-making bilingual English-French dictionary, his *Esclarcissement de la Langue françoyse*, was still a century away, whilst Cotgrave's dictionary of French and English was some two centuries in the future.

Looking beyond the confines of the British Isles, the phenomenon of mixed language is found in continental French as well as in the insular variety examined above. Dealing with thirteenth- and fourteenth-century vernacular wills in his book *Patois et Dialectes français*,[26] Pierre Guiraud describes them as follows: 'Ces testa-

[26]   Paris, 1968.

ments sont écrits dans une sorte de latin de cuisine entrelardé de formes indigènes, en particulier d'inventaires d'objets, de vêtements' (p. 43). The only viable solution in both countries would be the eventual vernacularisation of administrative records, a process that would mark the modern world off from the medieval, but the very difficulties experienced by the late medieval scribes could be used to increase our knowledge of the development of both English and French. A detailed comparison of documents similar to the *York Memorandum Book* drafted in different parts of England might show whether the vernacular trade terms used by various craftsmen were in current use on a national scale or were subject to regional or even dialectal variation,[27] whilst a comparison of such documents with those in mainland France referred to by Guiraud might reveal how much or how little technical and commercial terminology passed across the Channel. Finally, research into this type of document in the Provençal area, comparing the results with those gathered for northern France and England, could well cast new light on the transmission of different kinds of knowledge from the Mediterranean right up into England.[28]

Appendix
(Additional examples not discussed in the body of the paper)

(i) English words unmodified in a Latin text:
(a) unum lectum et unum *coverlet*, ij *blankettes* i 78

(b) unum par de *lynclathes* et j *kerechief* i 61

(c) lez *strynges* pro arcubus ii 123

(d) pro factura xij parium ocrearum in mundum, que linate fuerint, *quyssheld*, *lased* vel *clasped* i 194

(e) pro *chippyng* cujuslibet centene arcuum . . ., pro *thwytyng* . . . pro *dressyng* . . . i 199

(ii) English words unmodified in a French text:
(a) les *uphaldres* (i.e. upholsterers') quels vendount drape de leyne i 251

(b) que nul homme . . . ne *melte* ascun metal . . . i 94

(c) de les *stulpes* (i.e.'bollards') in Petirgate i 34

(d) que null . . . pende overtement en fenestres ou sur lez *rakkes* (i.e. 'racks for stretching cloth, etc.') aucun chose . . . i 89

(e) q'ils suffrent . . . D.F. . . . venir entre eux et franchement ové son *chafer* (i.e. 'goods, wares') passer ii 47

---

27 The Introduction to L. F. Salzman's *A Documentary History of Building in England down to 1540* (Oxford, 1952) contains a wealth of technical terms in tantalisingly brief snippets from many unresearched manuscripts from up and down the country.

28 E.g. 'calfatting'. See Laura Wright, *Sources of London English: Medieval Thames Vocabulary* (Oxford, 1996), pp. 36 and 162.

(iii) French words unmodified in a Latin text:

(a)   et quod lez *gistes* (i.e. 'joists') et aliud meremium . . . ii 93

(b)   cornerium domus predicto *buttans* (i.e. 'abutting') super venellam ii 109

(c)   j *geauge* (i.e. 'gauge') . . . pro latitudine et pro profunditate modiorum sigil-
landis ii 90

(d)   in auxilium reparacionis cujusdam nove *kaye* (i.e. 'quay') i 41

(e)   quod nullus magister . . . aperiat . . . nisi unam solam foliam *fenistre* (i.e.
'(window) shutter') shope sua i 197

(f)   si aliquis . . . gilde predicte *scandalizet* i 243

(g)   et ipsis in sua defensione *assisterent* laboribus et expensis i 20

(v) English words dressed up as Latin in a Latin text:

(a)   cum *crana* (i.e. 'crane') . . . sit jam de novo edificata i 81

(b)   pro *gabulagio* ('rent, gavel') de eisdem domo et gardino i 48

(c)   Ordinaciones *pewderariorum* (i.e. 'pewterers') i 211

(d)   dicta navis . . . cum *ankuris* ligata ad terram siccam i 229 (also 230, 232)

(ix) French words dressed up as Latin, used in an Anglo-French sense in a Latin text:

(a)   dederunt *possessionem* et *seisinam* . . . unius *mesuagii* cum tribus shoppis ii 48

(b)   predicti cives . . . *seisiti* fuerunt i 126 (127); *seisite* i 126; *seisitus* i 126 (128)

(c)   eam *disseisivit* de uno tenemento i 140; *disseisita* i 140; *disseisiverunt* i 146

(d)   *aretro* est de vij li. i 175

(e)   *arrainiaverunt* coram nobis ii 39

(f)   *attachiamentum* ii 39; dictus T. *attachiatus* fuit . . . *commissus* est gaole i 173

(g)   ille qui . . . debite *convincatur* imncurrat penes . . . i 217

(h)   per diversas *billas* suas i 120; per *billam* suam supponit quod . . . i 129

(i)   si dictus J. . . . *occasionetur* racione alicujus vendicionis . . . ii 14

(j)   tam de uno *banco* quam de alio i 47; coram justiariis de utroque *banco* i 147

(k)   collegit et recepit *parcellas* denariorum . . . et ipsas *parcellas* sic collectas
deliberavit annuatim predicto magistro J. i 218

(l)   infra *admirallitatem* predictam i 225 (*admiralté* 228)

(m)   pro uno *garetto* i 11

(n)   tondere aliquos pannos . . . qui non erunt de *fullitura* sua propria ii 159

(o)   J.D. et R.N. . . . sunt electi *serchatores* ejusdem artis ad eandem artem *super-
vivendum* i 31

(p)   cursus aque *guttere* predicte . . . nec habet ulteriorem exitum, nisi usque ad
murum lapideum ii 7

(q)   quod illa (*sc.* bargea) sit *frettata* usque Caleys cum lanis i 32

(r)   ad *supportacionem* pagine artis predicte i 101

Index

N.B.: This index does not list individual words discussed by contributors, nor does it list dictionaries when simply referred to in the text. Authors or works cited in footnotes are not normally included unless there is discussion of them beyond the basic bibliographical reference.